a
lent
6 Voice

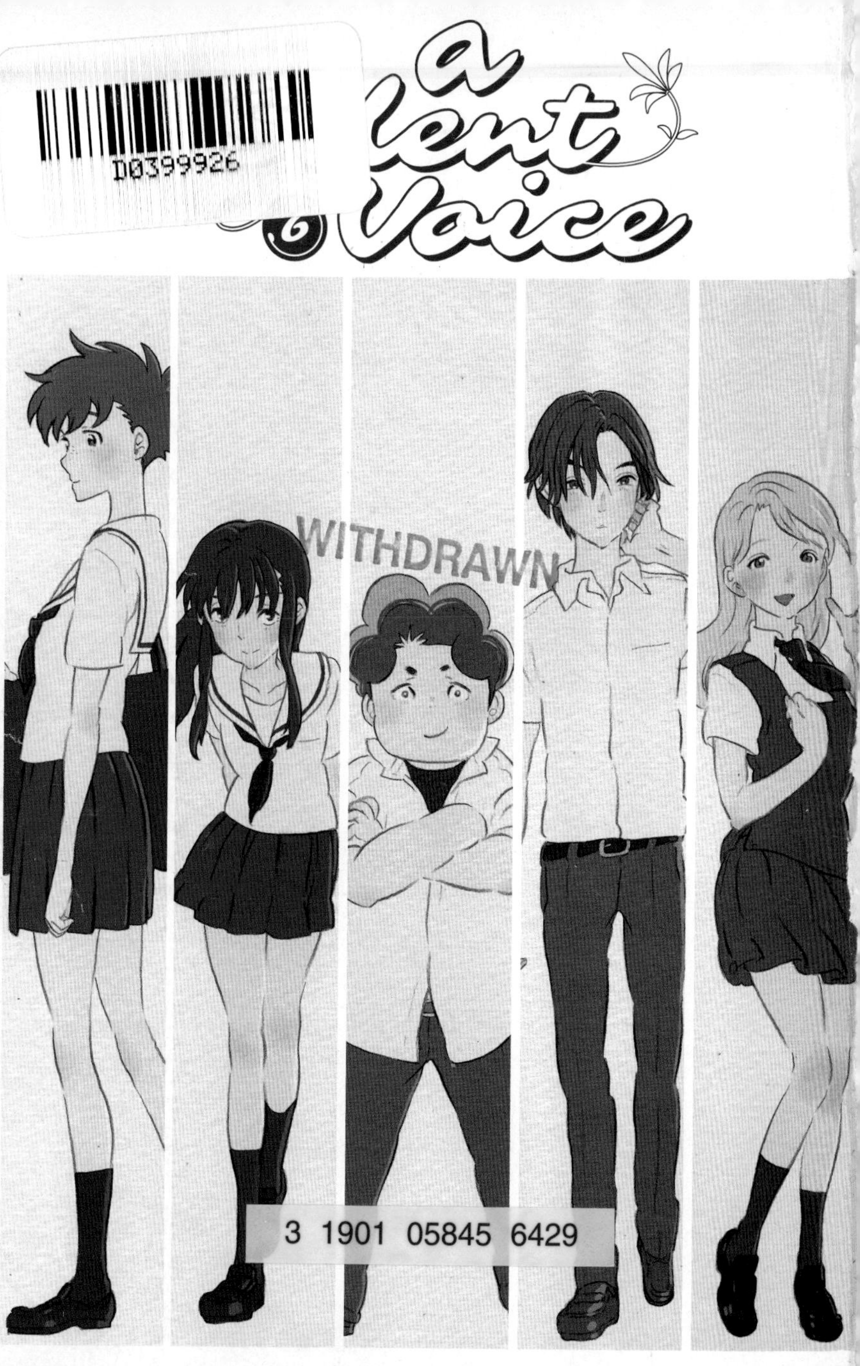

a Silent Voice

6

CONTENTS

Chapter 43
Daredevil _____ 3

Chapter 44
Blight _____ 23

Chapter 45
It Was All For Nothing? _____ 41

Chapter 46
Tomohiro Nagatsuka _____ 59

Chapter 47
Miyoko Sahara _____ 77

Chapter 48
Miki Kawai _____ 95

Chapter 49
Satoshi Mashiba _____ 113

Chapter 50
Naoka Ueno _____ 131

Chapter 51
Shoko Nishimiya _____ 149

Chapter 52
Silence _____ 167

CHAPTER 43: DAREDEVIL

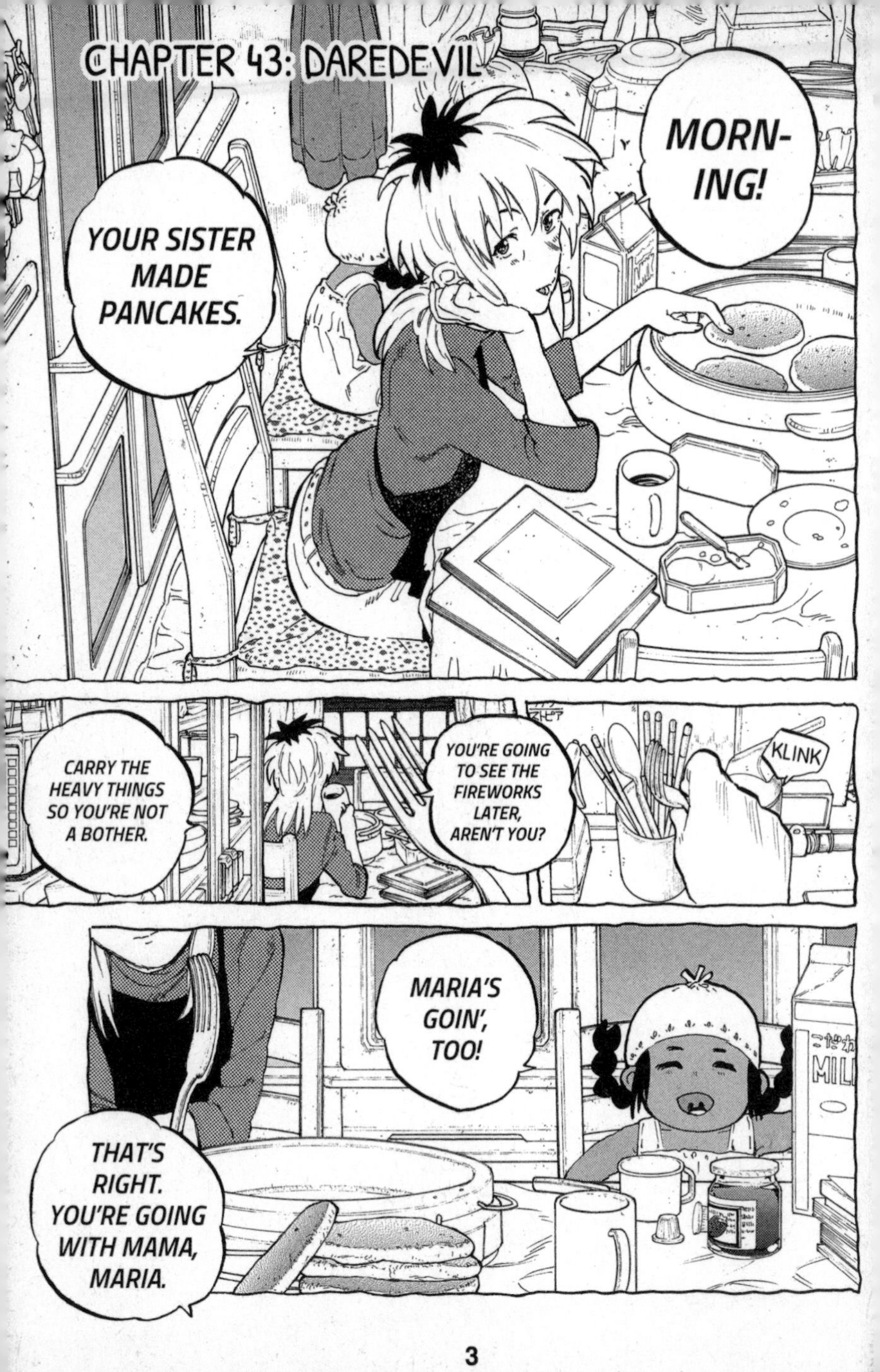
MORNING!
YOUR SISTER MADE PANCAKES.
KLINK
YOU'RE GOING TO SEE THE FIREWORKS LATER, AREN'T YOU?
CARRY THE HEAVY THINGS SO YOU'RE NOT A BOTHER.
MARIA'S GOIN', TOO!
THAT'S RIGHT. YOU'RE GOING WITH MAMA, MARIA.

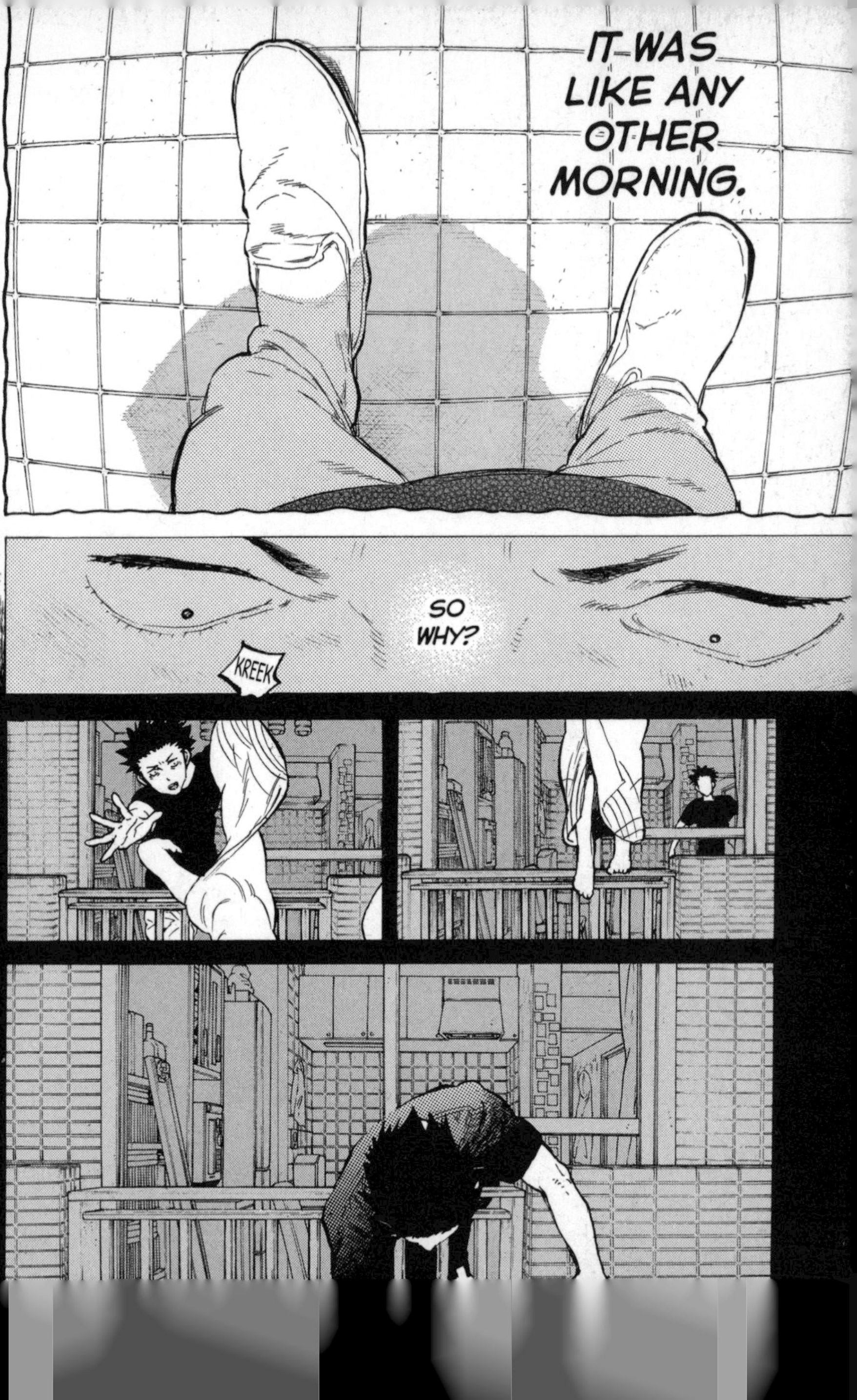
IT WAS LIKE ANY OTHER MORNING.
SO WHY?
KREEK

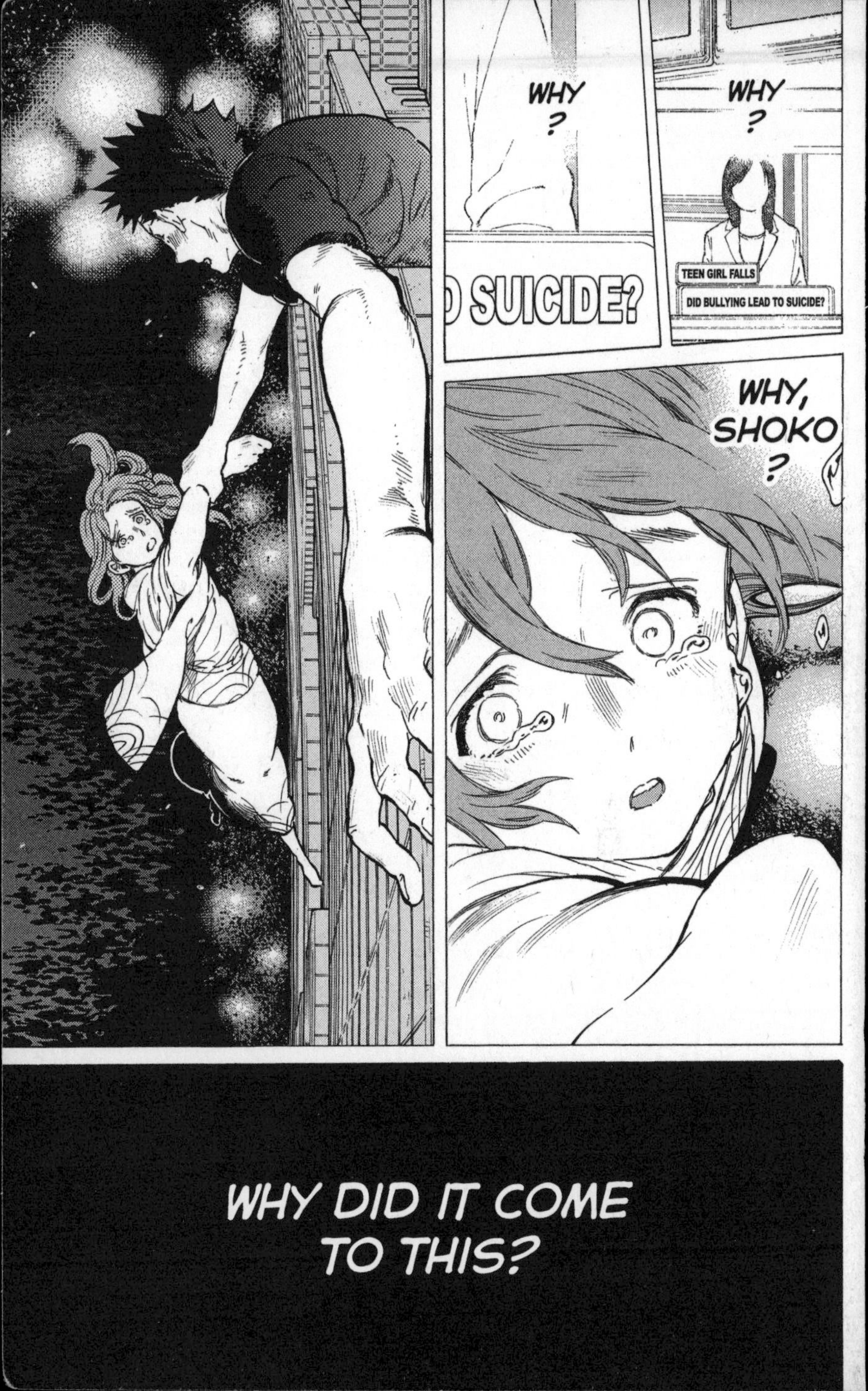
WHY?
TEEN GIRL FALLS
DID BULLYING LEAD TO SUICIDE?
WHY?
D SUICIDE?
WHY, SHOKO?
WHY DID IT COME TO THIS?

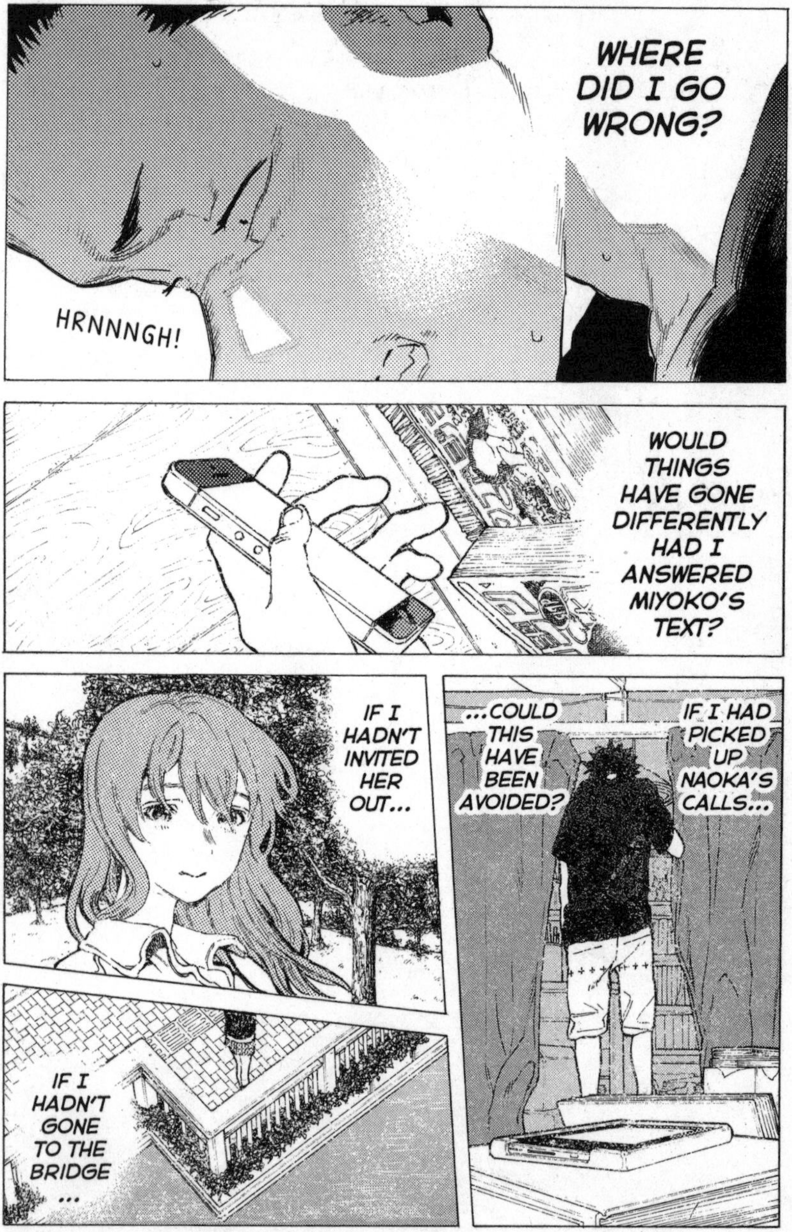
WHERE DID I GO WRONG?
HRNNNGH!
WOULD THINGS HAVE GONE DIFFERENTLY HAD I ANSWERED MIYOKO'S TEXT?
IF I HAD PICKED UP NAOKA'S CALLS...
...COULD THIS HAVE BEEN AVOIDED?
IF I HADN'T INVITED HER OUT...
IF I HADN'T GONE TO THE BRIDGE ...

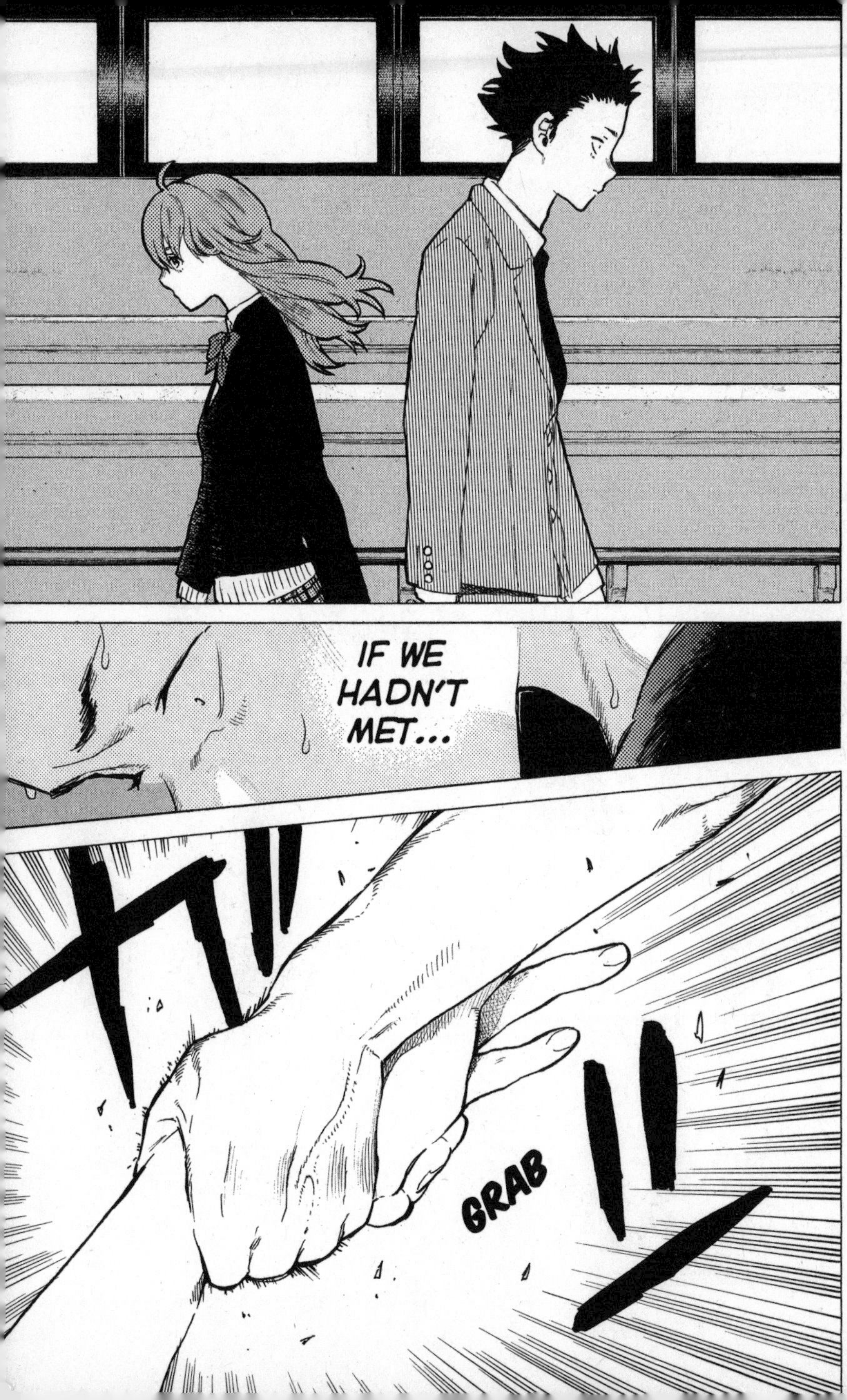
IF WE HADN'T MET...
GRAB

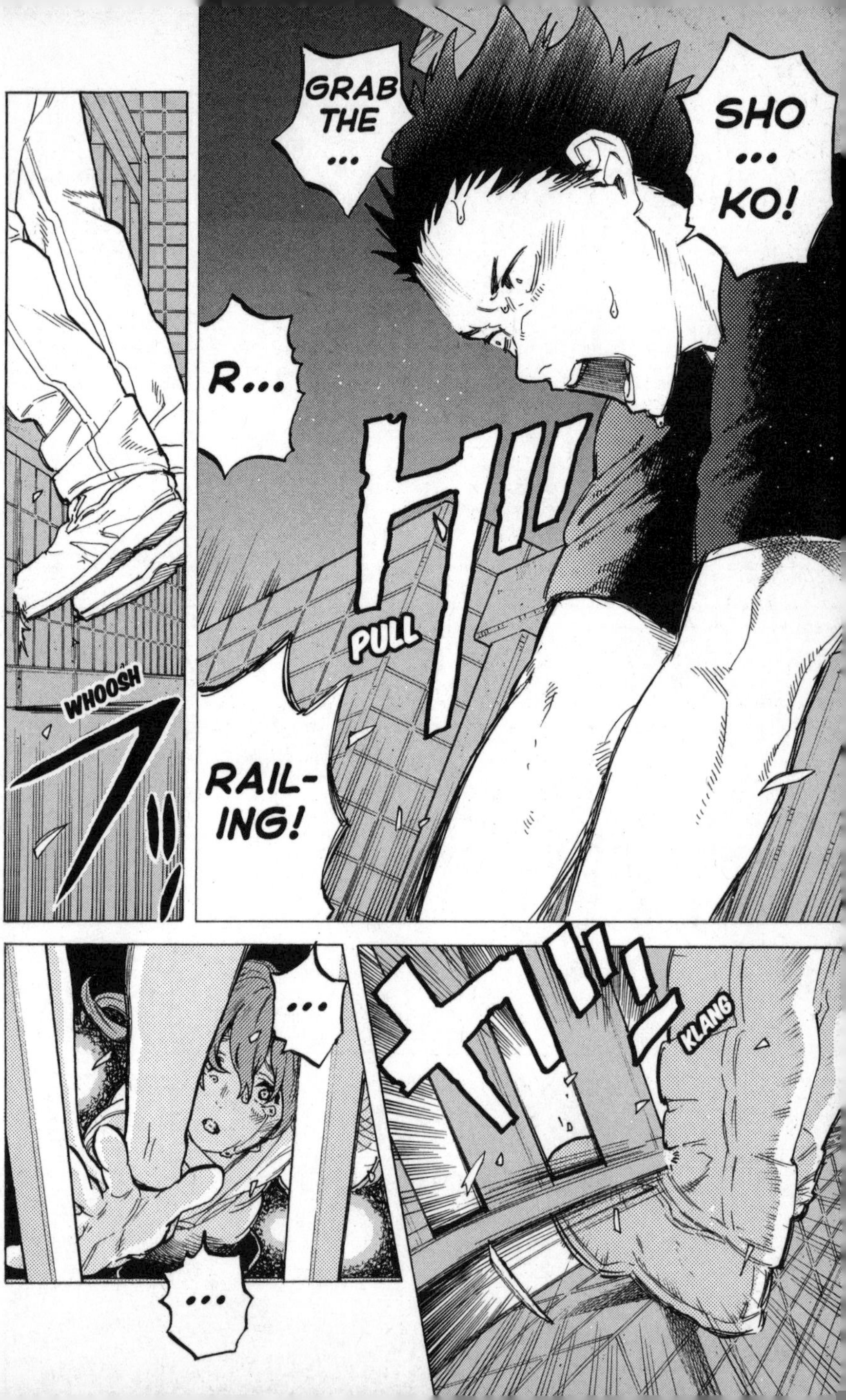
SHO ... KO!
GRAB THE ...
R...
PULL
RAIL-ING!
WHOOSH
KLANG
...
...

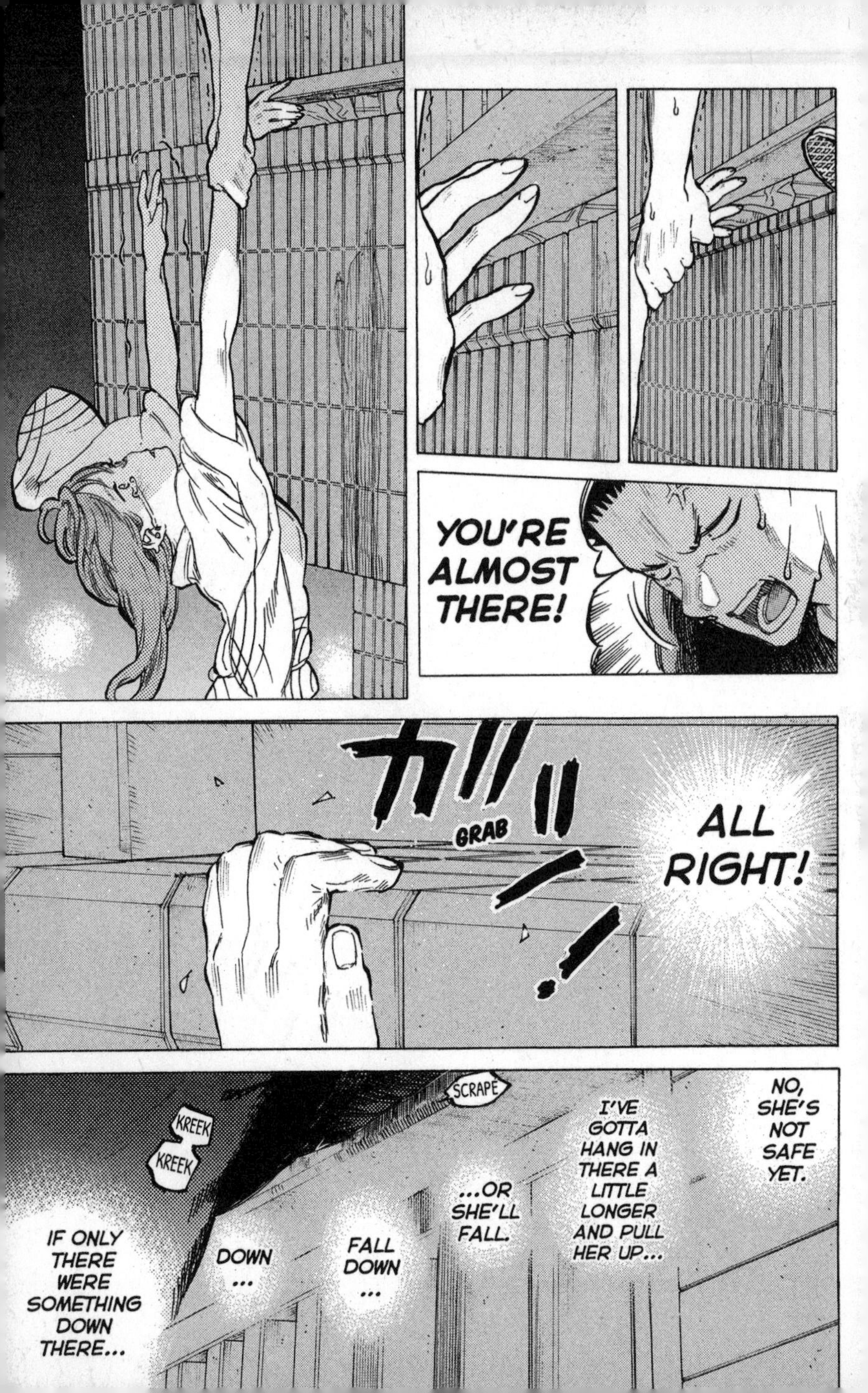
YOU'RE ALMOST THERE!
ALL RIGHT!
ガリ!!
GRAB
NO, SHE'S NOT SAFE YET.
I'VE GOTTA HANG IN THERE A LITTLE LONGER AND PULL HER UP...
...OR SHE'LL FALL.
SCRAPE
FALL DOWN...
DOWN...
KREEK
KREEK
IF ONLY THERE WERE SOMETHING DOWN THERE...

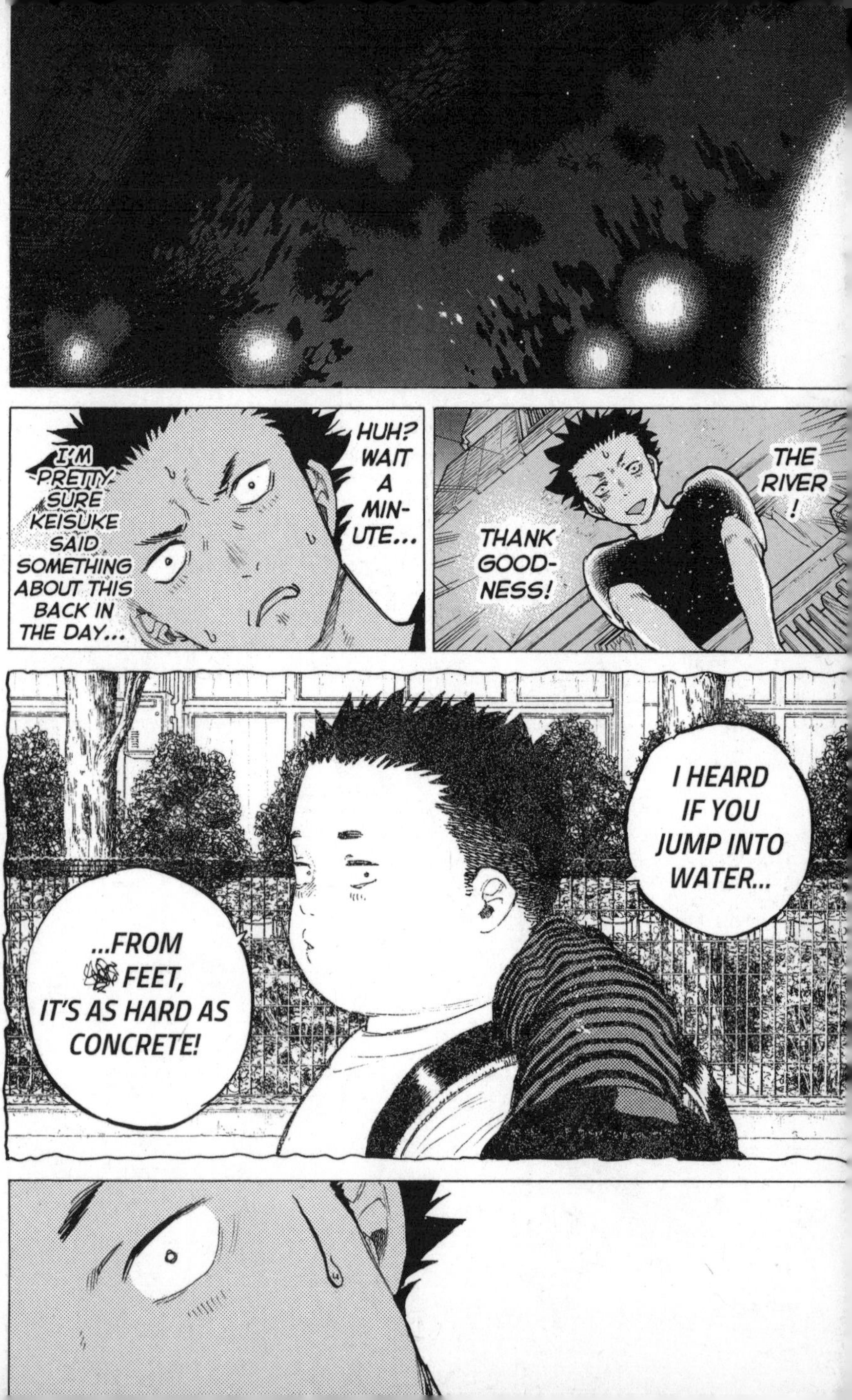
THE RIVER!
THANK GOODNESS!
HUH? WAIT A MINUTE...
I'M PRETTY SURE KEISUKE SAID SOMETHING ABOUT THIS BACK IN THE DAY...
I HEARD IF YOU JUMP INTO WATER...
...FROM FEET, IT'S AS HARD AS CONCRETE!

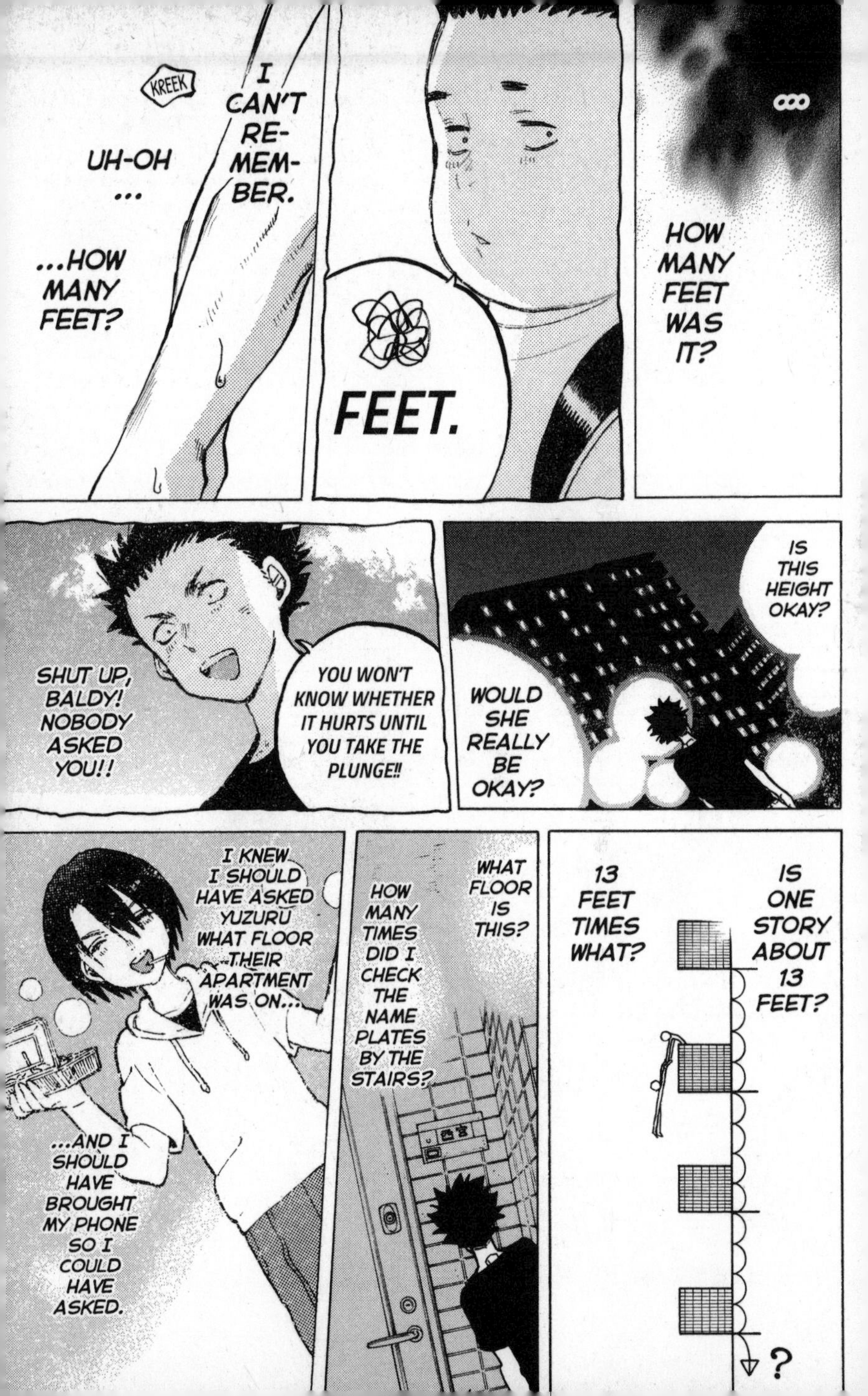
...
HOW MANY FEET WAS IT?
FEET.
I CAN'T REMEMBER.
KREEK
UH-OH ...
...HOW MANY FEET?
IS THIS HEIGHT OKAY?
WOULD SHE REALLY BE OKAY?
YOU WON'T KNOW WHETHER IT HURTS UNTIL YOU TAKE THE PLUNGE!!
SHUT UP, BALDY! NOBODY ASKED YOU!!
IS ONE STORY ABOUT 13 FEET?
13 FEET TIMES WHAT?
?
WHAT FLOOR IS THIS?
HOW MANY TIMES DID I CHECK THE NAME PLATES BY THE STAIRS?
I KNEW I SHOULD HAVE ASKED YUZURU WHAT FLOOR THEIR APARTMENT WAS ON...
...AND I SHOULD HAVE BROUGHT MY PHONE SO I COULD HAVE ASKED.

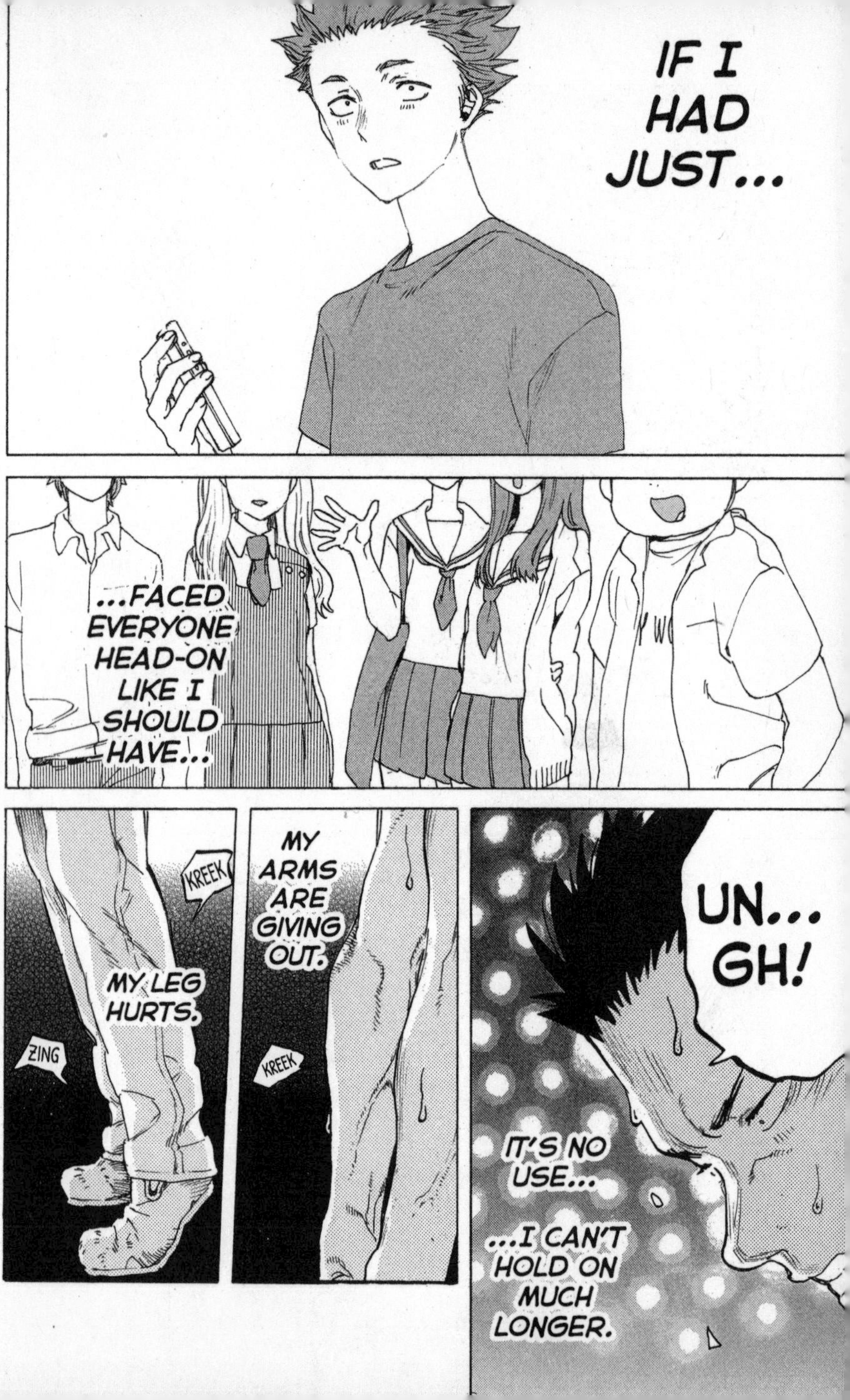
IF I HAD JUST...
...FACED EVERYONE HEAD-ON LIKE I SHOULD HAVE...
UN... GH!
IT'S NO USE...
...I CAN'T HOLD ON MUCH LONGER.
MY ARMS ARE GIVING OUT.
KREEK
KREEK
MY LEG HURTS.
ZING

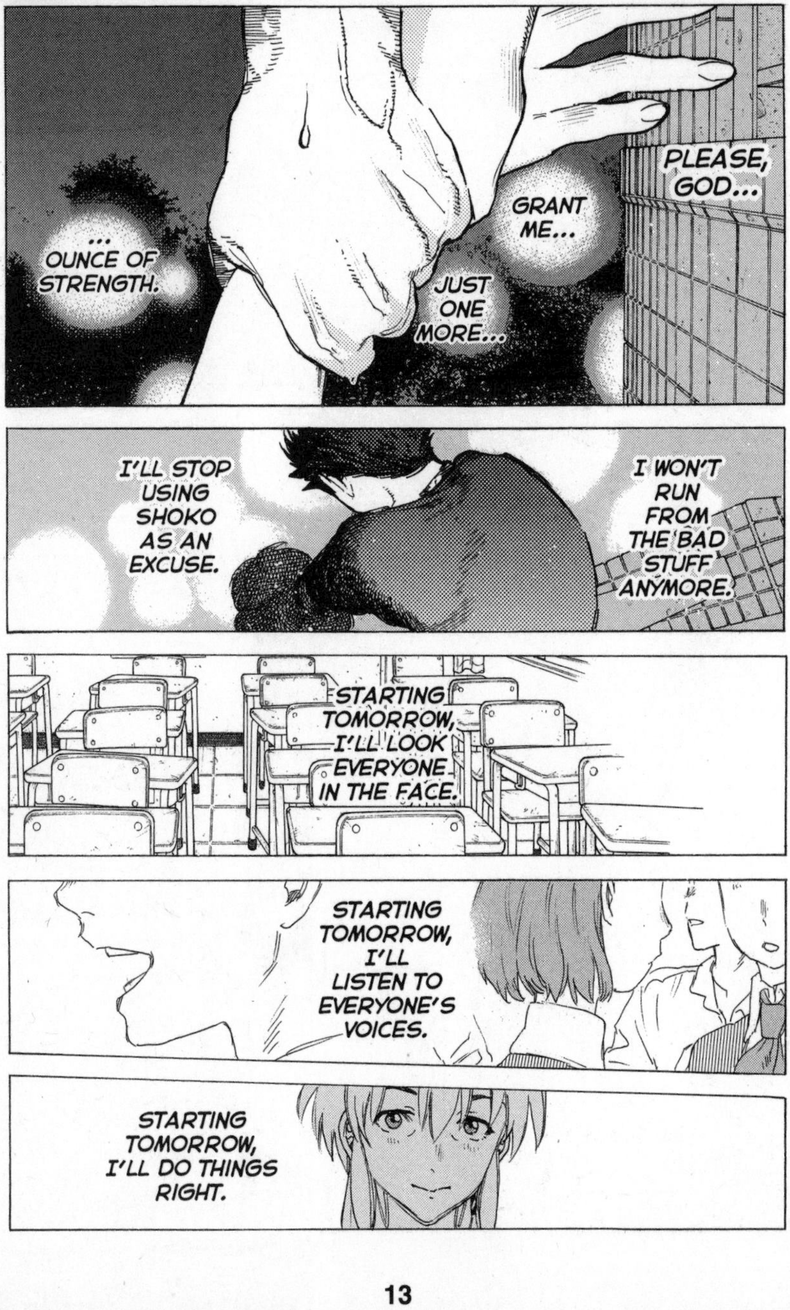
PLEASE, GOD...
GRANT ME...
JUST ONE MORE...
... OUNCE OF STRENGTH.
I WON'T RUN FROM THE BAD STUFF ANYMORE.
I'LL STOP USING SHOKO AS AN EXCUSE.
STARTING TOMORROW, I'LL LOOK EVERYONE IN THE FACE.
STARTING TOMORROW, I'LL LISTEN TO EVERYONE'S VOICES.
STARTING TOMORROW, I'LL DO THINGS RIGHT.

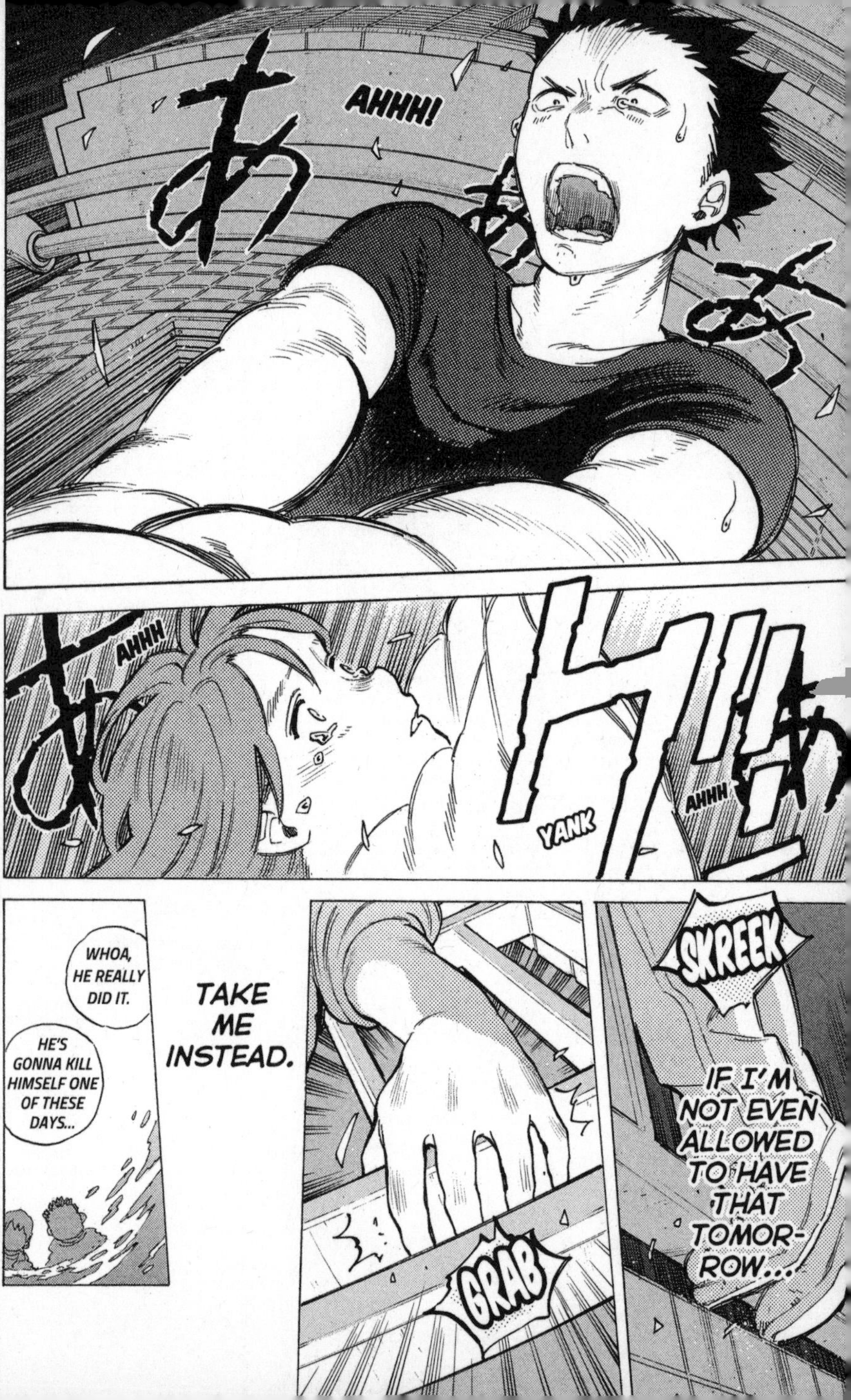
AHHH!
AHHH
YANK
AHHH
SKREEK
IF I'M NOT EVEN ALLOWED TO HAVE THAT TOMORROW...
GRAB
TAKE ME INSTEAD.
WHOA, HE REALLY DID IT.
HE'S GONNA KILL HIMSELF ONE OF THESE DAYS...

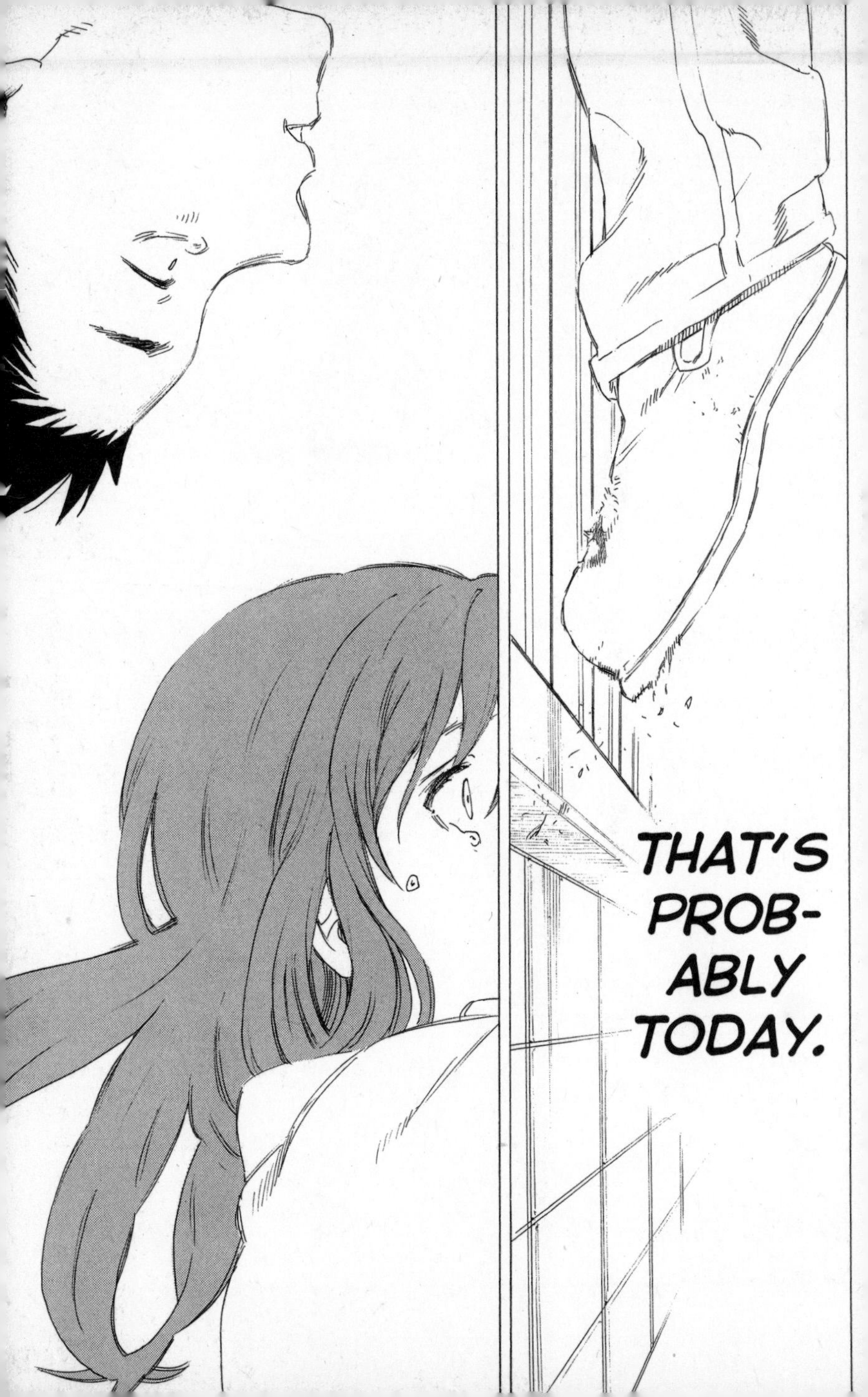
THAT'S PROB-ABLY TODAY.

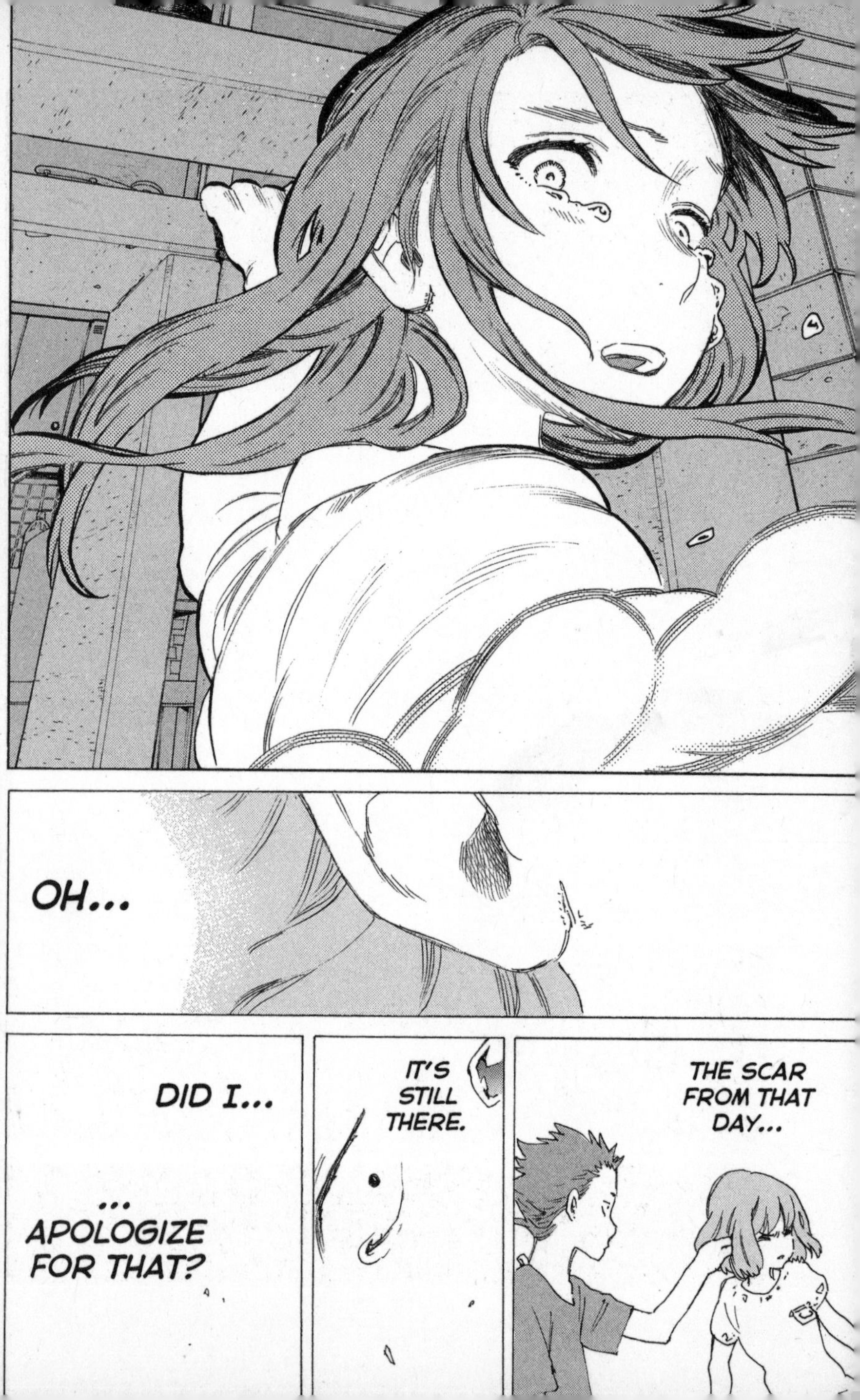
OH...
THE SCAR FROM THAT DAY...
IT'S STILL THERE.
DID I...
... APOLOGIZE FOR THAT?

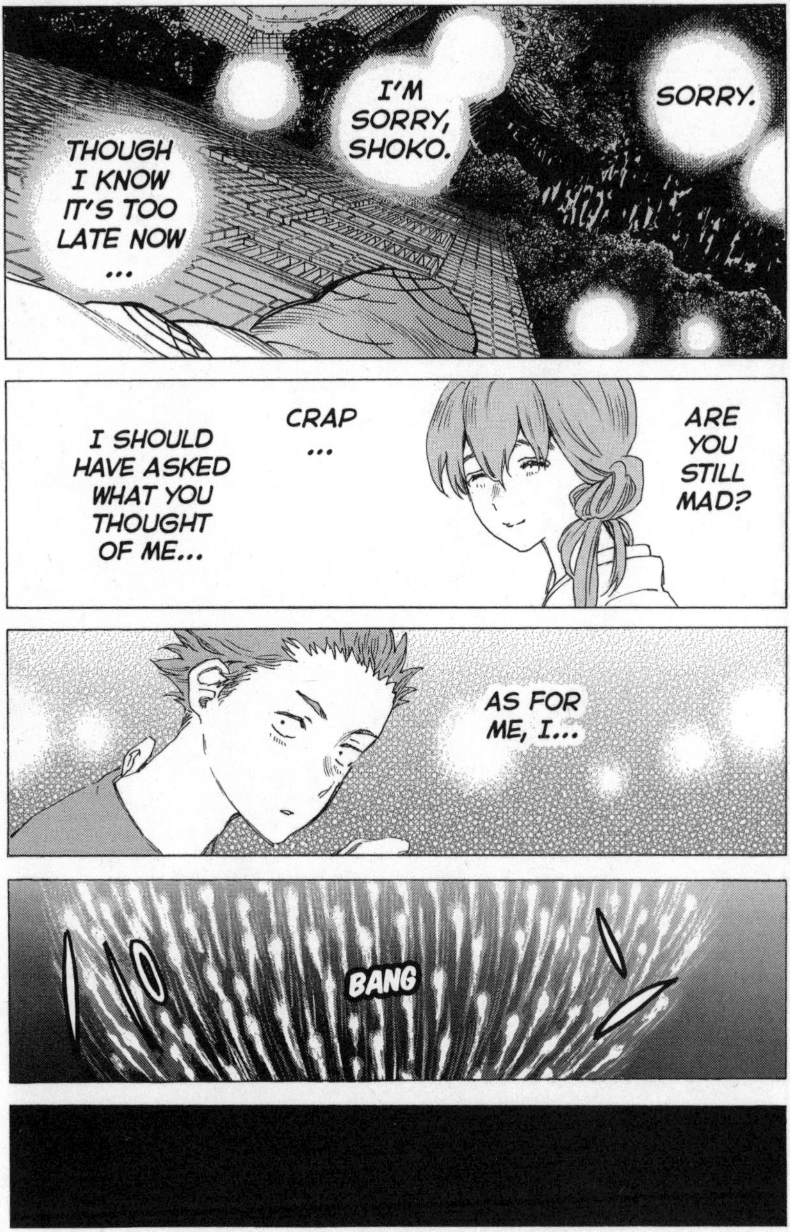
SORRY.
I'M SORRY, SHOKO.
THOUGH I KNOW IT'S TOO LATE NOW ...
ARE YOU STILL MAD?
CRAP ...
I SHOULD HAVE ASKED WHAT YOU THOUGHT OF ME...
AS FOR ME, I...
BANG

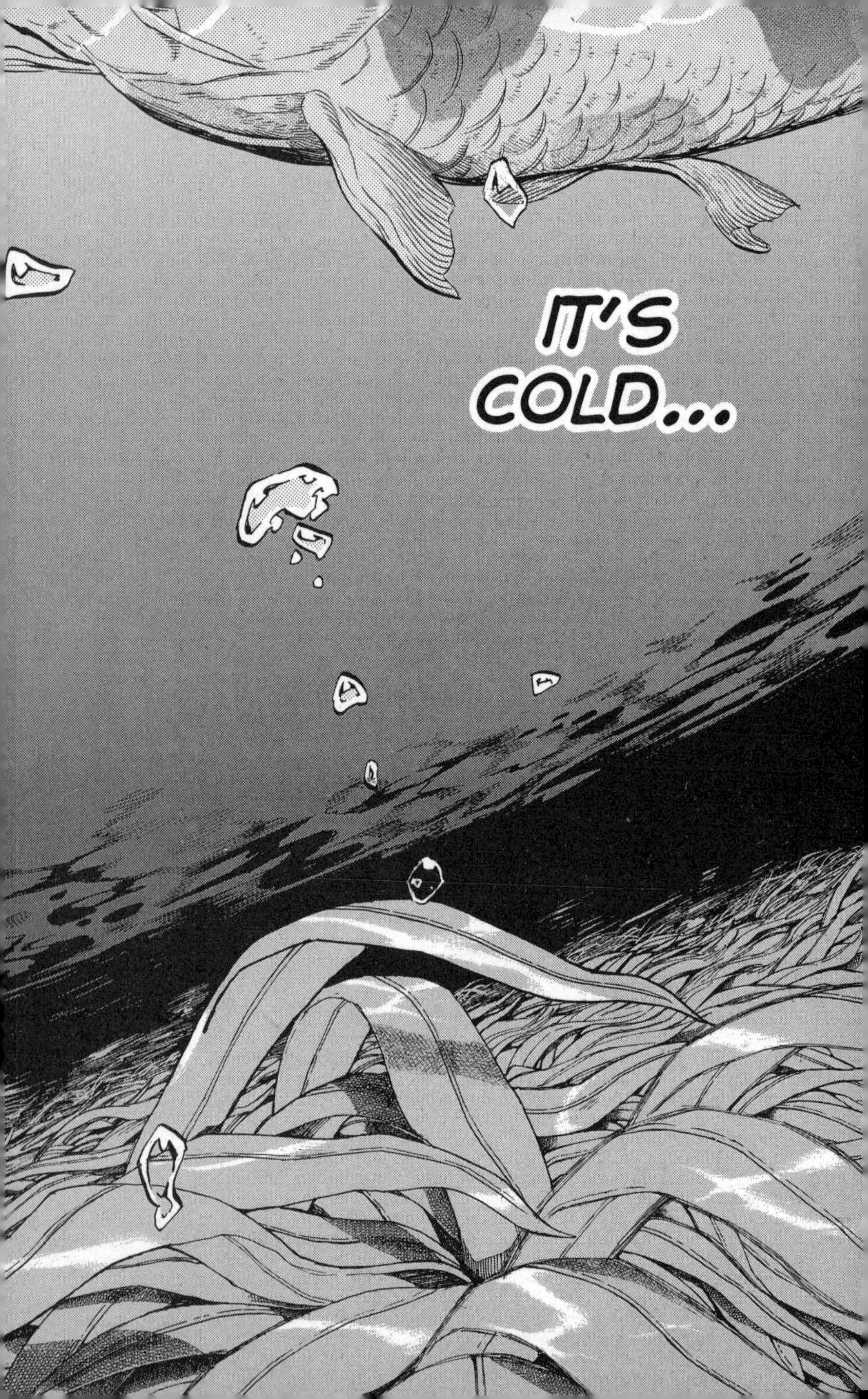
IT'S COLD...

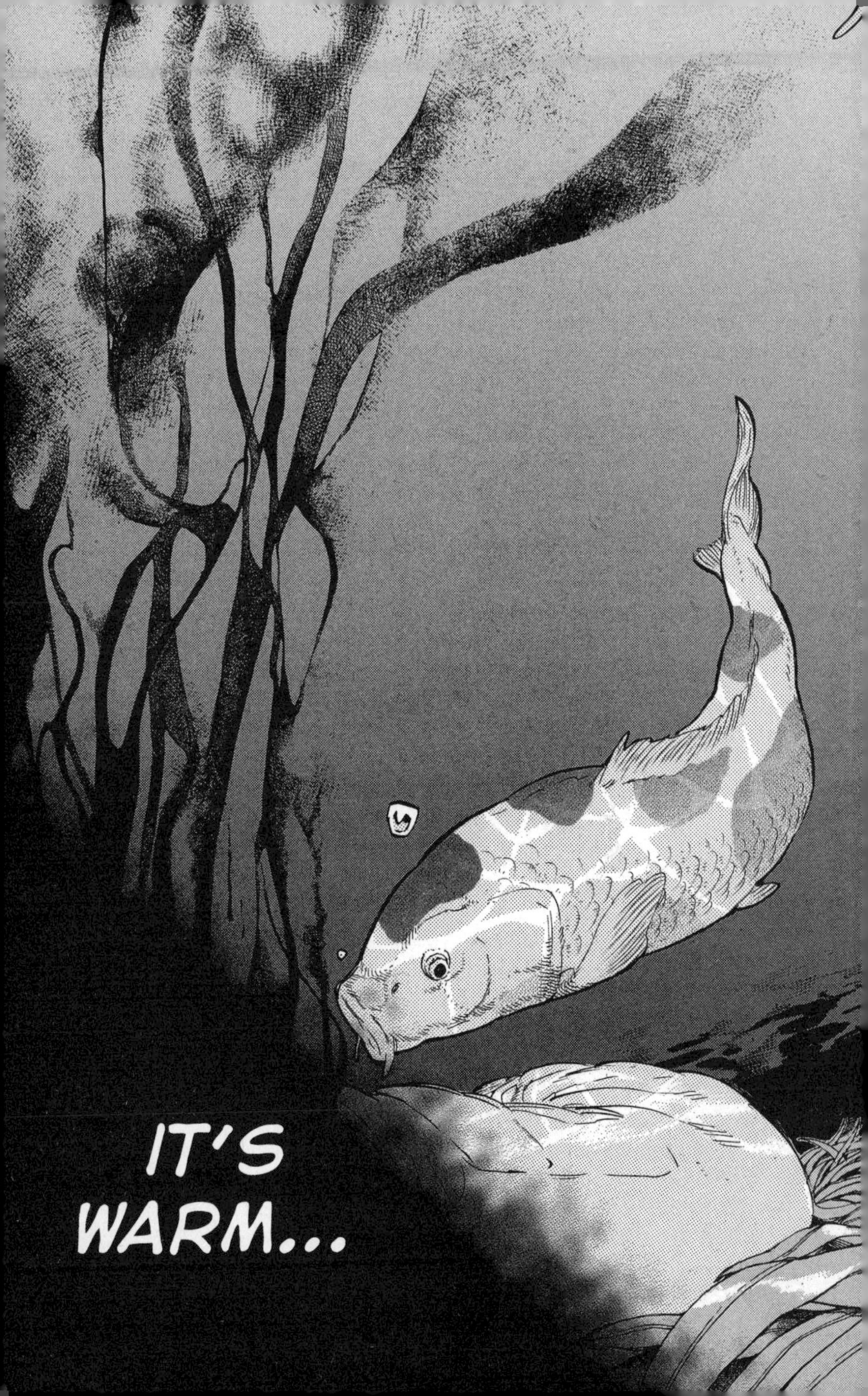
IT'S WARM...

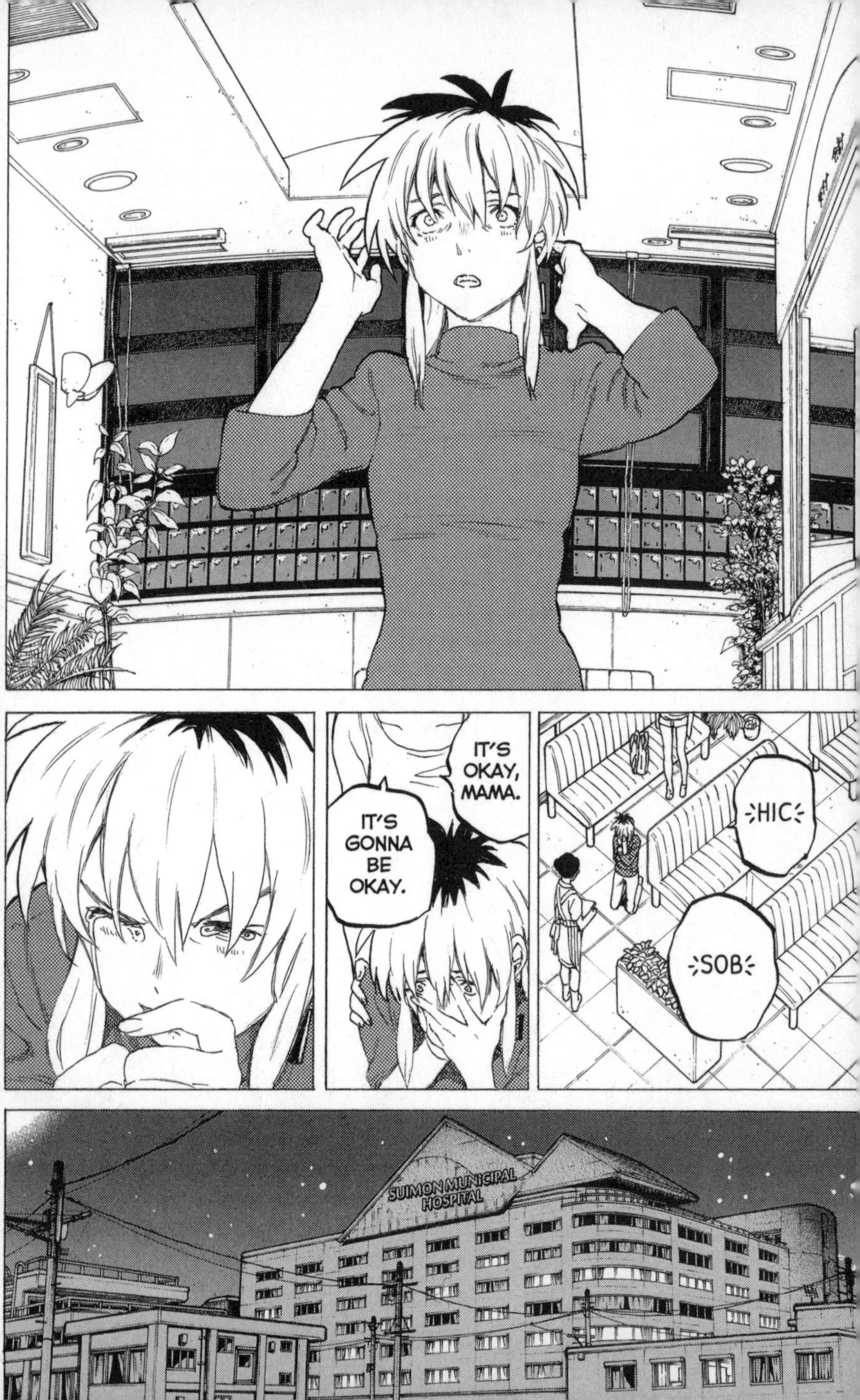
HIC
SOB
IT'S OKAY, MAMA.
IT'S GONNA BE OKAY.
SUIMON MUNICIPAL HOSPITAL

a Silent Voice

a Silent Voice

CHAPTER 44: BLIGHT

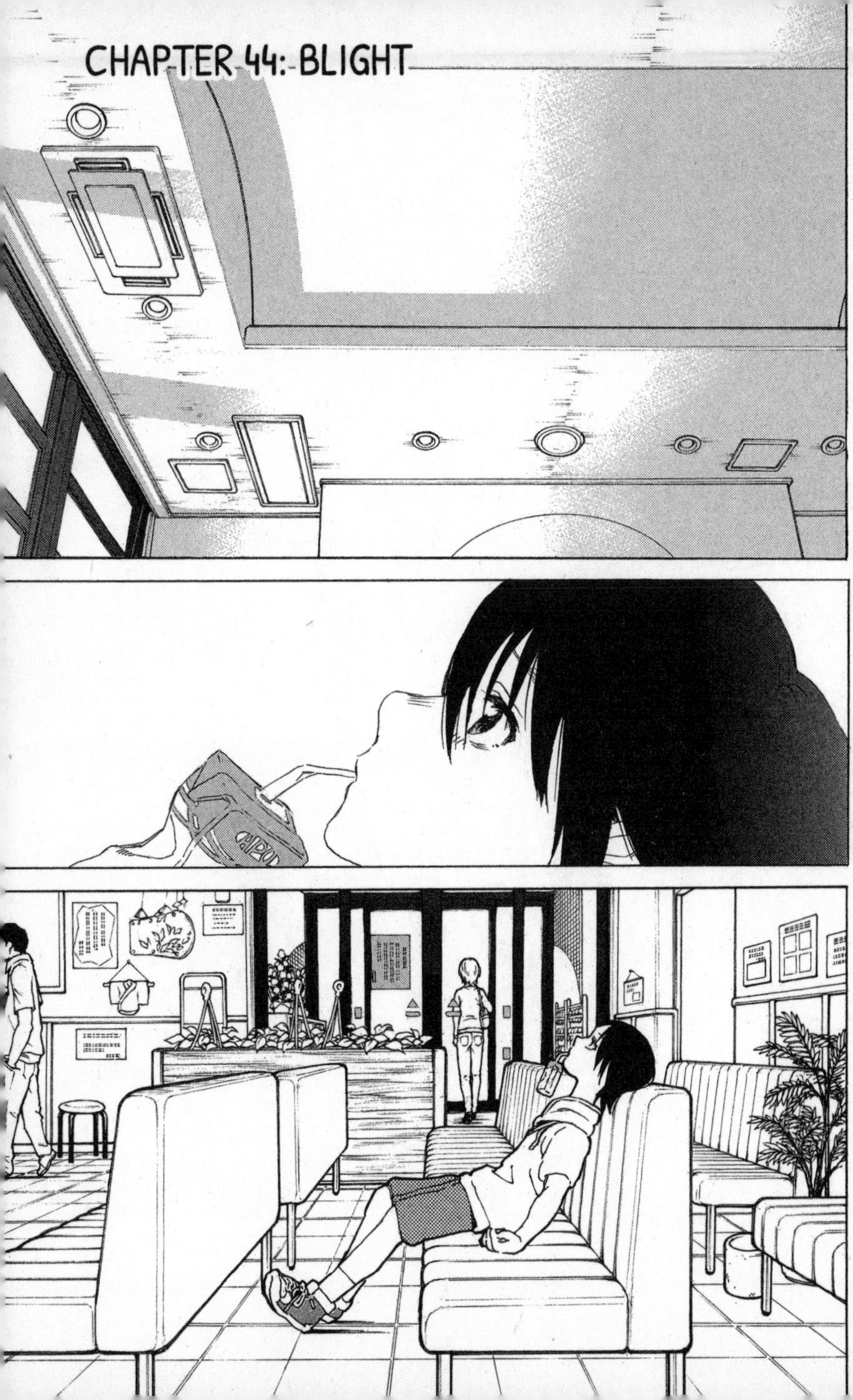

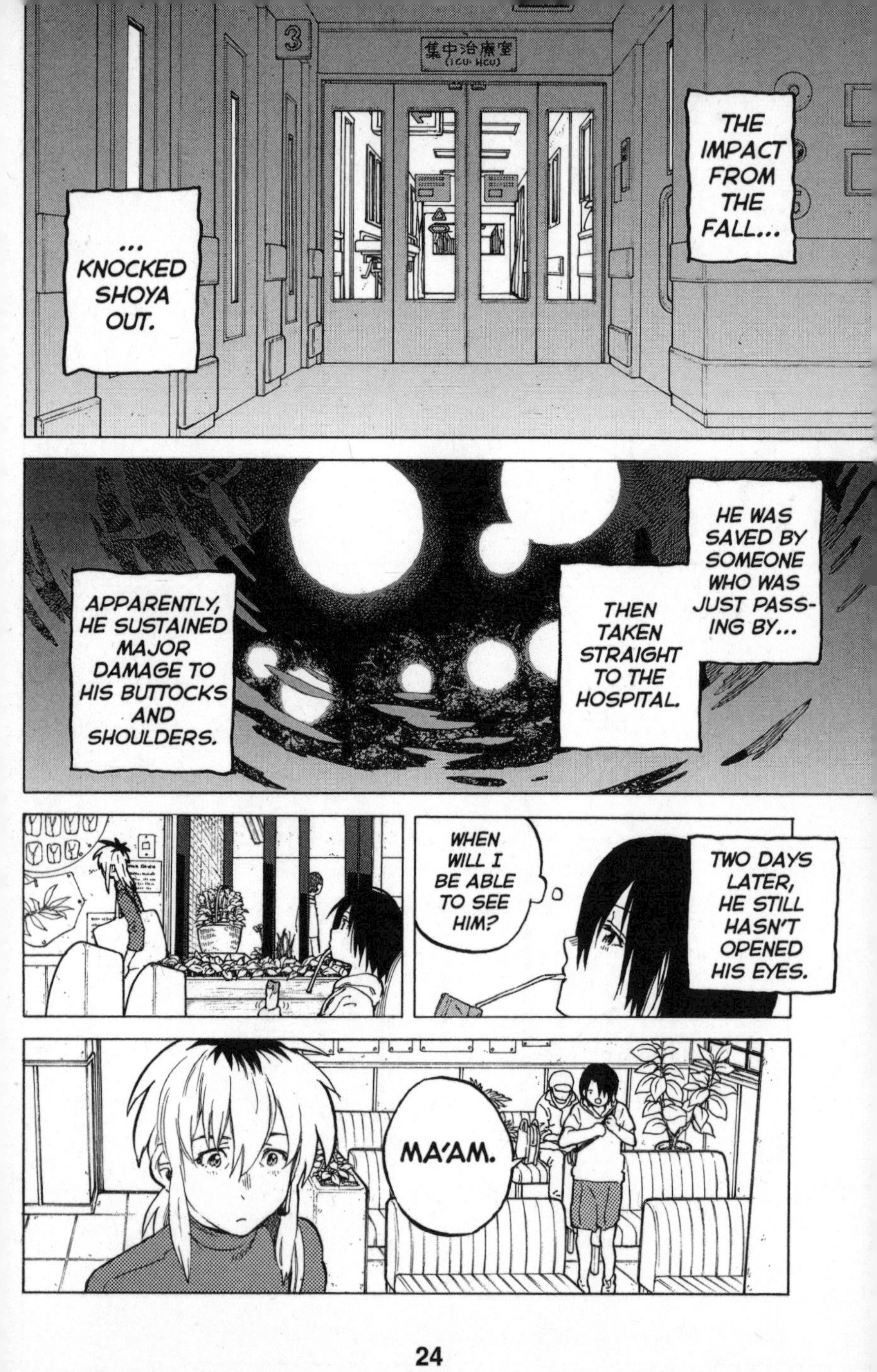
3
集中治療室
(ICU·HCU)
THE IMPACT FROM THE FALL...
... KNOCKED SHOYA OUT.
HE WAS SAVED BY SOMEONE WHO WAS JUST PASSING BY...
THEN TAKEN STRAIGHT TO THE HOSPITAL.
APPARENTLY, HE SUSTAINED MAJOR DAMAGE TO HIS BUTTOCKS AND SHOULDERS.
TWO DAYS LATER, HE STILL HASN'T OPENED HIS EYES.
WHEN WILL I BE ABLE TO SEE HIM?
MA'AM.

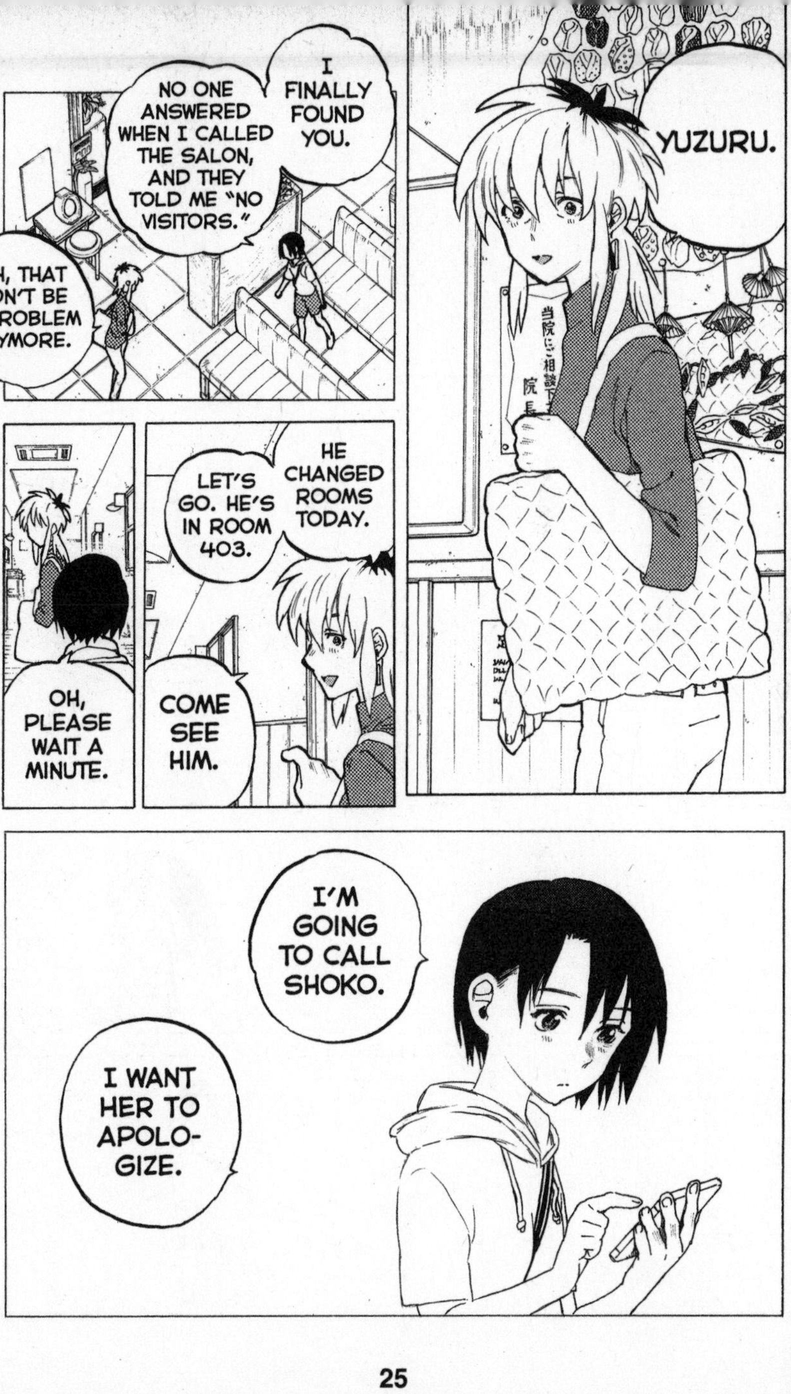
YUZURU.
I FINALLY FOUND YOU.
NO ONE ANSWERED WHEN I CALLED THE SALON, AND THEY TOLD ME "NO VISITORS."
OH, THAT WON'T BE A PROBLEM ANYMORE.
HE CHANGED ROOMS TODAY.
LET'S GO. HE'S IN ROOM 403.
COME SEE HIM.
OH, PLEASE WAIT A MINUTE.
I'M GOING TO CALL SHOKO.
I WANT HER TO APOLO-GIZE.

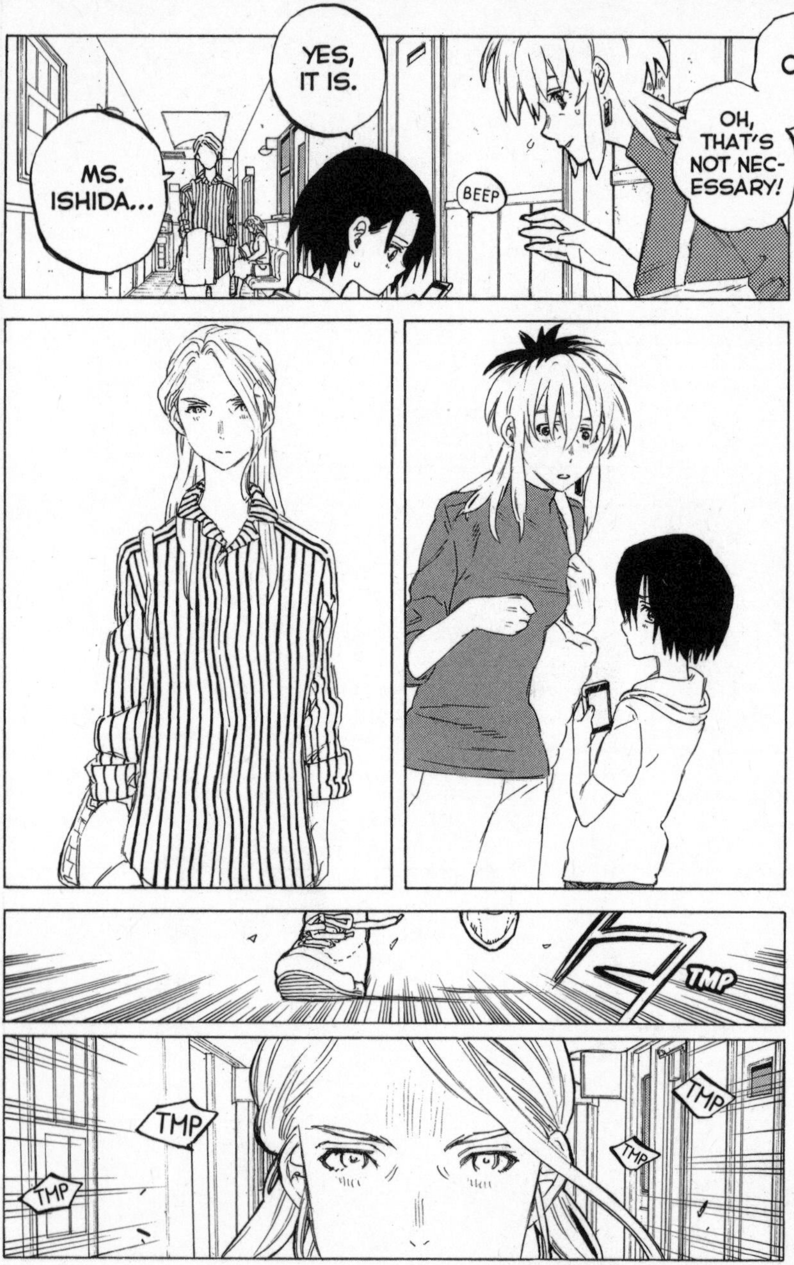
O-
OH, THAT'S NOT NEC-ESSARY!
BEEP
YES, IT IS.
MS. ISHIDA...
TMP
TMP
TMP
TMP
TMP

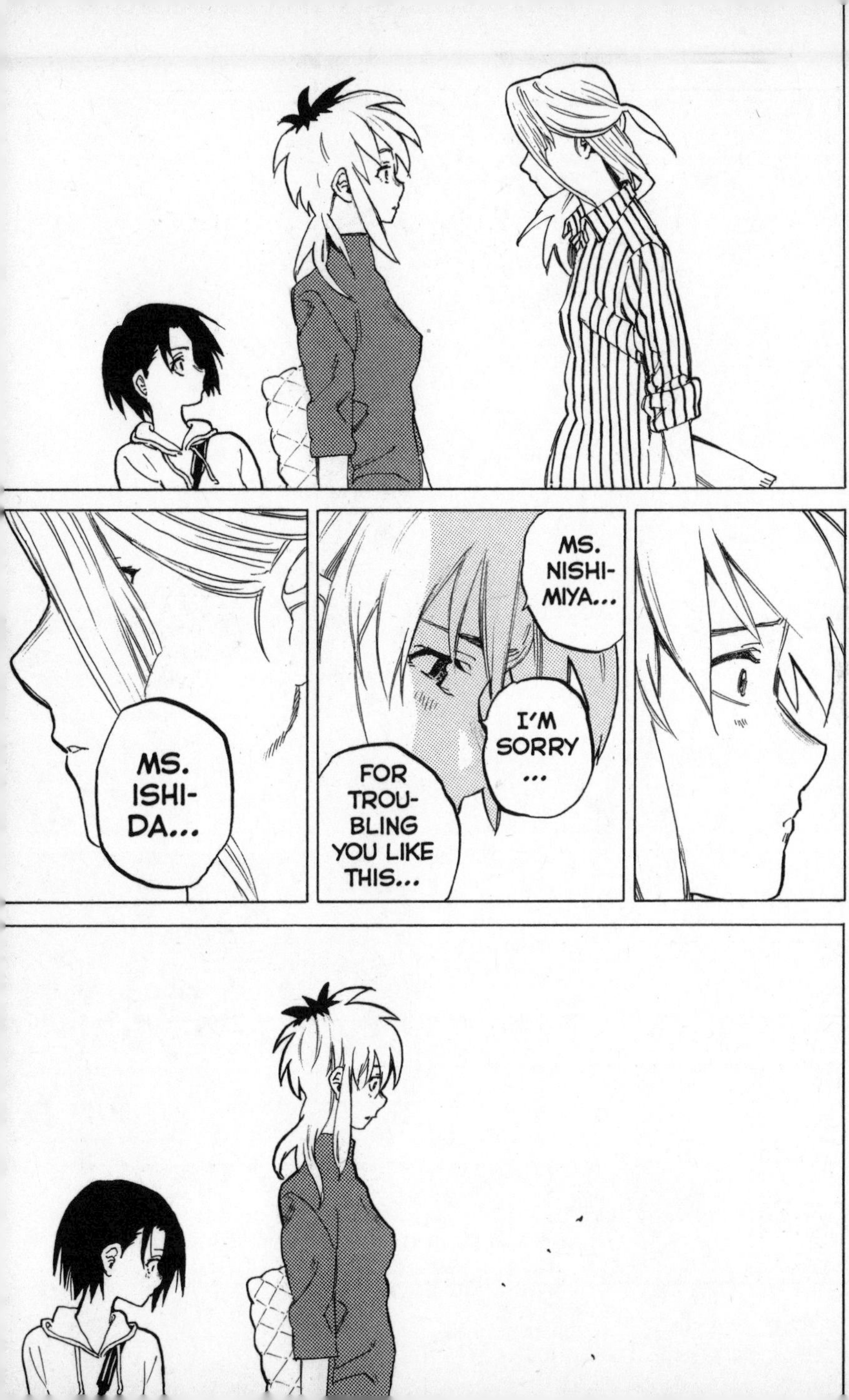
MS. NISHIMIYA...
I'M SORRY...
FOR TROUBLING YOU LIKE THIS...
MS. ISHIDA...

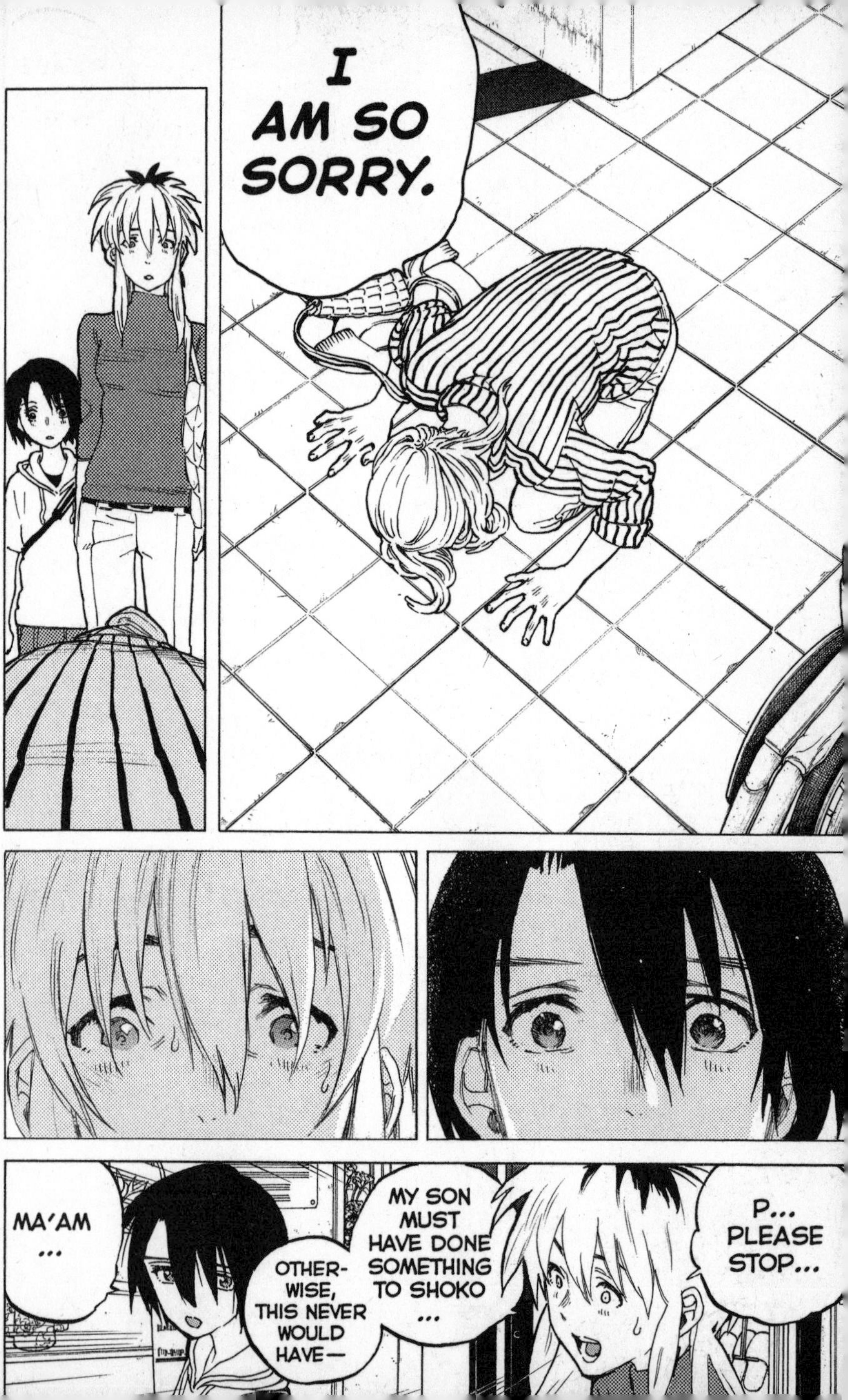
I AM SO SORRY.
P... PLEASE STOP...
MY SON MUST HAVE DONE SOMETHING TO SHOKO ...
OTHER-WISE, THIS NEVER WOULD HAVE—
MA'AM ...

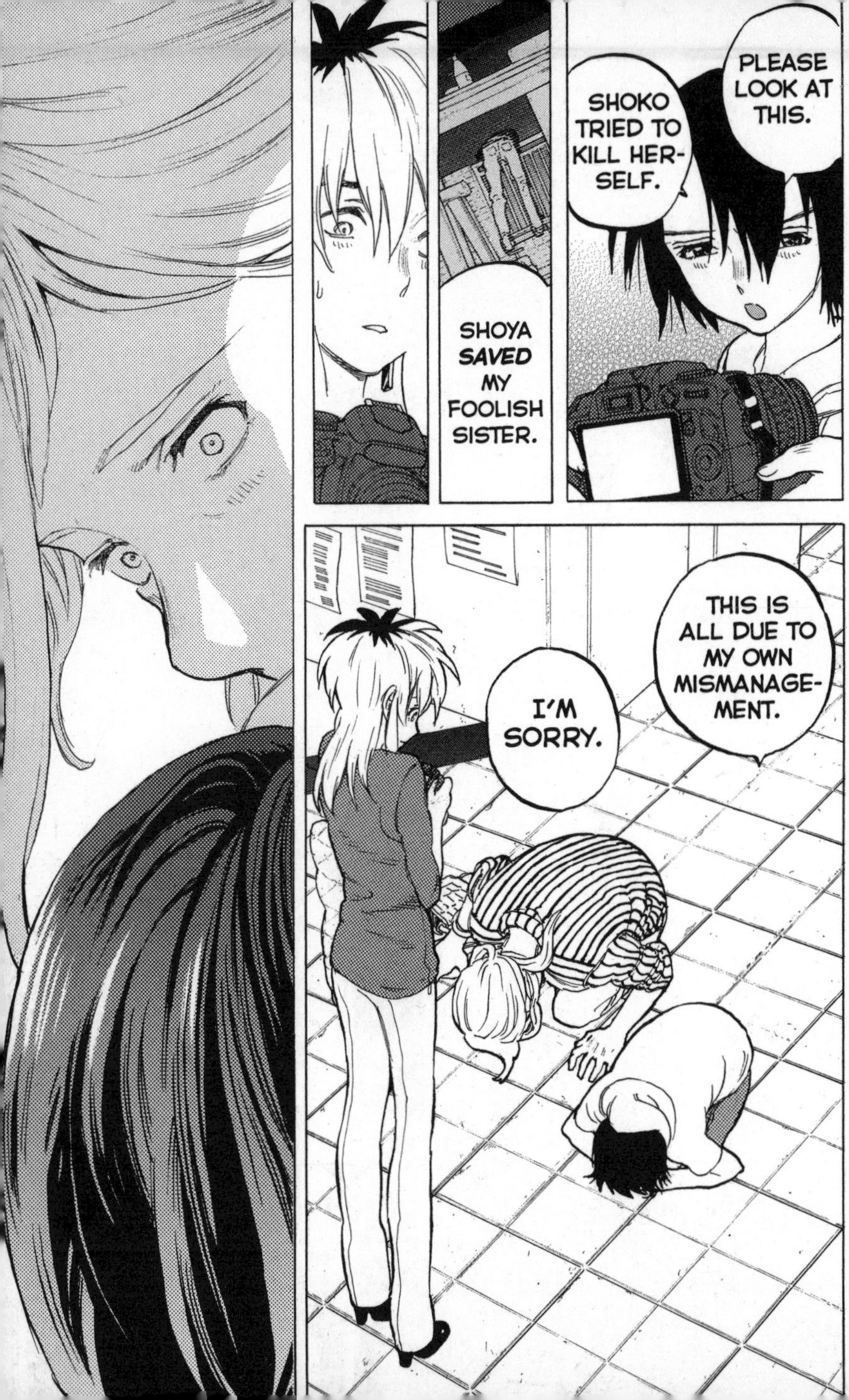
PLEASE LOOK AT THIS.
SHOKO TRIED TO KILL HER-SELF.
SHOYA **SAVED** MY FOOLISH SISTER.
THIS IS ALL DUE TO MY OWN MISMANAGE-MENT.
I'M SORRY.

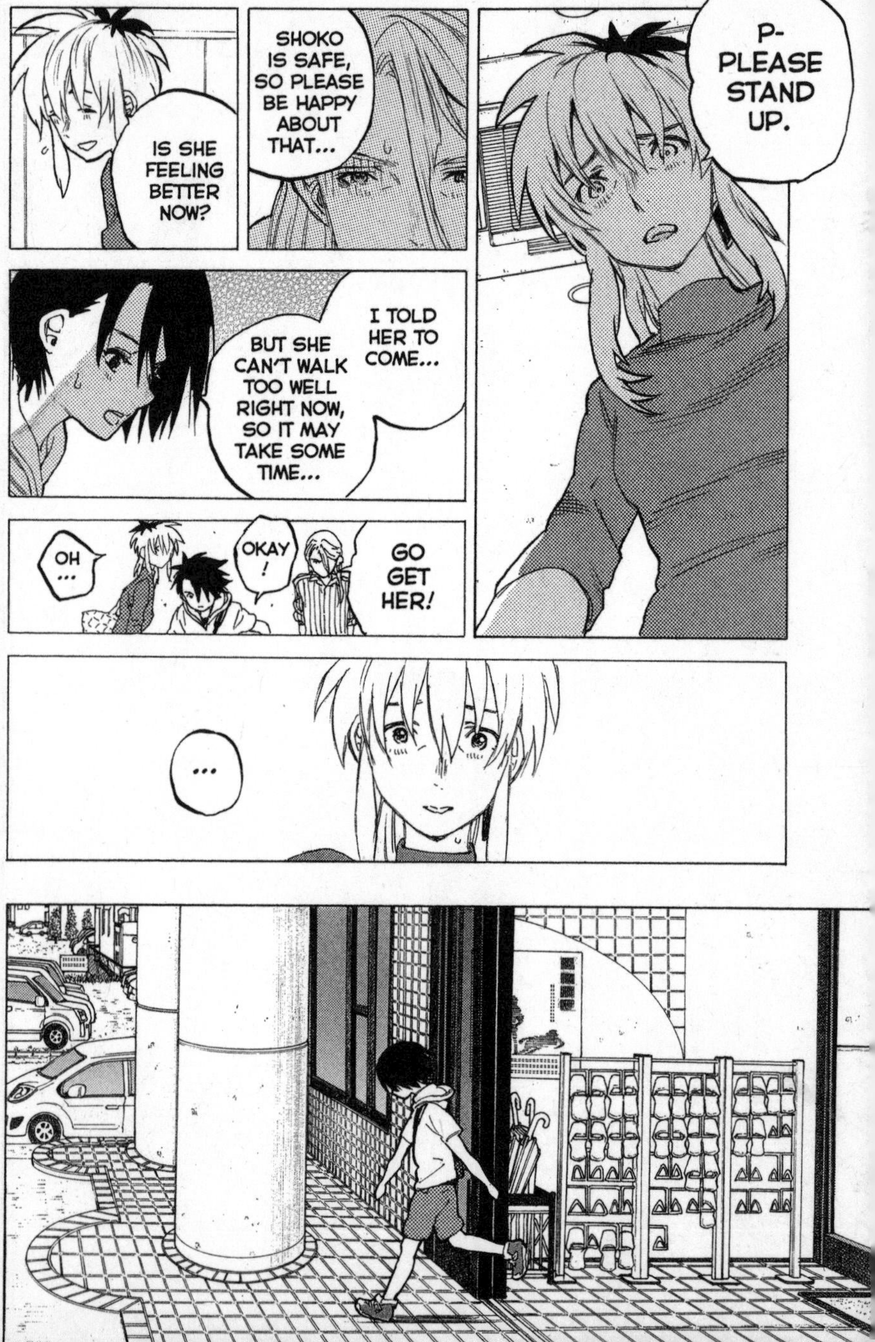
P-
PLEASE STAND UP.
SHOKO IS SAFE, SO PLEASE BE HAPPY ABOUT THAT...
IS SHE FEELING BETTER NOW?
I TOLD HER TO COME...
BUT SHE CAN'T WALK TOO WELL RIGHT NOW, SO IT MAY TAKE SOME TIME...
GO GET HER!
OKAY!
OH ...
...

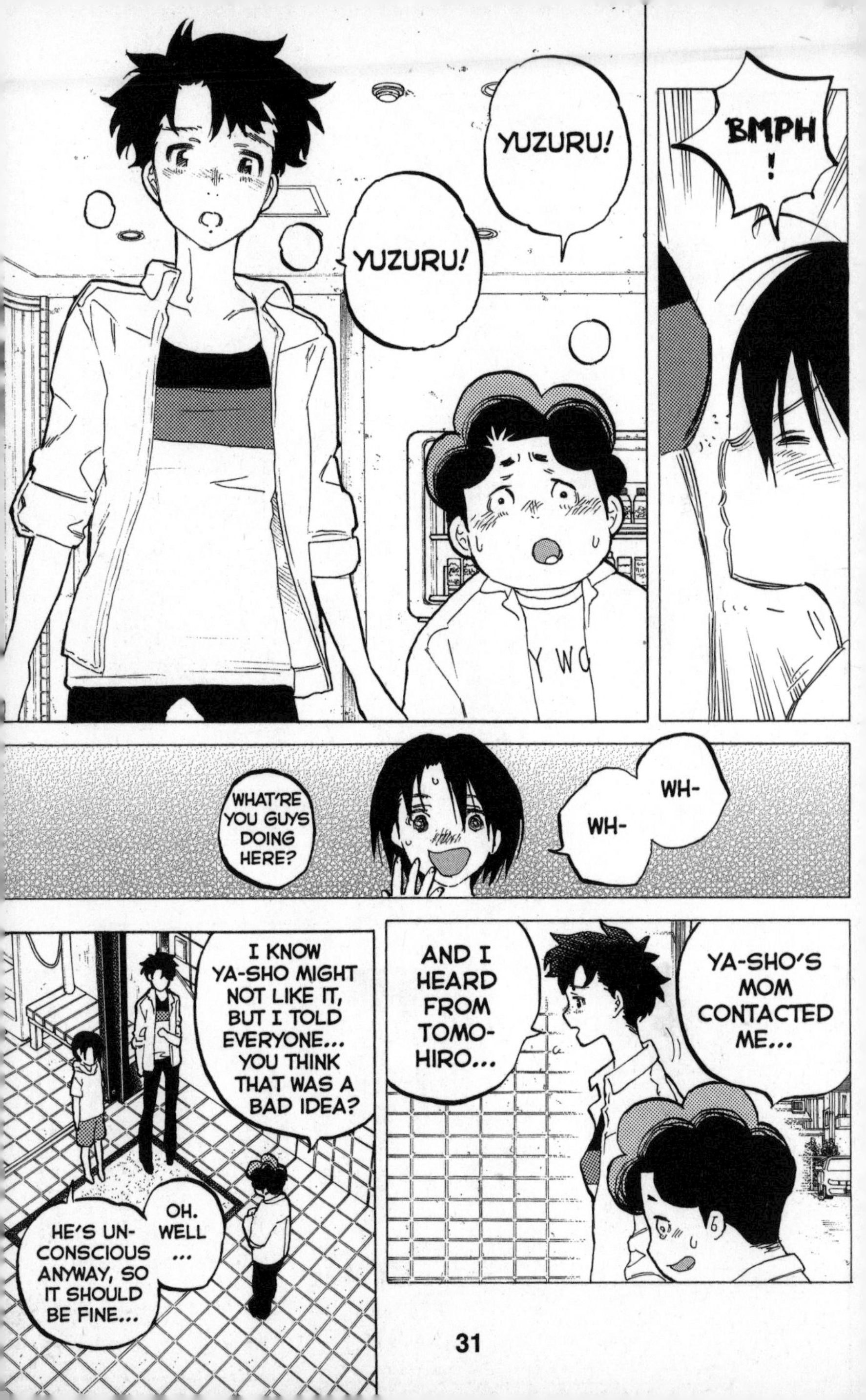
BMPH!
YUZURU!
YUZURU!
WH-
WH-
WHAT'RE YOU GUYS DOING HERE?
YA-SHO'S MOM CONTACTED ME...
AND I HEARD FROM TOMO-HIRO...
I KNOW YA-SHO MIGHT NOT LIKE IT, BUT I TOLD EVERYONE... YOU THINK THAT WAS A BAD IDEA?
OH. WELL ...
HE'S UN-CONSCIOUS ANYWAY, SO IT SHOULD BE FINE...

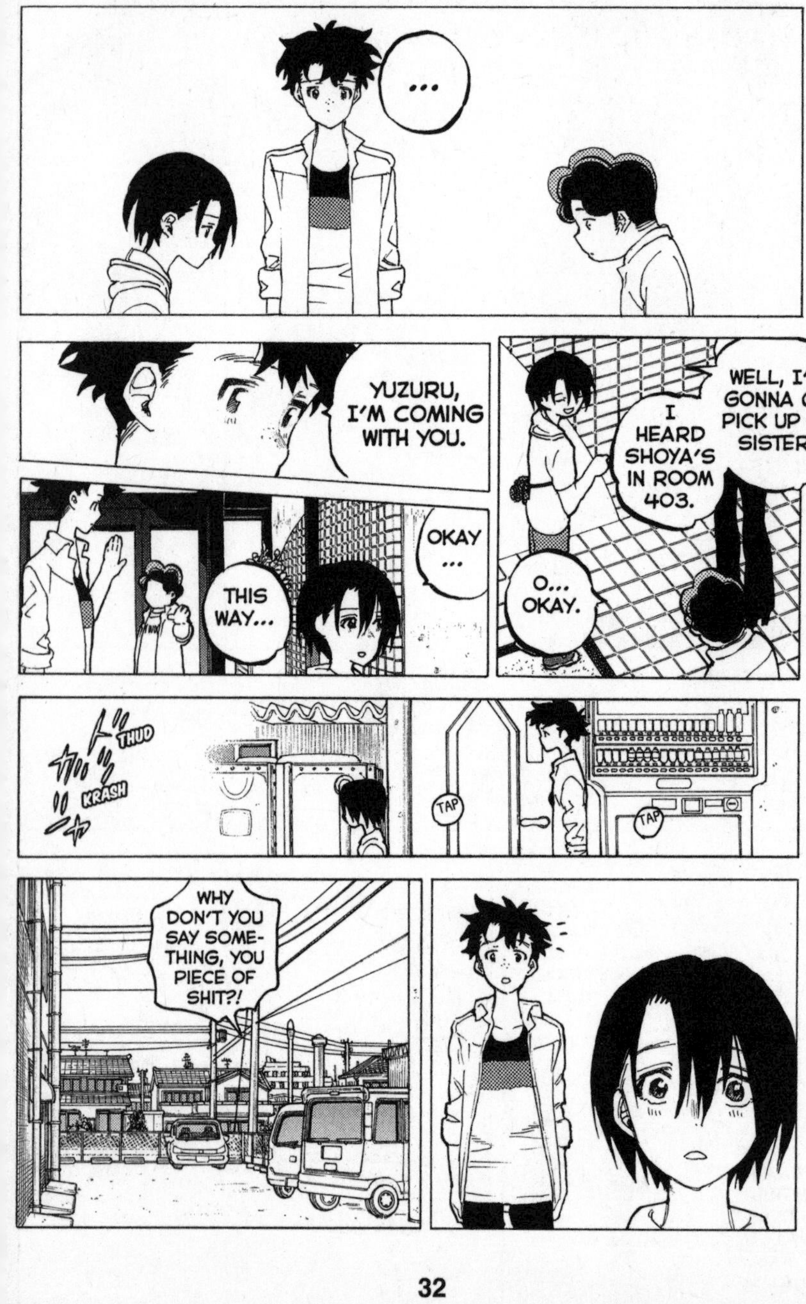
...
WELL, I'M GONNA GO PICK UP MY SISTER.
I HEARD SHOYA'S IN ROOM 403.
O... OKAY.
YUZURU, I'M COMING WITH YOU.
OKAY...
THIS WAY...
TAP
TAP
THUD
KRASH
WHY DON'T YOU SAY SOME-THING, YOU PIECE OF SHIT?!

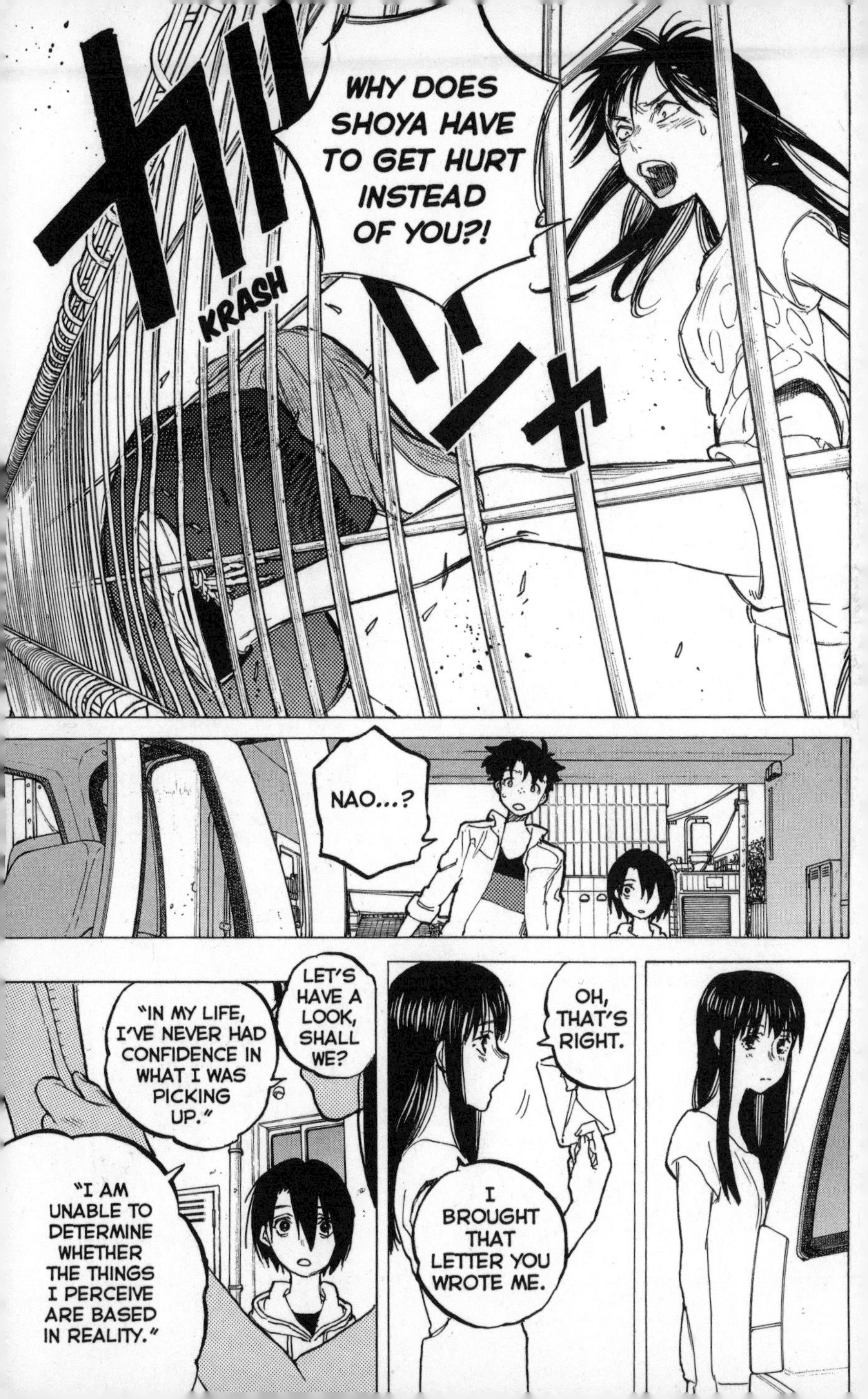
WHY DOES SHOYA HAVE TO GET HURT INSTEAD OF YOU?!
KRASH
NAO...?
OH, THAT'S RIGHT.
I BROUGHT THAT LETTER YOU WROTE ME.
LET'S HAVE A LOOK, SHALL WE?
"IN MY LIFE, I'VE NEVER HAD CONFIDENCE IN WHAT I WAS PICKING UP."
"I AM UNABLE TO DETERMINE WHETHER THE THINGS I PERCEIVE ARE BASED IN REALITY."

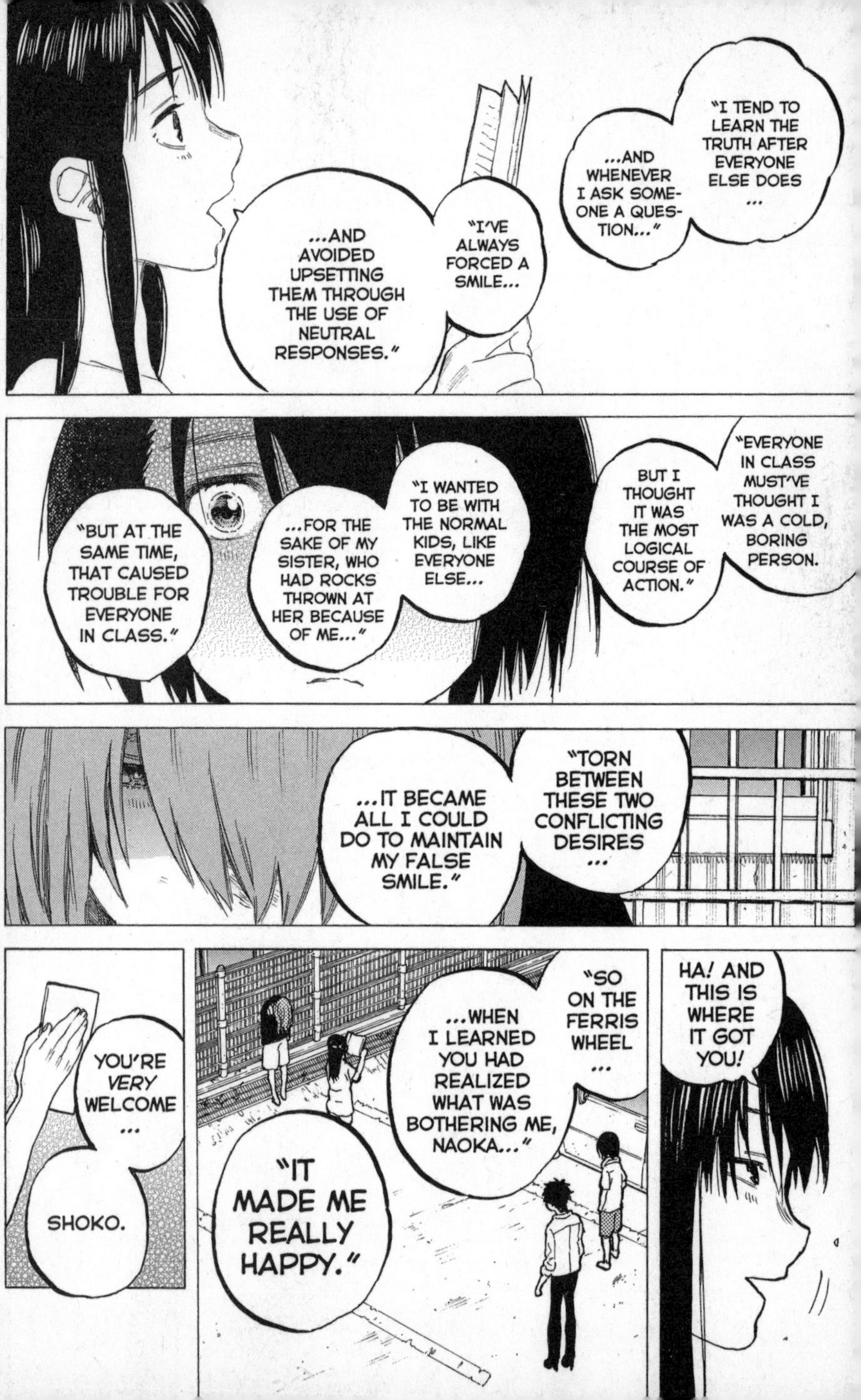
"I TEND TO LEARN THE TRUTH AFTER EVERYONE ELSE DOES...
...AND WHENEVER I ASK SOMEONE A QUESTION..."
"I'VE ALWAYS FORCED A SMILE...
...AND AVOIDED UPSETTING THEM THROUGH THE USE OF NEUTRAL RESPONSES."
"EVERYONE IN CLASS MUST'VE THOUGHT I WAS A COLD, BORING PERSON.
BUT I THOUGHT IT WAS THE MOST LOGICAL COURSE OF ACTION."
"I WANTED TO BE WITH THE NORMAL KIDS, LIKE EVERYONE ELSE...
...FOR THE SAKE OF MY SISTER, WHO HAD ROCKS THROWN AT HER BECAUSE OF ME..."
"BUT AT THE SAME TIME, THAT CAUSED TROUBLE FOR EVERYONE IN CLASS."
"TORN BETWEEN THESE TWO CONFLICTING DESIRES...
...IT BECAME ALL I COULD DO TO MAINTAIN MY FALSE SMILE."
HA! AND THIS IS WHERE IT GOT YOU!
"SO ON THE FERRIS WHEEL...
...WHEN I LEARNED YOU HAD REALIZED WHAT WAS BOTHERING ME, NAOKA..."
"IT MADE ME REALLY HAPPY."
YOU'RE *VERY* WELCOME...
SHOKO.

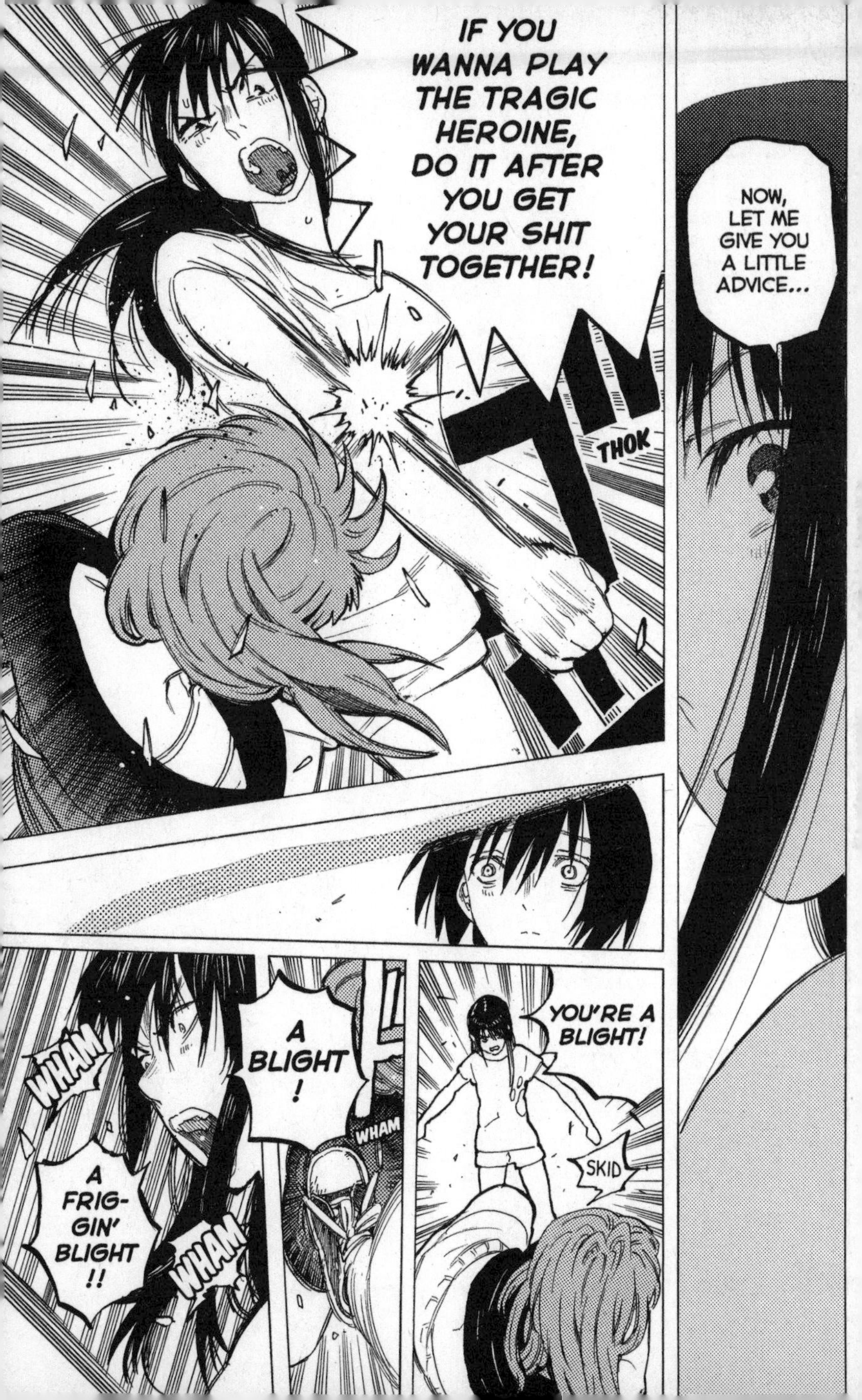
NOW, LET ME GIVE YOU A LITTLE ADVICE...
IF YOU WANNA PLAY THE TRAGIC HEROINE, DO IT AFTER YOU GET YOUR SHIT TOGETHER!
THOK
YOU'RE A BLIGHT!
SKID
A BLIGHT!
WHAM
WHAM
A FRIG-GIN' BLIGHT!!
WHAM

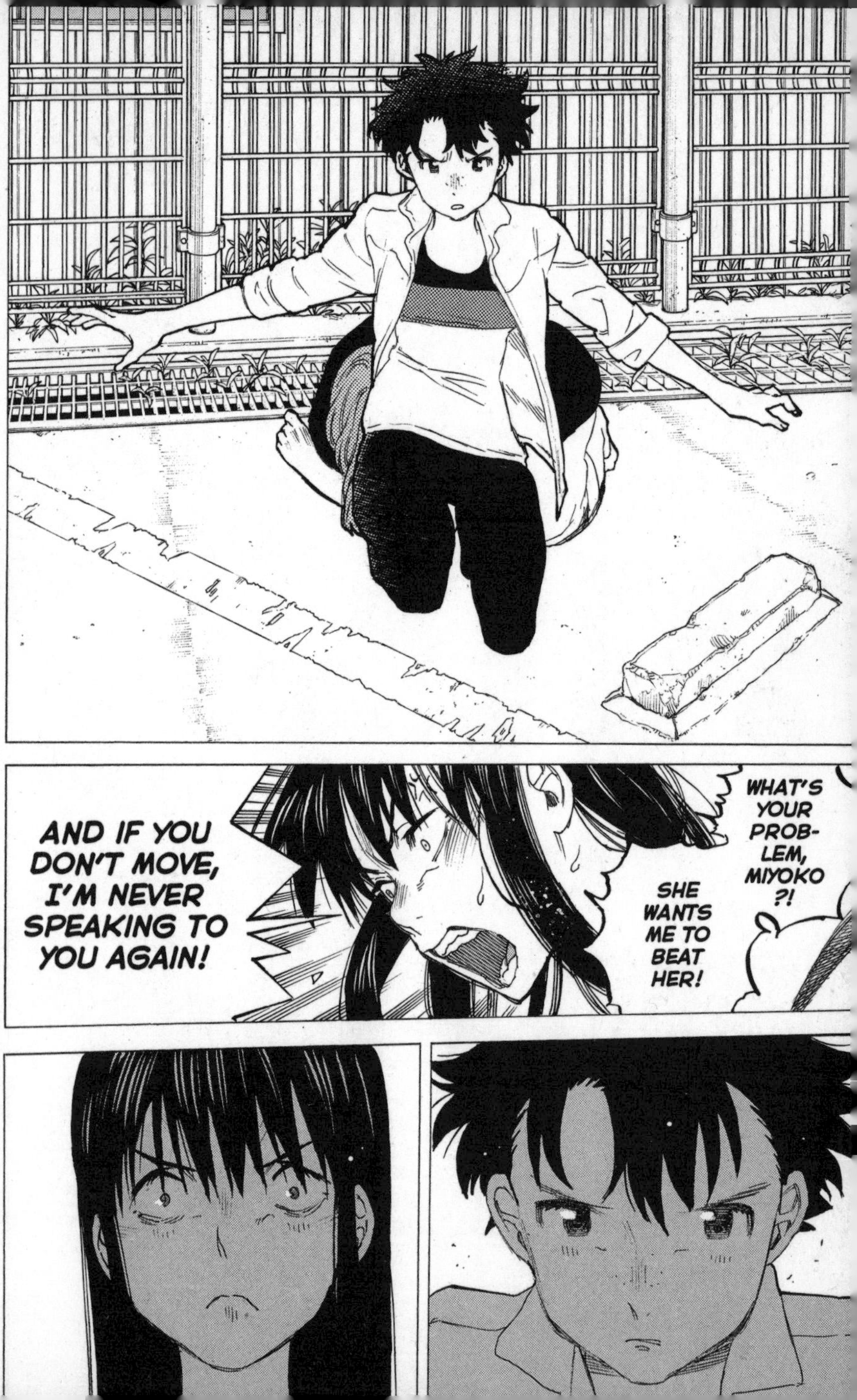
WHAT'S YOUR PROB-LEM, MIYOKO?!
SHE WANTS ME TO BEAT HER!
AND IF YOU DON'T MOVE, I'M NEVER SPEAKING TO YOU AGAIN!

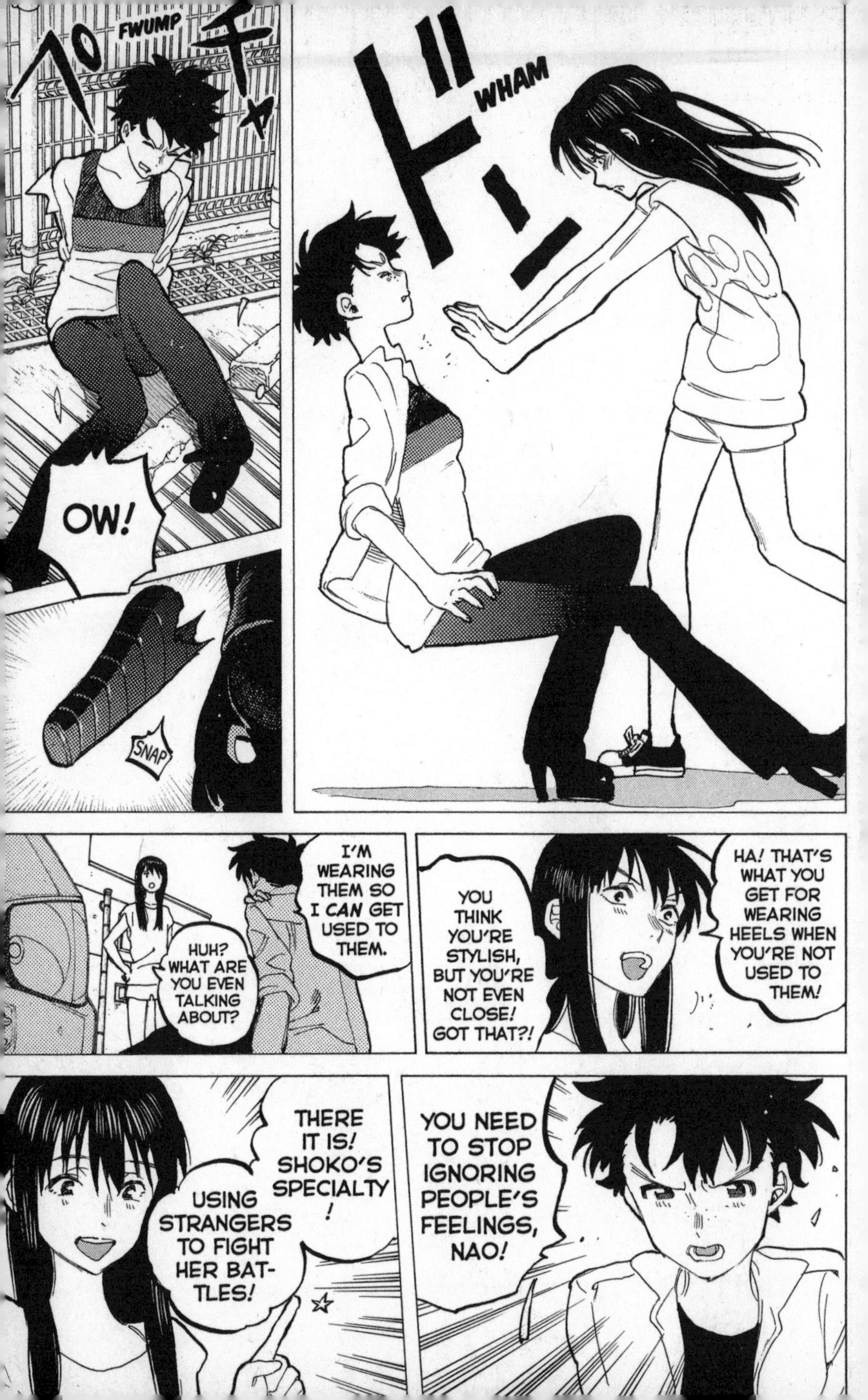
WHAM
FWUMP
OW!
SNAP
HA! THAT'S WHAT YOU GET FOR WEARING HEELS WHEN YOU'RE NOT USED TO THEM!
YOU THINK YOU'RE STYLISH, BUT YOU'RE NOT EVEN CLOSE! GOT THAT?!
I'M WEARING THEM SO I CAN GET USED TO THEM.
HUH? WHAT ARE YOU EVEN TALKING ABOUT?
YOU NEED TO STOP IGNORING PEOPLE'S FEELINGS, NAO!
THERE IT IS! SHOKO'S SPECIALTY!
USING STRANGERS TO FIGHT HER BAT-TLES!

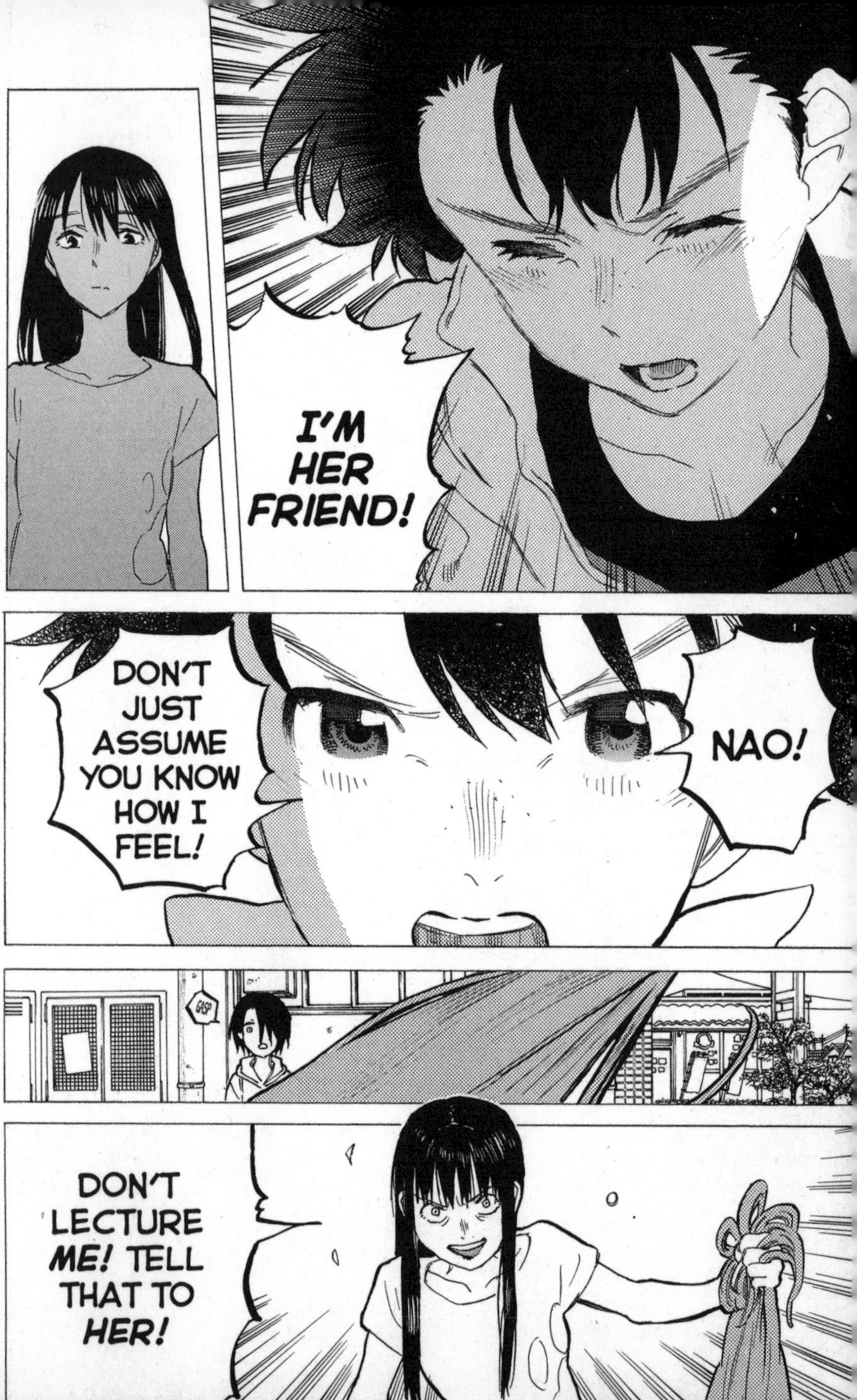
I'M HER FRIEND!
NAO!
DON'T JUST ASSUME YOU KNOW HOW I FEEL!
GASP
DON'T LECTURE *ME!* TELL THAT TO *HER!*

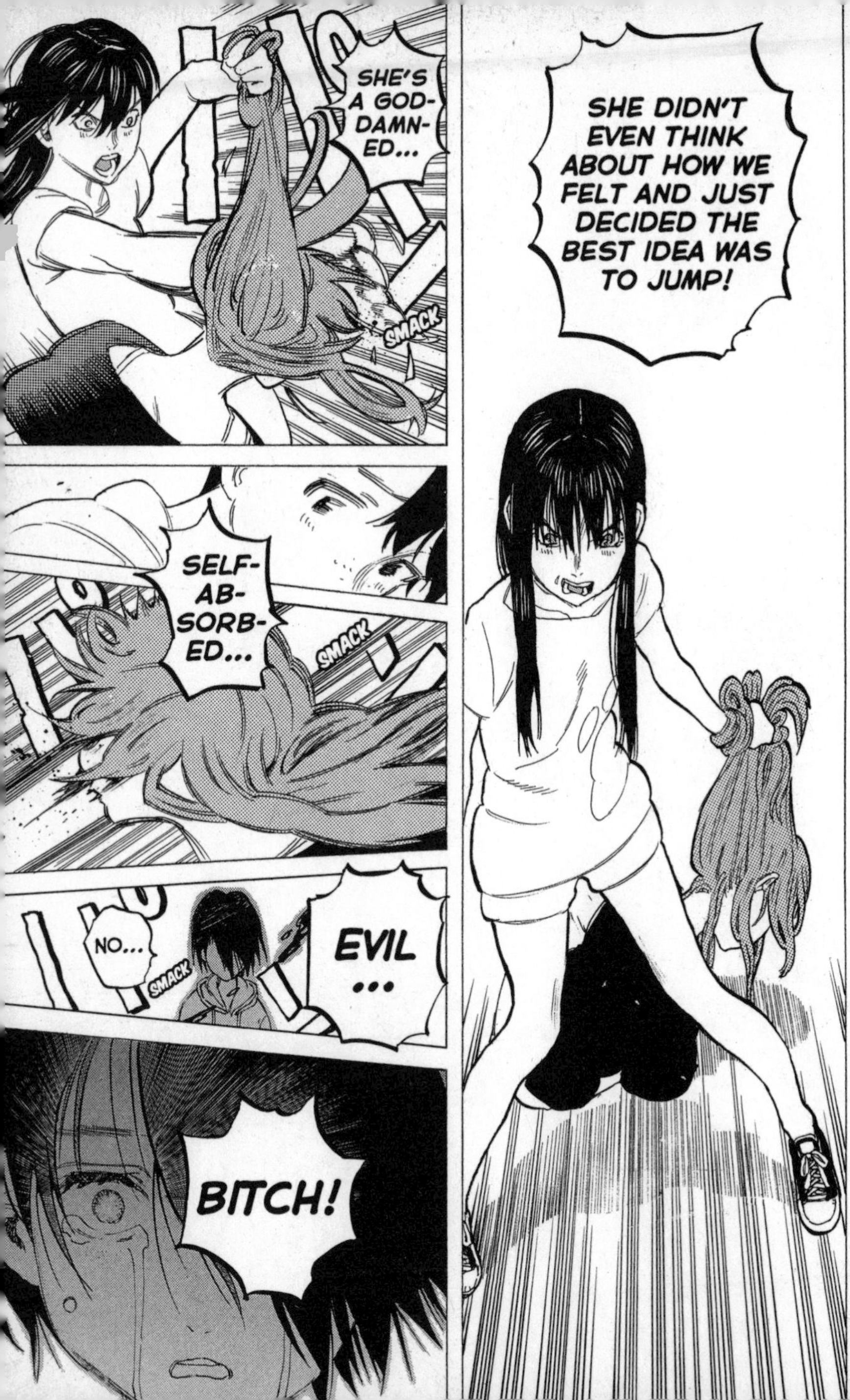

SHE DIDN'T EVEN THINK ABOUT HOW WE FELT AND JUST DECIDED THE BEST IDEA WAS TO JUMP!
SHE'S A GOD-DAMN-ED...
SMACK
SELF-AB-SORB-ED...
SMACK
EVIL...
SMACK
NO...
BITCH!

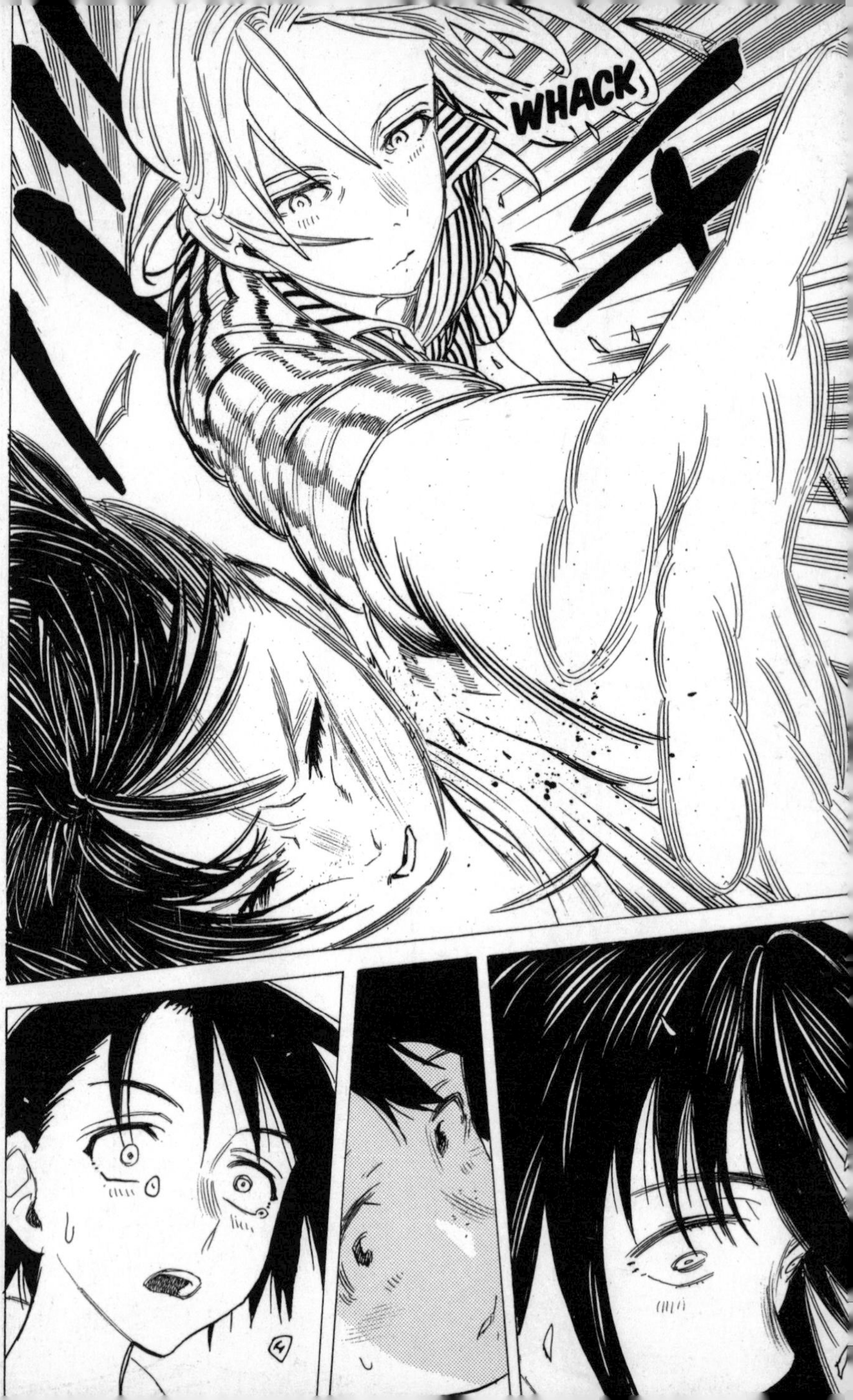
WHACK

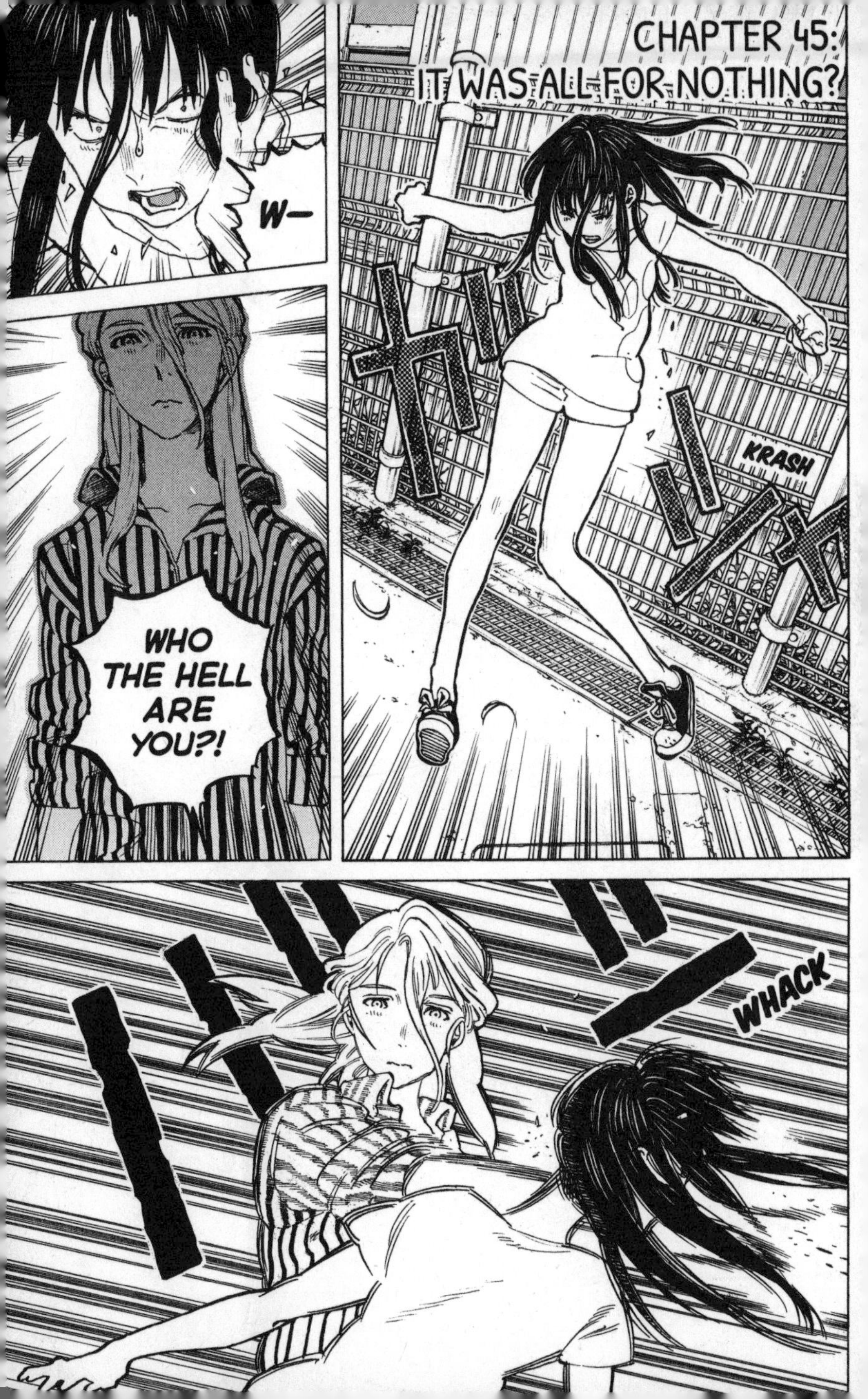
CHAPTER 45:
IT WAS ALL FOR NOTHING?
KRASH
W—
WHO THE HELL ARE YOU?!
WHACK

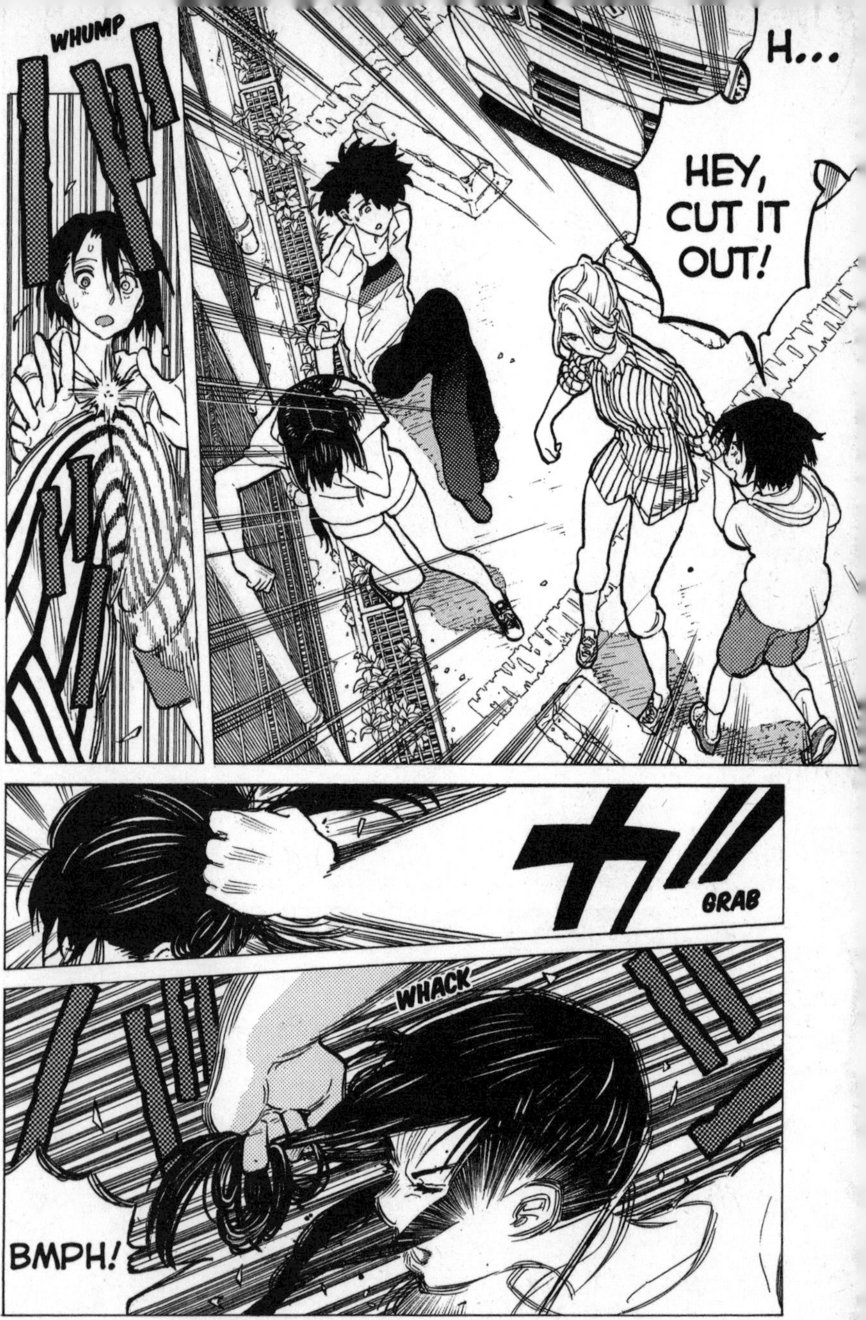
H...
HEY, CUT IT OUT!
WHUMP
GRAB
WHACK
BMPH!

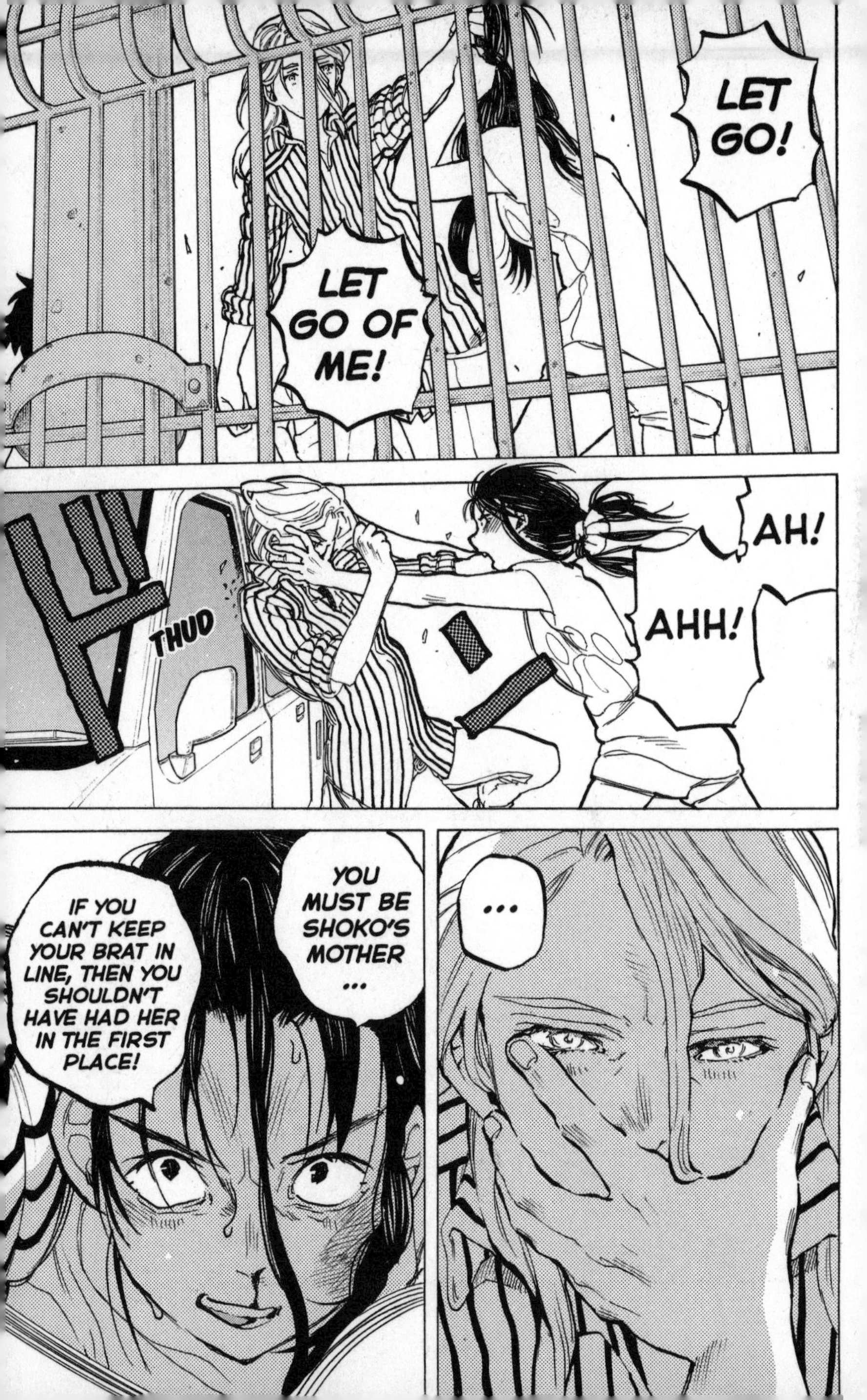
LET GO!
LET GO OF ME!
AH!
AHH!
THUD
...
YOU MUST BE SHOKO'S MOTHER ...
IF YOU CAN'T KEEP YOUR BRAT IN LINE, THEN YOU SHOULDN'T HAVE HAD HER IN THE FIRST PLACE!

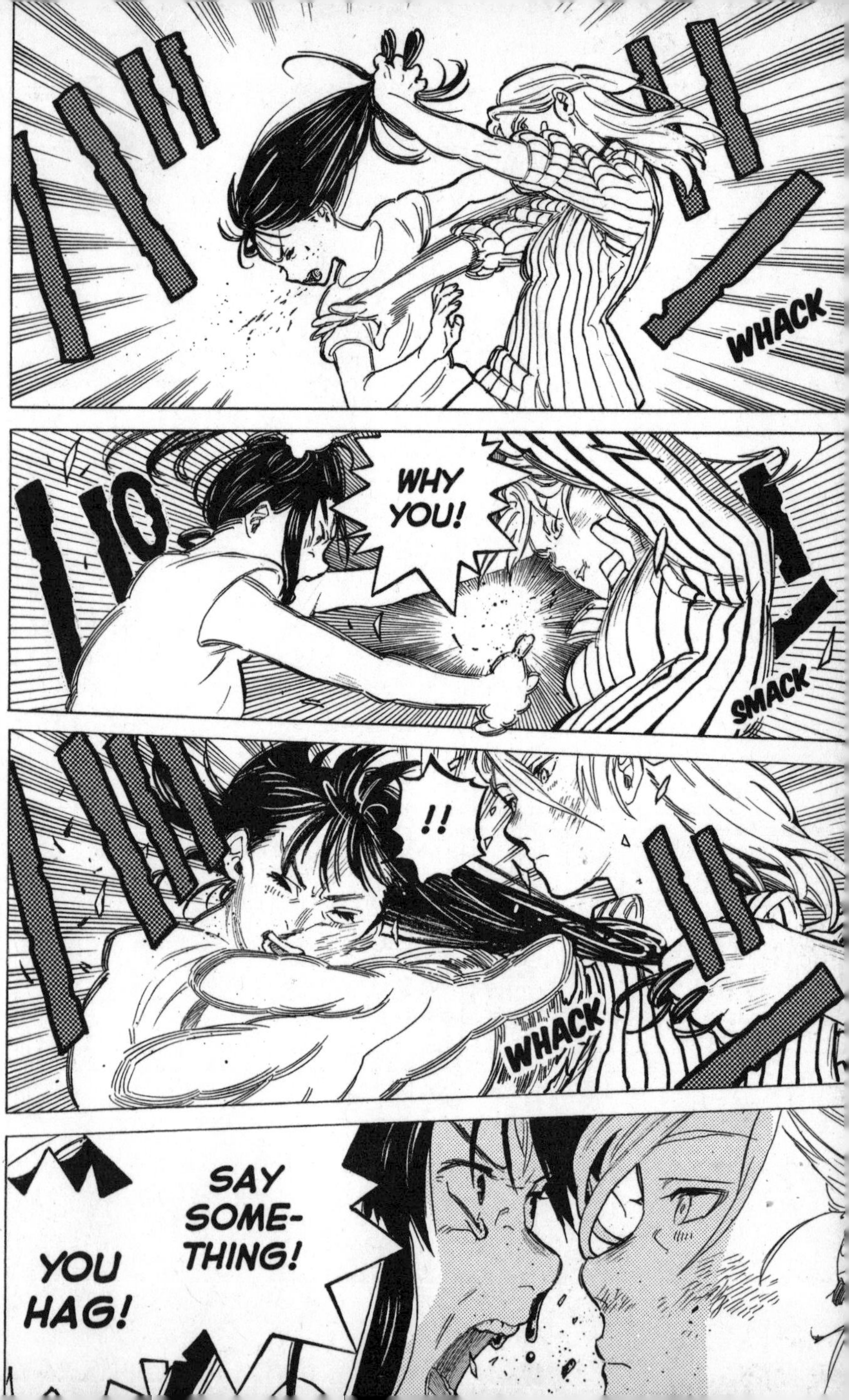
WHACK
WHY YOU!
SMACK
!!
WHACK
SAY SOME-THING!
YOU HAG!

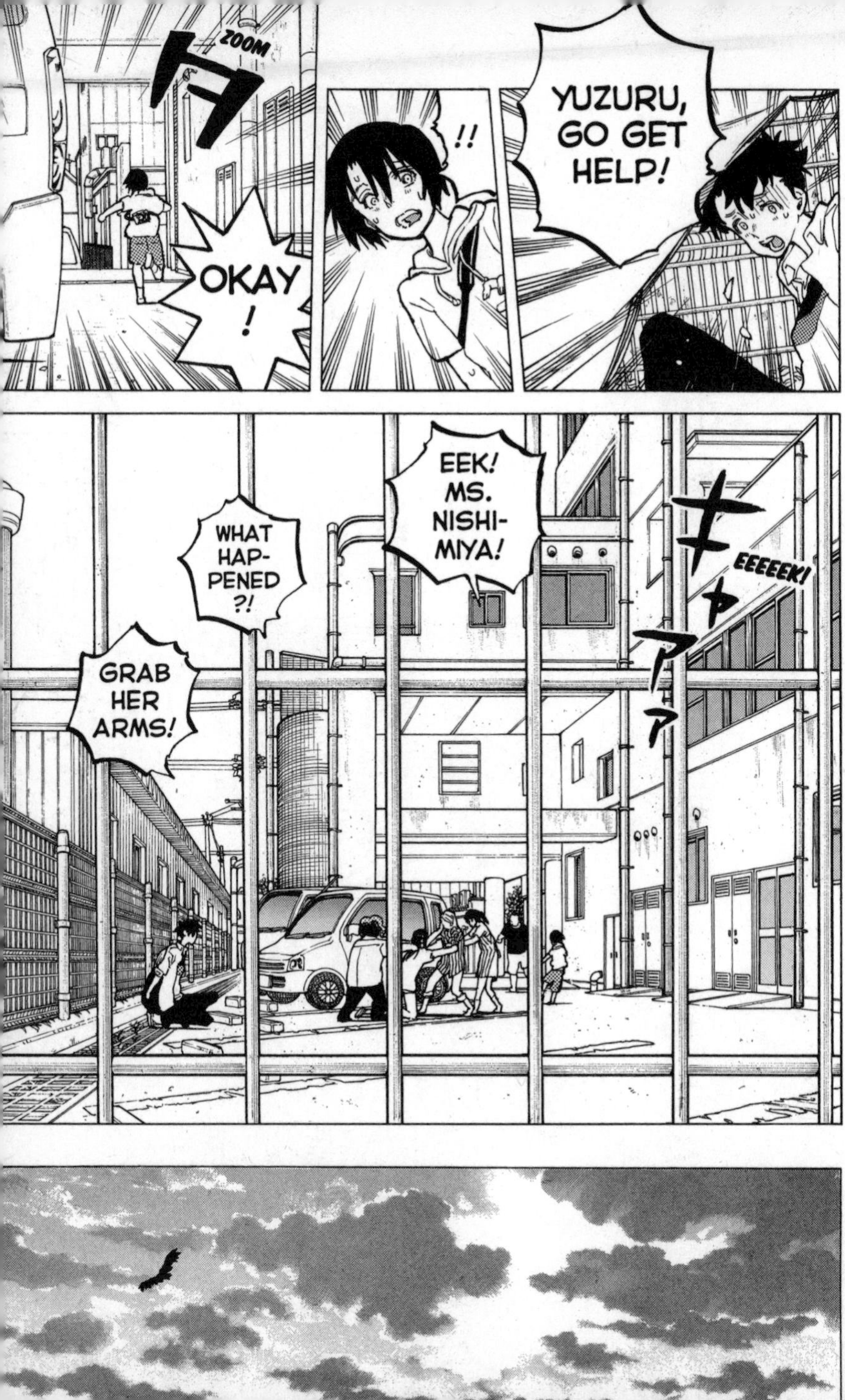
YUZURU, GO GET HELP!
!!
ZOOM
OKAY!
キャアア
EEEEEK!
EEK! MS. NISHIMIYA!
WHAT HAPPENED?!
GRAB HER ARMS!

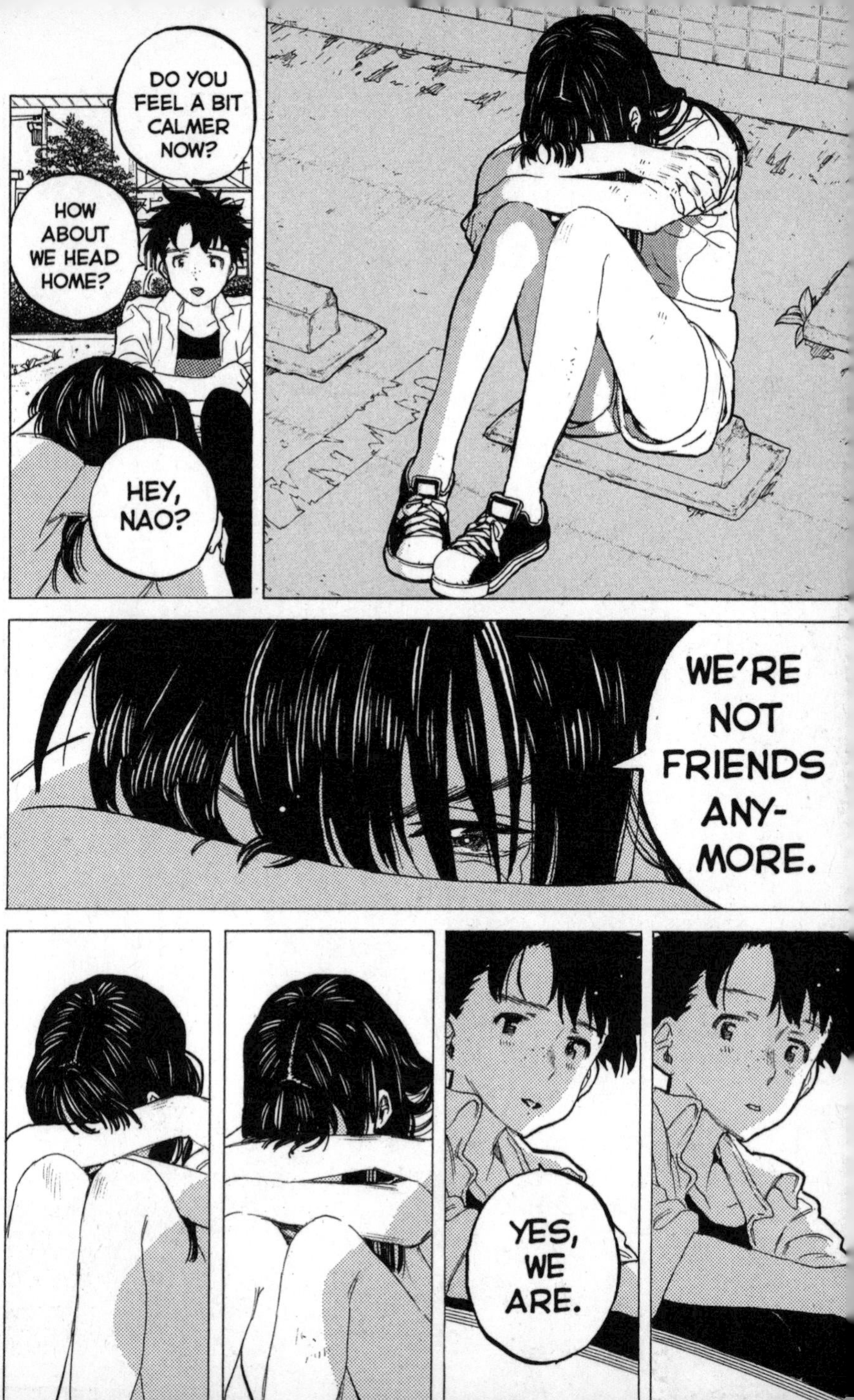
DO YOU FEEL A BIT CALMER NOW?
HOW ABOUT WE HEAD HOME?
HEY, NAO?
WE'RE NOT FRIENDS ANY-MORE.
YES, WE ARE.

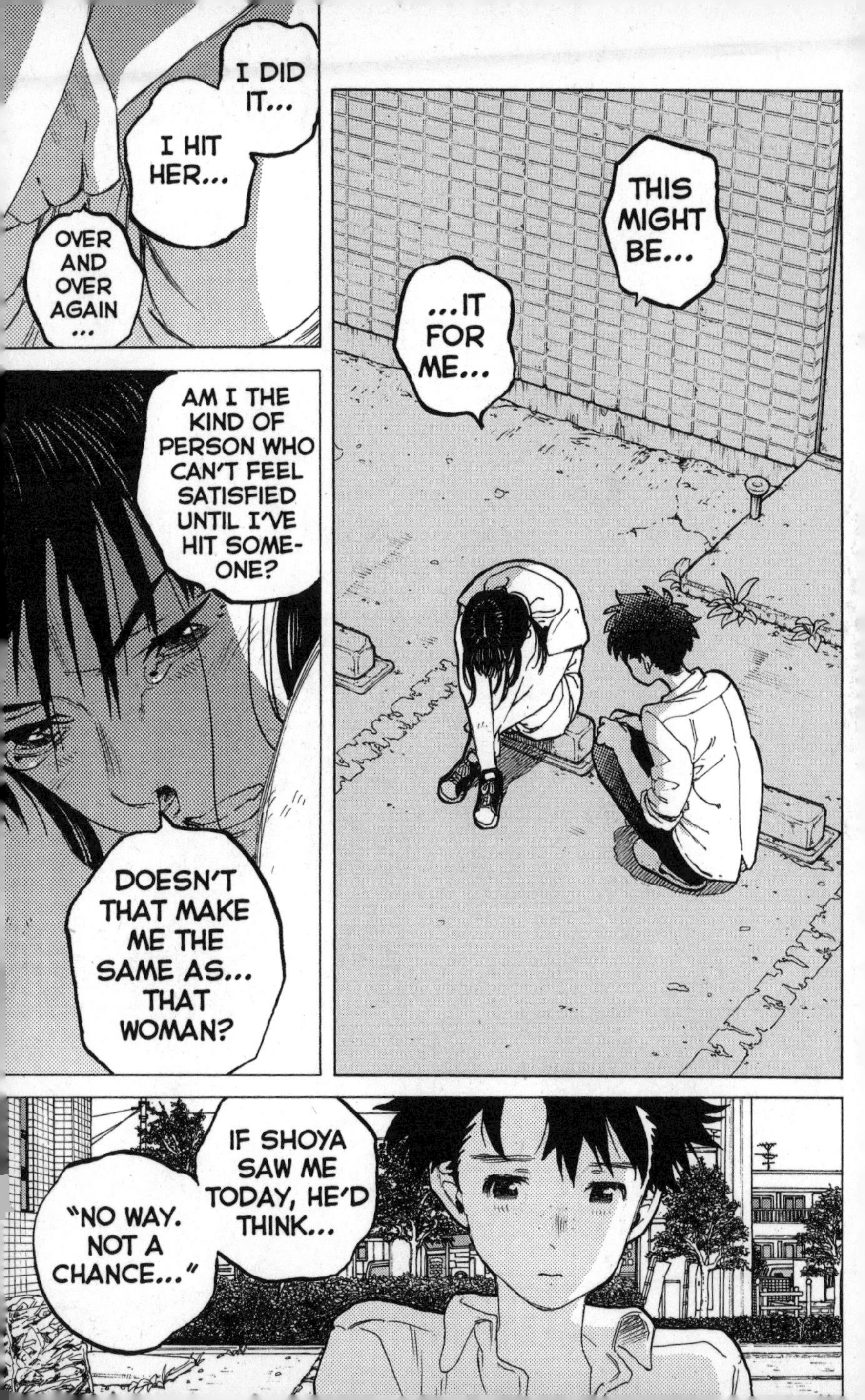
THIS MIGHT BE...
...IT FOR ME...
I DID IT...
I HIT HER...
OVER AND OVER AGAIN...
AM I THE KIND OF PERSON WHO CAN'T FEEL SATISFIED UNTIL I'VE HIT SOME-ONE?
DOESN'T THAT MAKE ME THE SAME AS... THAT WOMAN?
IF SHOYA SAW ME TODAY, HE'D THINK...
"NO WAY. NOT A CHANCE..."

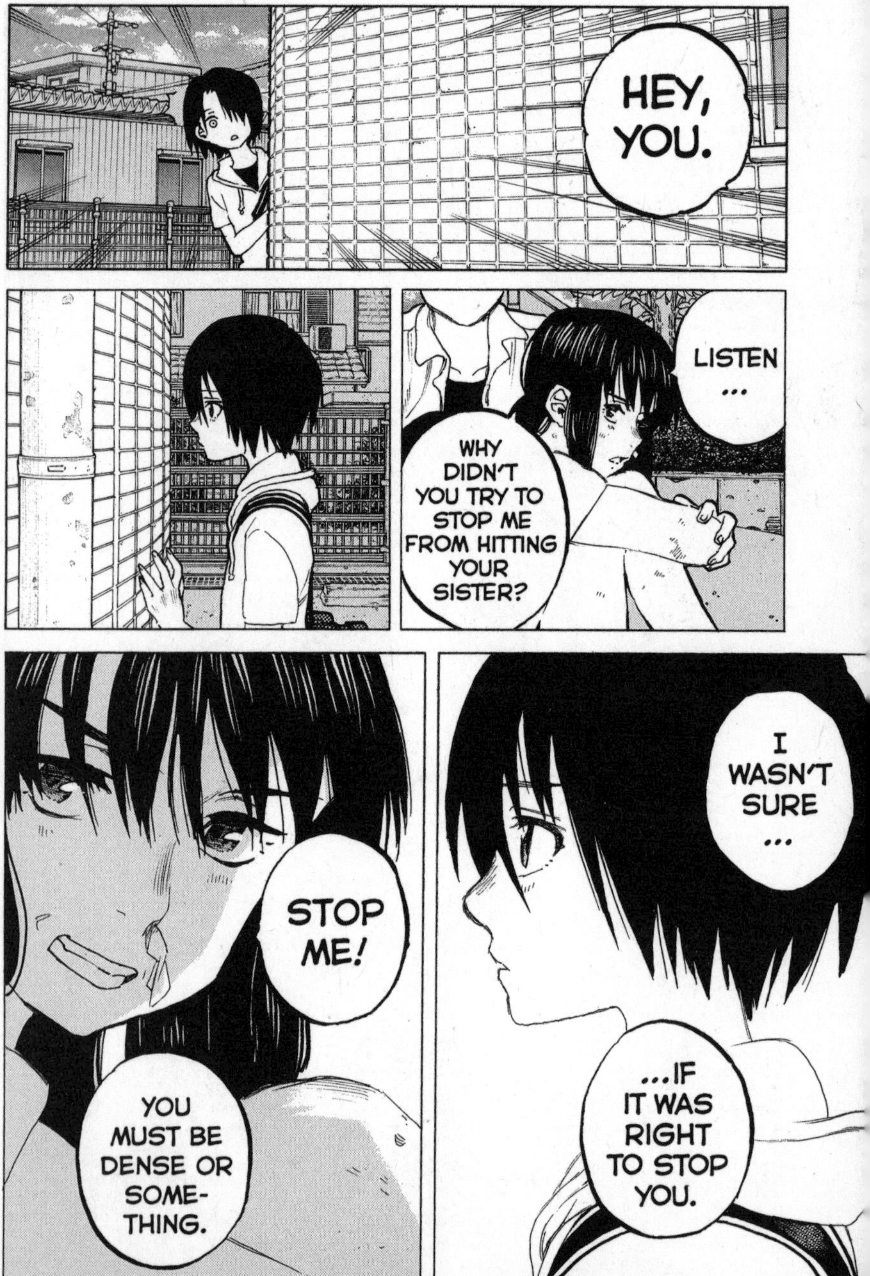
HEY, YOU.
LISTEN ...
WHY DIDN'T YOU TRY TO STOP ME FROM HITTING YOUR SISTER?
I WASN'T SURE ...
...IF IT WAS RIGHT TO STOP YOU.
STOP ME!
YOU MUST BE DENSE OR SOME-THING.

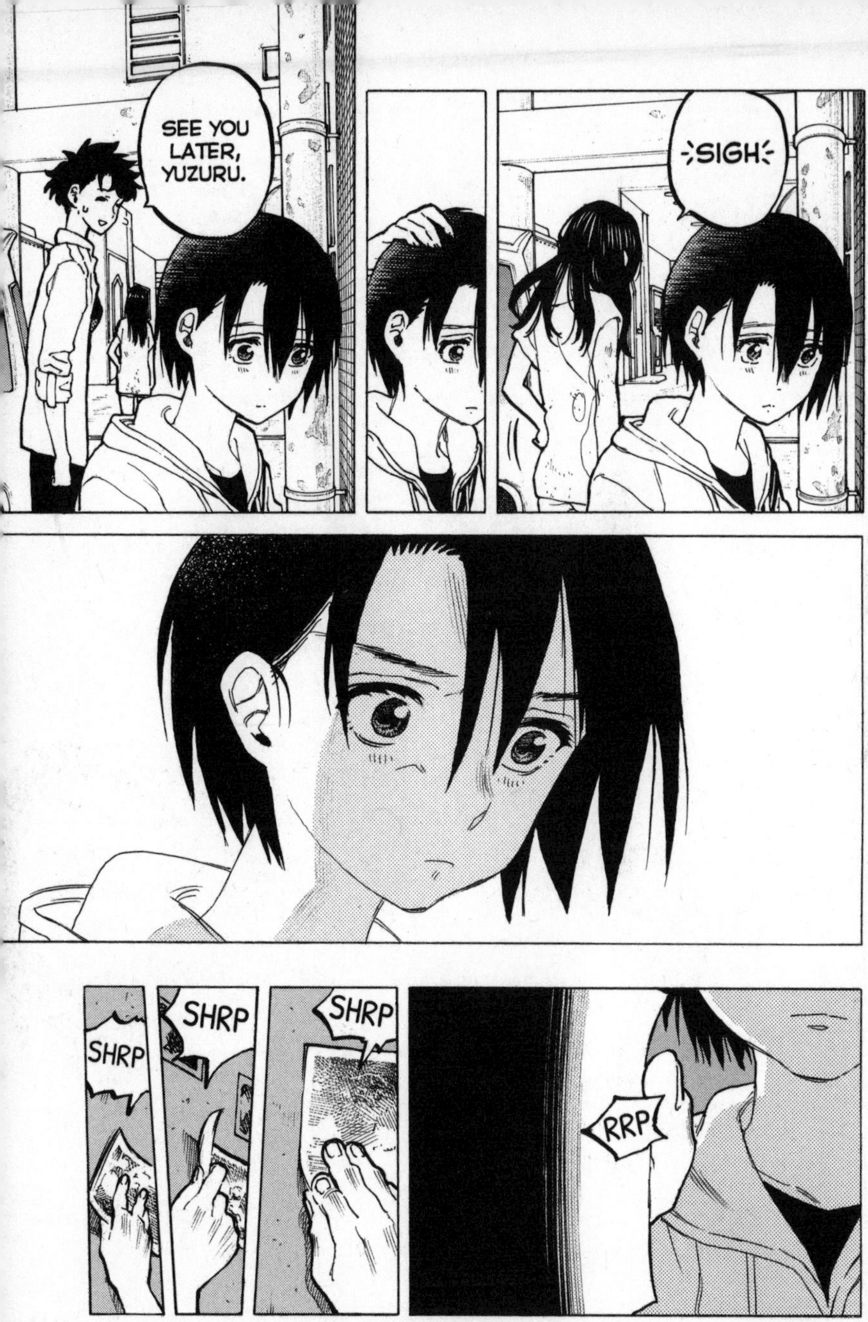

SIGH
SEE YOU LATER, YUZURU.
RRP
SHRP
SHRP
SHRP

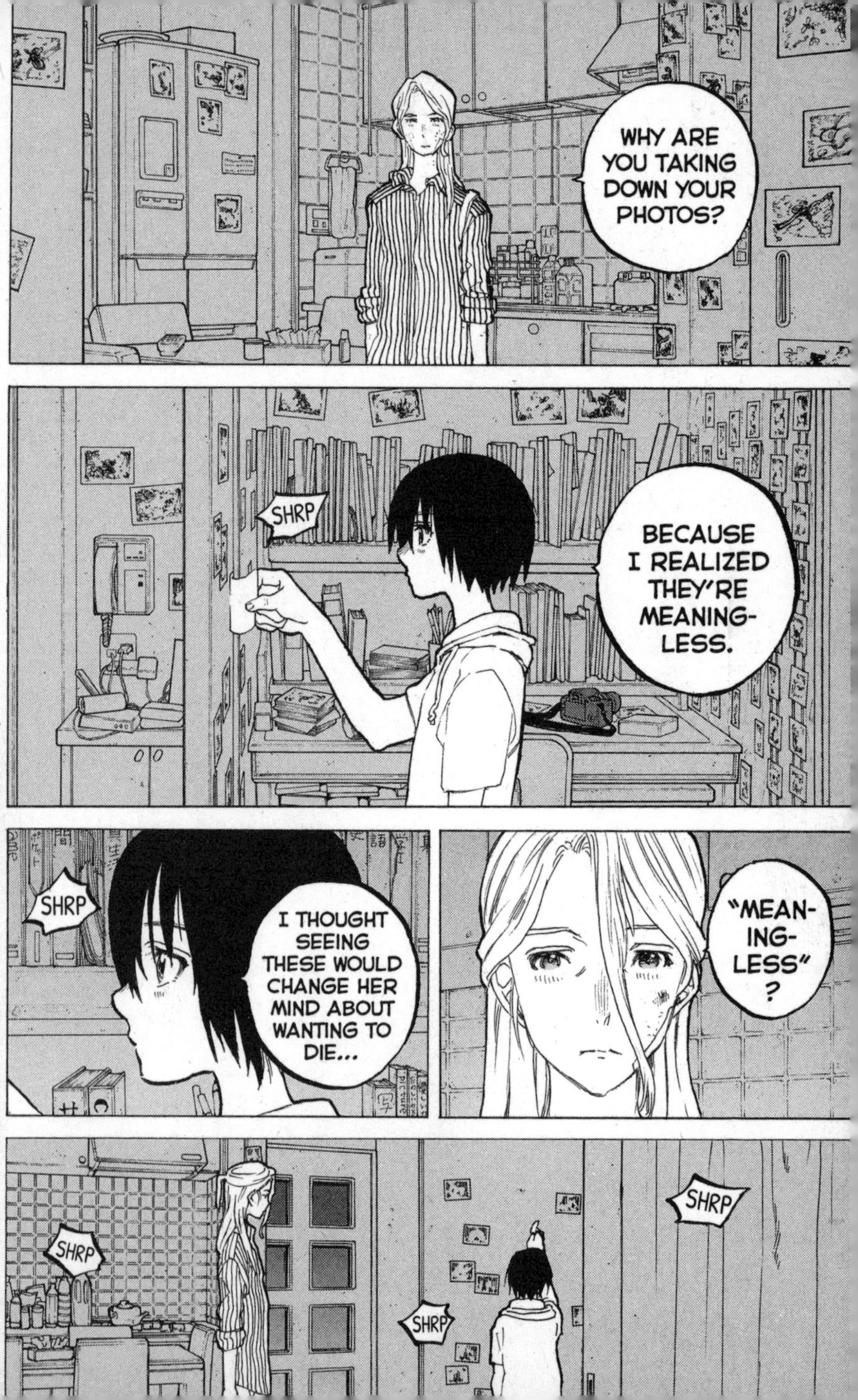
WHY ARE YOU TAKING DOWN YOUR PHOTOS?
BECAUSE I REALIZED THEY'RE MEANING-LESS.
SHRP
"MEAN-ING-LESS"?
SHRP
I THOUGHT SEEING THESE WOULD CHANGE HER MIND ABOUT WANTING TO DIE...
SHRP
SHRP
SHRP

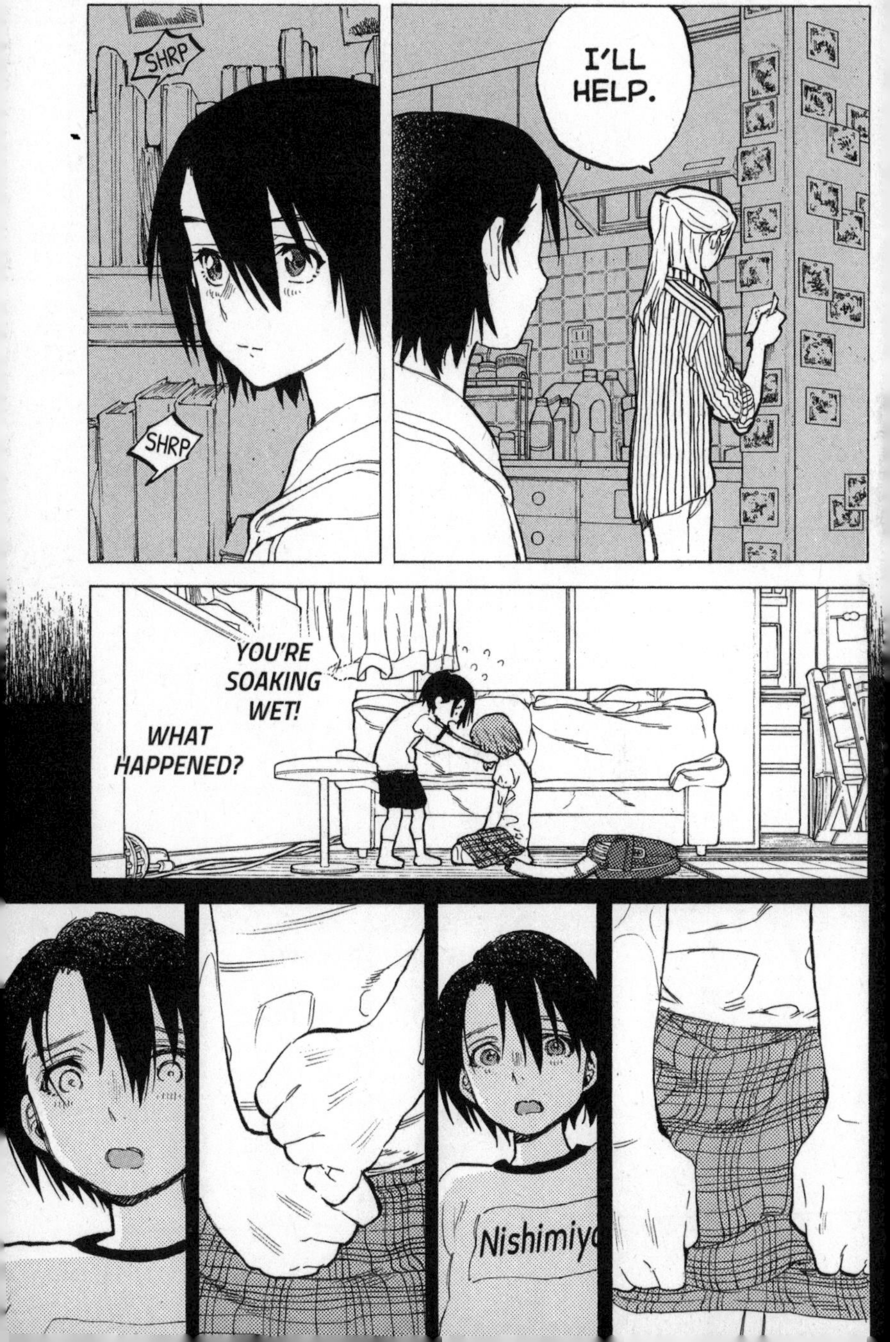
I'LL HELP.
SHRP
SHRP
YOU'RE SOAKING WET!
WHAT HAPPENED?
Nishimiy

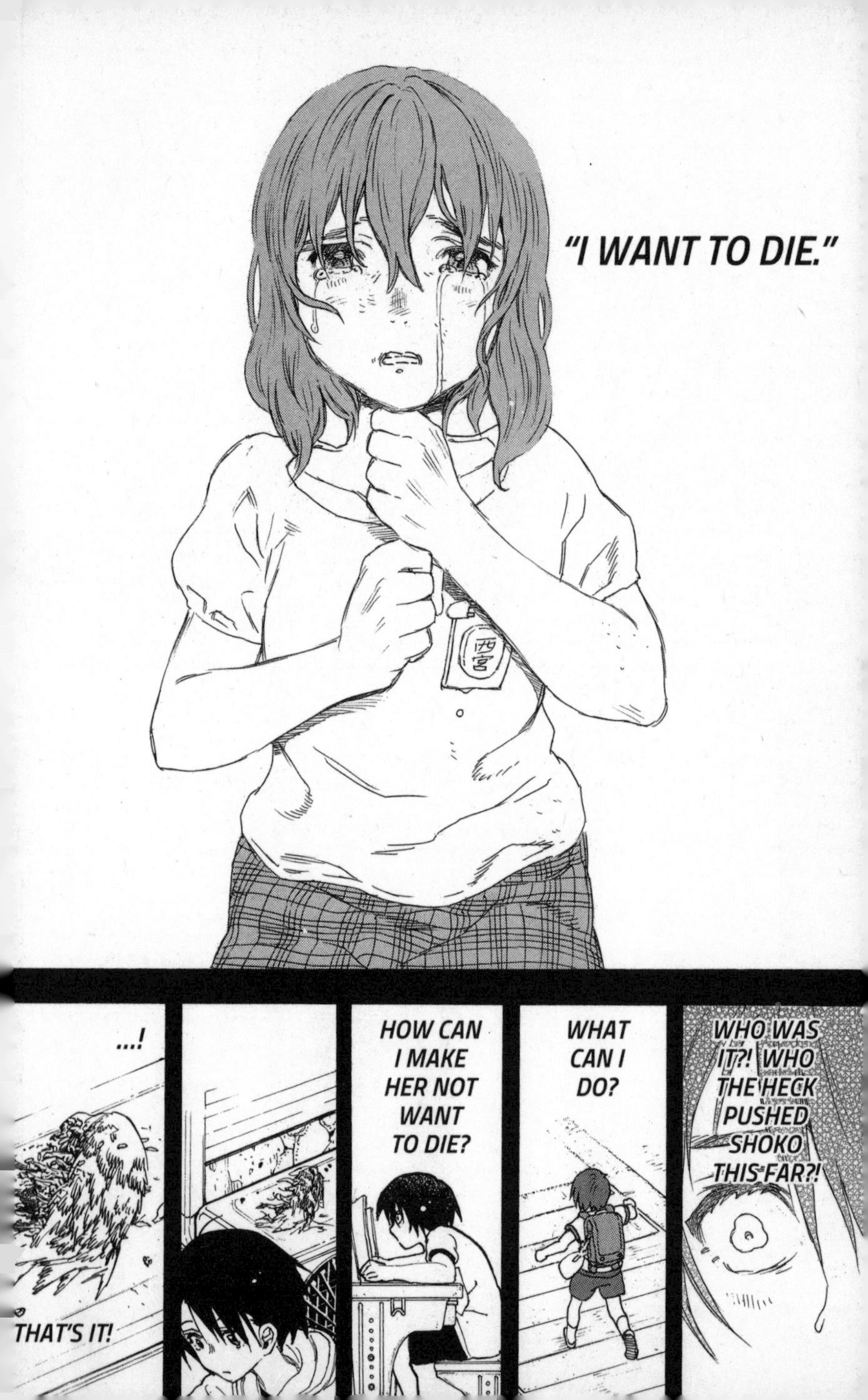
"I WANT TO DIE."
WHO WAS IT?! WHO THE HECK PUSHED SHOKO THIS FAR?!
WHAT CAN I DO?
HOW CAN I MAKE HER NOT WANT TO DIE?
...!
THAT'S IT!

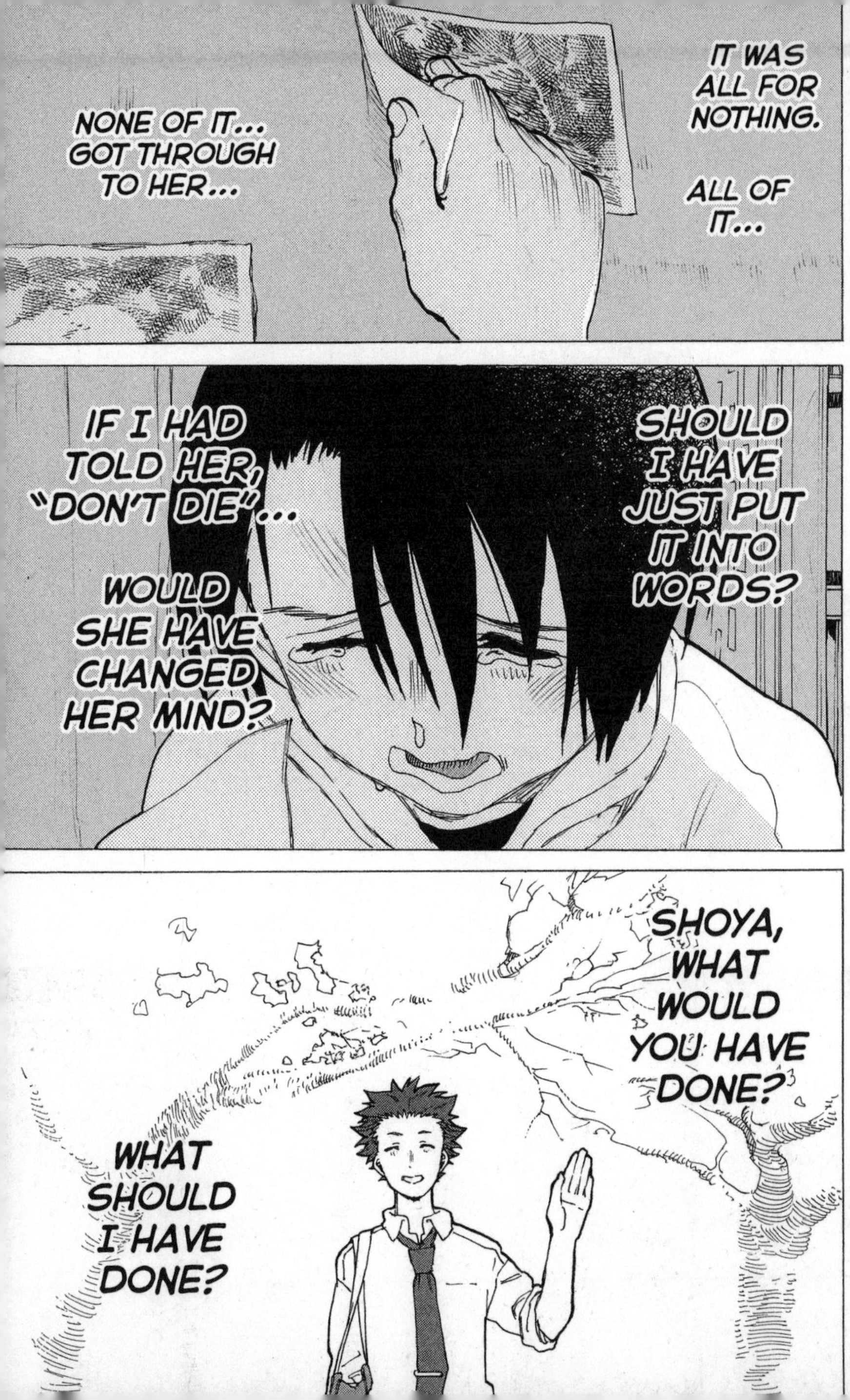
IT WAS ALL FOR NOTHING.
ALL OF IT...
NONE OF IT... GOT THROUGH TO HER...
SHOULD I HAVE JUST PUT IT INTO WORDS?
IF I HAD TOLD HER, "DON'T DIE"...
WOULD SHE HAVE CHANGED HER MIND?
SHOYA, WHAT WOULD YOU HAVE DONE?
WHAT SHOULD I HAVE DONE?

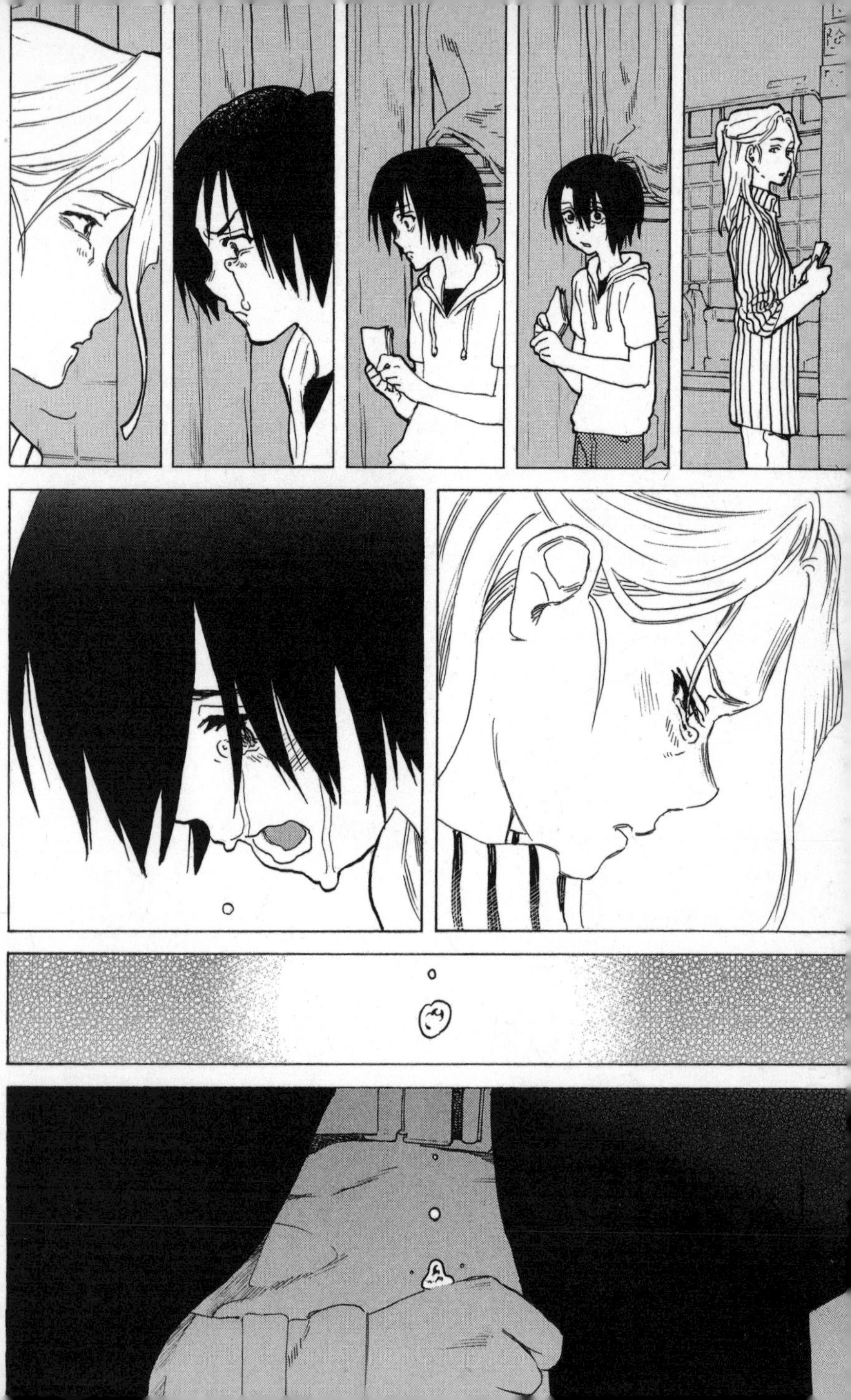

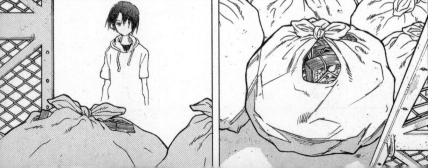

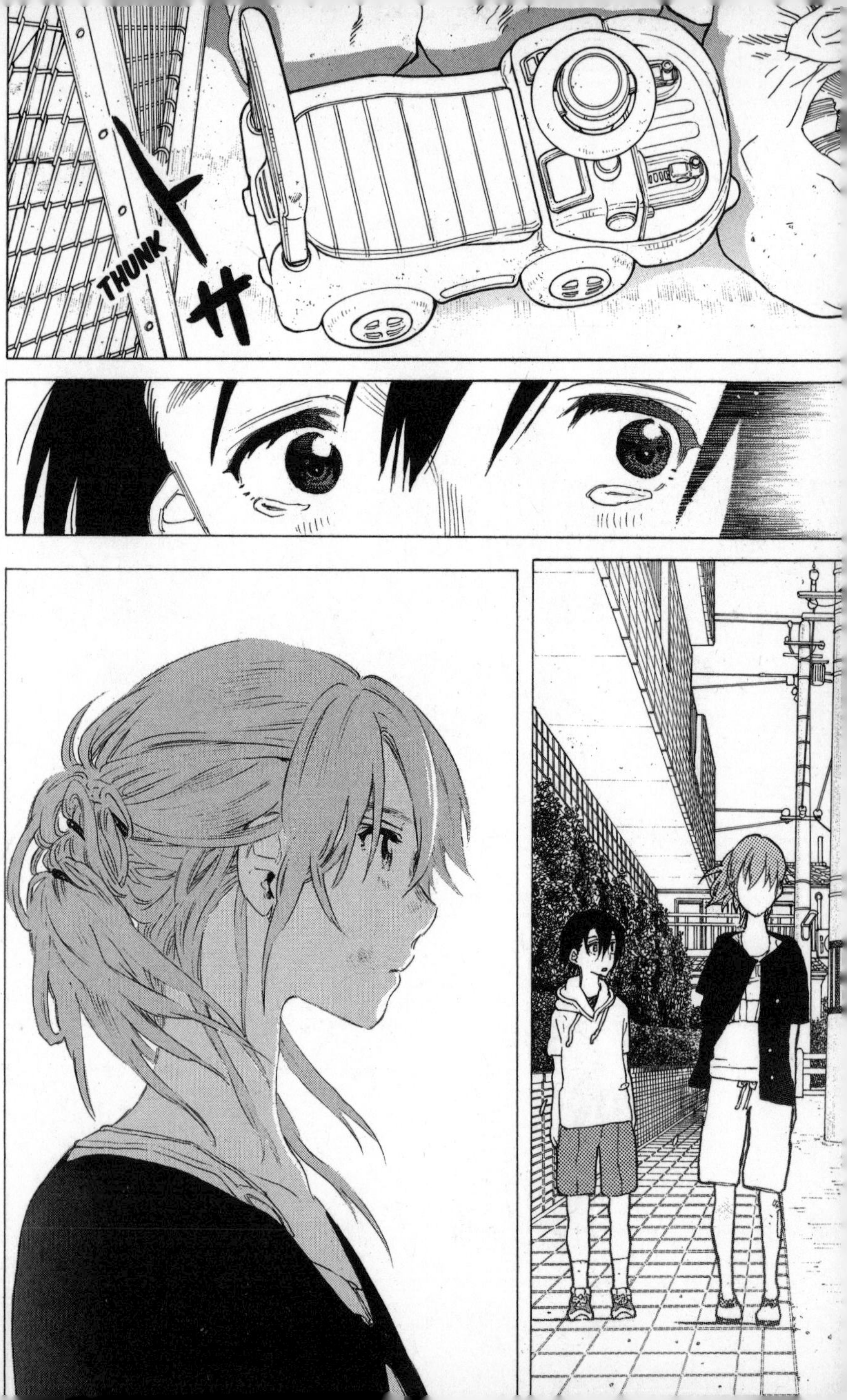
THUNK

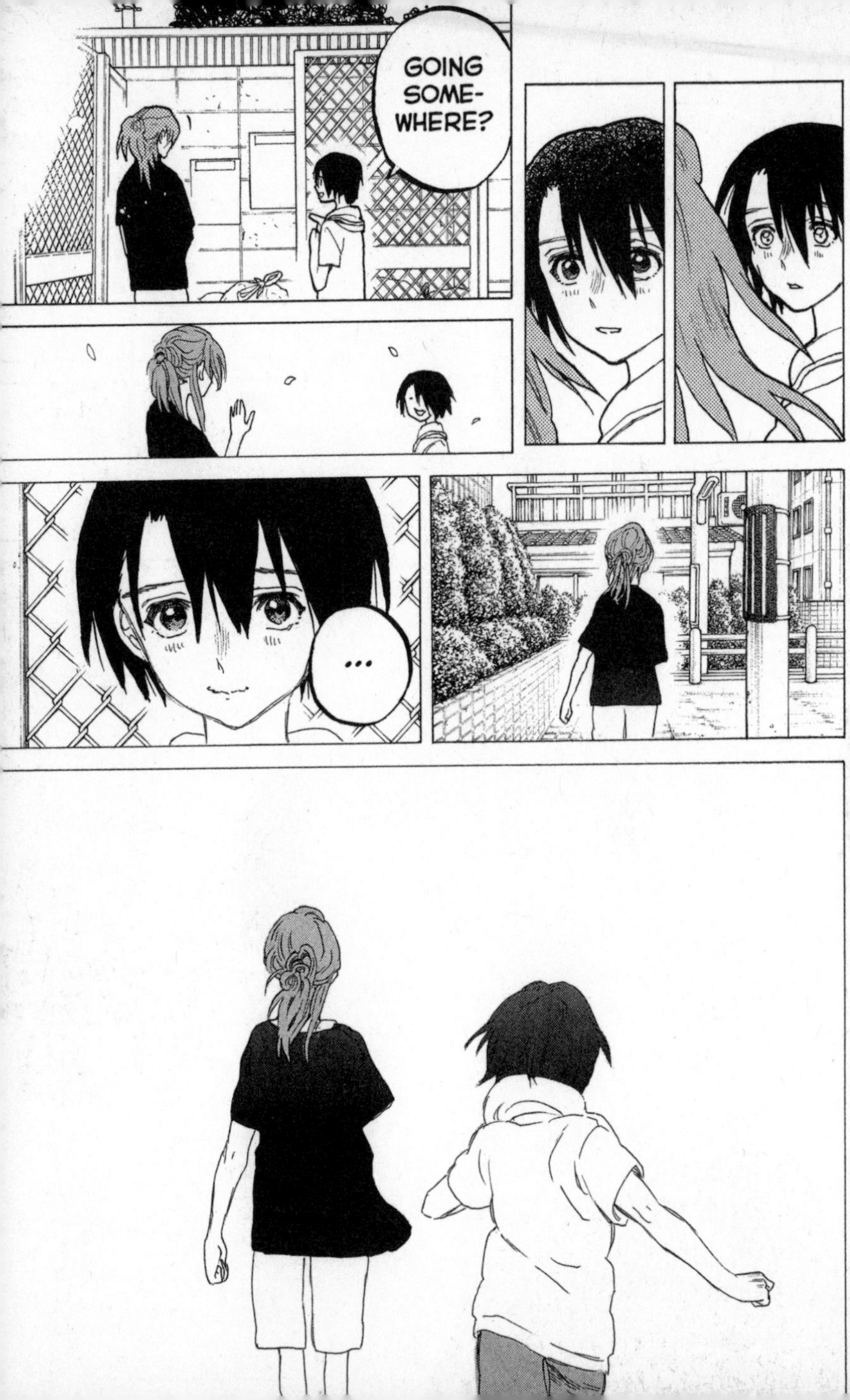
GOING SOME-WHERE?
...

a Silent Voice

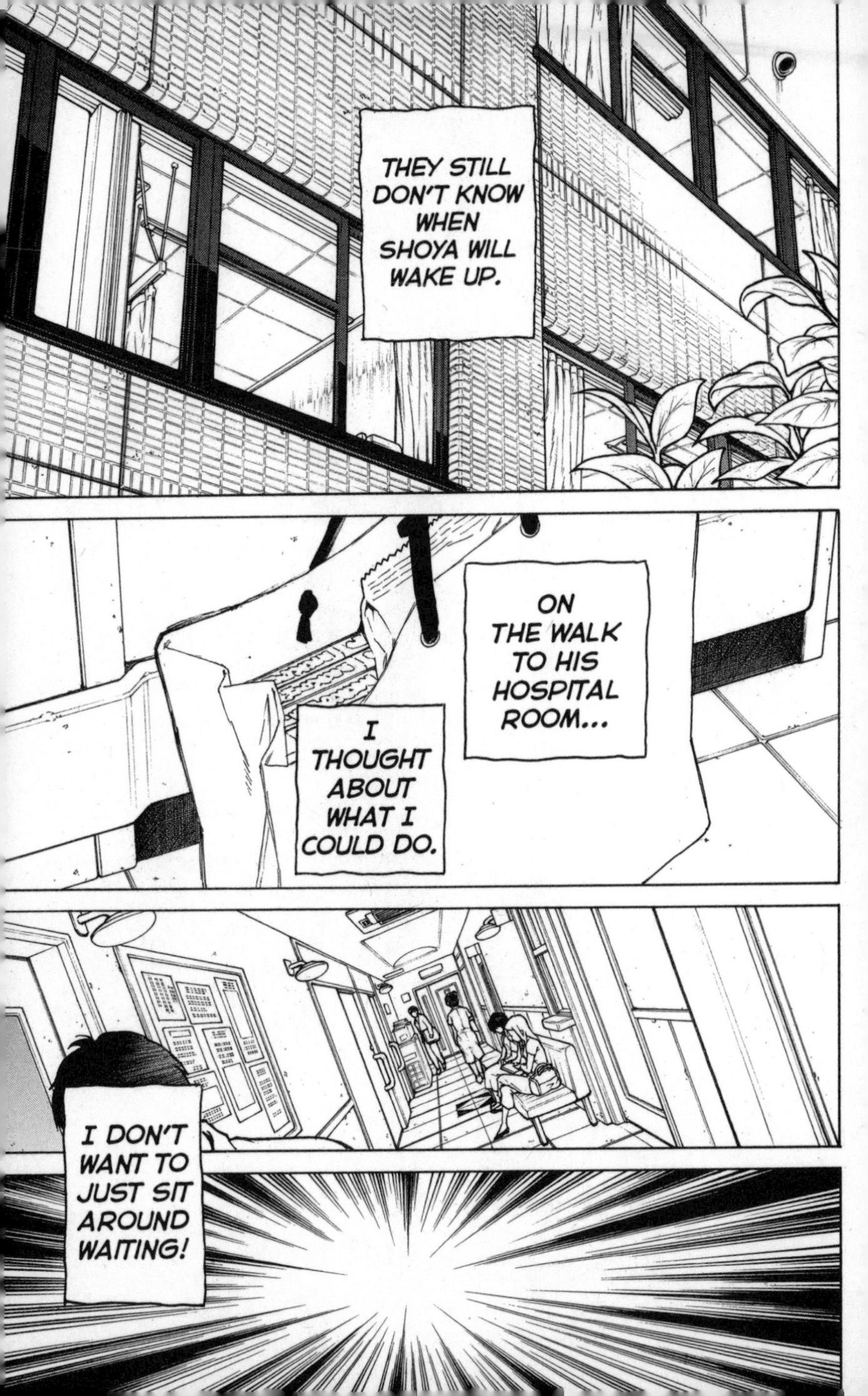
THEY STILL DON'T KNOW WHEN SHOYA WILL WAKE UP.
ON THE WALK TO HIS HOSPITAL ROOM...
I THOUGHT ABOUT WHAT I COULD DO.
I DON'T WANT TO JUST SIT AROUND WAITING!

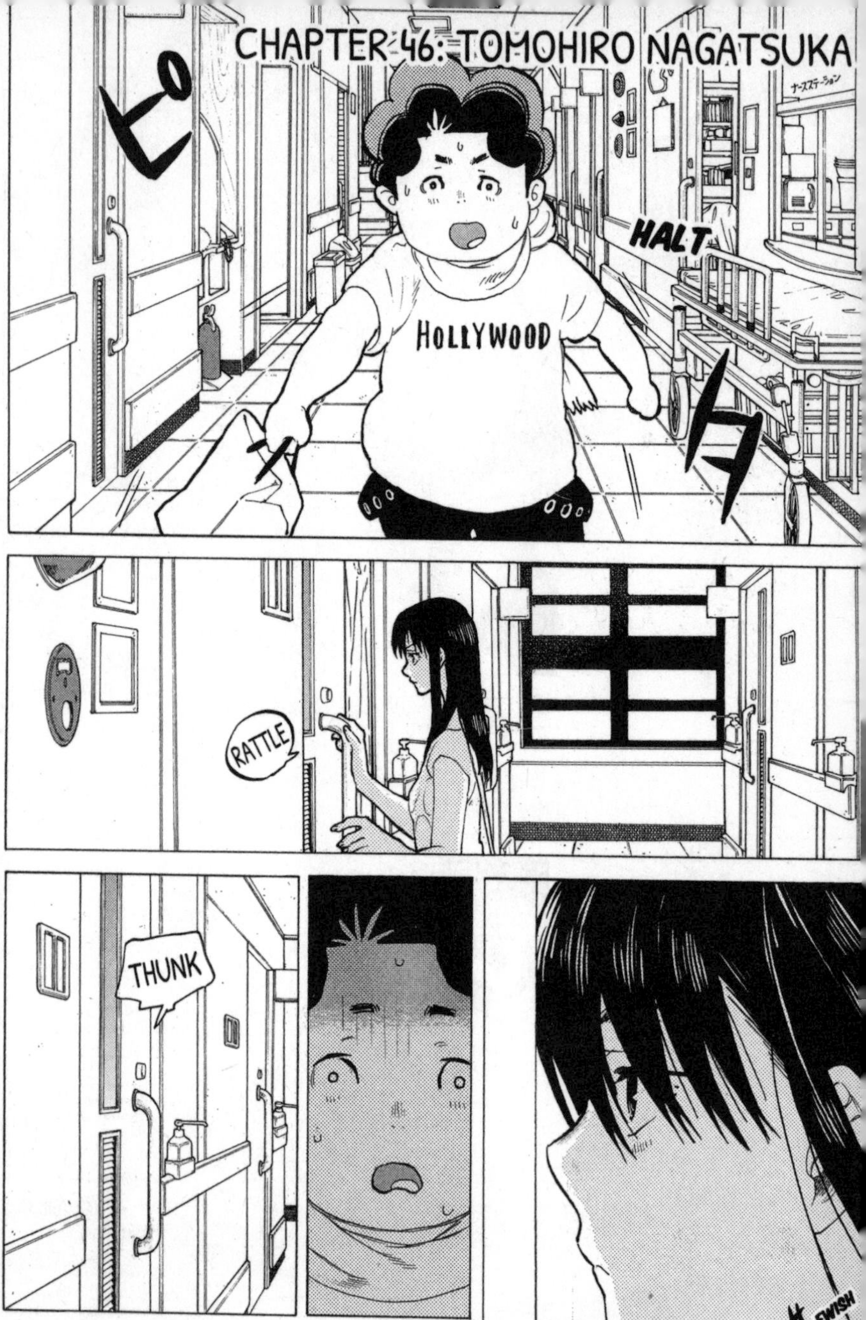
CHAPTER 46: TOMOHIRO NAGATSUKA
ナースステーション
HALT
RATTLE
FWISH
THUNK

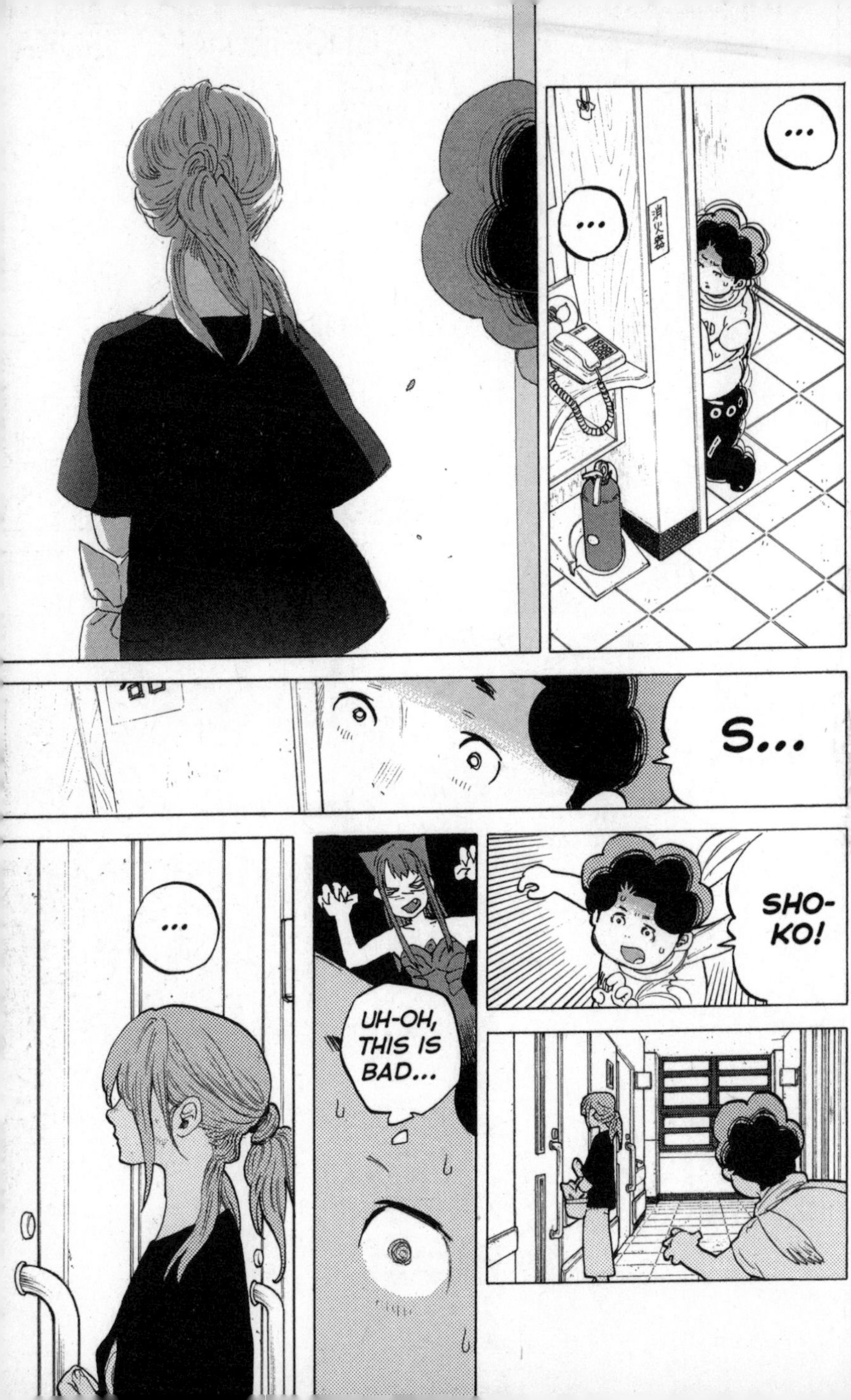
...
消火器
...
S...
SHO-KO!
UH-OH, THIS IS BAD...
...

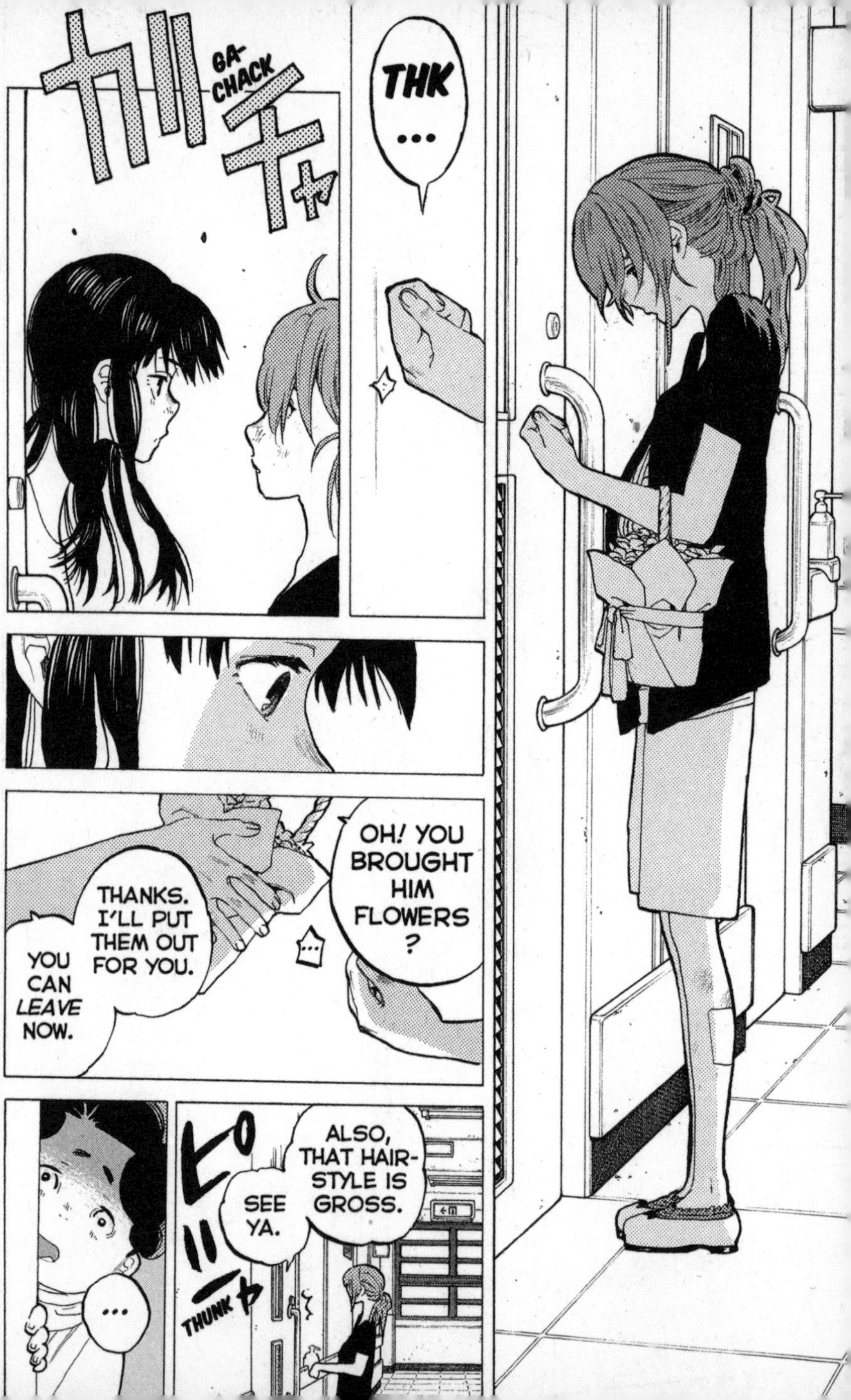
THK
...
GA-CHACK
OH! YOU BROUGHT HIM FLOWERS?
THANKS. I'LL PUT THEM OUT FOR YOU.
YOU CAN *LEAVE* NOW.
ALSO, THAT HAIR-STYLE IS GROSS.
SEE YA.
THUNK
...

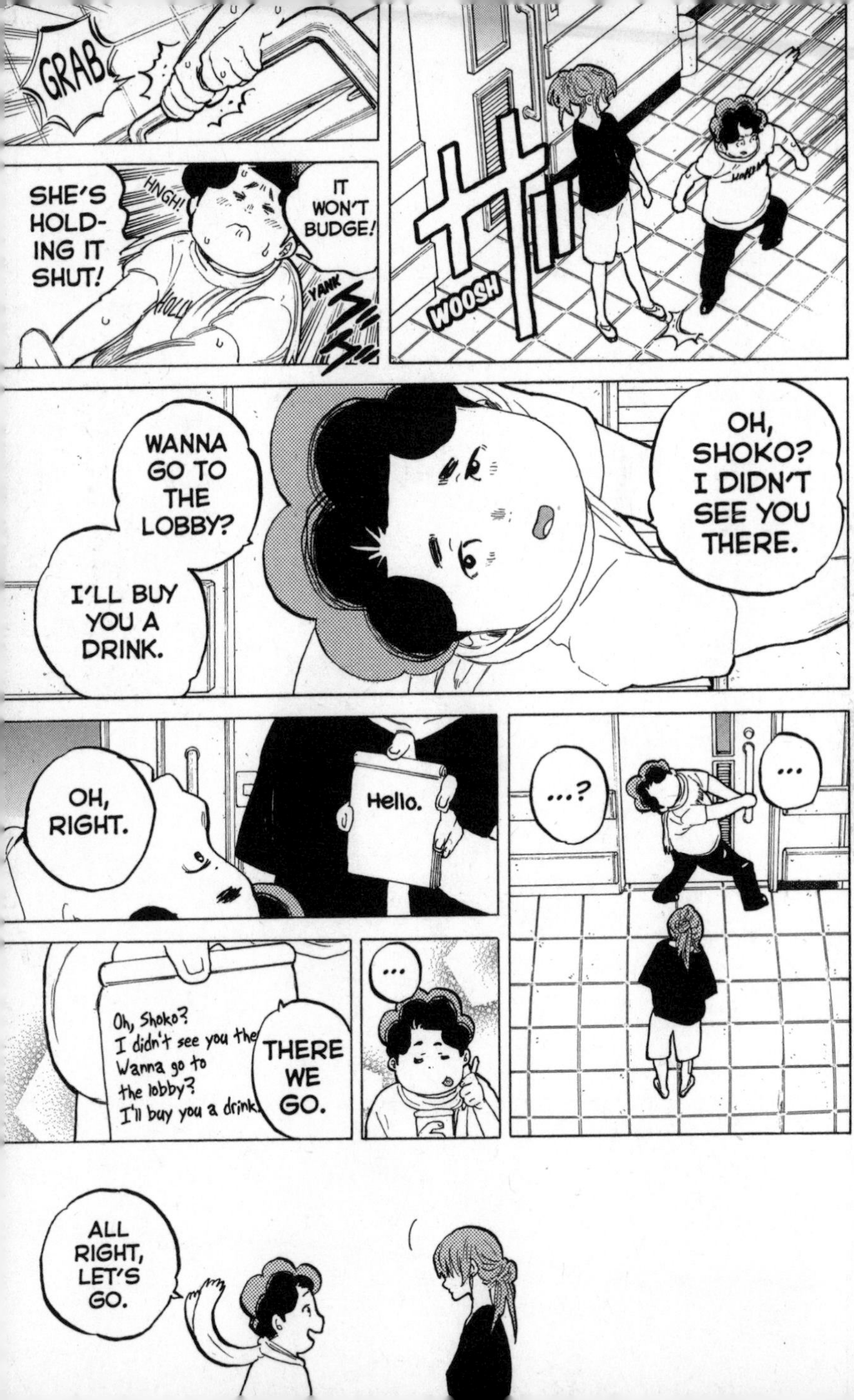
WOOSH
GRAB
IT WON'T BUDGE!
HNGH!
SHE'S HOLDING-ING IT SHUT!
YANK
OH, SHOKO? I DIDN'T SEE YOU THERE.
WANNA GO TO THE LOBBY?
I'LL BUY YOU A DRINK.
...
...?
Hello.
OH, RIGHT.
...
Oh, Shoko? I didn't see you the Wanna go to the lobby? I'll buy you a drink.
THERE WE GO.
ALL RIGHT, LET'S GO.

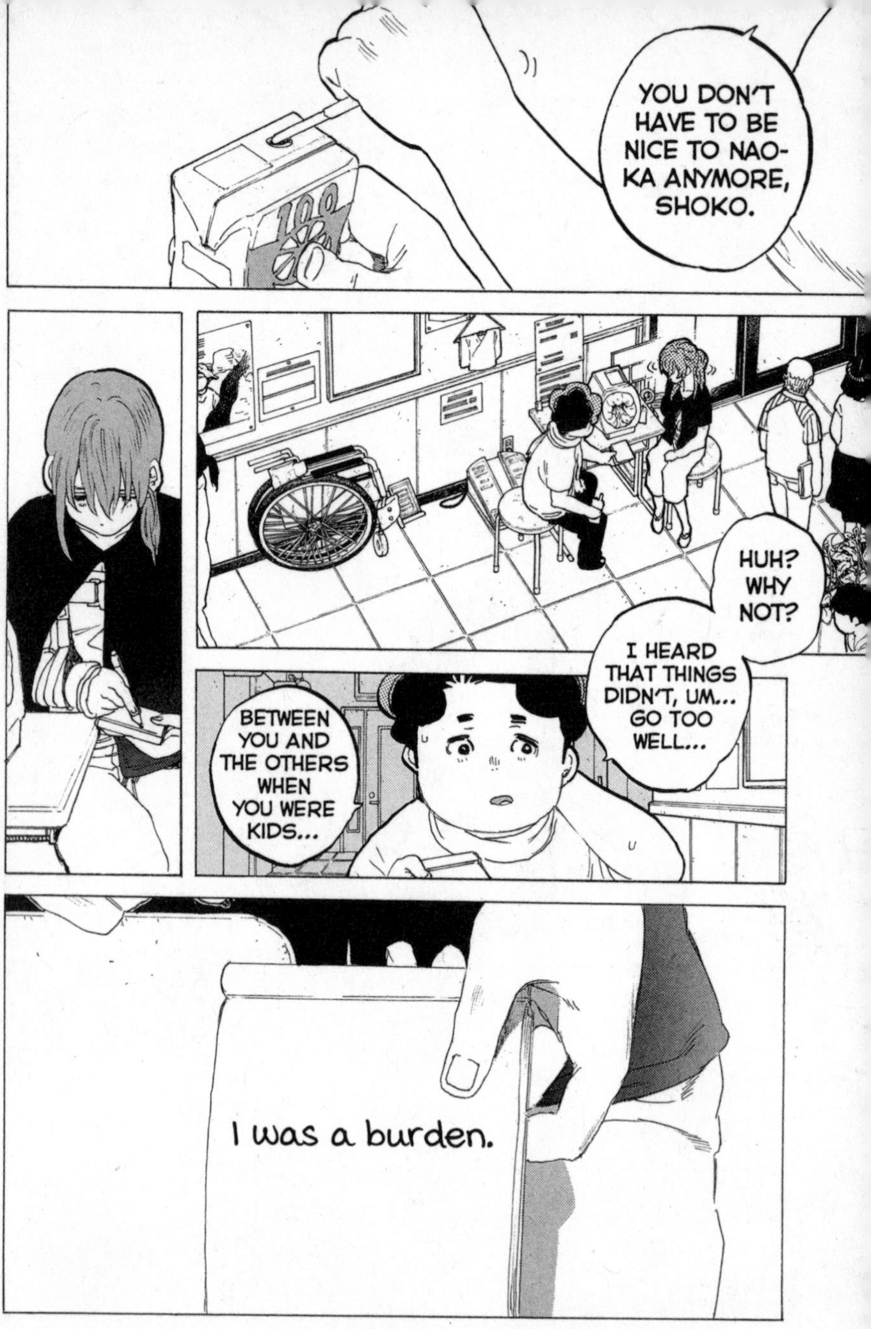
YOU DON'T HAVE TO BE NICE TO NAO-KA ANYMORE, SHOKO.
HUH? WHY NOT?
I HEARD THAT THINGS DIDN'T, UM... GO TOO WELL...
BETWEEN YOU AND THE OTHERS WHEN YOU WERE KIDS...
I was a burden.

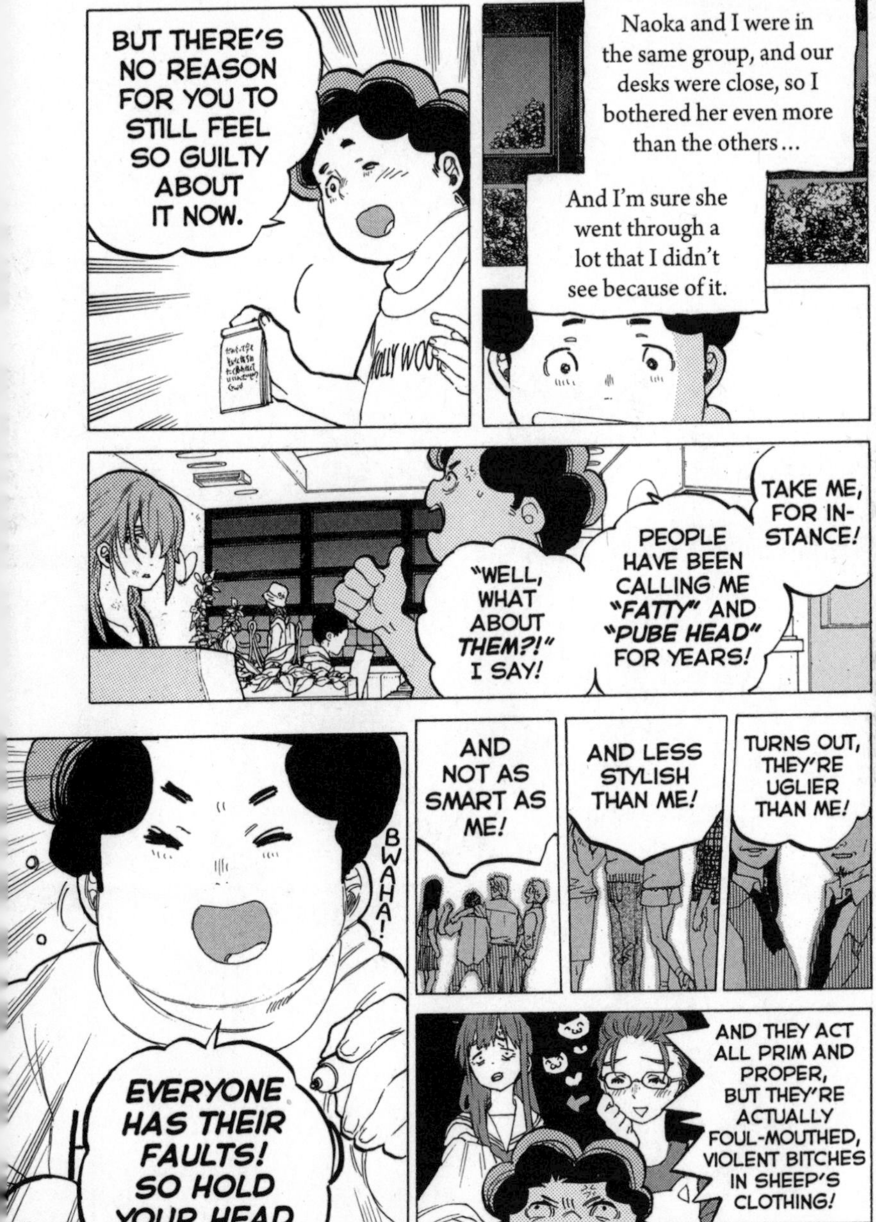
Naoka and I were in the same group, and our desks were close, so I bothered her even more than the others…
And I'm sure she went through a lot that I didn't see because of it.
BUT THERE'S NO REASON FOR YOU TO STILL FEEL SO GUILTY ABOUT IT NOW.
TAKE ME, FOR INSTANCE!
PEOPLE HAVE BEEN CALLING ME *"FATTY"* AND *"PUBE HEAD"* FOR YEARS!
"WELL, WHAT ABOUT *THEM?!"* I SAY!
TURNS OUT, THEY'RE UGLIER THAN ME!
AND LESS STYLISH THAN ME!
AND NOT AS SMART AS ME!
AND THEY ACT ALL PRIM AND PROPER, BUT THEY'RE ACTUALLY FOUL-MOUTHED, VIOLENT BITCHES IN SHEEP'S CLOTHING!
BWAHAHA!
EVERYONE HAS THEIR FAULTS! SO HOLD YOUR HEAD UP HIGH!

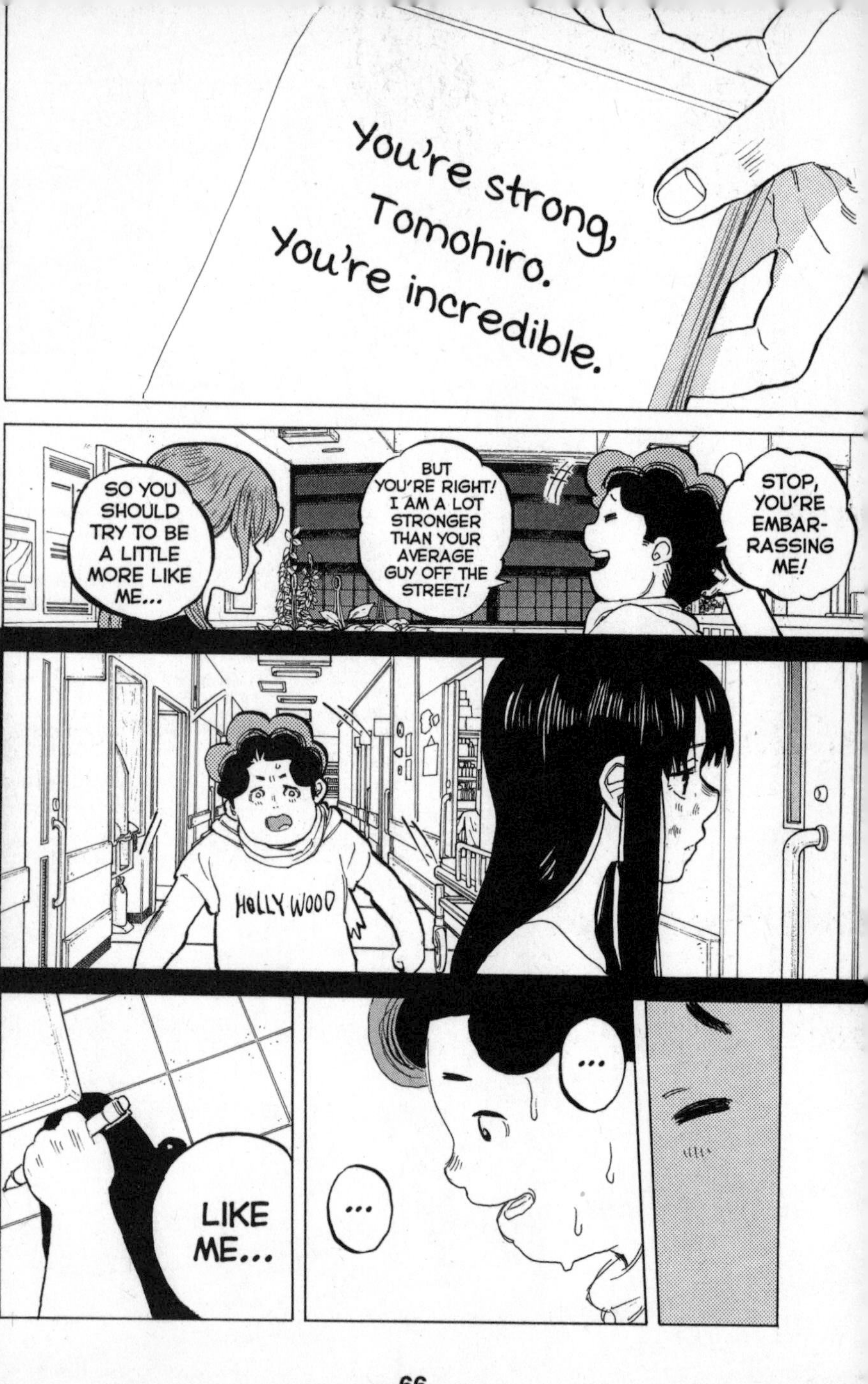
You're strong, Tomohiro. You're incredible.
STOP, YOU'RE EMBARRASSING ME!
BUT YOU'RE RIGHT! I AM A LOT STRONGER THAN YOUR AVERAGE GUY OFF THE STREET!
SO YOU SHOULD TRY TO BE A LITTLE MORE LIKE ME...
...
...
LIKE ME...

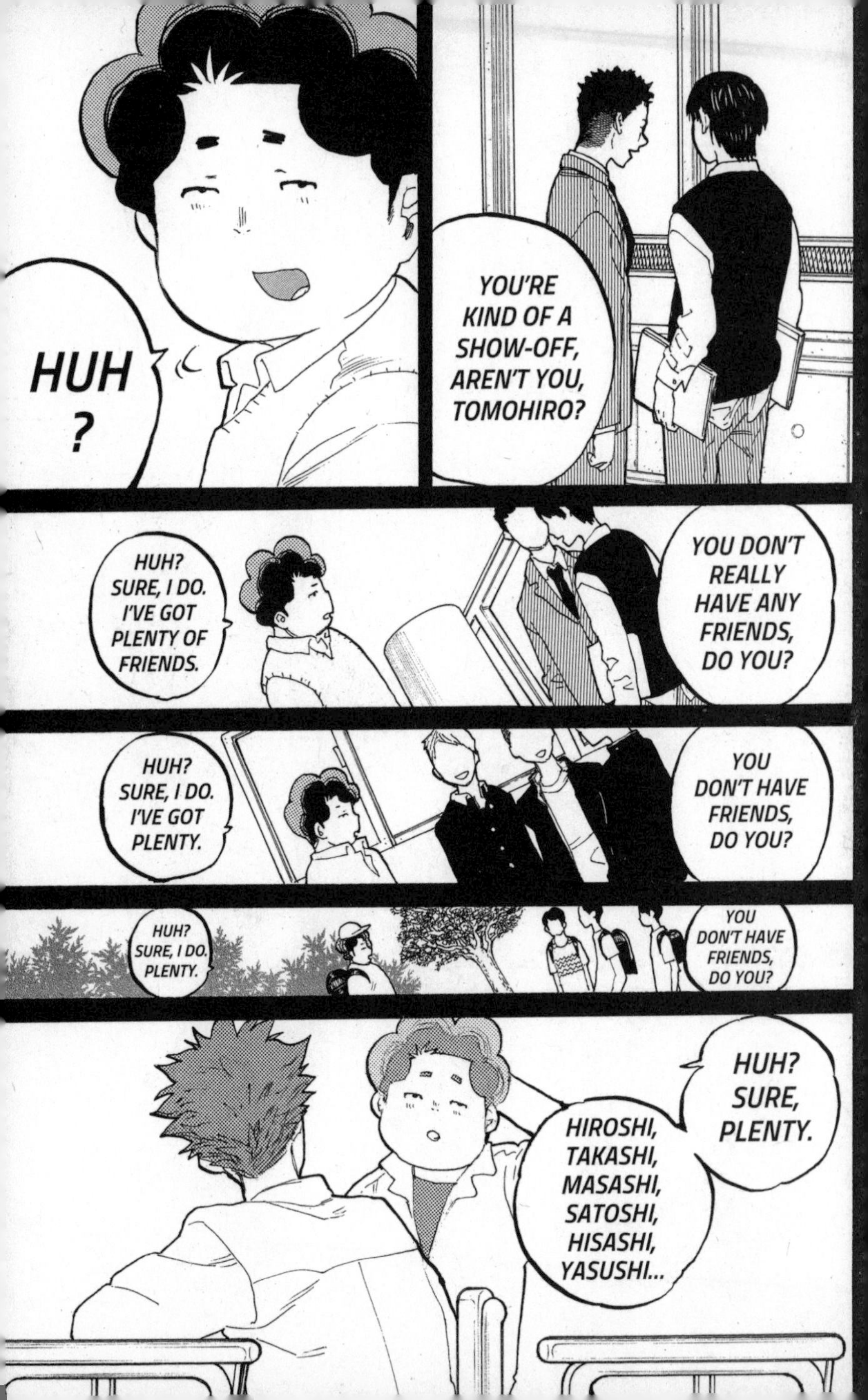
YOU'RE KIND OF A SHOW-OFF, AREN'T YOU, TOMOHIRO?
HUH?
YOU DON'T REALLY HAVE ANY FRIENDS, DO YOU?
HUH? SURE, I DO. I'VE GOT PLENTY OF FRIENDS.
YOU DON'T HAVE FRIENDS, DO YOU?
HUH? SURE, I DO. I'VE GOT PLENTY.
YOU DON'T HAVE FRIENDS, DO YOU?
HUH? SURE, I DO. PLENTY.
HUH? SURE, PLENTY.
HIROSHI, TAKASHI, MASASHI, SATOSHI, HISASHI, YASUSHI...

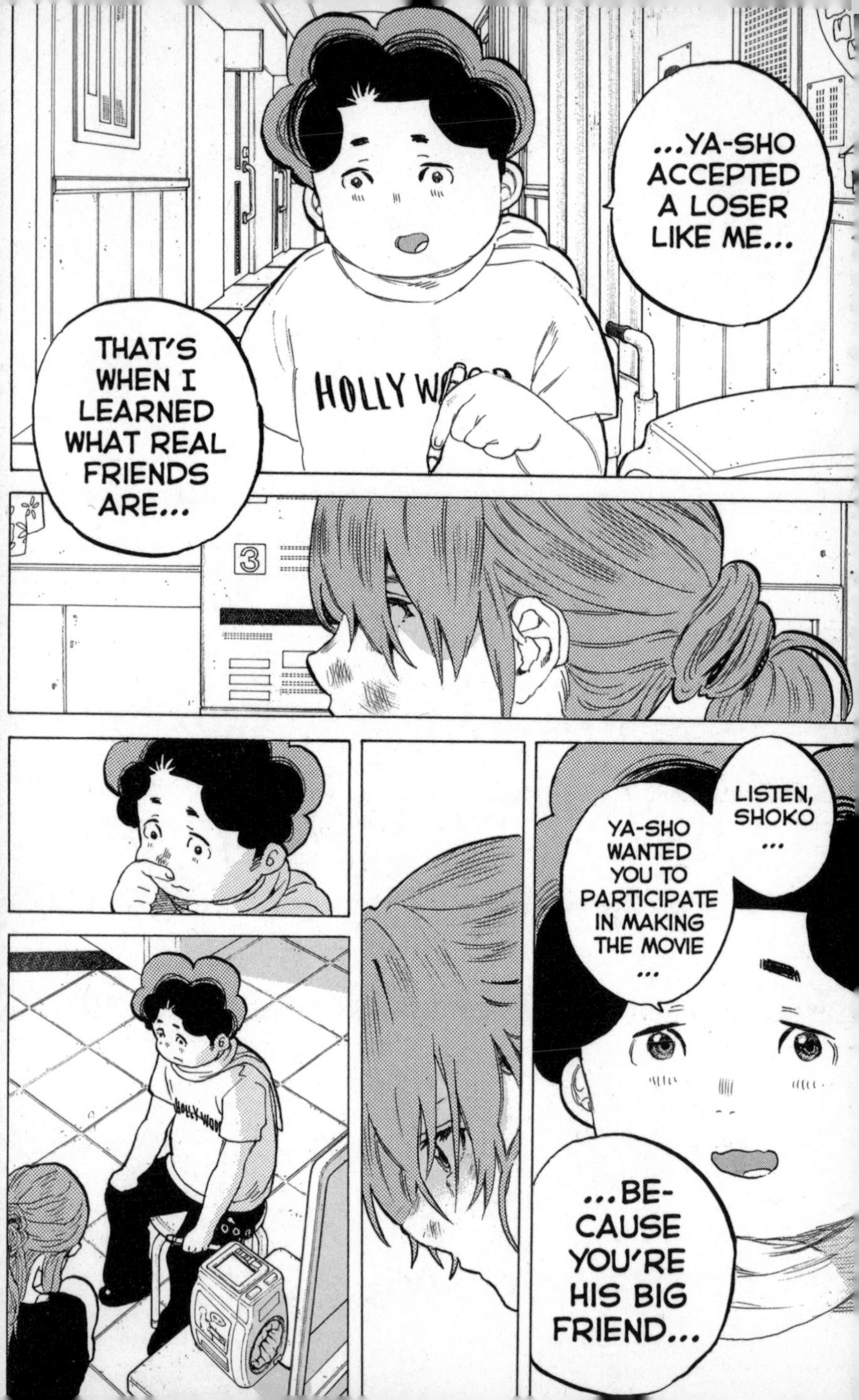
...YA-SHO ACCEPTED A LOSER LIKE ME...
THAT'S WHEN I LEARNED WHAT REAL FRIENDS ARE...
LISTEN, SHOKO...
YA-SHO WANTED YOU TO PARTICIPATE IN MAKING THE MOVIE...
...BE-CAUSE YOU'RE HIS BIG FRIEND...

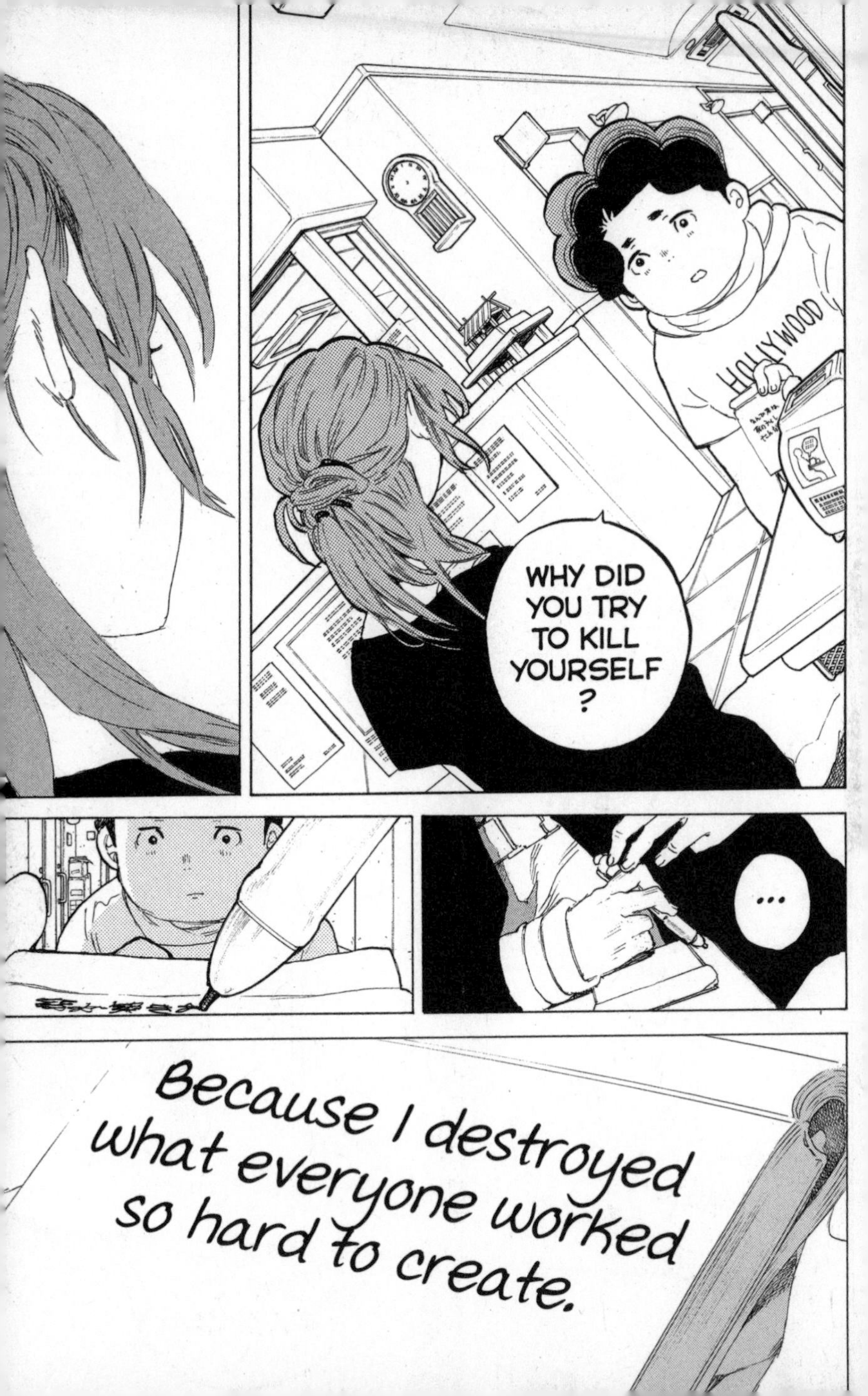
WHY DID YOU TRY TO KILL YOURSELF?
...
Because I destroyed what everyone worked so hard to create.

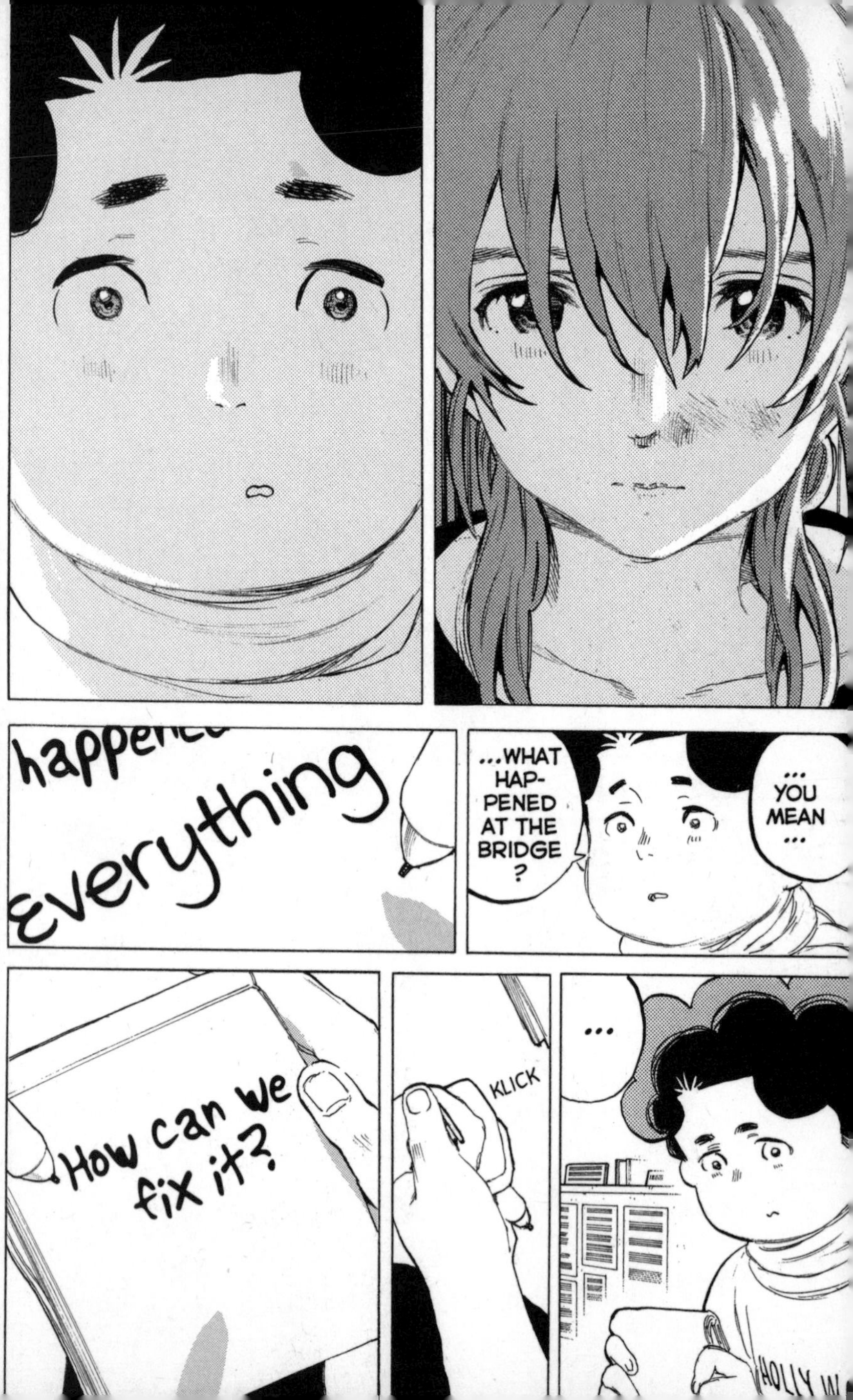
... YOU MEAN ...
...WHAT HAP-PENED AT THE BRIDGE?
Everything
...
KLICK
How can we fix it?

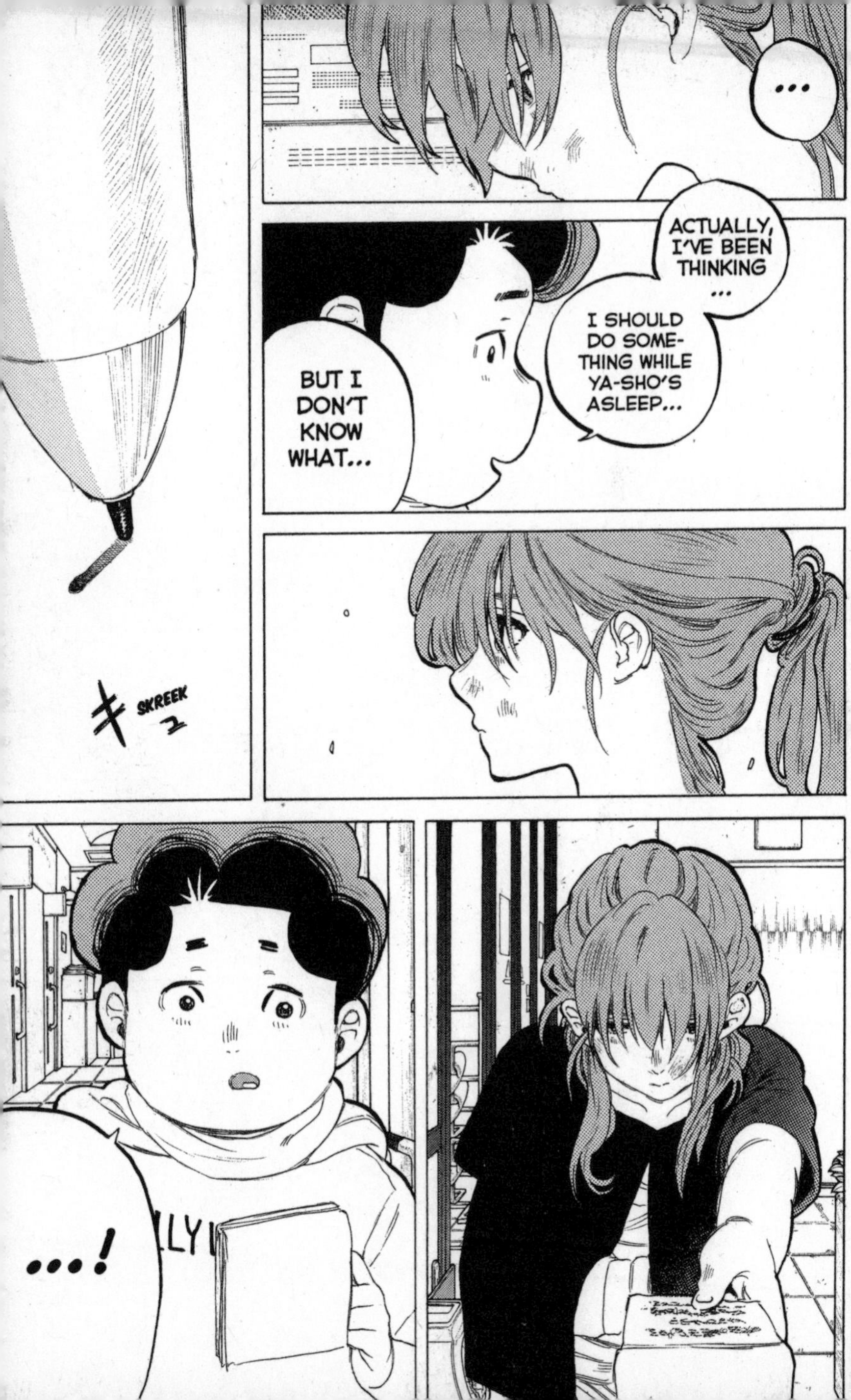
...
ACTUALLY, I'VE BEEN THINKING ...
I SHOULD DO SOMETHING WHILE YA-SHO'S ASLEEP...
BUT I DON'T KNOW WHAT...
SKREEK
...!

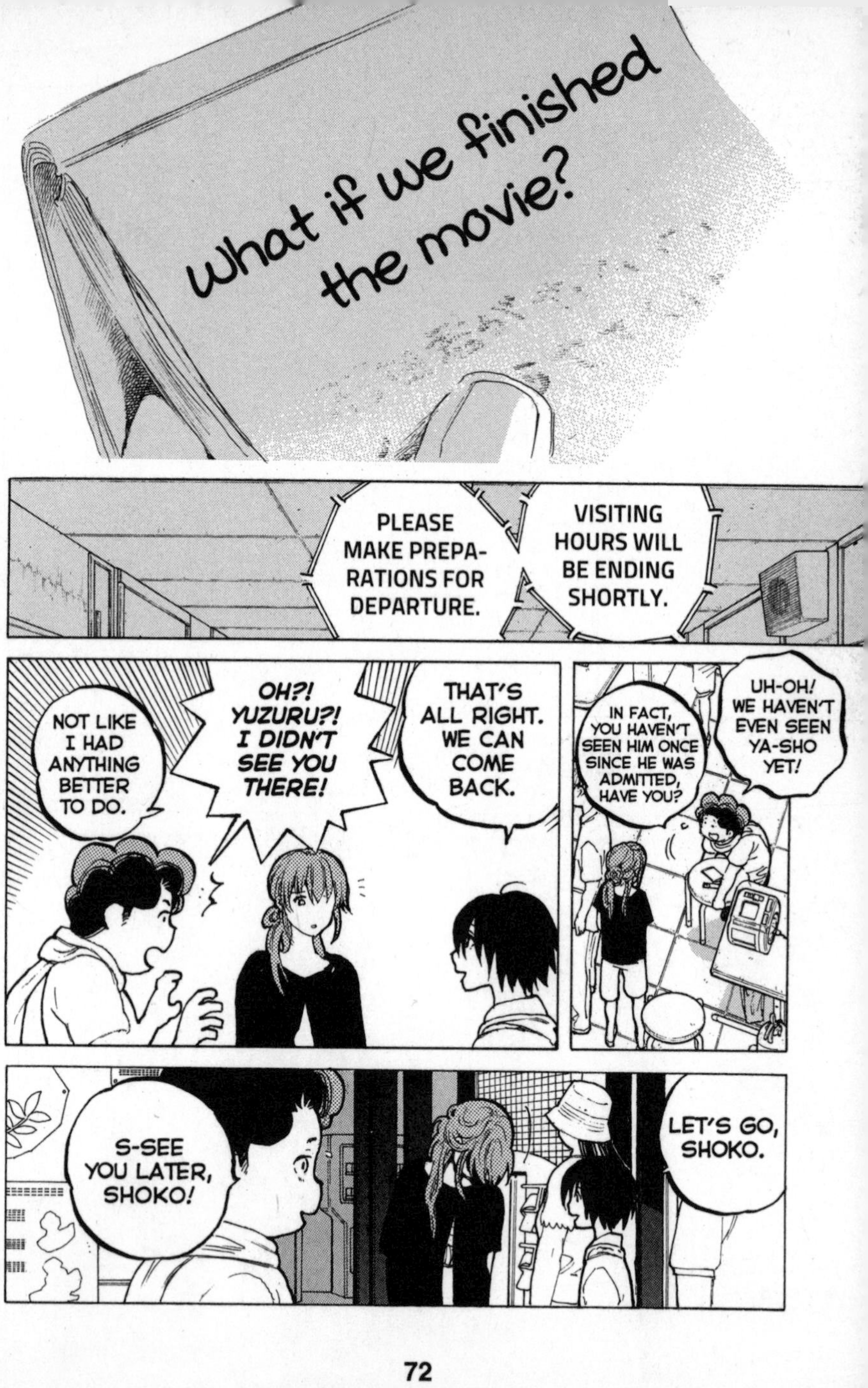
What if we finished the movie?
VISITING HOURS WILL BE ENDING SHORTLY.
PLEASE MAKE PREPARATIONS FOR DEPARTURE.
UH-OH! WE HAVEN'T EVEN SEEN YA-SHO YET!
IN FACT, YOU HAVEN'T SEEN HIM ONCE SINCE HE WAS ADMITTED, HAVE YOU?
THAT'S ALL RIGHT. WE CAN COME BACK.
OH?! YUZURU?! I DIDN'T SEE YOU THERE!
NOT LIKE I HAD ANYTHING BETTER TO DO.
LET'S GO, SHOKO.
S-SEE YOU LATER, SHOKO!

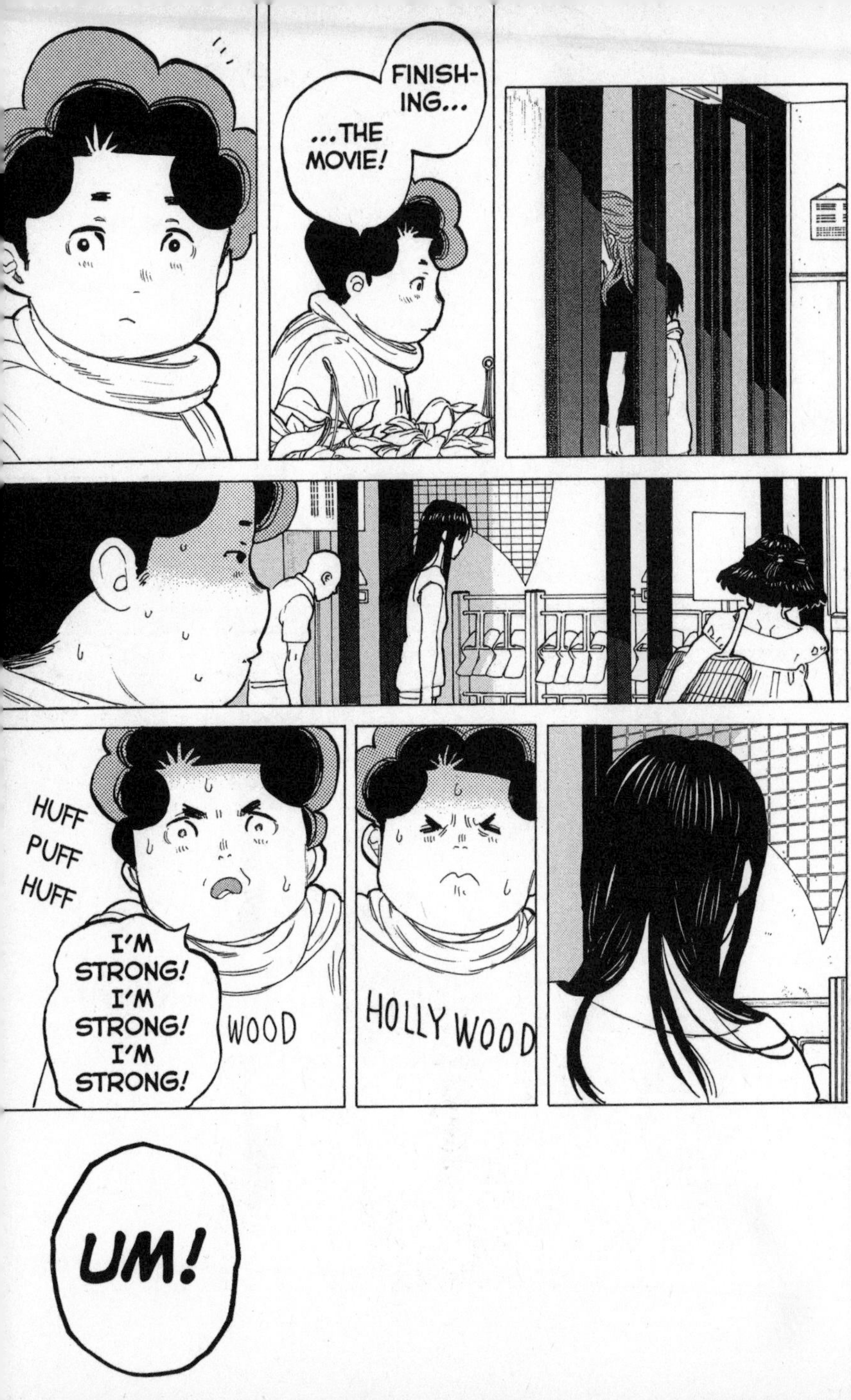
FINISHING...
...THE MOVIE!
HOLLYWOOD
HUFF PUFF HUFF
I'M STRONG! I'M STRONG! I'M STRONG!
WOOD
UM!

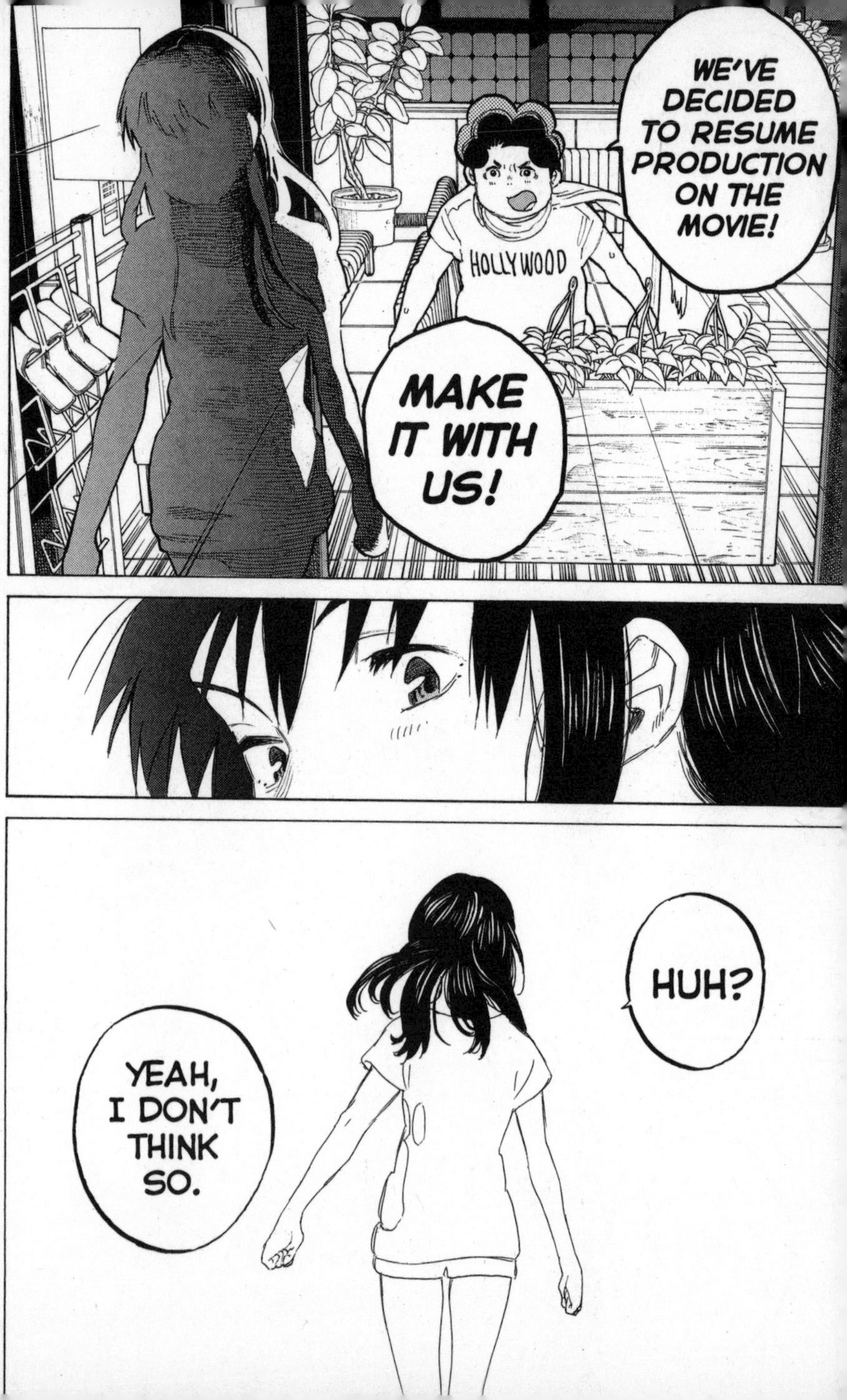
WE'VE DECIDED TO RESUME PRODUCTION ON THE MOVIE!
MAKE IT WITH US!
HUH?
YEAH, I DON'T THINK SO.

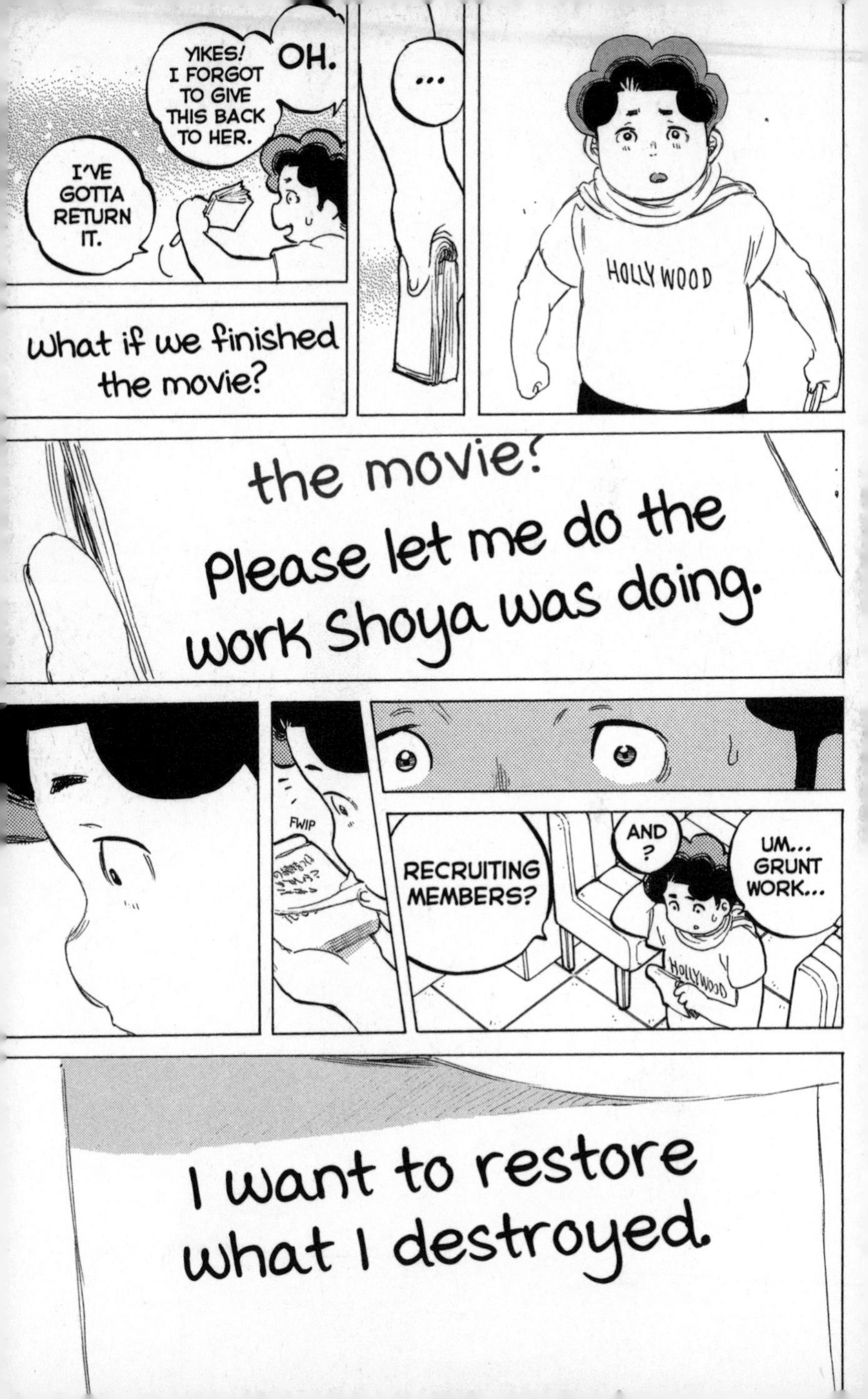
...
OH.
YIKES! I FORGOT TO GIVE THIS BACK TO HER.
I'VE GOTTA RETURN IT.
what if we finished the movie?
the movie?
Please let me do the work Shoya was doing.
UM... GRUNT WORK...
AND ?
RECRUITING MEMBERS?
FWIP
I want to restore what I destroyed.

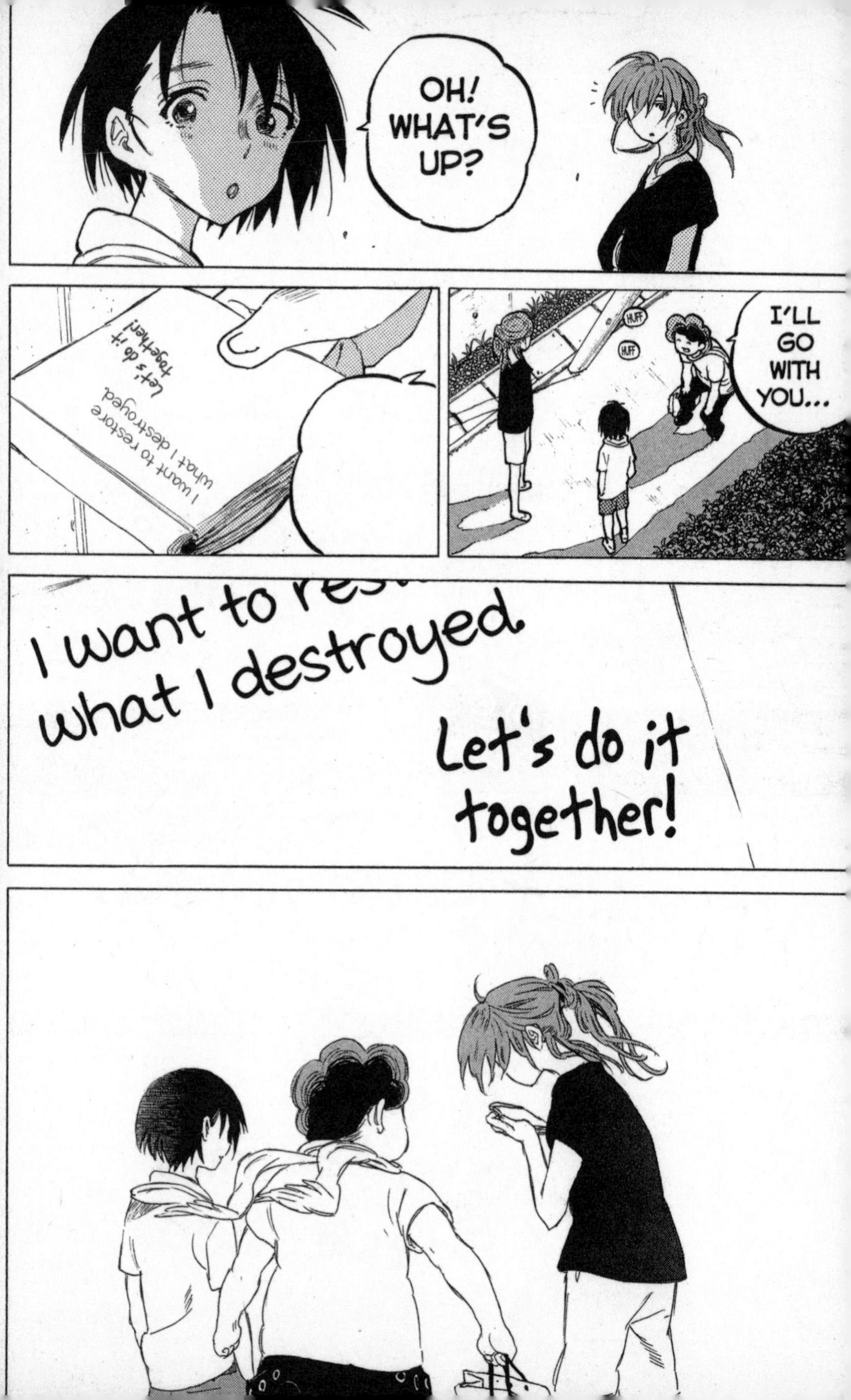
OH! WHAT'S UP?
HUFF
HUFF
I'LL GO WITH YOU...
I want to restore what I destroyed.
Let's do it together!
I want to
what I destroyed.
Let's do it together!

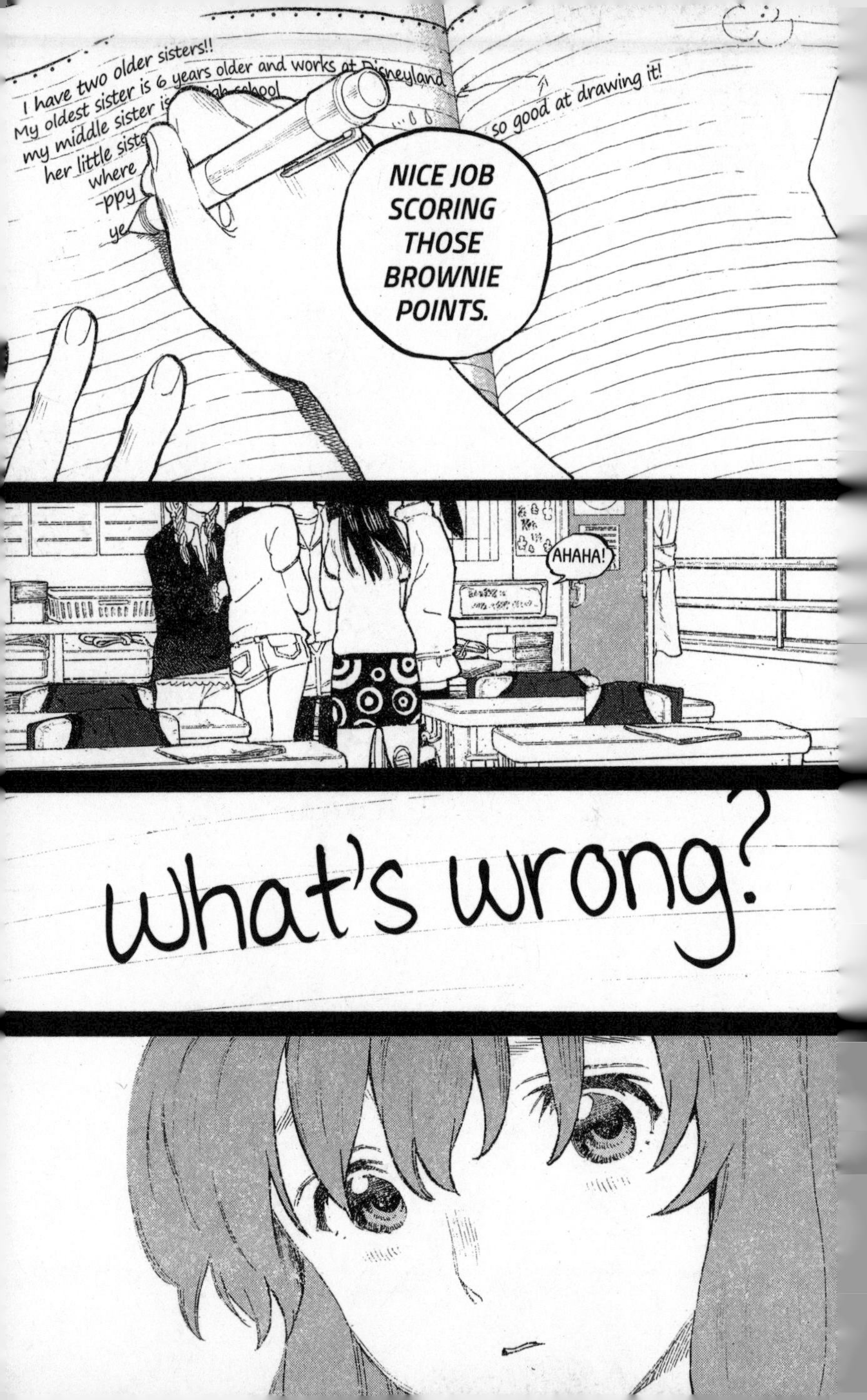
so good at drawing it!
I have two older sisters!!
My oldest sister is 6 years older and works at Disneyland
NICE JOB SCORING THOSE BROWNIE POINTS.
AHAHA!
what's wrong?

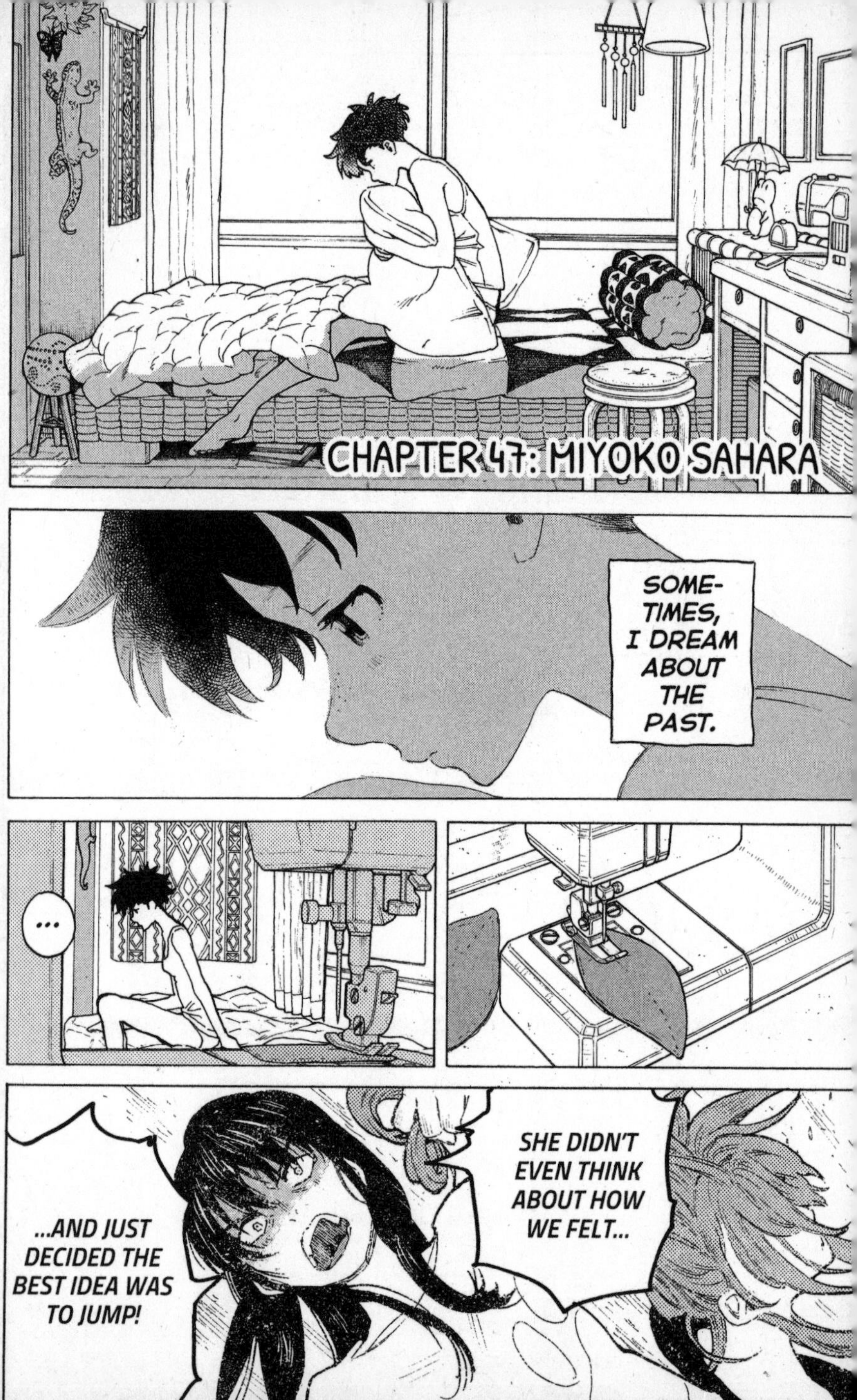
CHAPTER 47: MIYOKO SAHARA
SOME-TIMES, I DREAM ABOUT THE PAST.
...
SHE DIDN'T EVEN THINK ABOUT HOW WE FELT...
...AND JUST DECIDED THE BEST IDEA WAS TO JUMP!

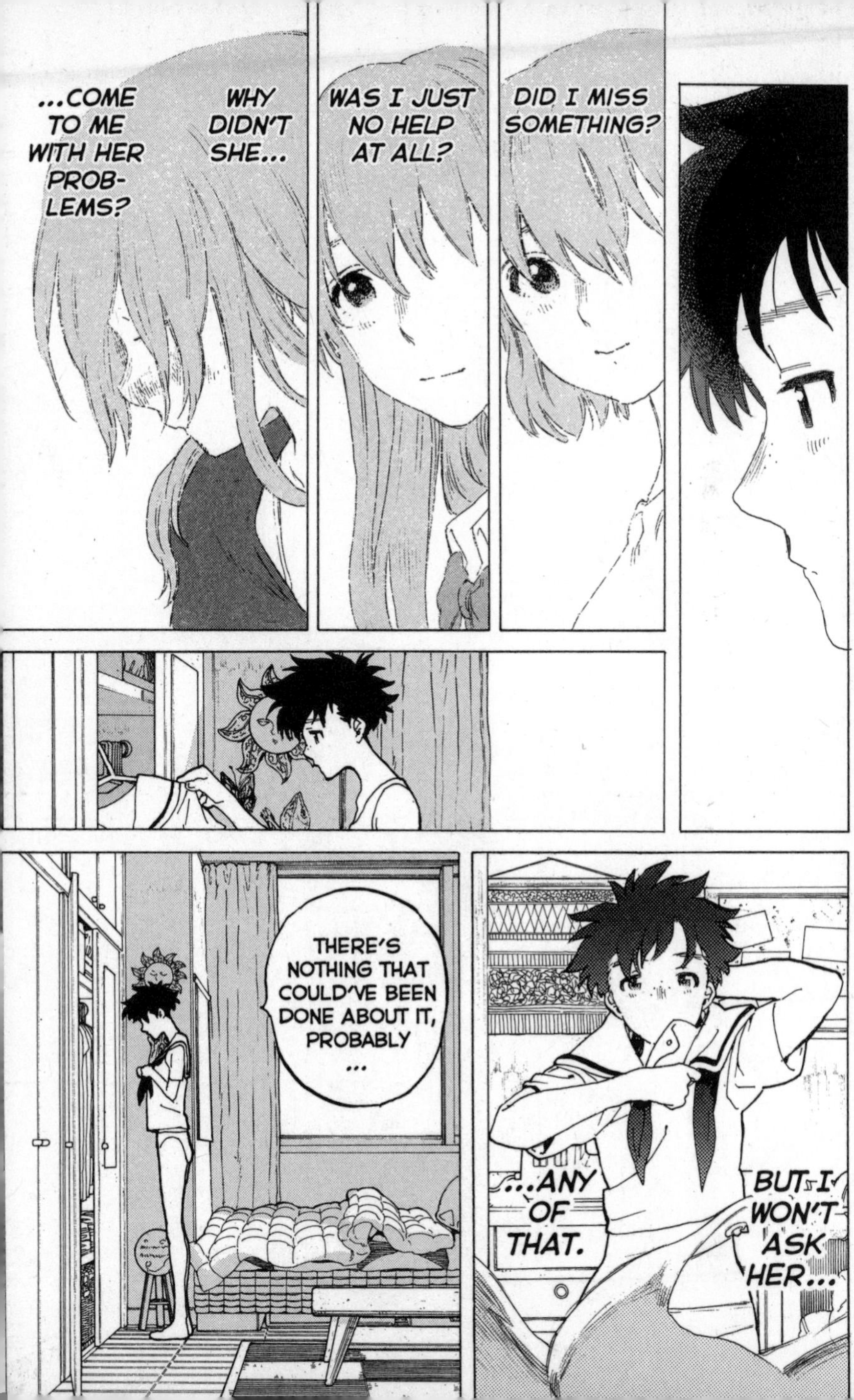
DID I MISS SOMETHING?
WAS I JUST NO HELP AT ALL?
WHY DIDN'T SHE...
...COME TO ME WITH HER PROB-LEMS?
BUT I WON'T ASK HER...
...ANY OF THAT.
THERE'S NOTHING THAT COULD'VE BEEN DONE ABOUT IT, PROBABLY
...

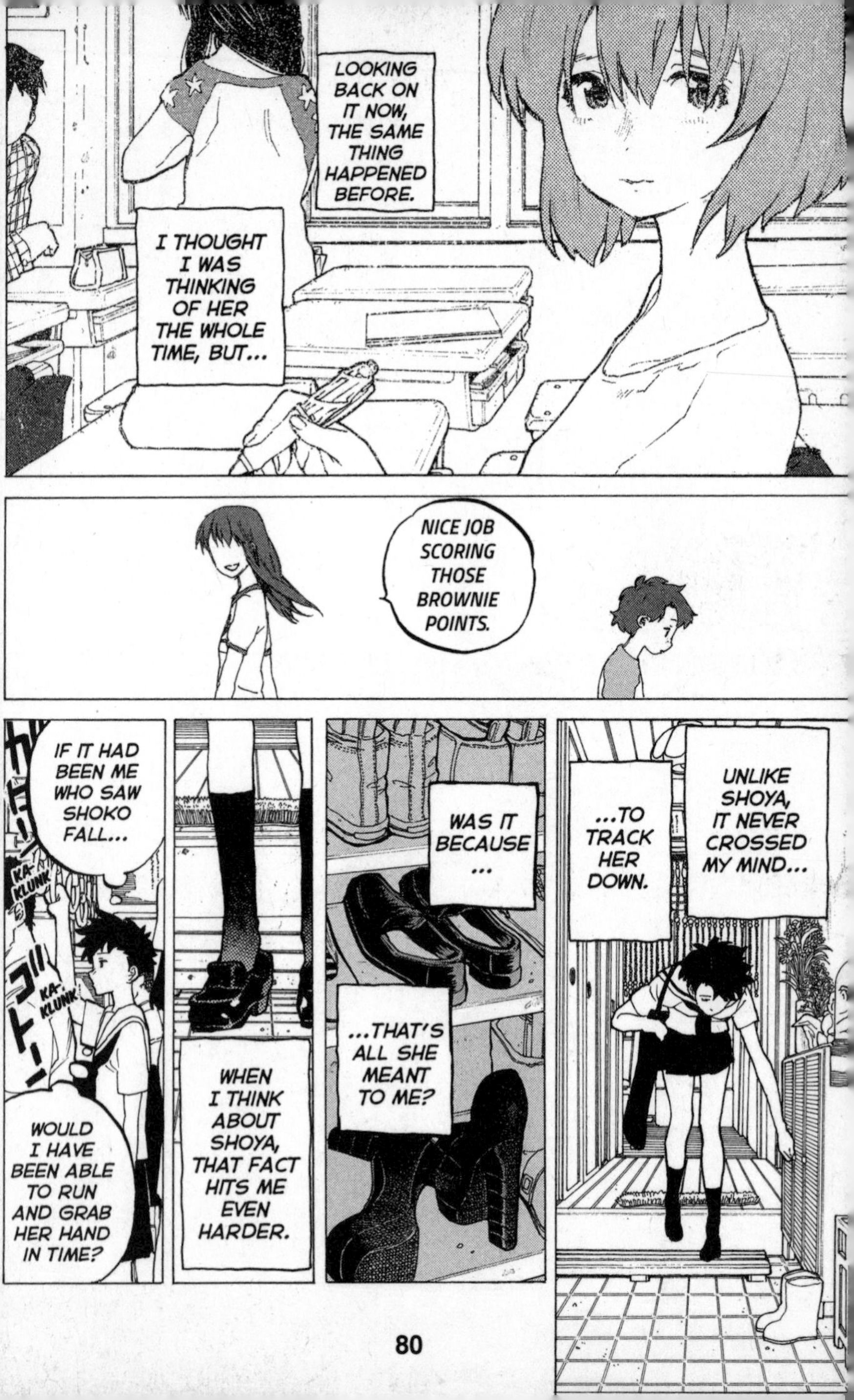
LOOKING BACK ON IT NOW, THE SAME THING HAPPENED BEFORE.
I THOUGHT I WAS THINKING OF HER THE WHOLE TIME, BUT...
NICE JOB SCORING THOSE BROWNIE POINTS.
UNLIKE SHOYA, IT NEVER CROSSED MY MIND...
...TO TRACK HER DOWN.
WAS IT BECAUSE...
...THAT'S ALL SHE MEANT TO ME?
WHEN I THINK ABOUT SHOYA, THAT FACT HITS ME EVEN HARDER.
IF IT HAD BEEN ME WHO SAW SHOKO FALL...
KA-KLUNK
KA-KLUNK
WOULD I HAVE BEEN ABLE TO RUN AND GRAB HER HAND IN TIME?

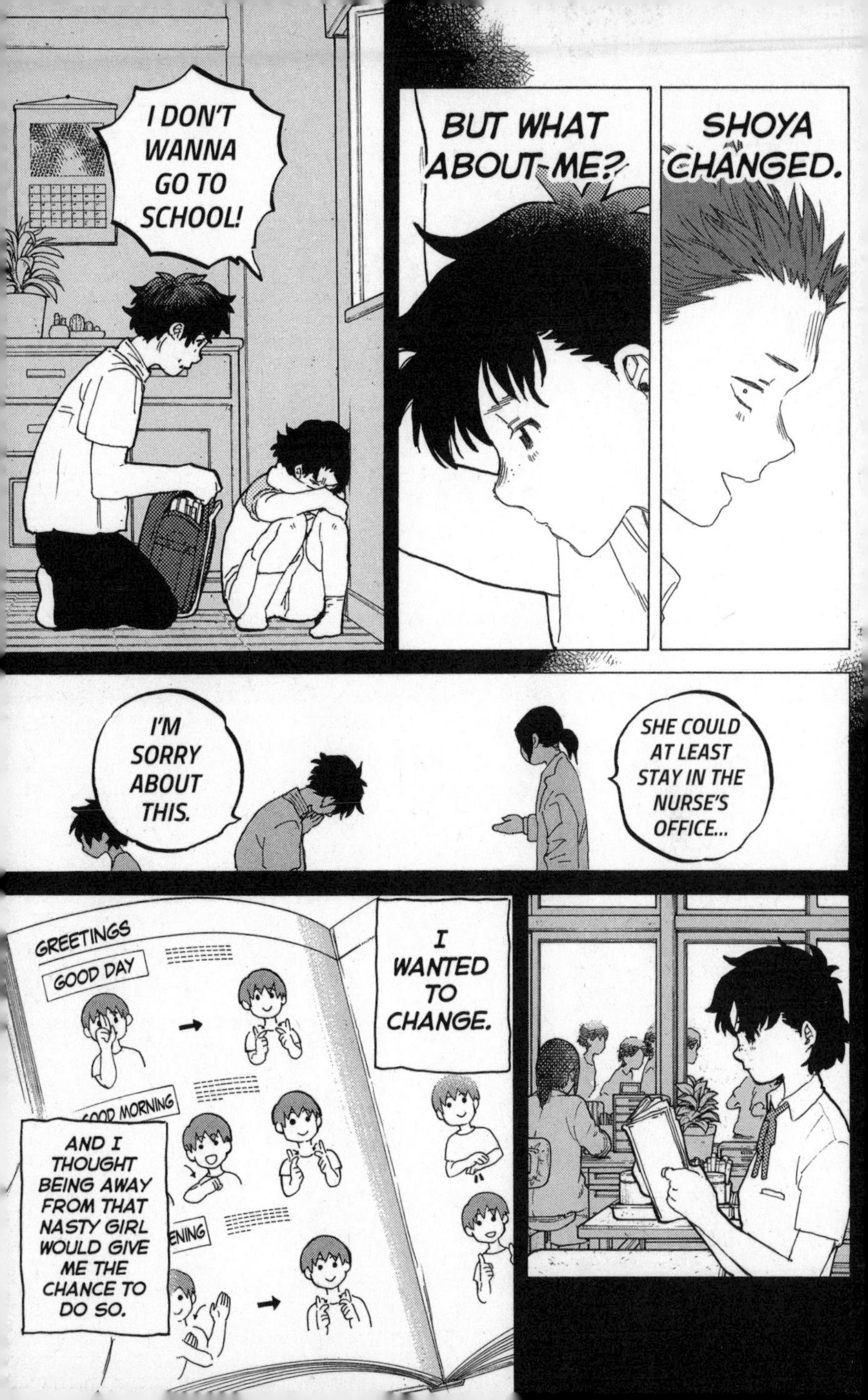
SHOYA CHANGED.
BUT WHAT ABOUT ME?
I DON'T WANNA GO TO SCHOOL!
SHE COULD AT LEAST STAY IN THE NURSE'S OFFICE...
I'M SORRY ABOUT THIS.
I WANTED TO CHANGE.
AND I THOUGHT BEING AWAY FROM THAT NASTY GIRL WOULD GIVE ME THE CHANCE TO DO SO.
GREETINGS
GOOD DAY

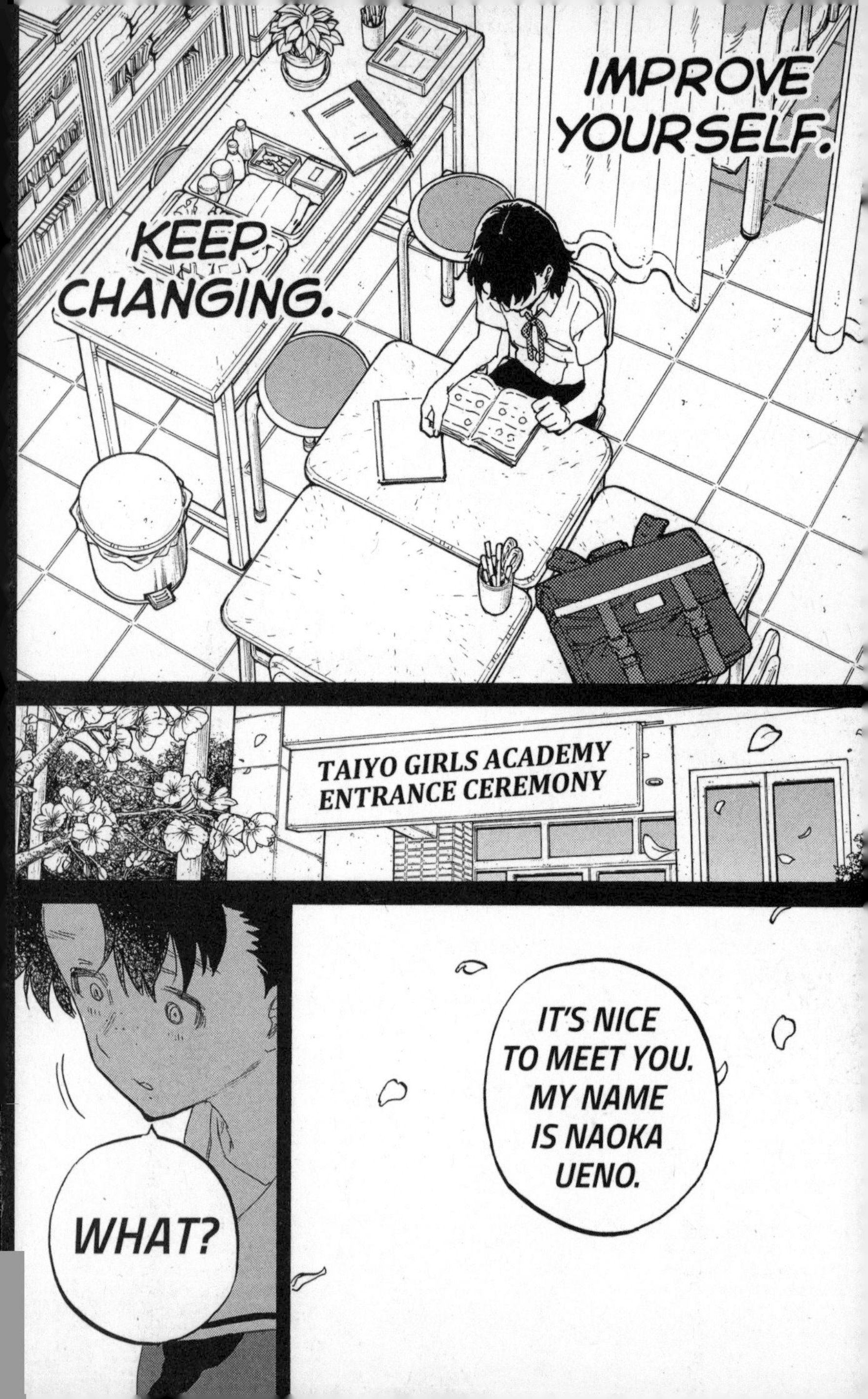
IMPROVE YOURSELF.
KEEP CHANGING.
TAIYO GIRLS ACADEMY ENTRANCE CEREMONY
IT'S NICE TO MEET YOU. MY NAME IS NAOKA UENO.
WHAT?

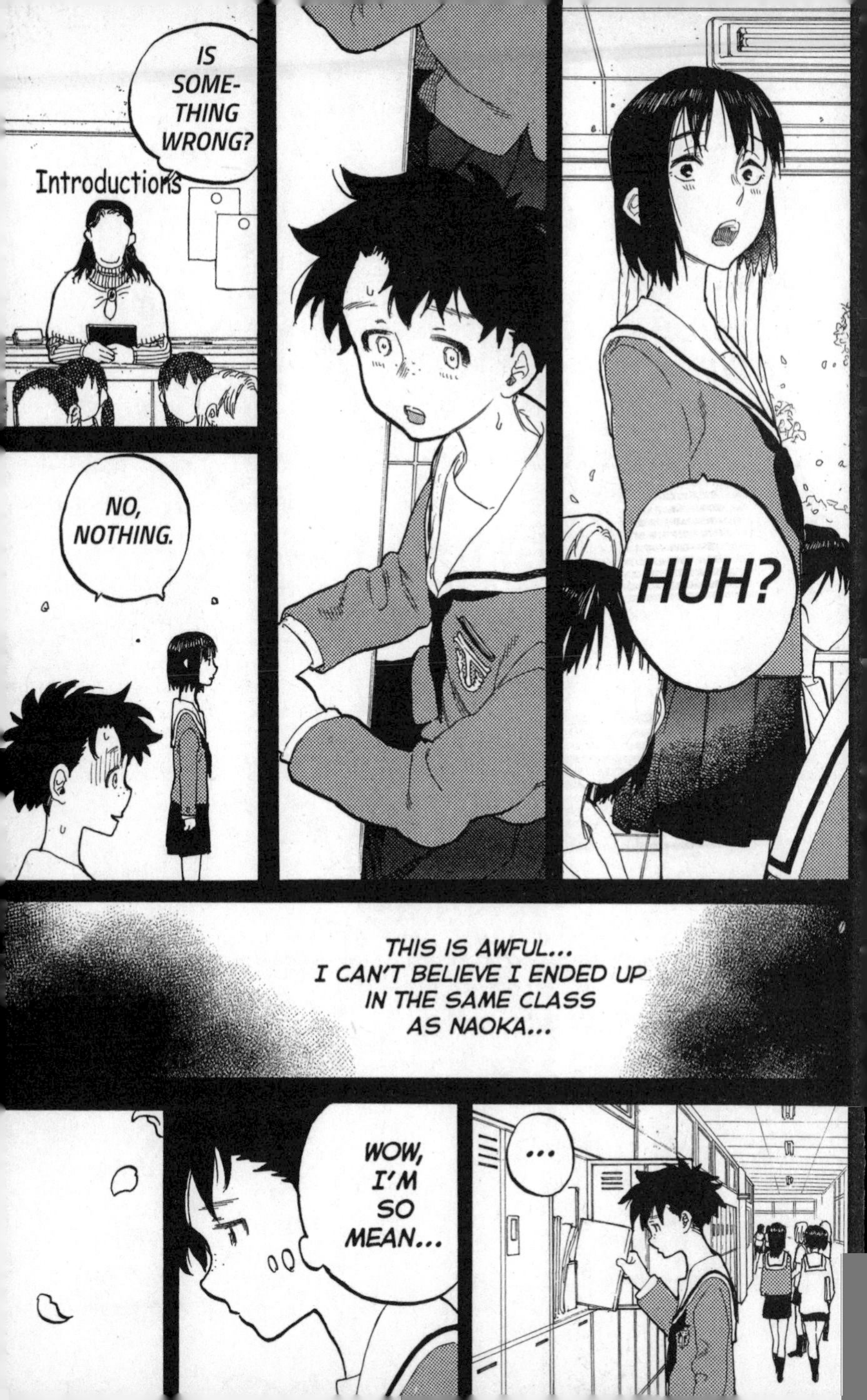
HUH?
IS SOMETHING WRONG?
Introductions
NO, NOTHING.
THIS IS AWFUL... I CAN'T BELIEVE I ENDED UP IN THE SAME CLASS AS NAOKA...
...
WOW, I'M SO MEAN...

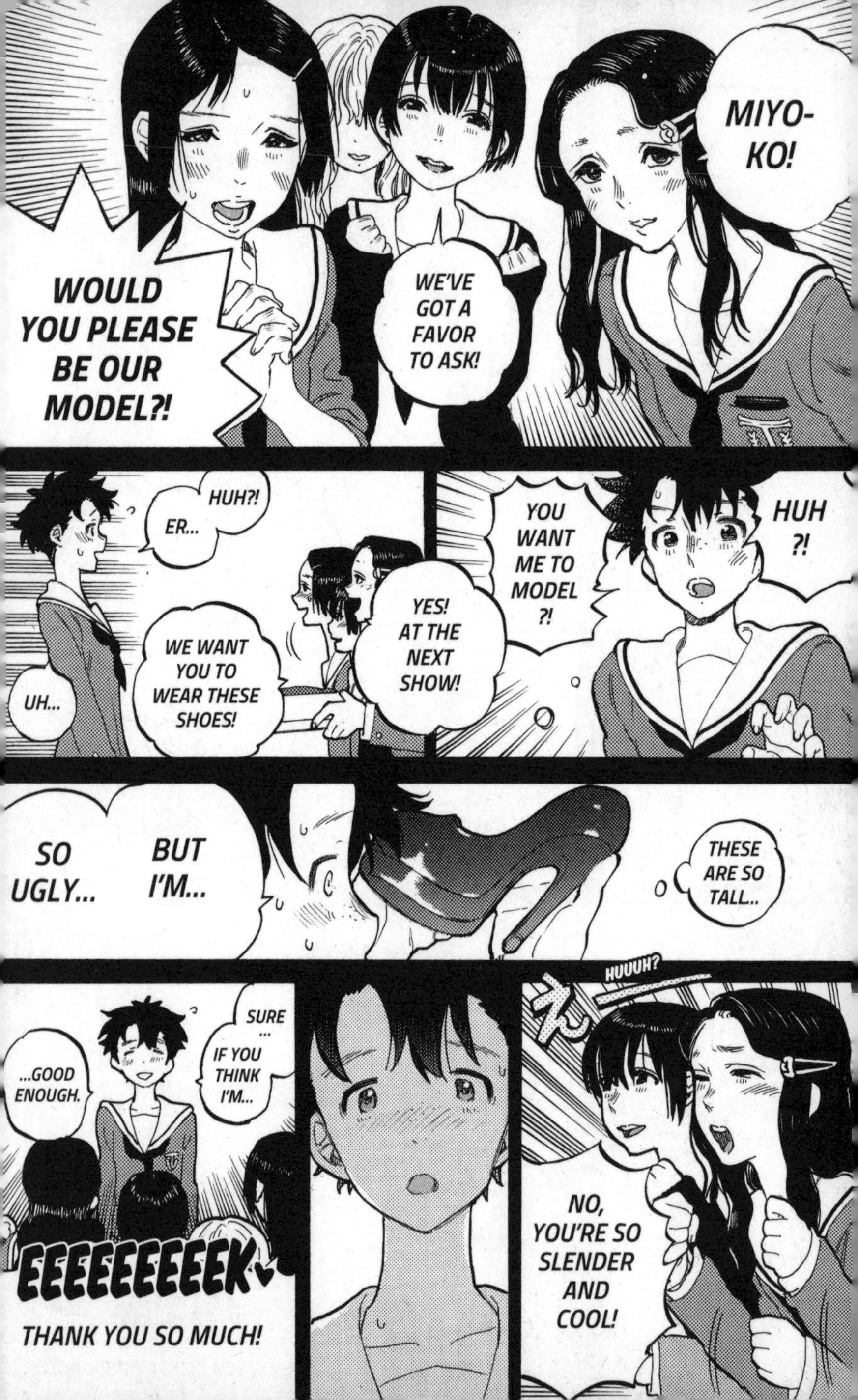
MIYO-KO!
WE'VE GOT A FAVOR TO ASK!
WOULD YOU PLEASE BE OUR MODEL?!
HUH ?!
YOU WANT ME TO MODEL ?!
YES! AT THE NEXT SHOW!
WE WANT YOU TO WEAR THESE SHOES!
HUH?! ER...
UH...
THESE ARE SO TALL...
BUT I'M...
SO UGLY...
HUUUH?
NO, YOU'RE SO SLENDER AND COOL!
SURE... IF YOU THINK I'M...
...GOOD ENOUGH.
EEEEEEEEEEK
THANK YOU SO MUCH!

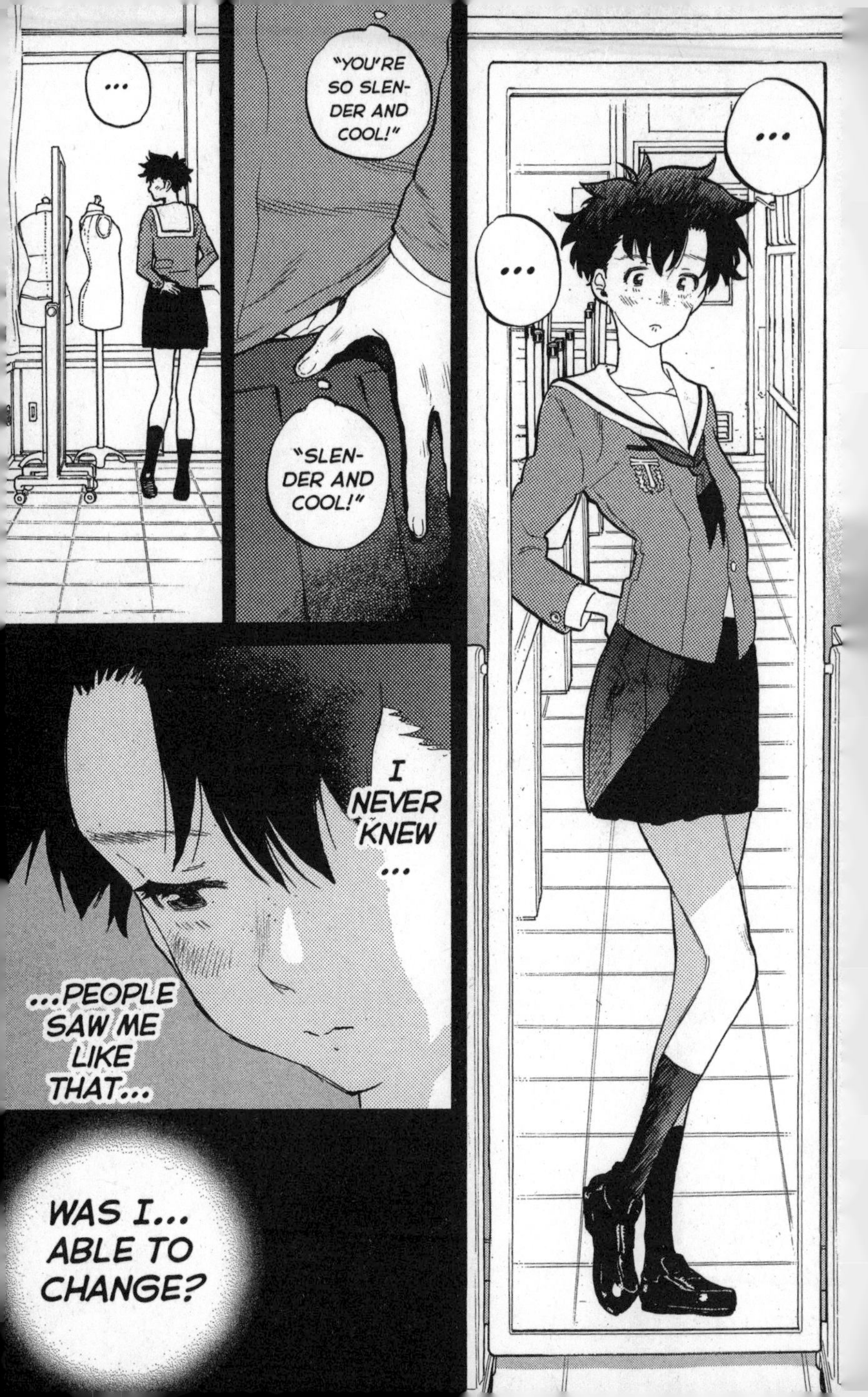
...
...
"YOU'RE SO SLENDER AND COOL!"
"SLENDER AND COOL!"
...
I NEVER KNEW...
...PEOPLE SAW ME LIKE THAT...
WAS I... ABLE TO CHANGE?

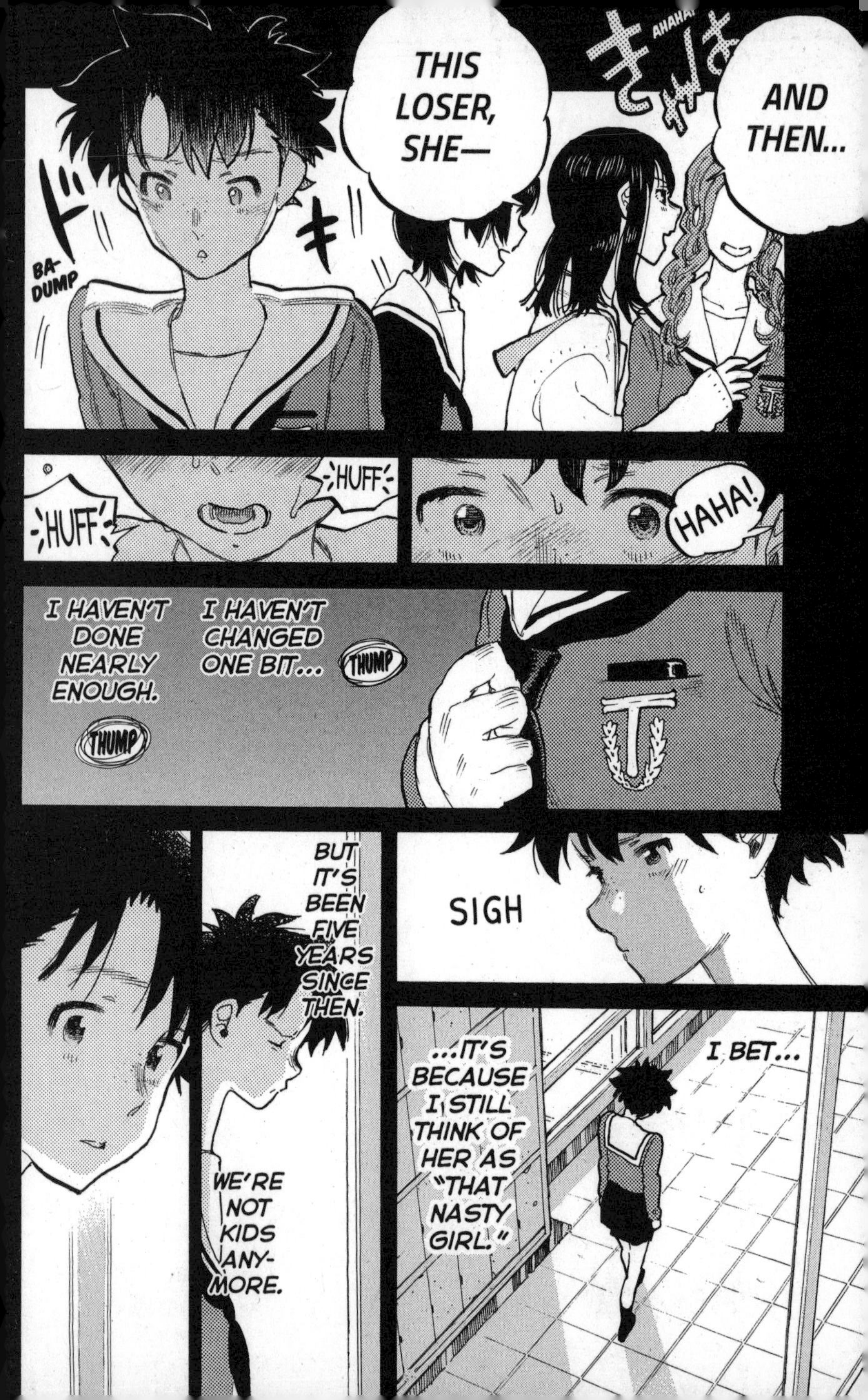
AND THEN...
AHAHA
THIS LOSER, SHE—
BA-DUMP
HAHA!
HUFF
HUFF
I HAVEN'T CHANGED ONE BIT...
THUMP
I HAVEN'T DONE NEARLY ENOUGH.
THUMP
SIGH
I BET...
...IT'S BECAUSE I STILL THINK OF HER AS "THAT NASTY GIRL."
BUT IT'S BEEN FIVE YEARS SINCE THEN.
WE'RE NOT KIDS ANYMORE.

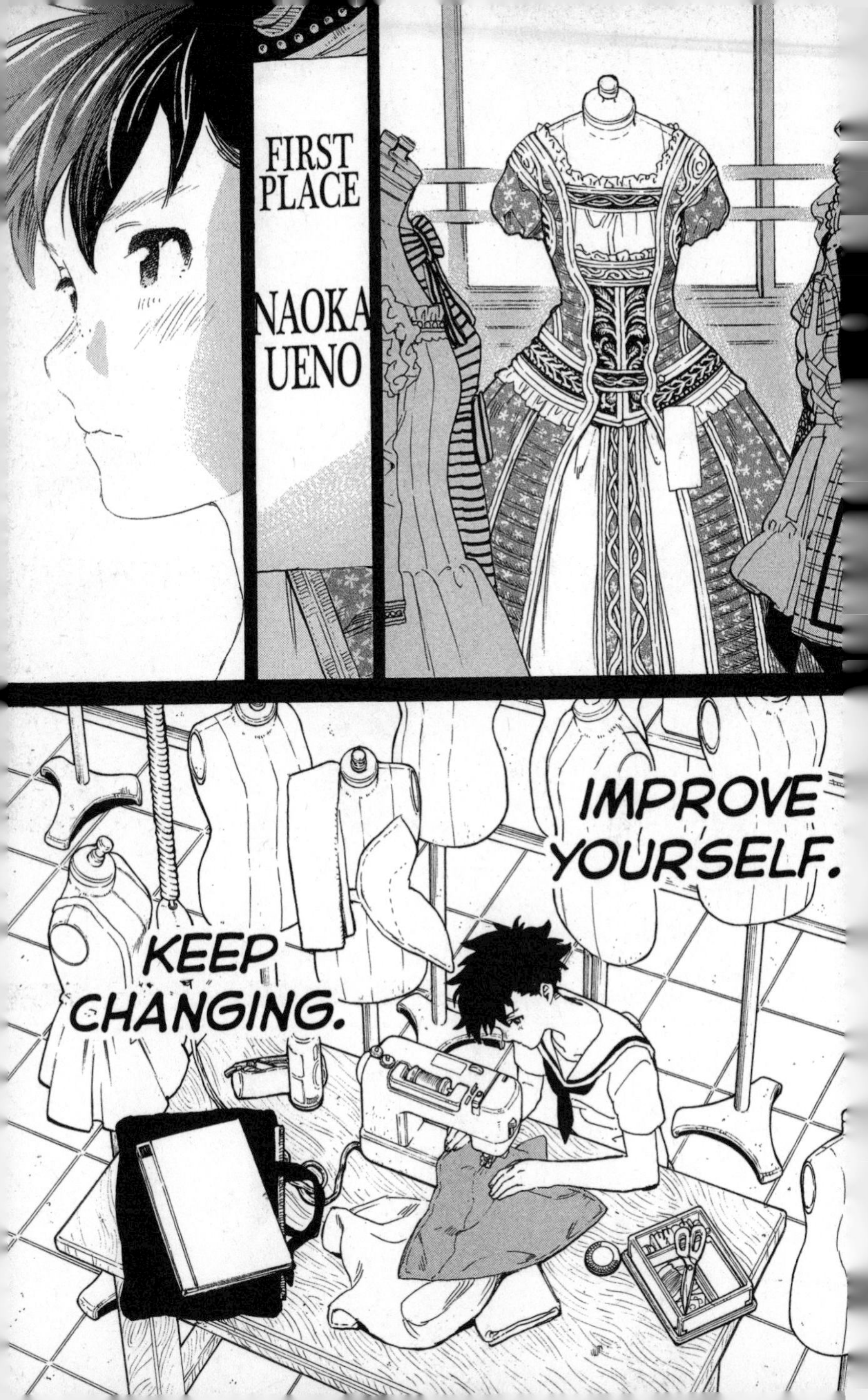
FIRST PLACE
NAOKA UENO
IMPROVE YOURSELF.
KEEP CHANGING.

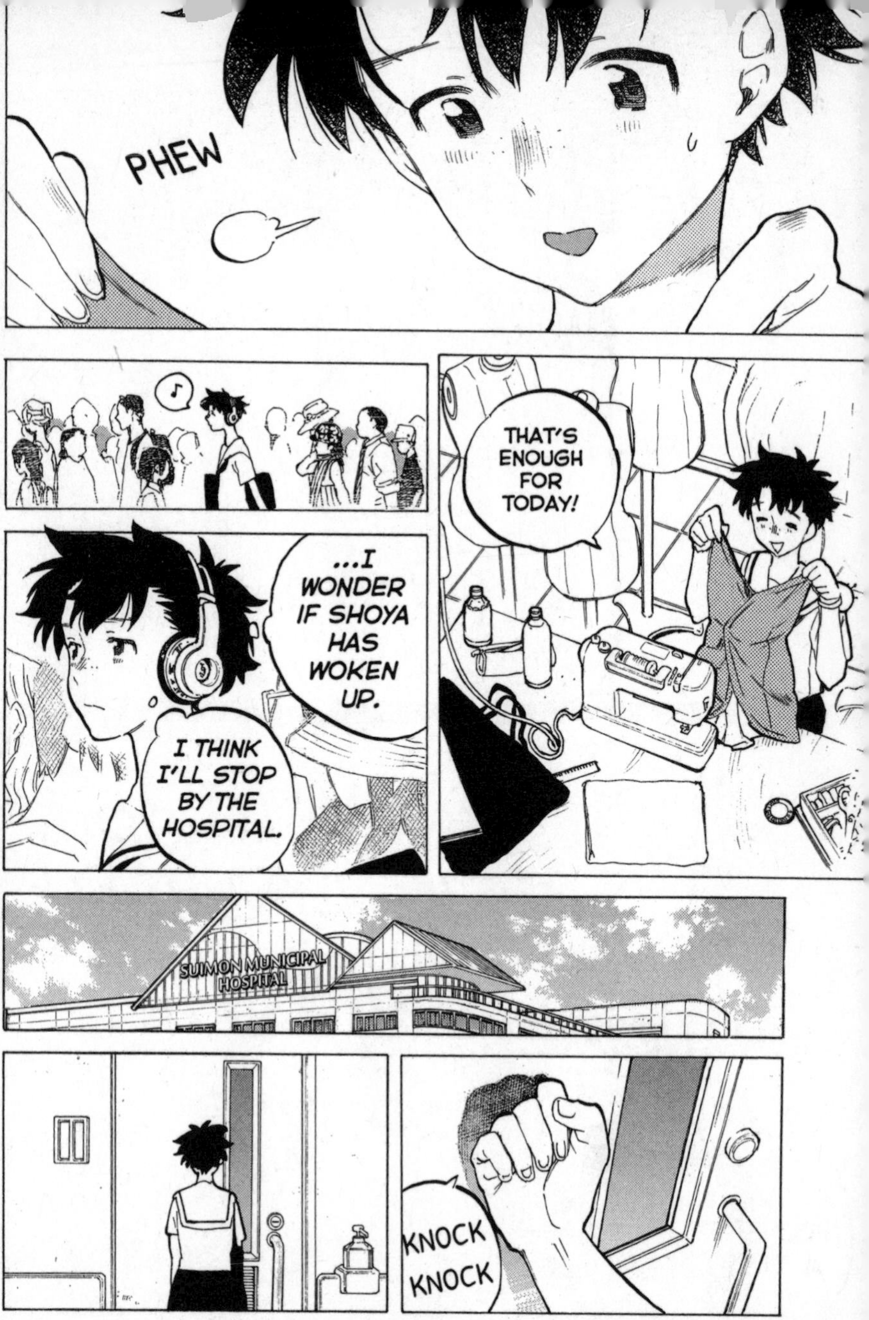
PHEW
THAT'S ENOUGH FOR TODAY!
♪
...I WONDER IF SHOYA HAS WOKEN UP.
I THINK I'LL STOP BY THE HOSPITAL.
SUIMON MUNICIPAL HOSPITAL
KNOCK KNOCK

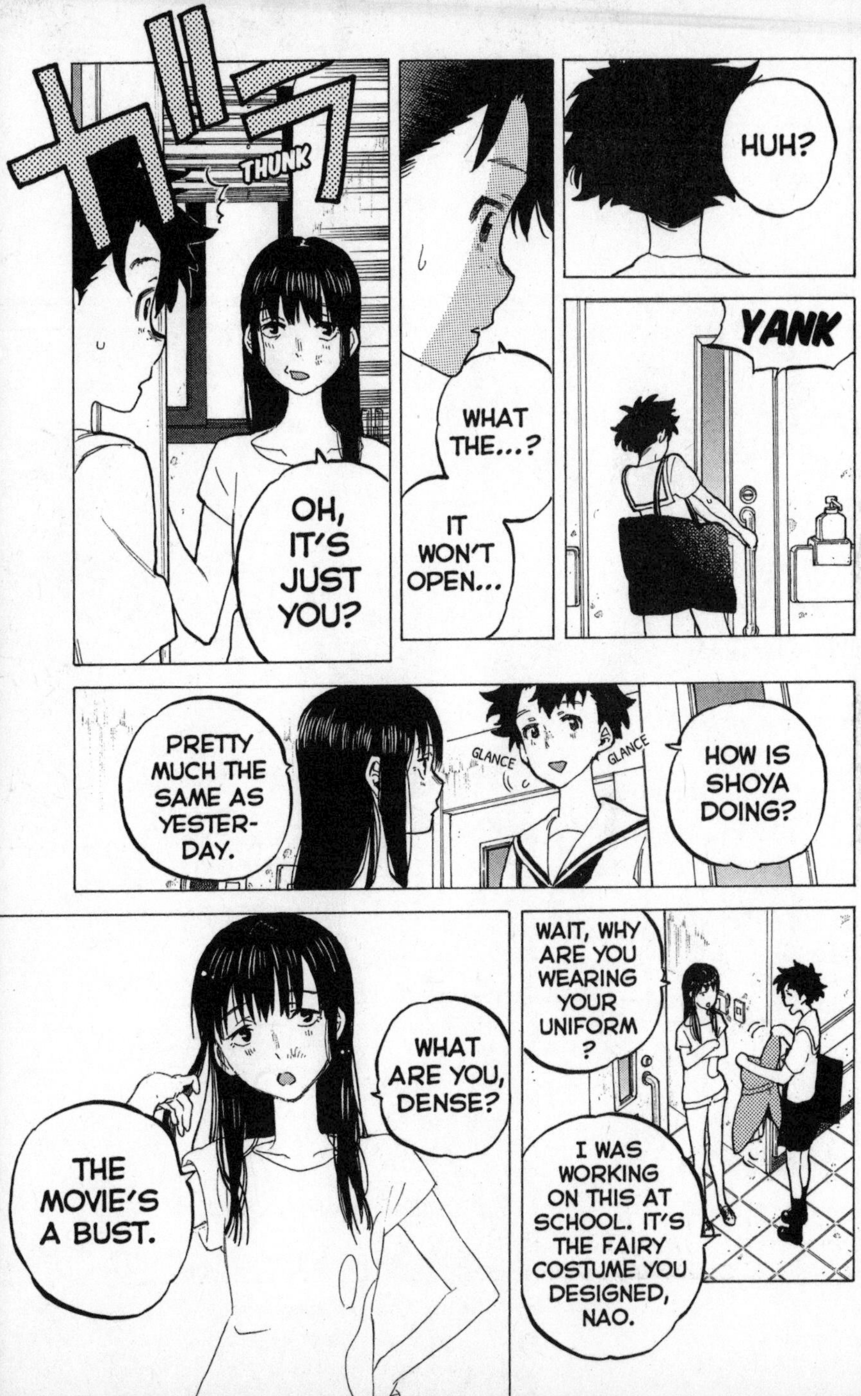
HUH?
YANK
WHAT THE...?
IT WON'T OPEN...
THUNK
OH, IT'S JUST YOU?
HOW IS SHOYA DOING?
GLANCE
GLANCE
PRETTY MUCH THE SAME AS YESTER-DAY.
WAIT, WHY ARE YOU WEARING YOUR UNIFORM?
I WAS WORKING ON THIS AT SCHOOL. IT'S THE FAIRY COSTUME YOU DESIGNED, NAO.
WHAT ARE YOU, DENSE?
THE MOVIE'S A BUST.

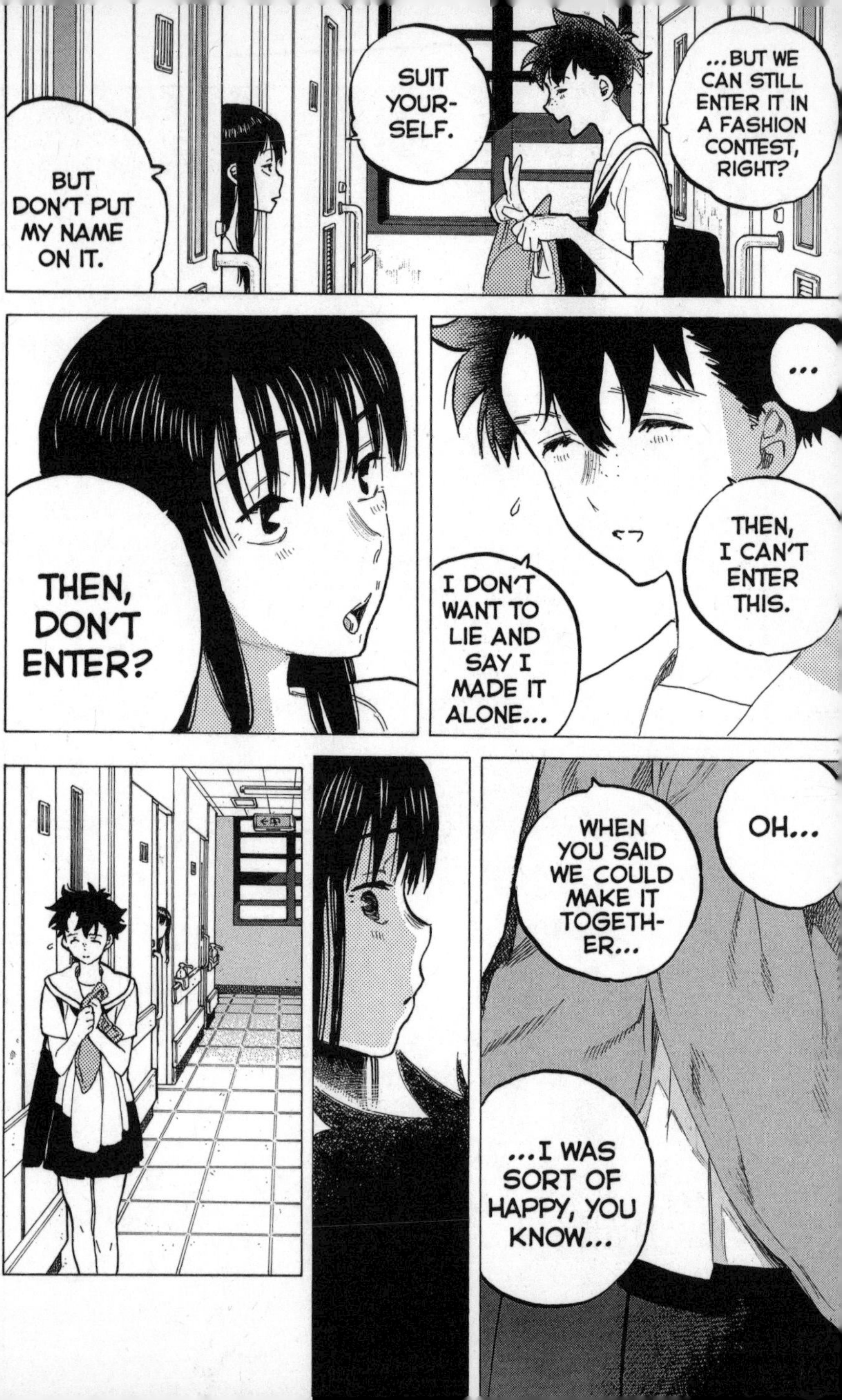
...BUT WE CAN STILL ENTER IT IN A FASHION CONTEST, RIGHT?
SUIT YOUR-SELF.
BUT DON'T PUT MY NAME ON IT.
...
THEN, I CAN'T ENTER THIS.
I DON'T WANT TO LIE AND SAY I MADE IT ALONE...
THEN, DON'T ENTER?
OH...
WHEN YOU SAID WE COULD MAKE IT TOGETH-ER...
...I WAS SORT OF HAPPY, YOU KNOW...

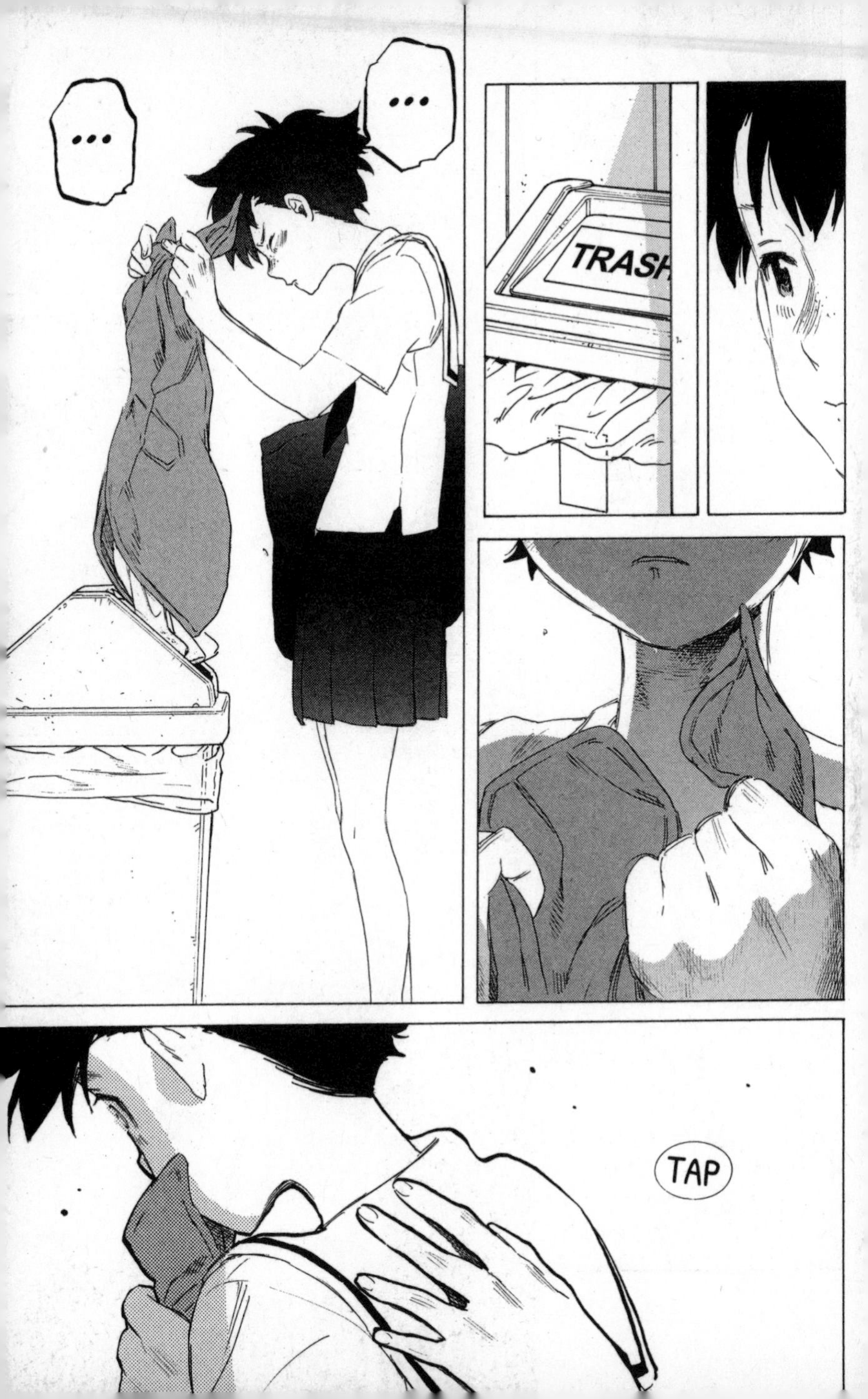

TRASH
...
...
TAP

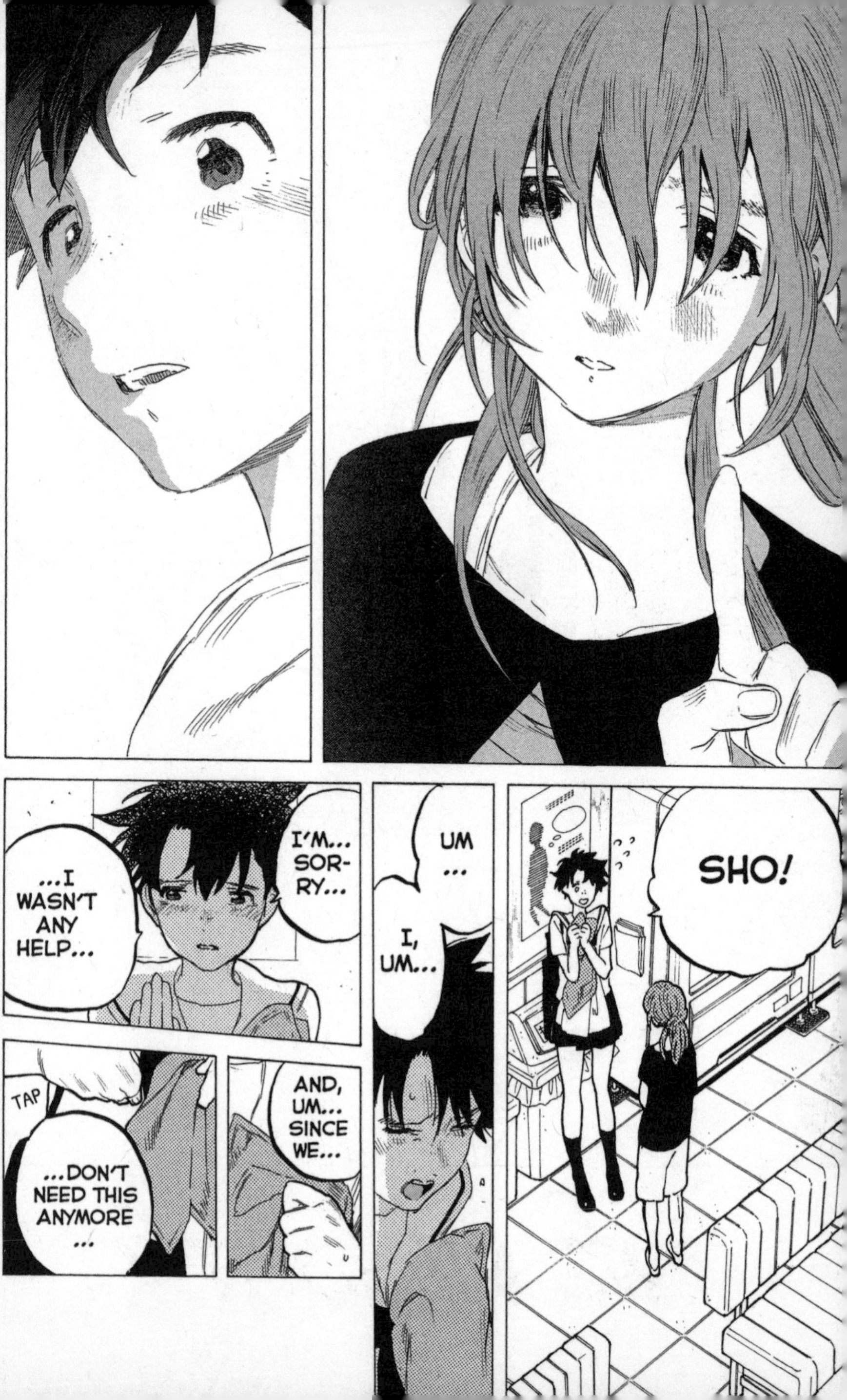
SHO!
UM ...
I, UM...
I'M... SORRY...
...I WASN'T ANY HELP...
AND, UM... SINCE WE...
TAP
...DON'T NEED THIS ANYMORE ...

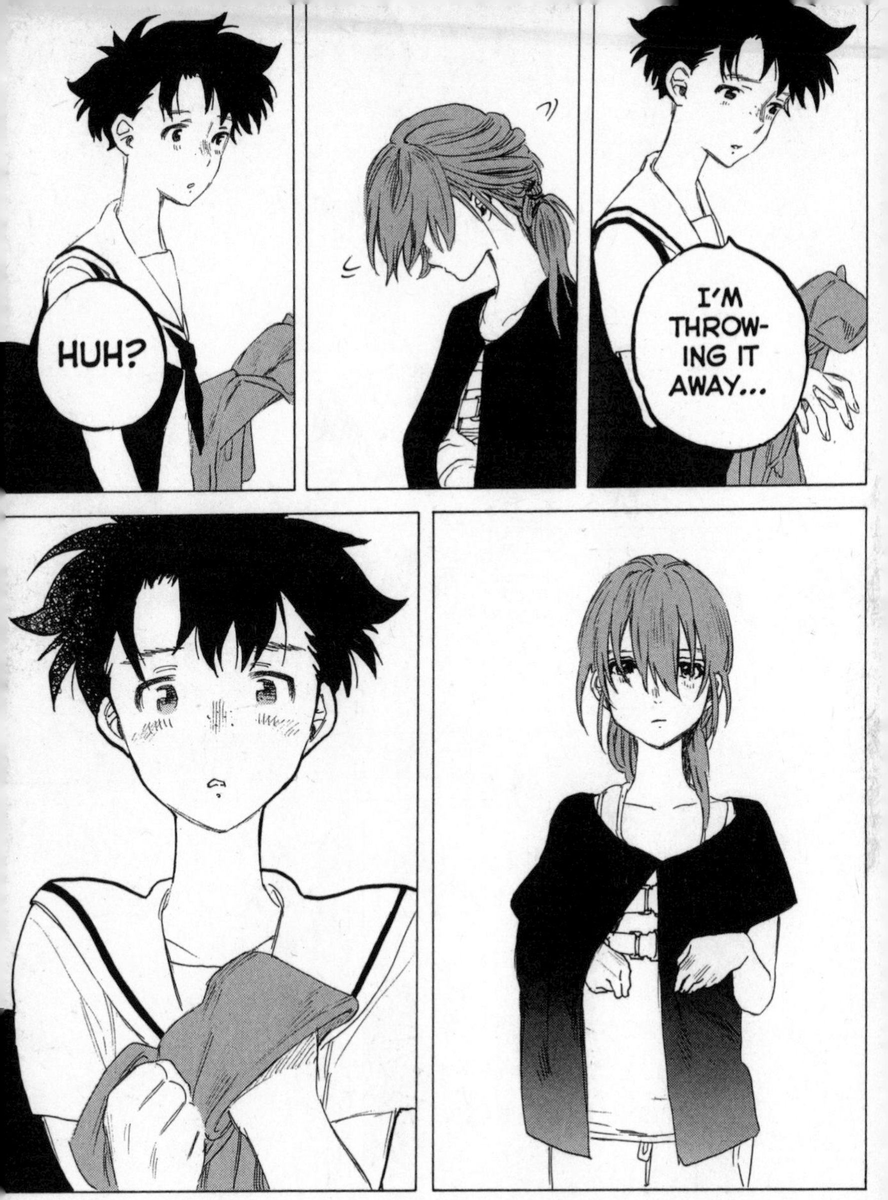
I'M THROWING IT AWAY...
HUH?

"WE NEED IT."

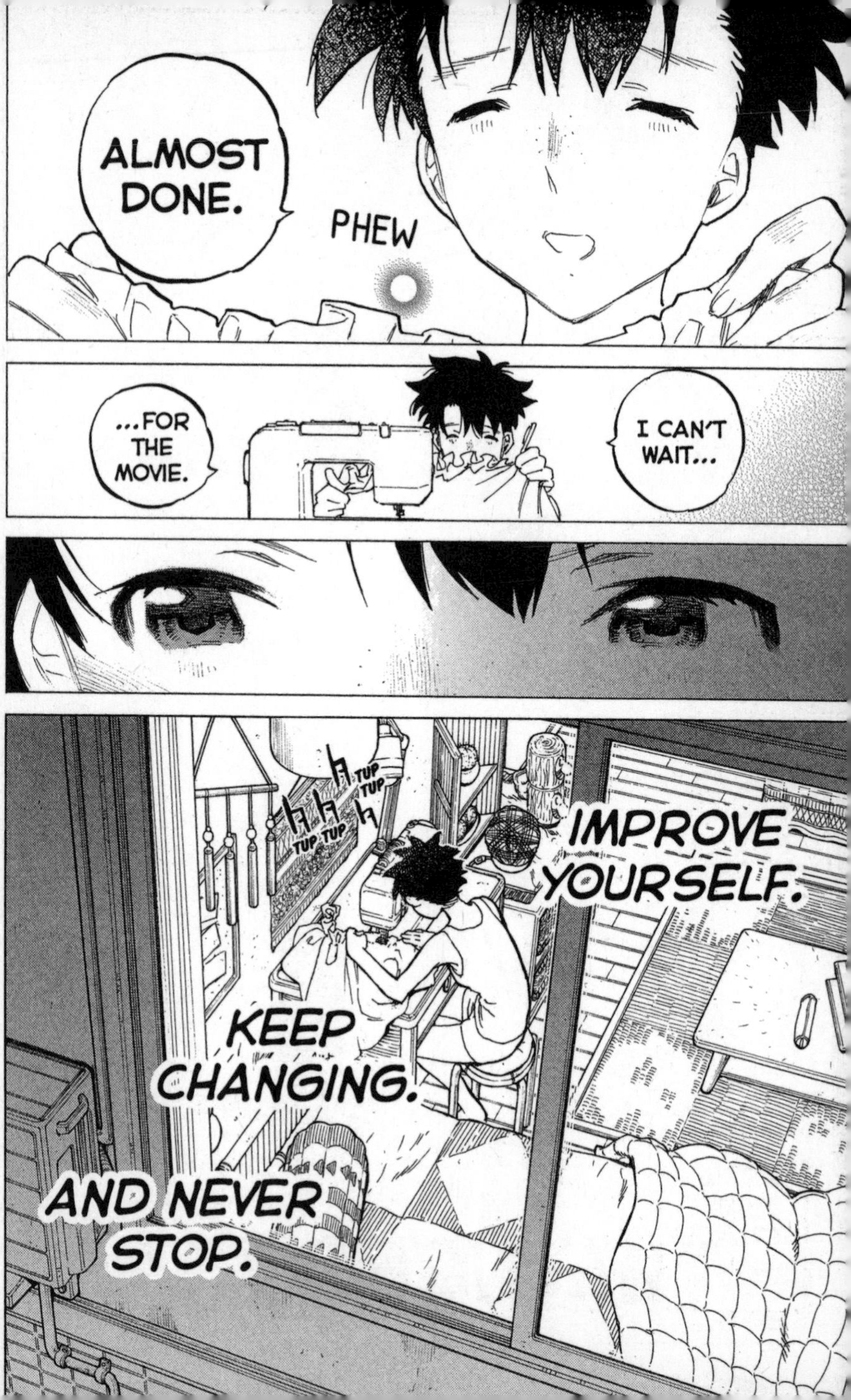
ALMOST DONE.
PHEW
I CAN'T WAIT...
...FOR THE MOVIE.
TUP TUP
TUP TUP
IMPROVE YOURSELF.
KEEP CHANGING.
AND NEVER STOP.

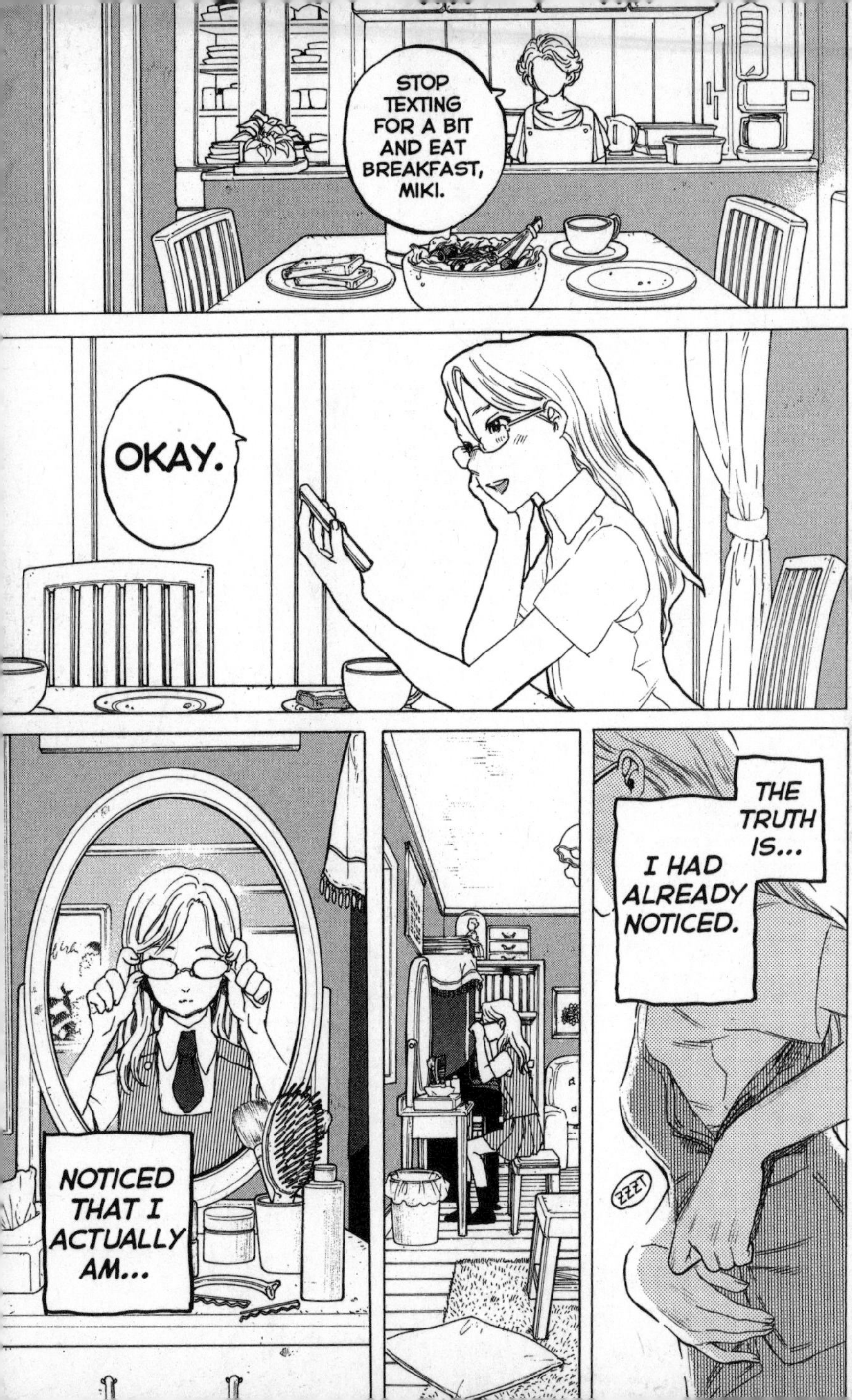
STOP TEXTING FOR A BIT AND EAT BREAKFAST, MIKI.
OKAY.
THE TRUTH IS...
I HAD ALREADY NOTICED.
ZZZT
NOTICED THAT I ACTUALLY AM...

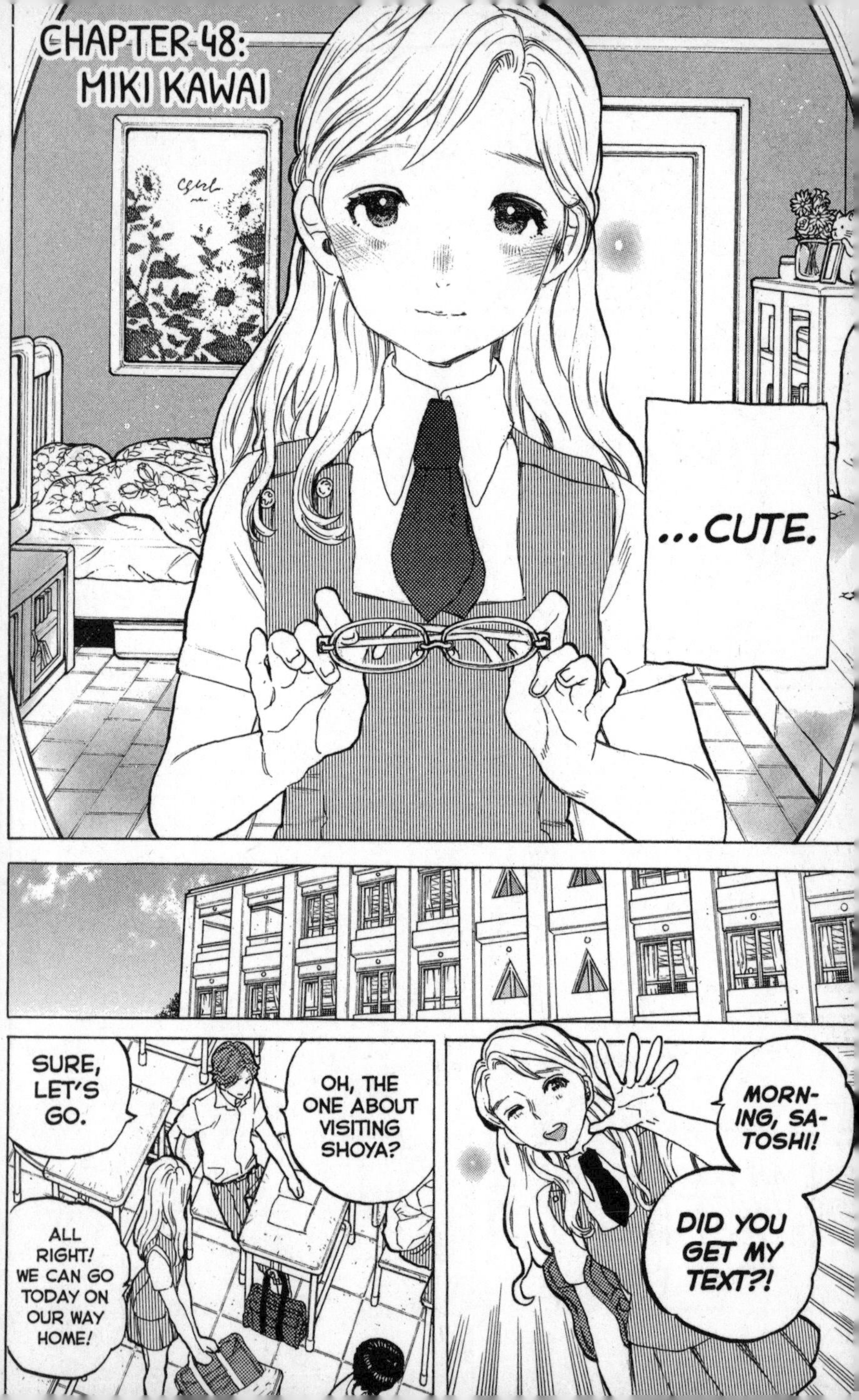
CHAPTER 48: MIKI KAWAI
...CUTE.
MORNING, SATOSHI!
DID YOU GET MY TEXT?!
OH, THE ONE ABOUT VISITING SHOYA?
SURE, LET'S GO.
ALL RIGHT! WE CAN GO TODAY ON OUR WAY HOME!

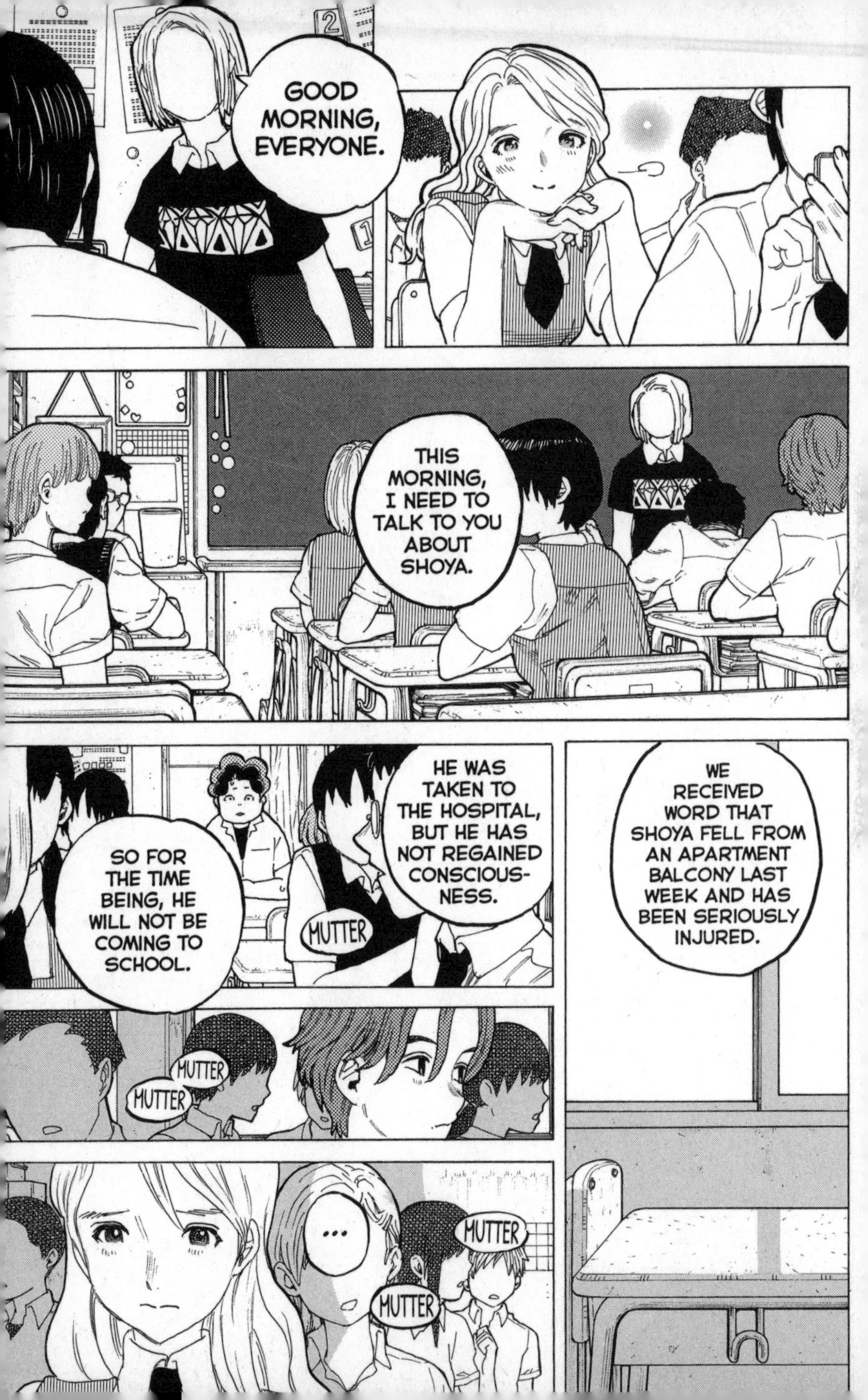
GOOD MORNING, EVERYONE.
THIS MORNING, I NEED TO TALK TO YOU ABOUT SHOYA.
WE RECEIVED WORD THAT SHOYA FELL FROM AN APARTMENT BALCONY LAST WEEK AND HAS BEEN SERIOUSLY INJURED.
HE WAS TAKEN TO THE HOSPITAL, BUT HE HAS NOT REGAINED CONSCIOUS-NESS.
MUTTER
SO FOR THE TIME BEING, HE WILL NOT BE COMING TO SCHOOL.
MUTTER
MUTTER
MUTTER
...
MUTTER

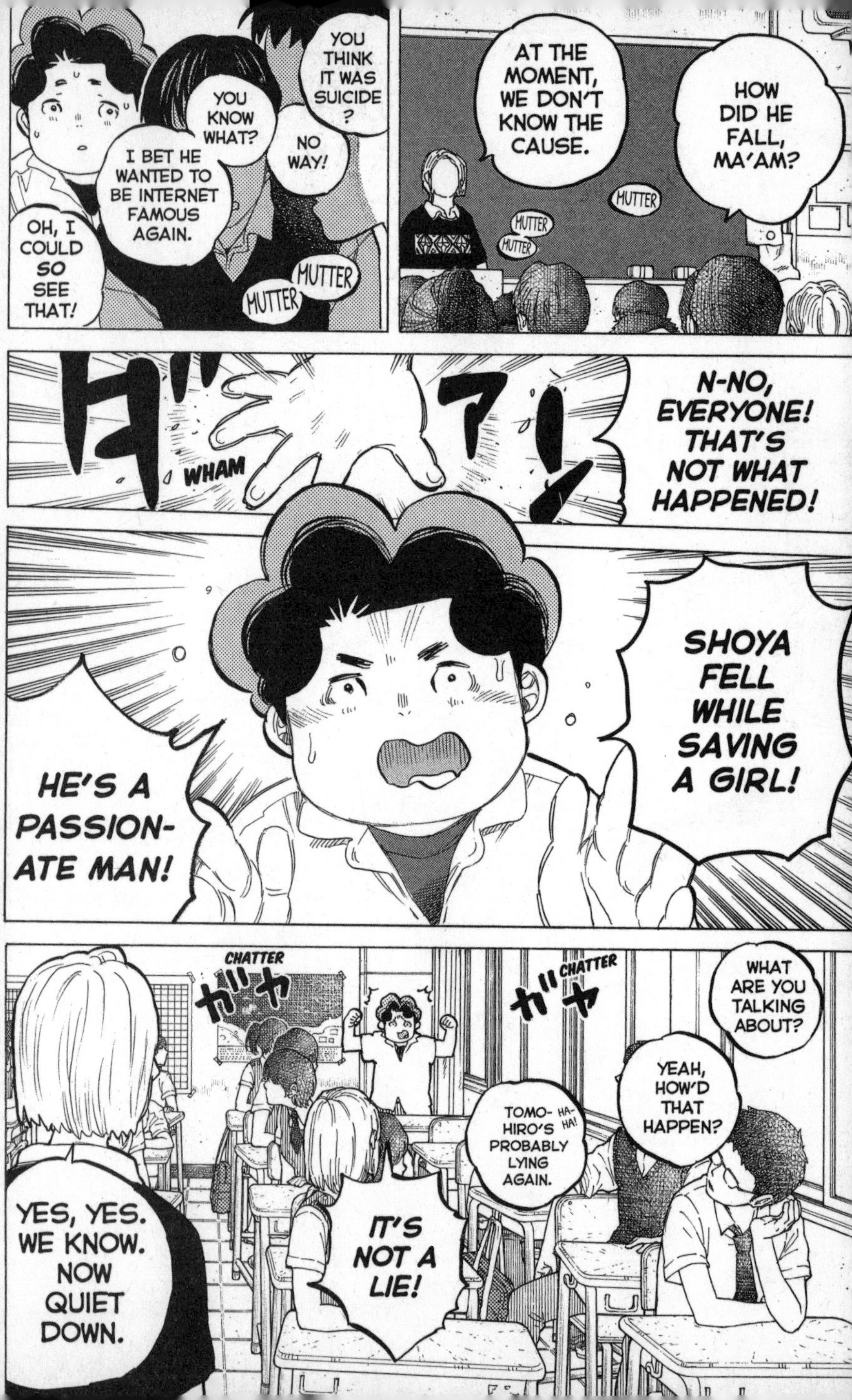
HOW DID HE FALL, MA'AM?
AT THE MOMENT, WE DON'T KNOW THE CAUSE.
MUTTER
MUTTER
MUTTER
YOU THINK IT WAS SUICIDE?
NO WAY!
YOU KNOW WHAT?
I BET HE WANTED TO BE INTERNET FAMOUS AGAIN.
OH, I COULD SO SEE THAT!
MUTTER
MUTTER
N-NO, EVERYONE! THAT'S NOT WHAT HAPPENED!
WHAM
SHOYA FELL WHILE SAVING A GIRL!
HE'S A PASSION-ATE MAN!
WHAT ARE YOU TALKING ABOUT?
YEAH, HOW'D THAT HAPPEN?
CHATTER
TOMO-HIRO'S PROBABLY LYING AGAIN.
HA-HA!
IT'S NOT A LIE!
CHATTER
YES, YES. WE KNOW. NOW QUIET DOWN.

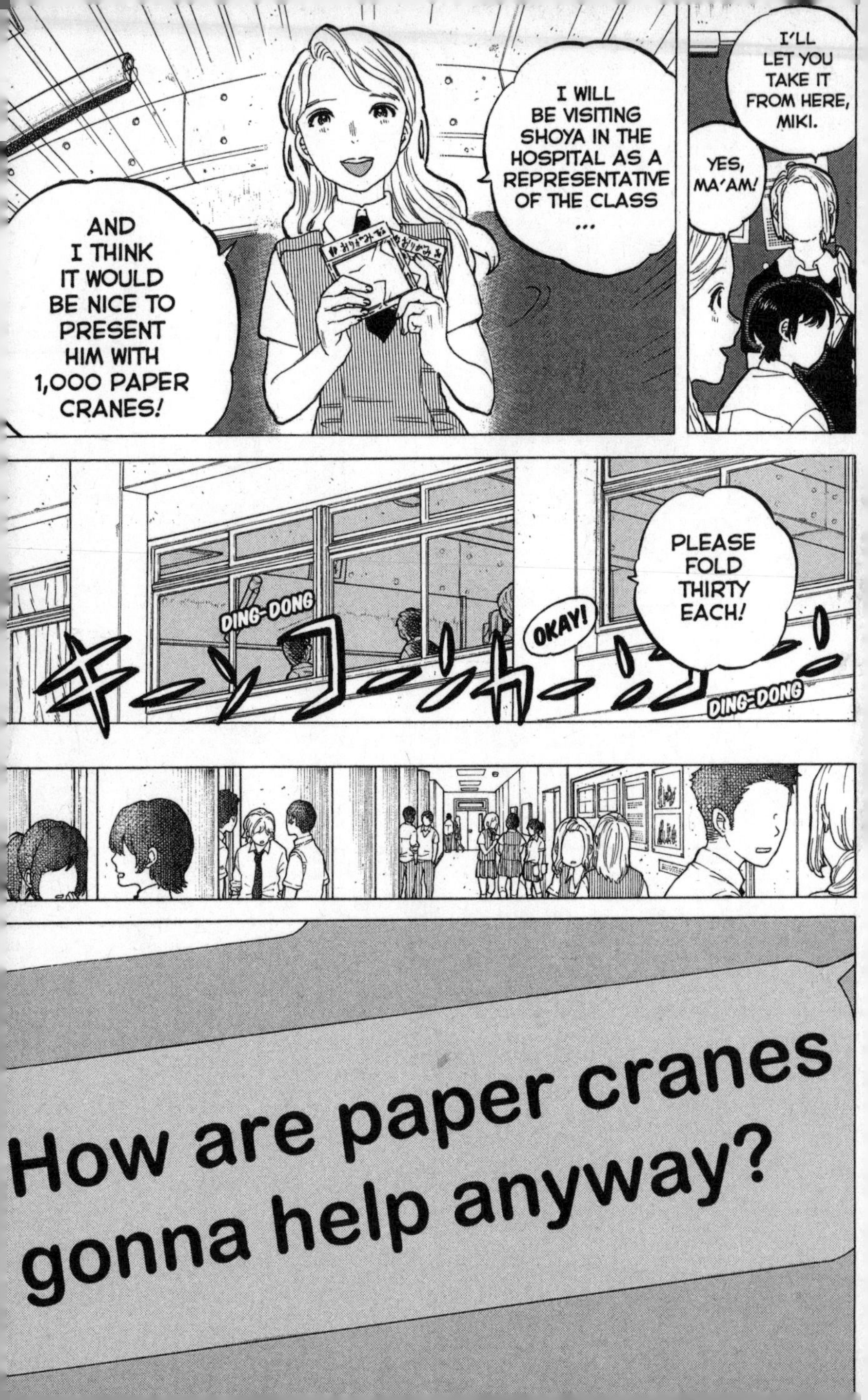
I'LL LET YOU TAKE IT FROM HERE, MIKI.
YES, MA'AM!
I WILL BE VISITING SHOYA IN THE HOSPITAL AS A REPRESENTATIVE OF THE CLASS ...
AND I THINK IT WOULD BE NICE TO PRESENT HIM WITH 1,000 PAPER CRANES!
PLEASE FOLD THIRTY EACH!
OKAY!
DING-DONG
キーンコーンカーンコーン
DING-DONG
How are paper cranes gonna help anyway?

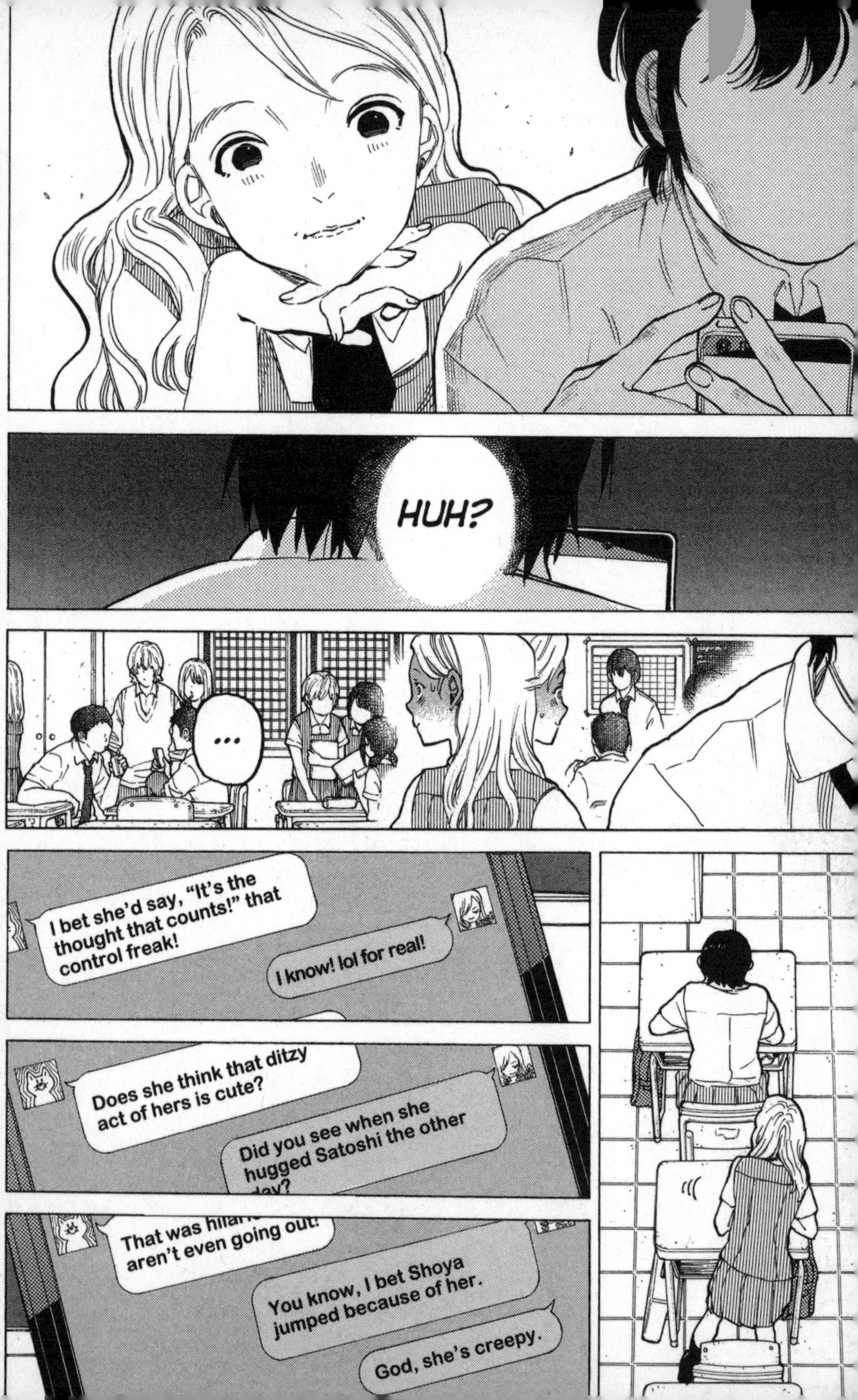
HUH?
...
I bet she'd say, "It's the thought that counts!" that control freak!
I know! lol for real!
Does she think that ditzy act of hers is cute?
Did you see when she hugged Satoshi the other
That was
aren't even going out!
You know, I bet Shoya jumped because of her.
God, she's creepy.

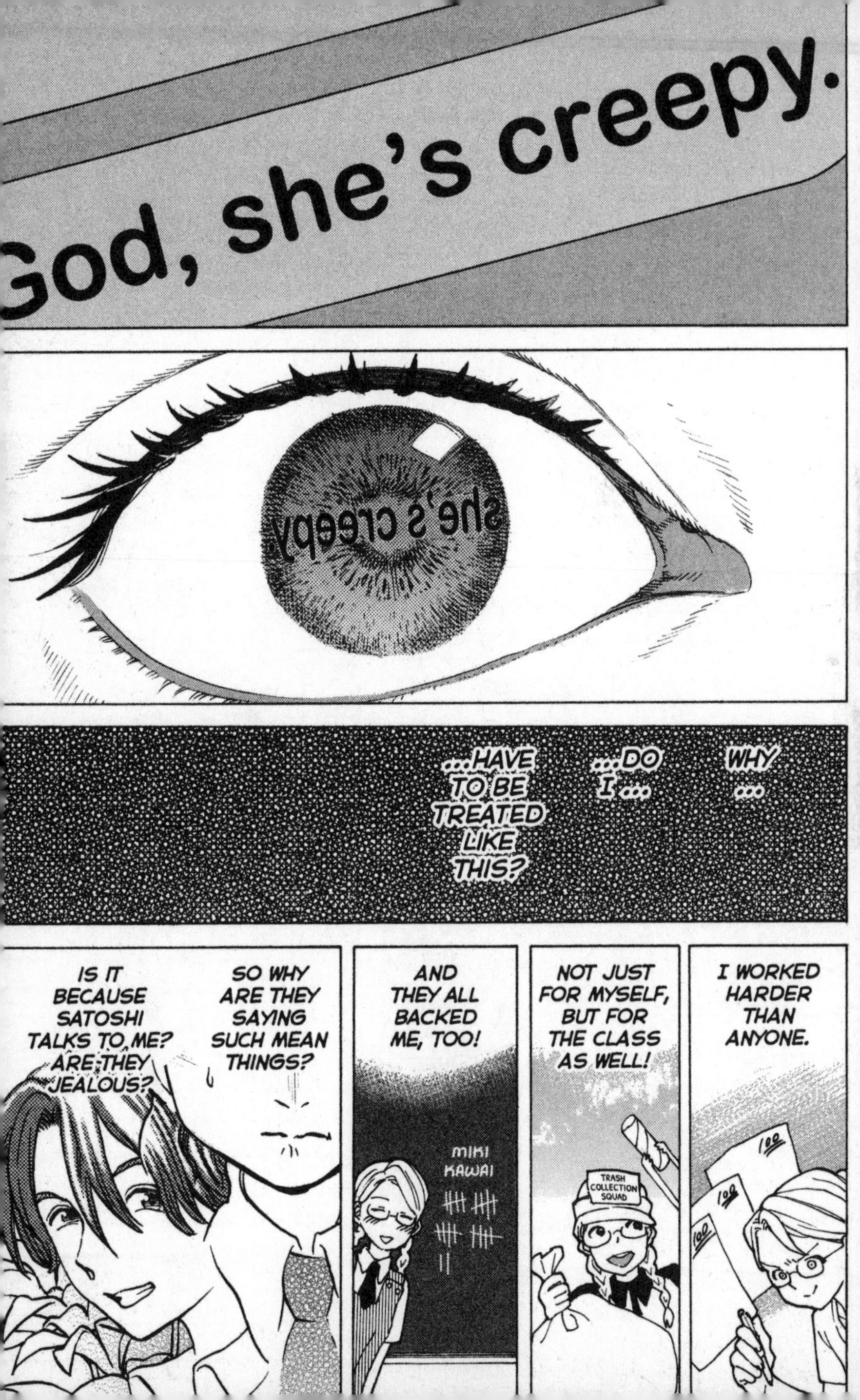
God, she's creepy.
she's creepy.
WHY...
...DO I...
...HAVE TO BE TREATED LIKE THIS?
I WORKED HARDER THAN ANYONE.
NOT JUST FOR MYSELF, BUT FOR THE CLASS AS WELL!
TRASH COLLECTION SQUAD
AND THEY ALL BACKED ME, TOO!
MIKI KAWAI
SO WHY ARE THEY SAYING SUCH MEAN THINGS?
IS IT BECAUSE SATOSHI TALKS TO ME? ARE THEY JEALOUS?

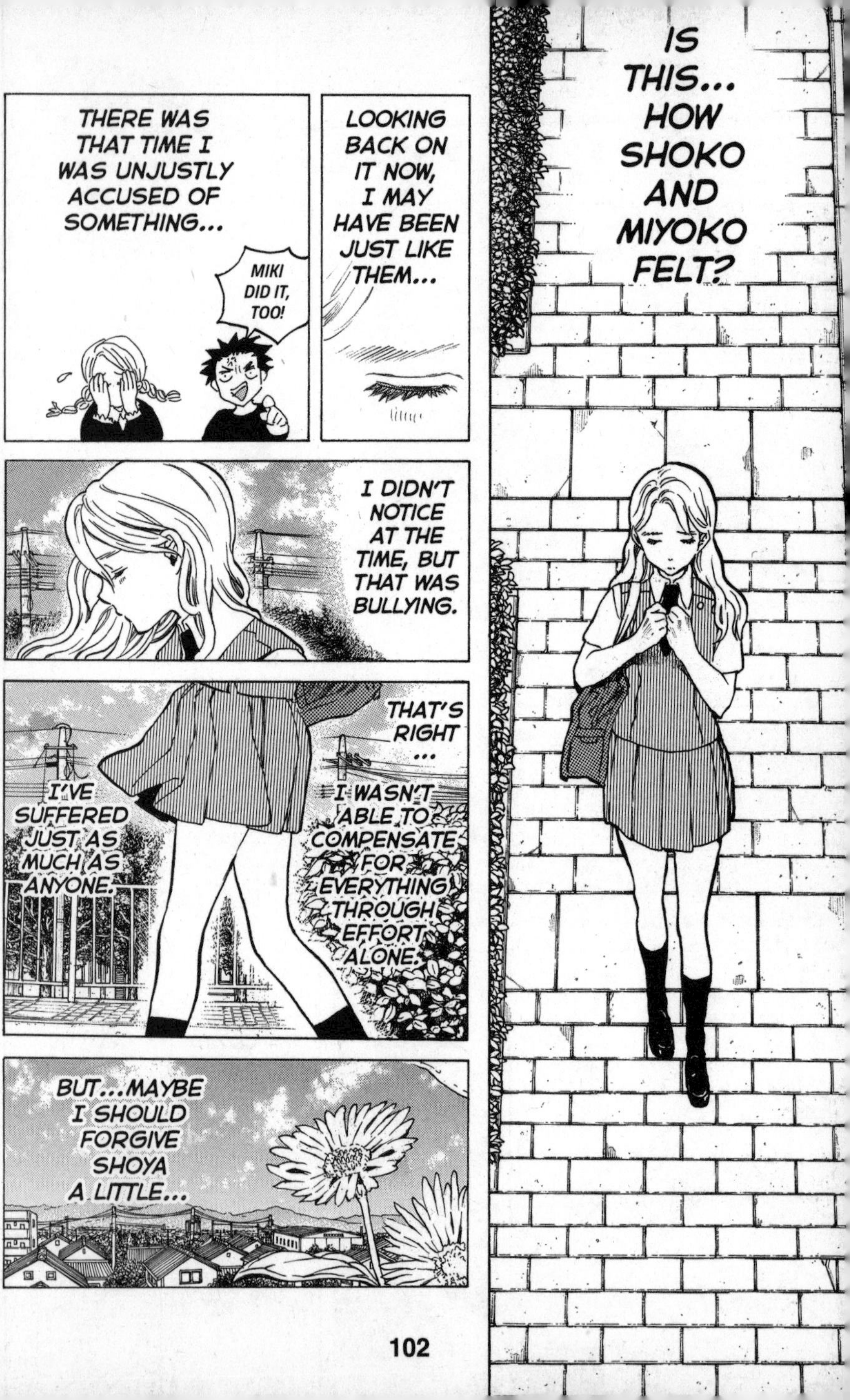
IS THIS... HOW SHOKO AND MIYOKO FELT?
LOOKING BACK ON IT NOW, I MAY HAVE BEEN JUST LIKE THEM...
THERE WAS THAT TIME I WAS UNJUSTLY ACCUSED OF SOMETHING...
MIKI DID IT, TOO!
I DIDN'T NOTICE AT THE TIME, BUT THAT WAS BULLYING.
THAT'S RIGHT...
I WASN'T ABLE TO COMPENSATE FOR EVERYTHING THROUGH EFFORT ALONE.
I'VE SUFFERED JUST AS MUCH AS ANYONE.
BUT...MAYBE I SHOULD FORGIVE SHOYA A LITTLE...

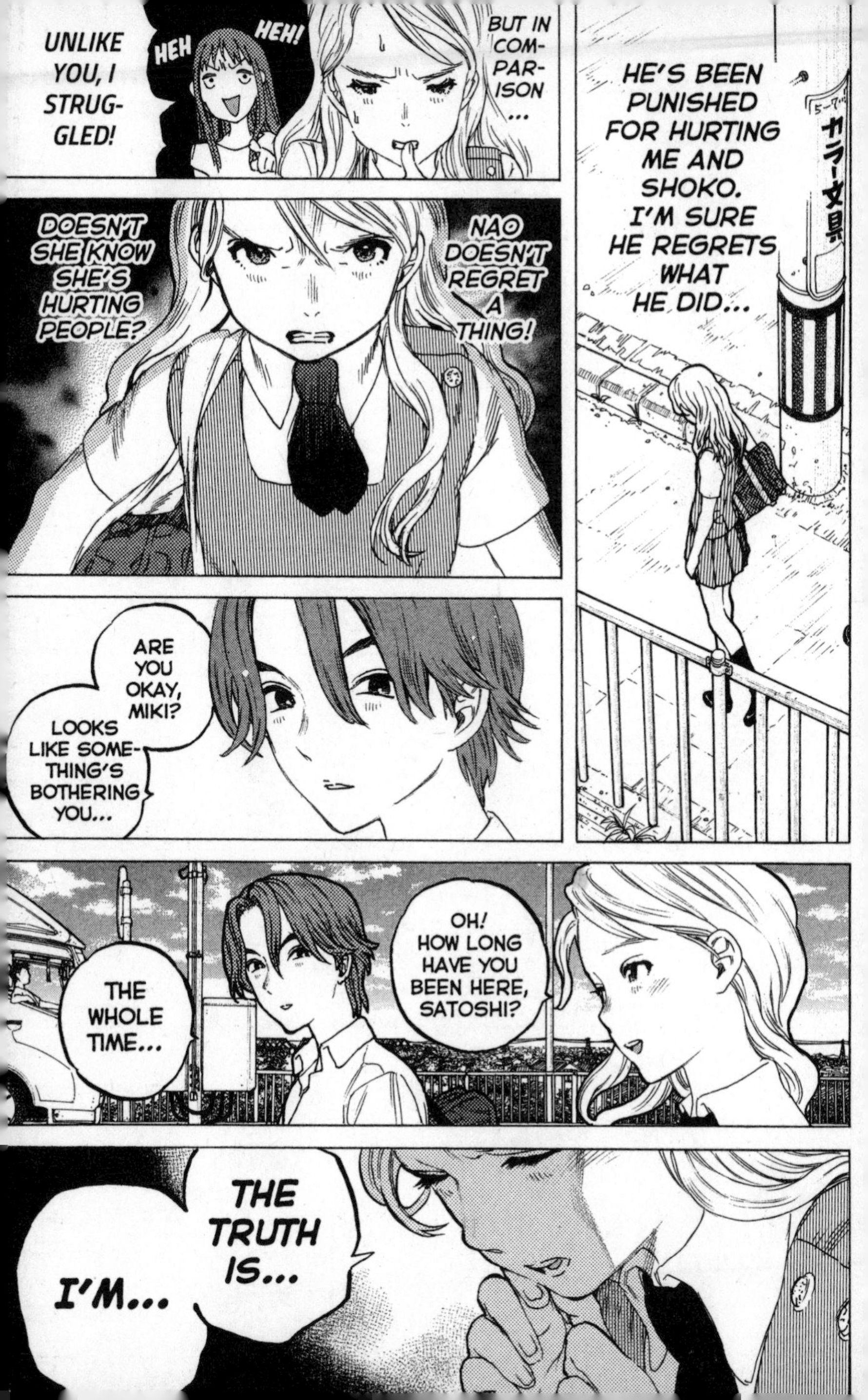

HE'S BEEN PUNISHED FOR HURTING ME AND SHOKO. I'M SURE HE REGRETS WHAT HE DID...
カラー文具
BUT IN COMPARISON...
HEH HEH!
UNLIKE YOU, I STRUGGLED!
NAO DOESN'T REGRET A THING!
DOESN'T SHE KNOW SHE'S HURTING PEOPLE?
ARE YOU OKAY, MIKI?
LOOKS LIKE SOMETHING'S BOTHERING YOU...
OH! HOW LONG HAVE YOU BEEN HERE, SATOSHI?
THE WHOLE TIME...
THE TRUTH IS...
I'M...

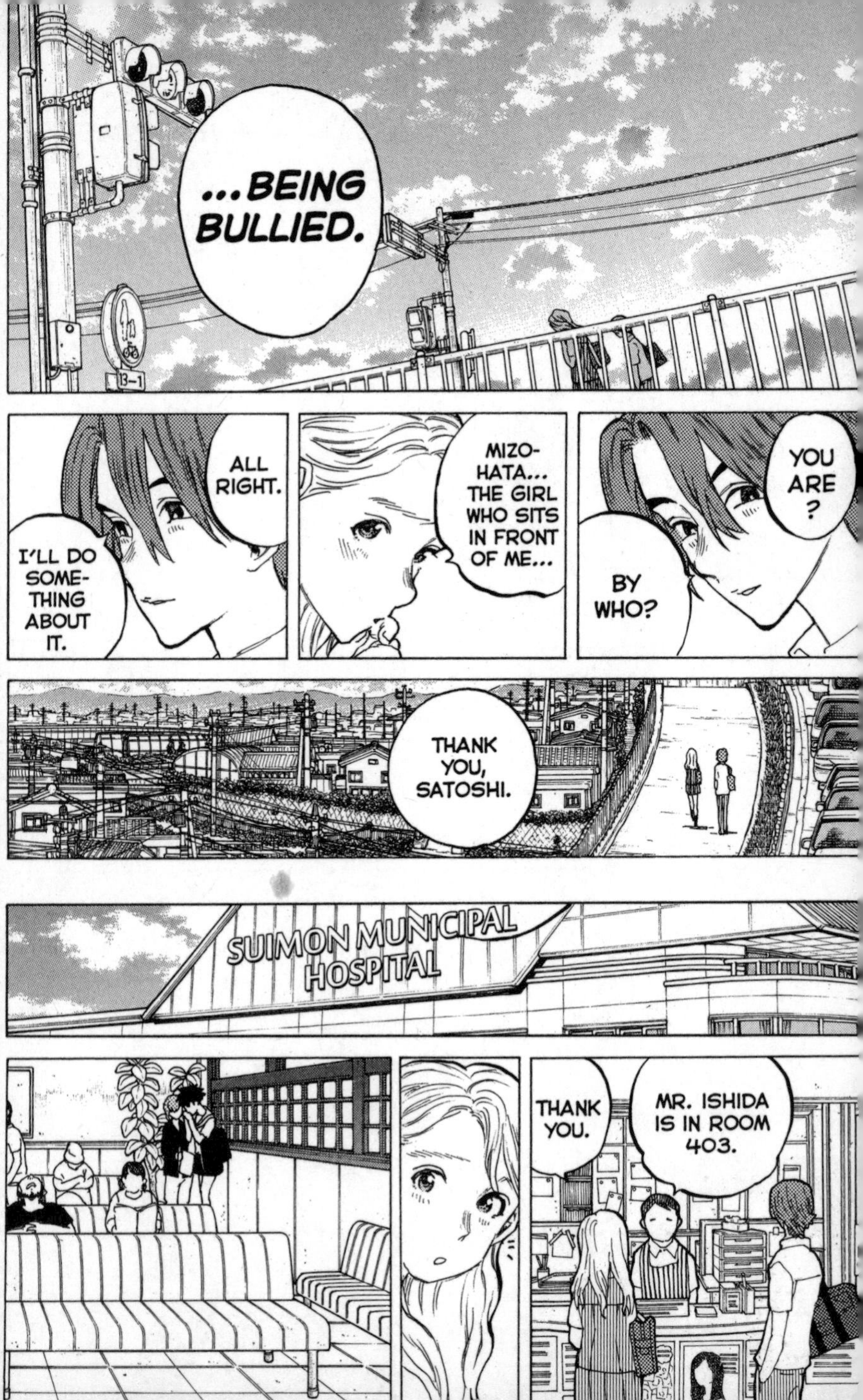
...BEING BULLIED.
13-1
YOU ARE?
BY WHO?
MIZO-HATA... THE GIRL WHO SITS IN FRONT OF ME...
ALL RIGHT.
I'LL DO SOME-THING ABOUT IT.
THANK YOU, SATOSHI.
SUIMON MUNICIPAL HOSPITAL
MR. ISHIDA IS IN ROOM 403.
THANK YOU.

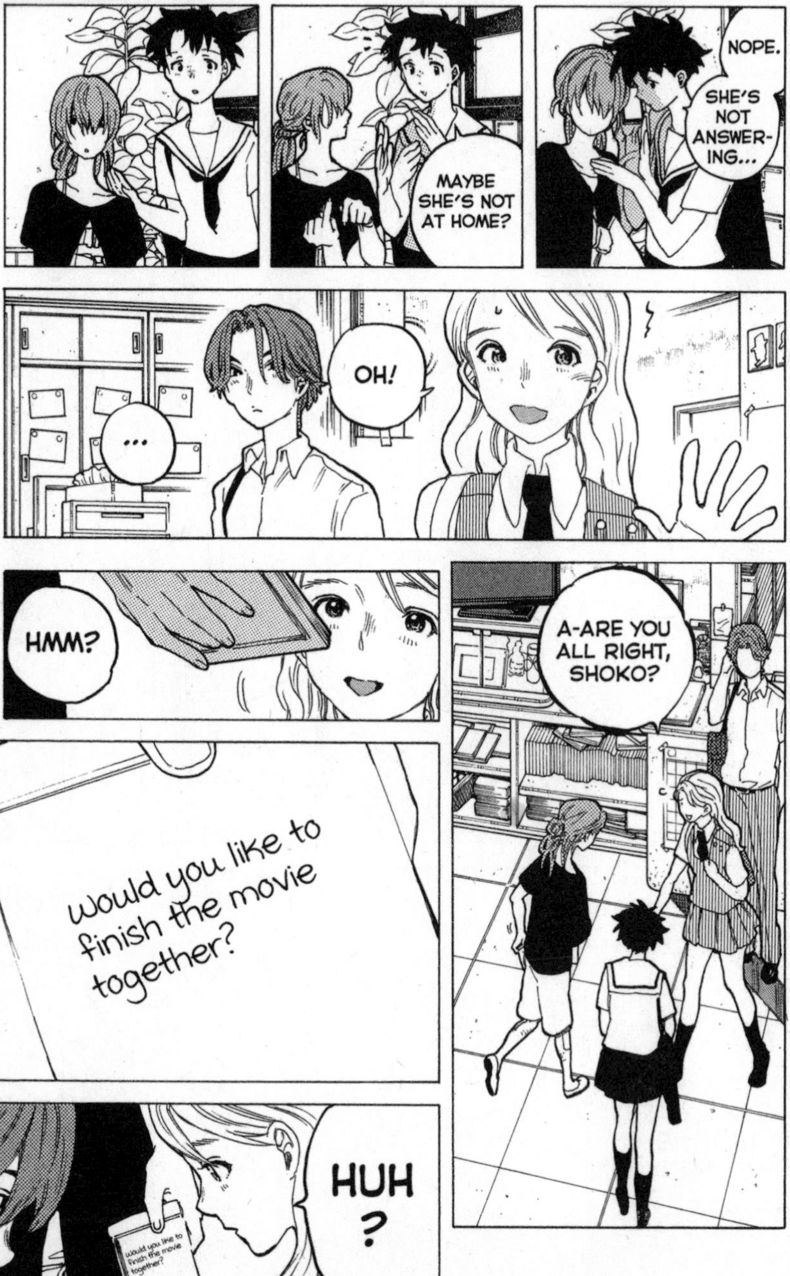
NOPE.
SHE'S NOT ANSWERING...
MAYBE SHE'S NOT AT HOME?
OH!
...
A-ARE YOU ALL RIGHT, SHOKO?
HMM?
Would you like to finish the movie together?
HUH ?
Would you like to finish the movie together?

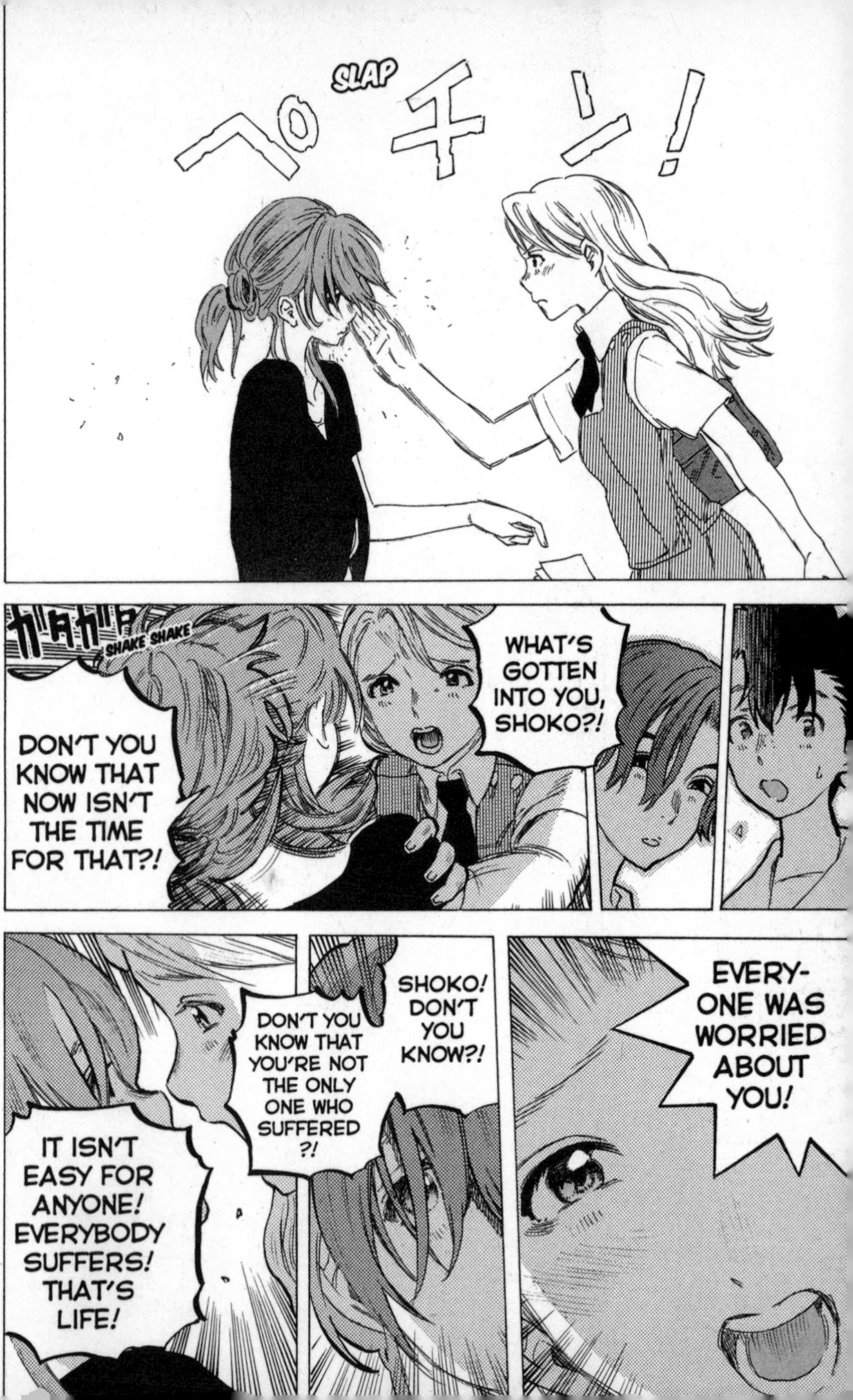
SLAP
ペチン!
WHAT'S GOTTEN INTO YOU, SHOKO?!
ガクガク
SHAKE SHAKE
DON'T YOU KNOW THAT NOW ISN'T THE TIME FOR THAT?!
EVERY-ONE WAS WORRIED ABOUT YOU!
SHOKO! DON'T YOU KNOW?!
DON'T YOU KNOW THAT YOU'RE NOT THE ONLY ONE WHO SUFFERED?!
IT ISN'T EASY FOR ANYONE! EVERYBODY SUFFERS! THAT'S LIFE!

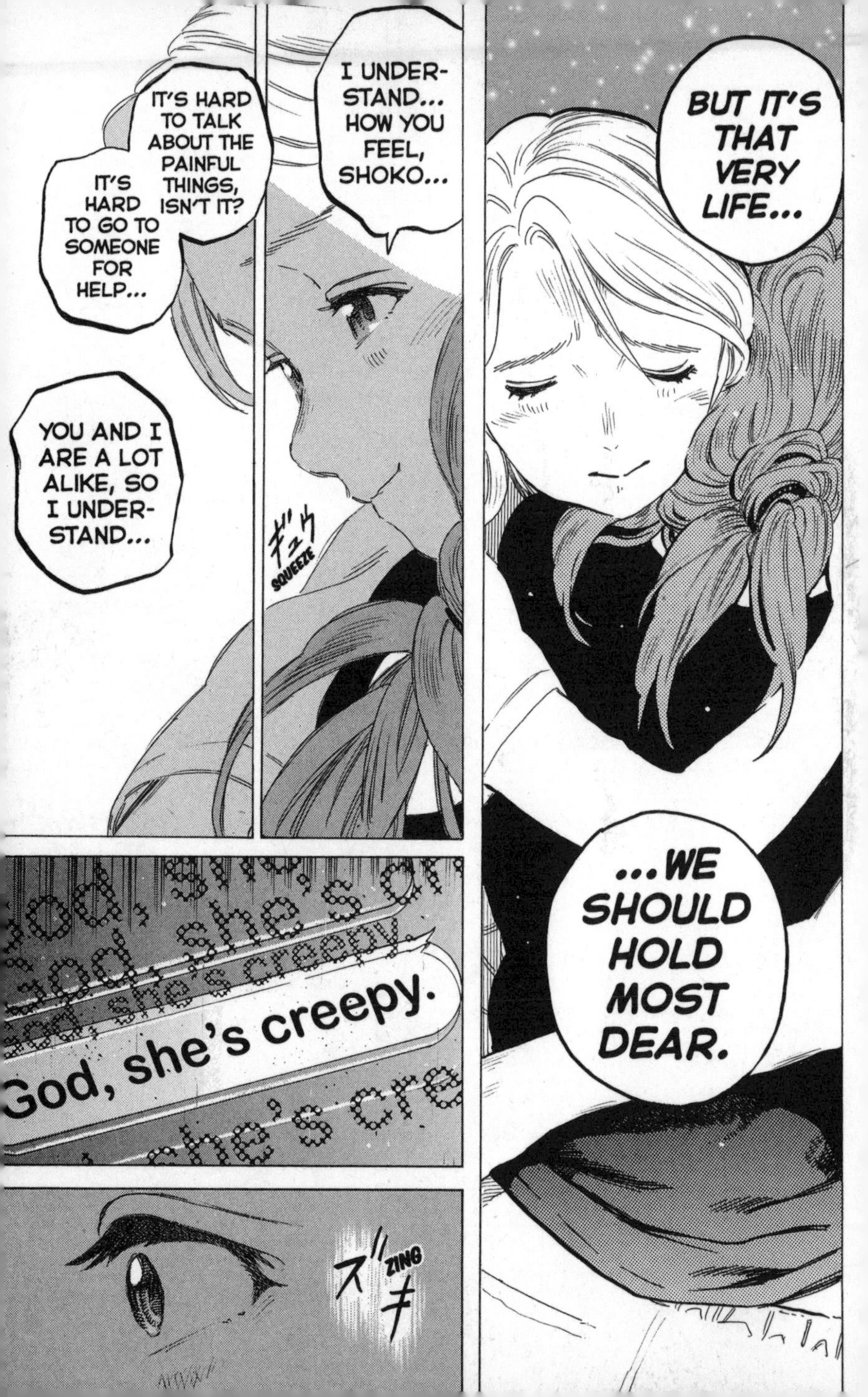
I UNDER-
STAND...
HOW YOU
FEEL,
SHOKO...
SQUEEZE
IT'S HARD
TO TALK
ABOUT THE
PAINFUL
THINGS,
ISN'T IT?
IT'S
HARD
TO GO TO
SOMEONE
FOR
HELP...
YOU AND I
ARE A LOT
ALIKE, SO
I UNDER-
STAND...
God, she's creepy.
ZING
BUT IT'S
THAT
VERY
LIFE...
...WE
SHOULD
HOLD
MOST
DEAR.

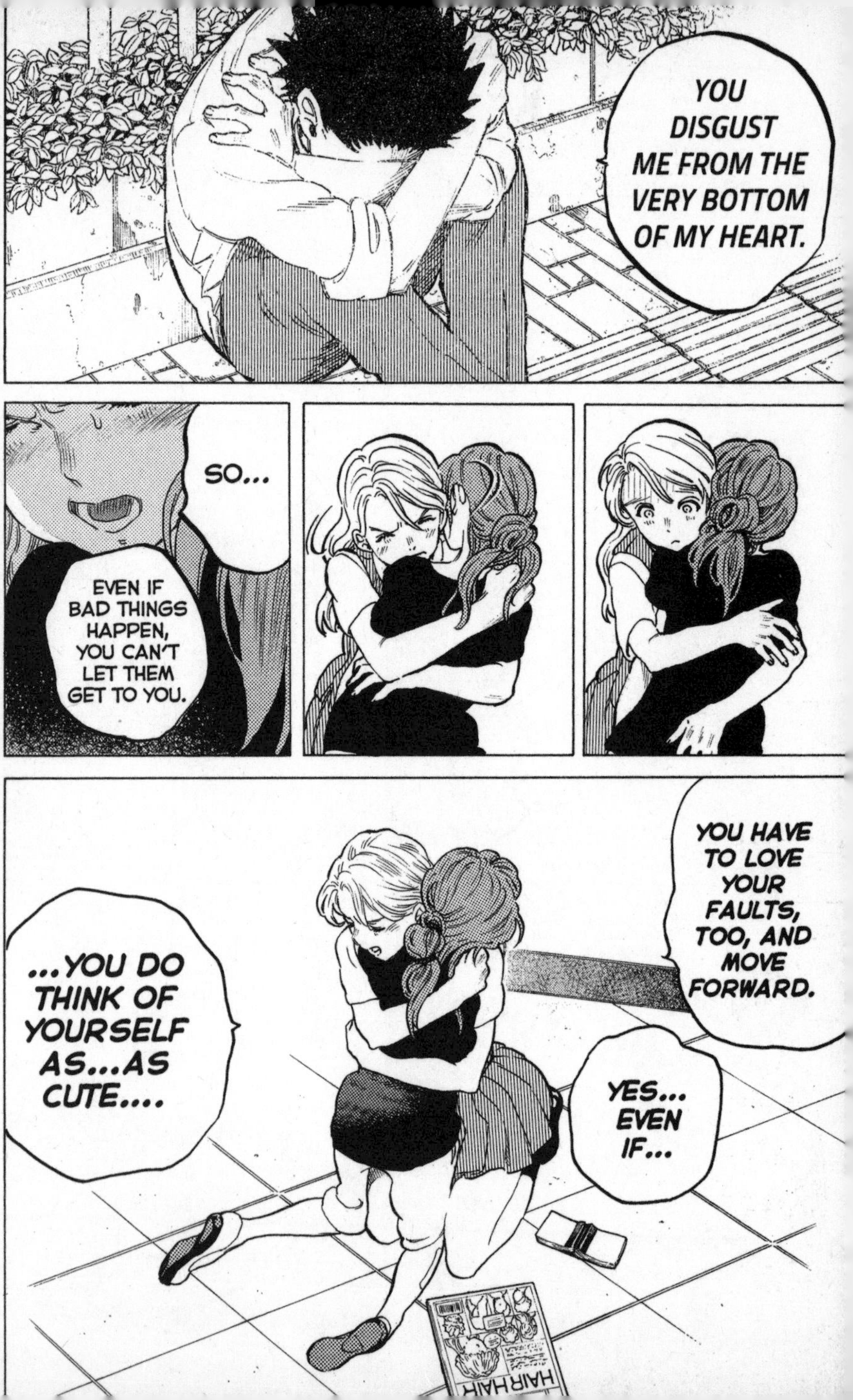
YOU DISGUST ME FROM THE VERY BOTTOM OF MY HEART.
SO...
EVEN IF BAD THINGS HAPPEN, YOU CAN'T LET THEM GET TO YOU.
YOU HAVE TO LOVE YOUR FAULTS, TOO, AND MOVE FORWARD.
YES... EVEN IF...
...YOU DO THINK OF YOURSELF AS...AS CUTE....

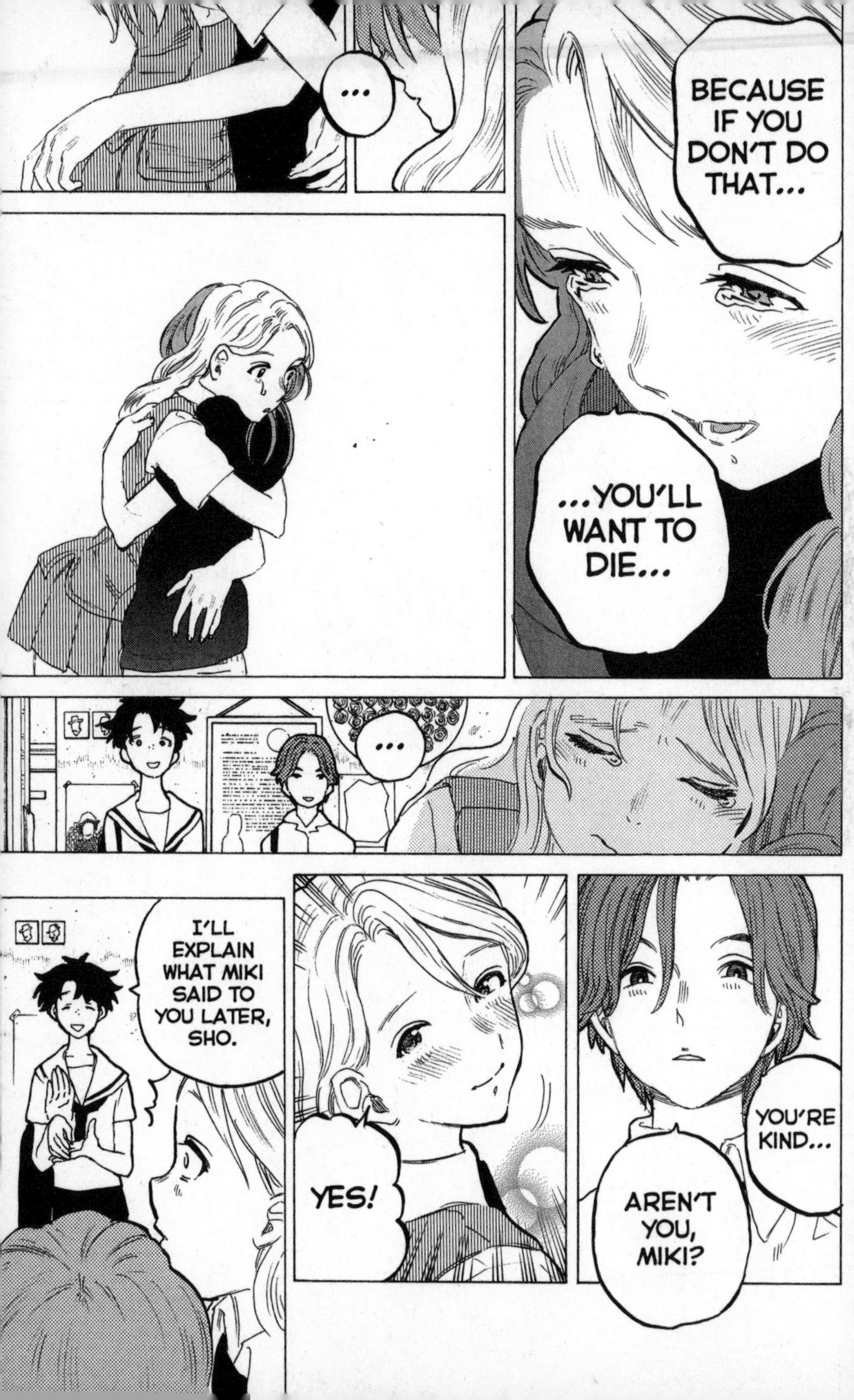

BECAUSE IF YOU DON'T DO THAT...
...YOU'LL WANT TO DIE...
...
...
YOU'RE KIND...
AREN'T YOU, MIKI?
YES!
I'LL EXPLAIN WHAT MIKI SAID TO YOU LATER, SHO.

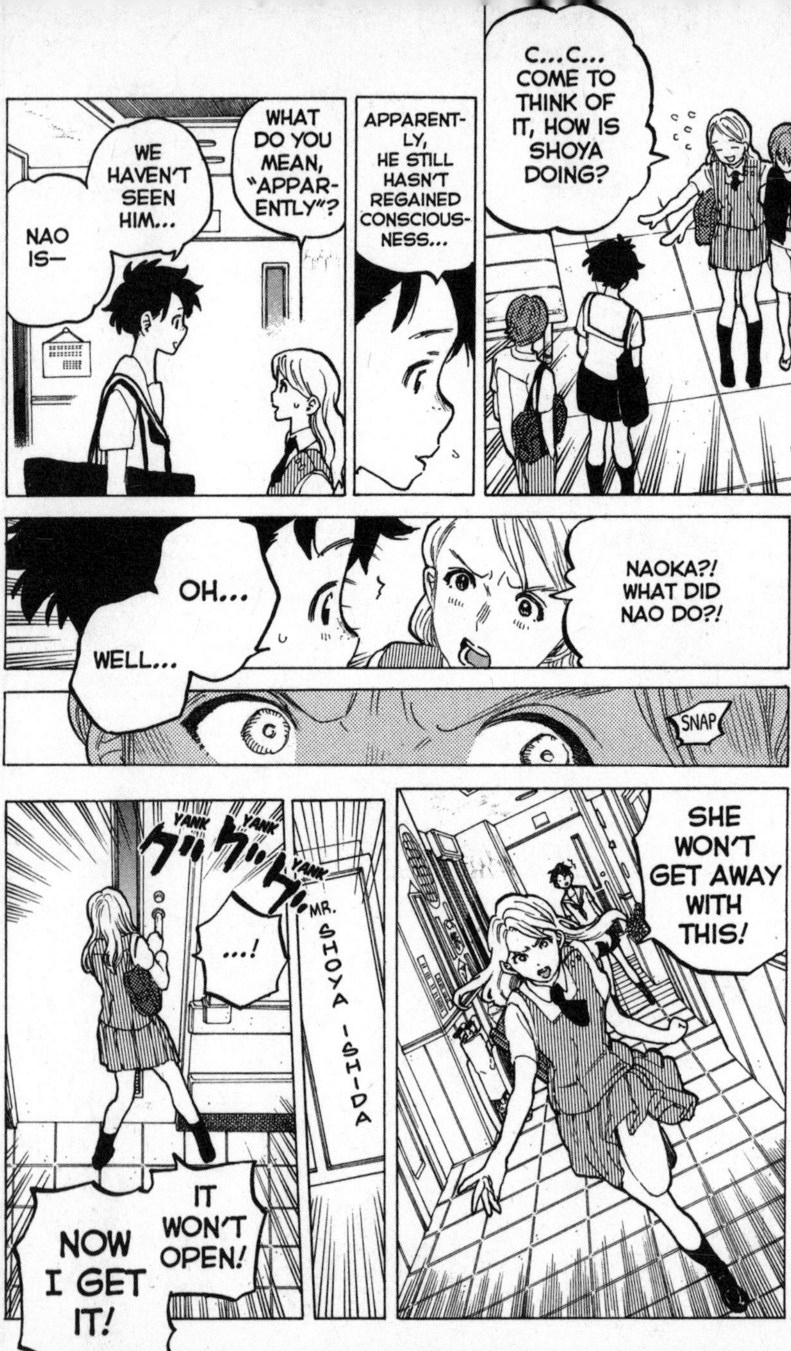
C...C... COME TO THINK OF IT, HOW IS SHOYA DOING?
APPARENT-LY, HE STILL HASN'T REGAINED CONSCIOUS-NESS...
WHAT DO YOU MEAN, "APPAR-ENTLY"?
WE HAVEN'T SEEN HIM...
NAO IS—
NAOKA?! WHAT DID NAO DO?!
OH...
WELL...
SNAP
SHE WON'T GET AWAY WITH THIS!
MR. SHOYA ISHIDA
YANK
YANK
YANK
...!
IT WON'T OPEN!
NOW I GET IT!

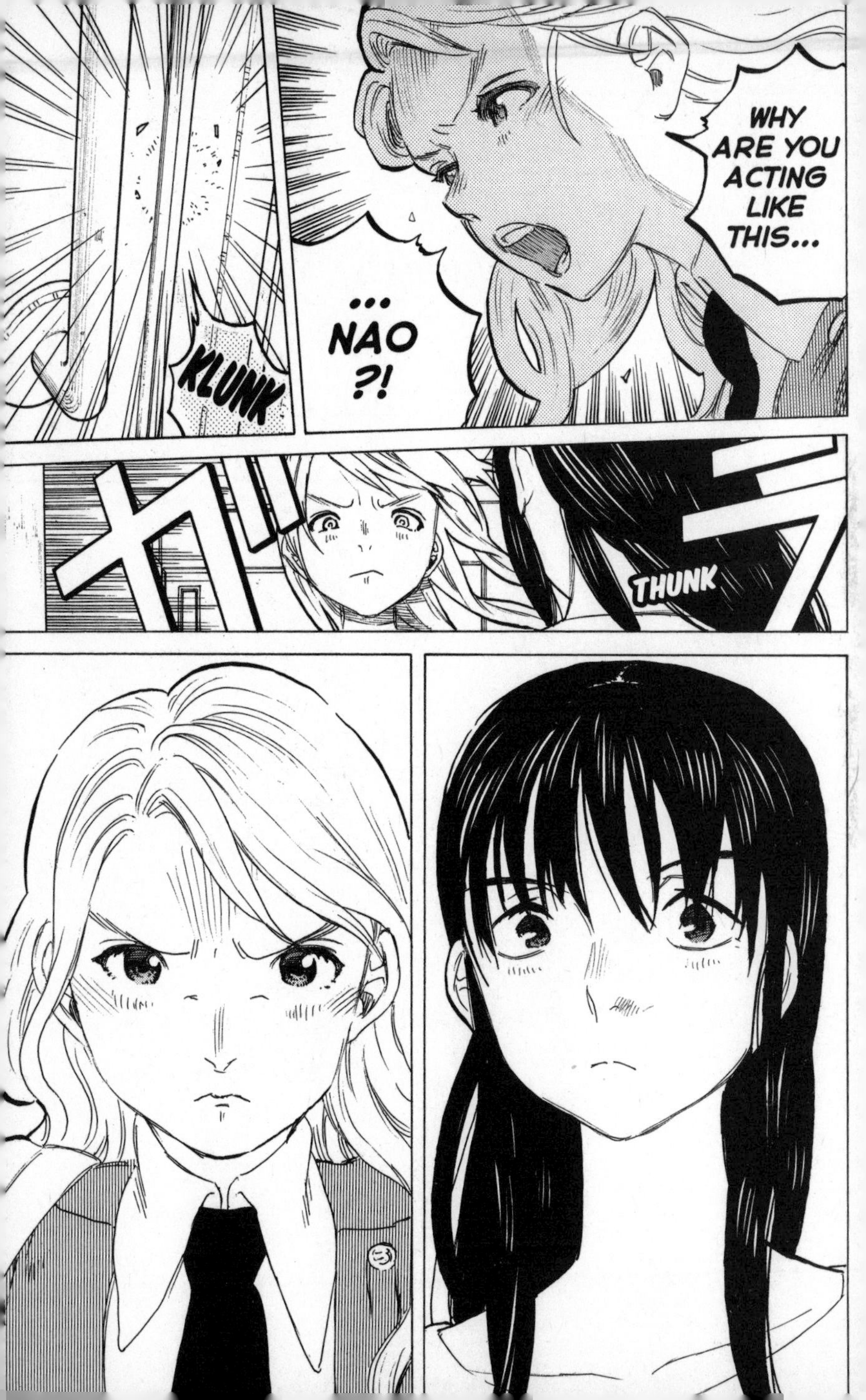
WHY ARE YOU ACTING LIKE THIS...
...NAO ?!
KLUNK
THUNK

a Silent Voice

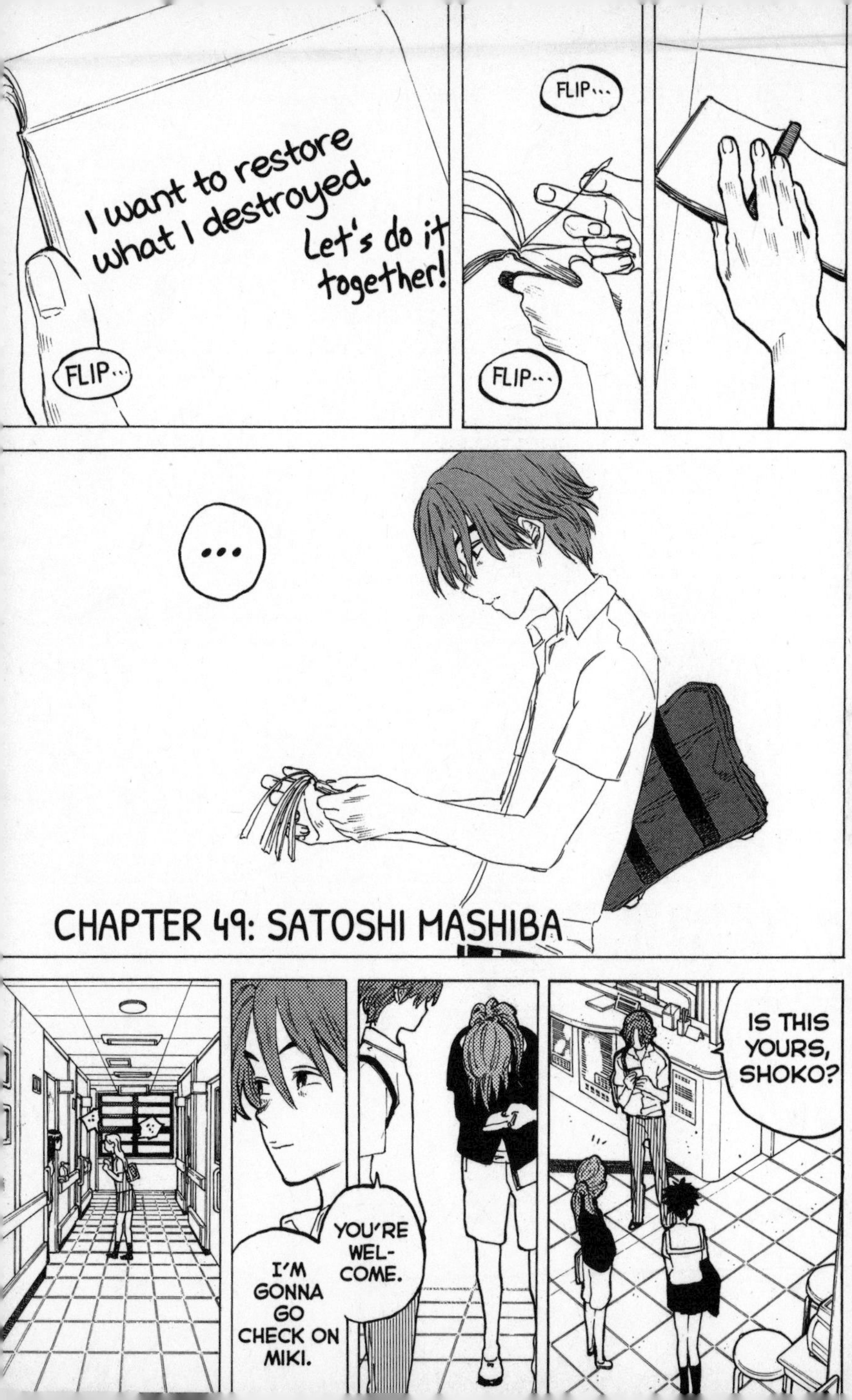
FLIP...
FLIP...
I want to restore what I destroyed.
Let's do it together!
FLIP...
...
CHAPTER 49: SATOSHI MASHIBA
IS THIS YOURS, SHOKO?
YOU'RE WEL-COME.
I'M GONNA GO CHECK ON MIKI.

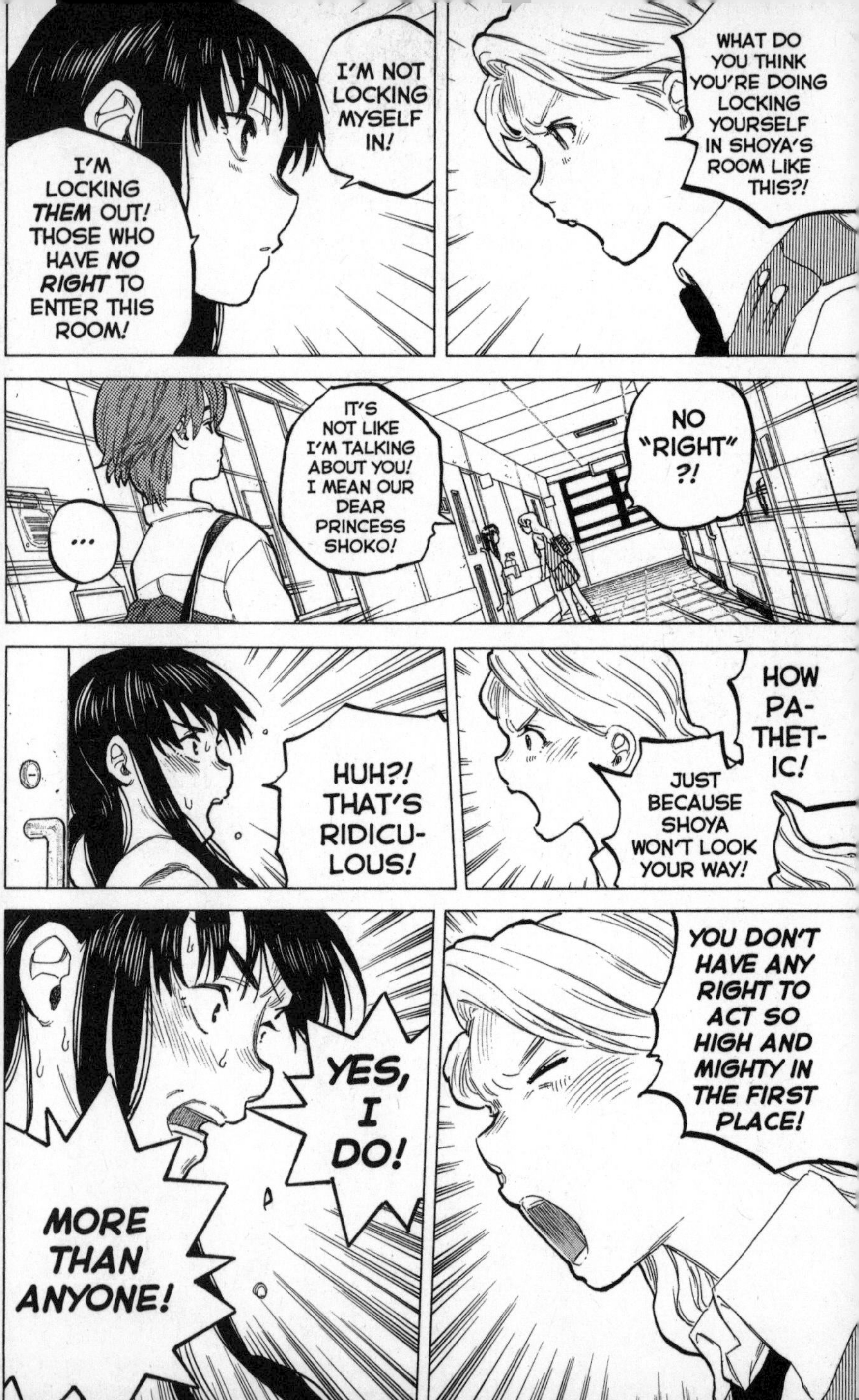
WHAT DO YOU THINK YOU'RE DOING LOCKING YOURSELF IN SHOYA'S ROOM LIKE THIS?!
I'M NOT LOCKING MYSELF IN!
I'M LOCKING THEM OUT! THOSE WHO HAVE NO RIGHT TO ENTER THIS ROOM!
NO "RIGHT"?!
IT'S NOT LIKE I'M TALKING ABOUT YOU! I MEAN OUR DEAR PRINCESS SHOKO!
...
HOW PA-THET-IC!
JUST BECAUSE SHOYA WON'T LOOK YOUR WAY!
HUH?! THAT'S RIDICU-LOUS!
YOU DON'T HAVE ANY RIGHT TO ACT SO HIGH AND MIGHTY IN THE FIRST PLACE!
YES, I DO!
MORE THAN ANYONE!

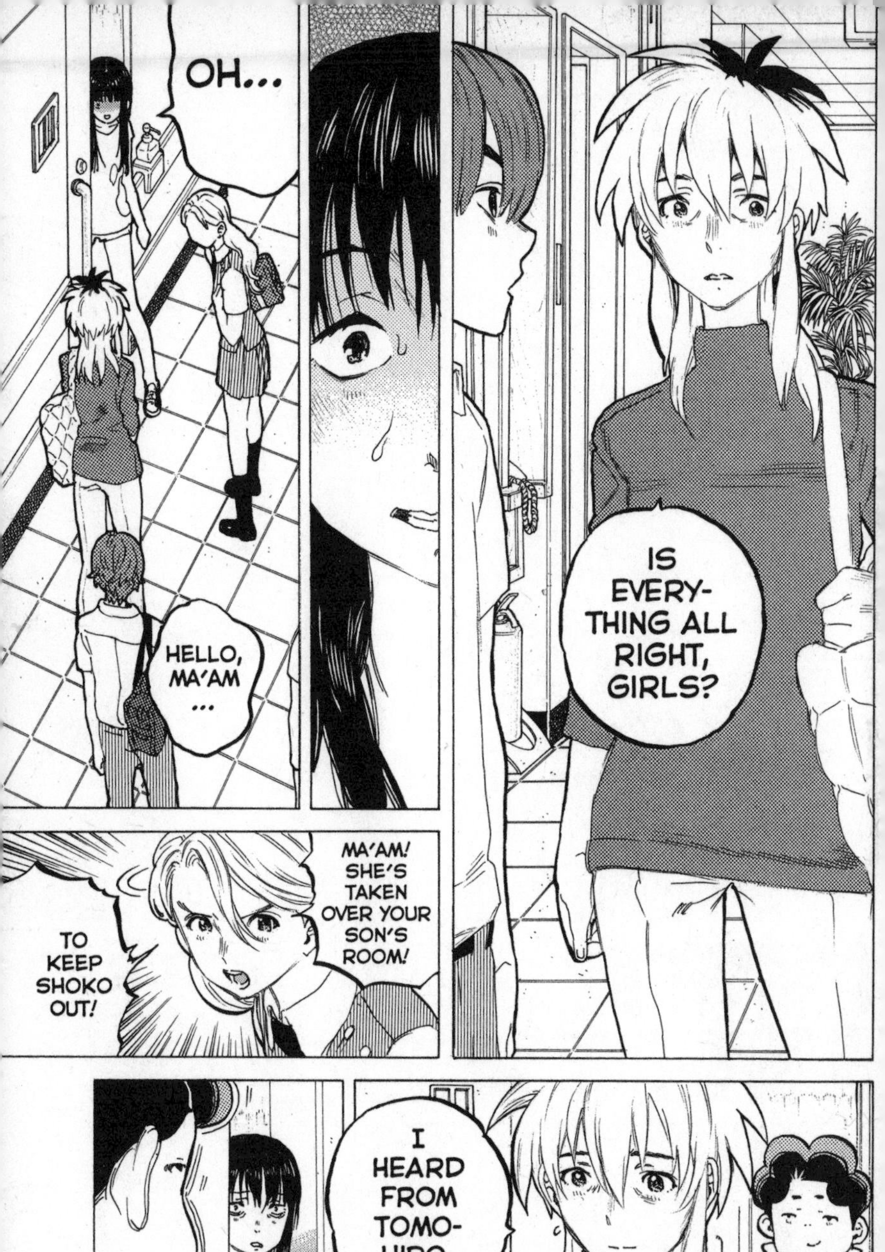
IS EVERYTHING ALL RIGHT, GIRLS?
OH...
HELLO, MA'AM ...
MA'AM! SHE'S TAKEN OVER YOUR SON'S ROOM!
TO KEEP SHOKO OUT!
I HEARD FROM TOMOHIRO.

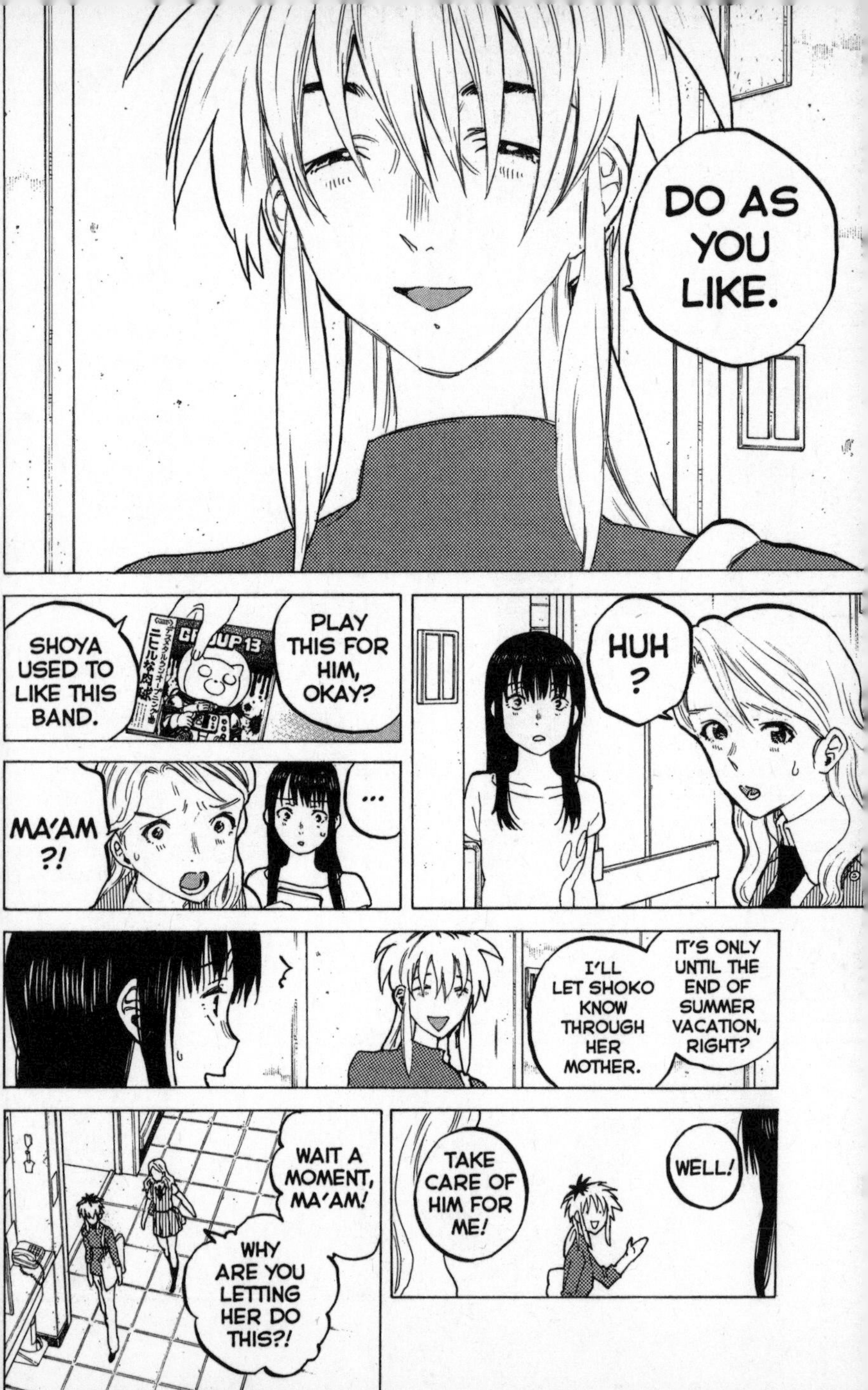
DO AS YOU LIKE.
HUH ?
PLAY THIS FOR HIM, OKAY?
GROUP 13
SHOYA USED TO LIKE THIS BAND.
...
MA'AM ?!
IT'S ONLY UNTIL THE END OF SUMMER VACATION, RIGHT?
I'LL LET SHOKO KNOW THROUGH HER MOTHER.
WELL!
TAKE CARE OF HIM FOR ME!
WAIT A MOMENT, MA'AM!
WHY ARE YOU LETTING HER DO THIS?!

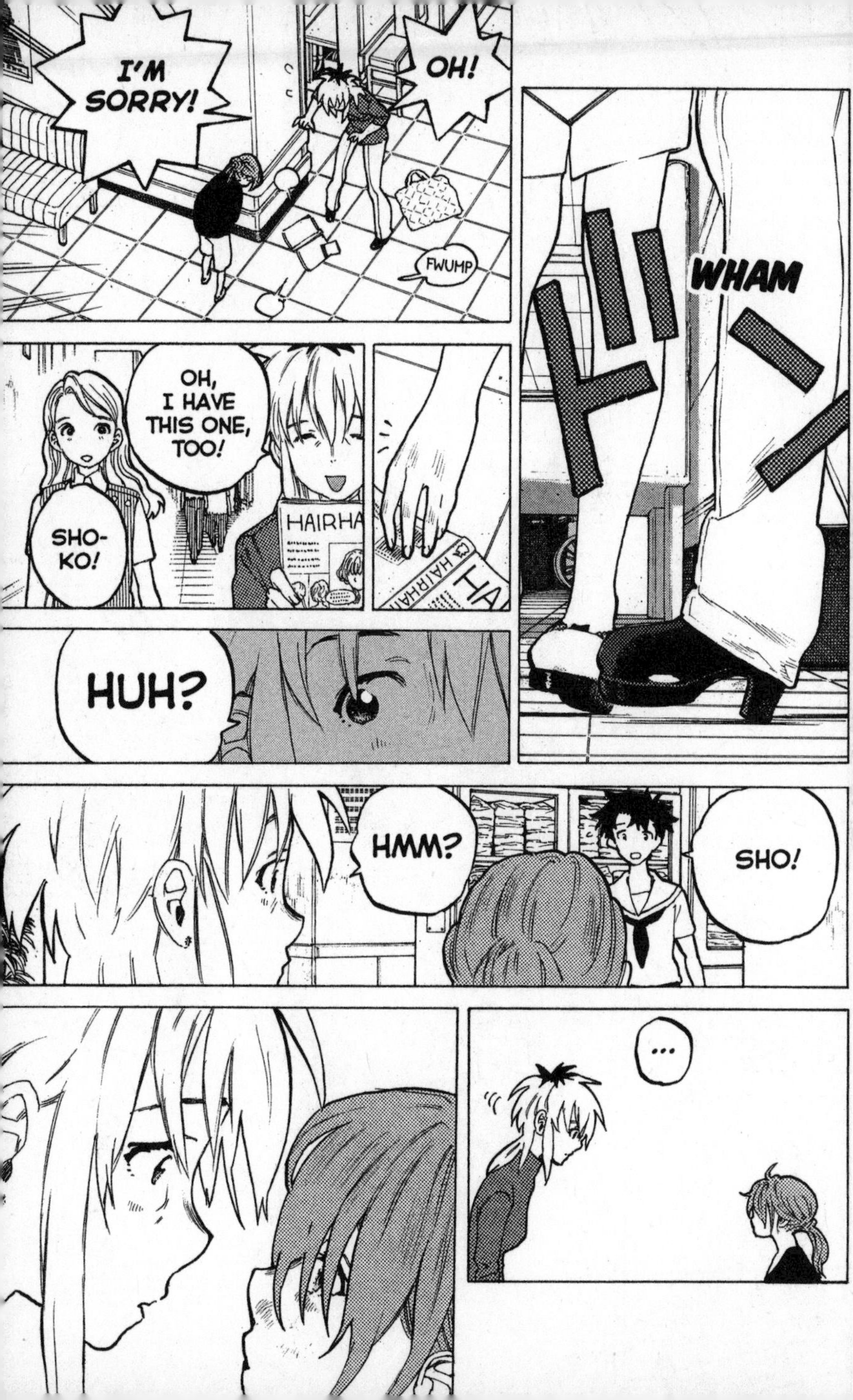
OH!
I'M SORRY!
FWUMP
WHAM
OH, I HAVE THIS ONE, TOO!
SHO-KO!
HAIRHA
HUH?
SHO!
HMM?
...

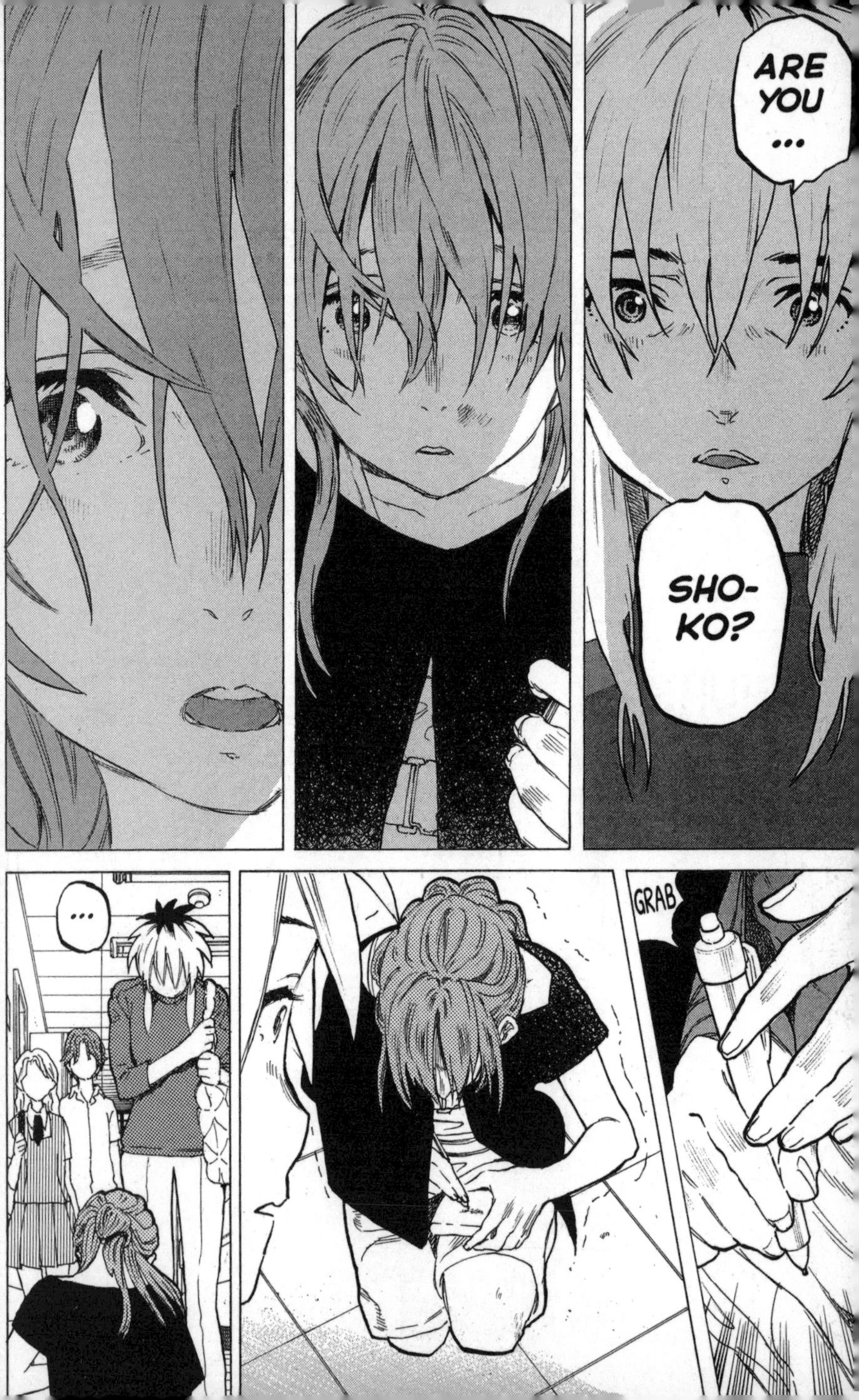
ARE YOU ...
SHO-KO?
GRAB
...

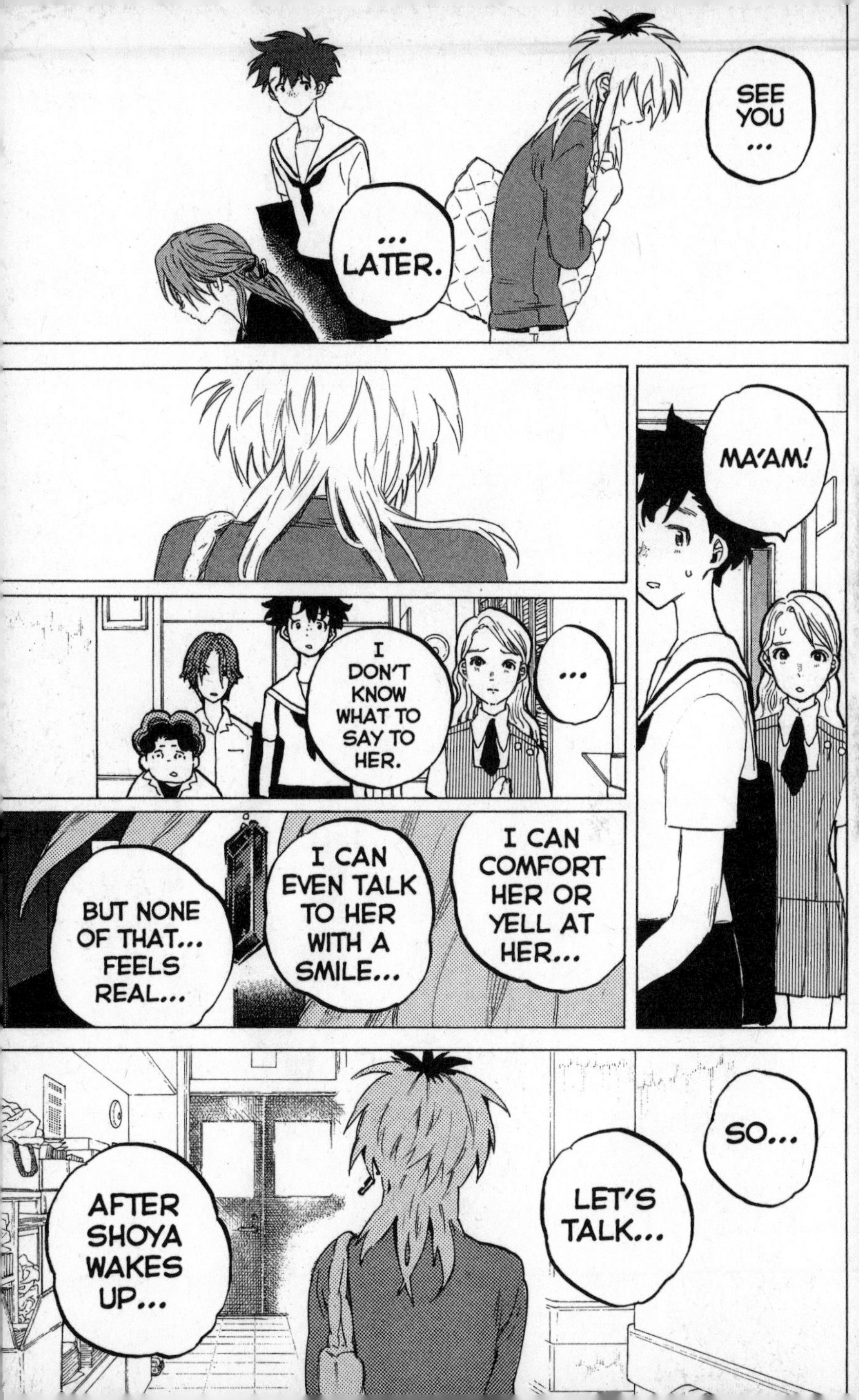
SEE YOU ...
... LATER.
MA'AM!
...
I DON'T KNOW WHAT TO SAY TO HER.
I CAN COMFORT HER OR YELL AT HER...
I CAN EVEN TALK TO HER WITH A SMILE...
BUT NONE OF THAT... FEELS REAL...
SO...
LET'S TALK...
AFTER SHOYA WAKES UP...

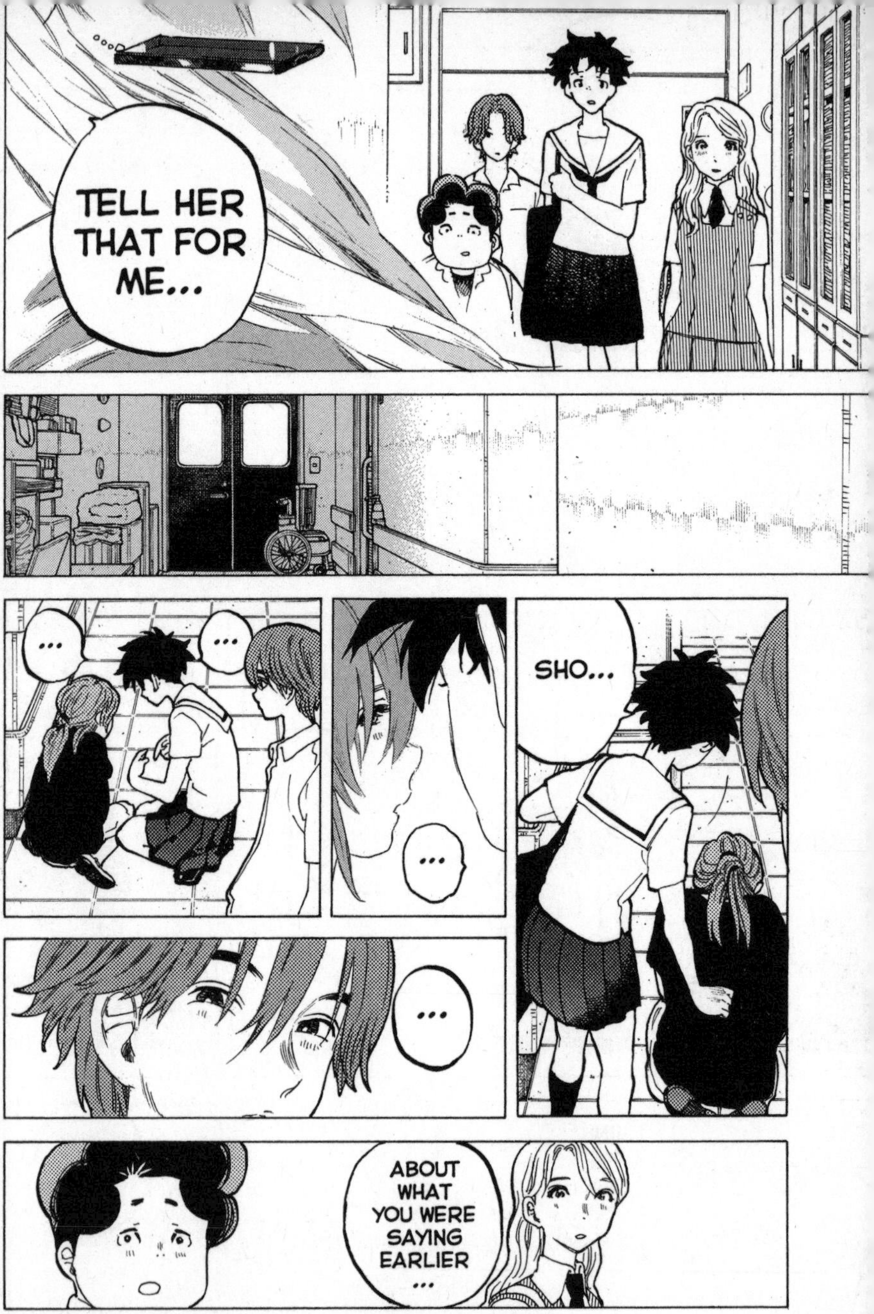
TELL HER THAT FOR ME...
SHO...
...
...
...
...
ABOUT WHAT YOU WERE SAYING EARLIER ...

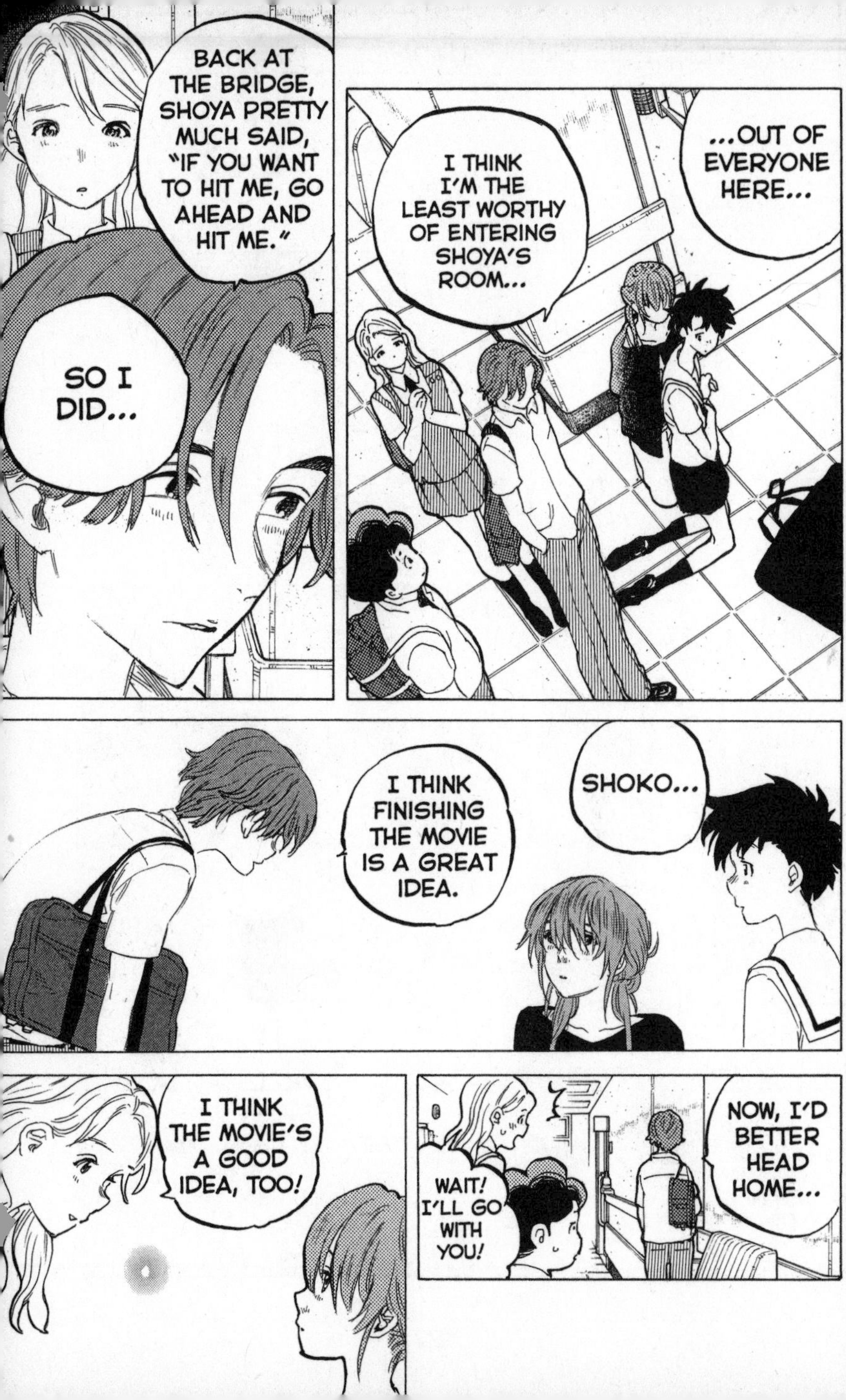
...OUT OF EVERYONE HERE...
I THINK I'M THE LEAST WORTHY OF ENTERING SHOYA'S ROOM...
BACK AT THE BRIDGE, SHOYA PRETTY MUCH SAID, "IF YOU WANT TO HIT ME, GO AHEAD AND HIT ME."
SO I DID...
SHOKO...
I THINK FINISHING THE MOVIE IS A GREAT IDEA.
NOW, I'D BETTER HEAD HOME...
WAIT! I'LL GO WITH YOU!
I THINK THE MOVIE'S A GOOD IDEA, TOO!

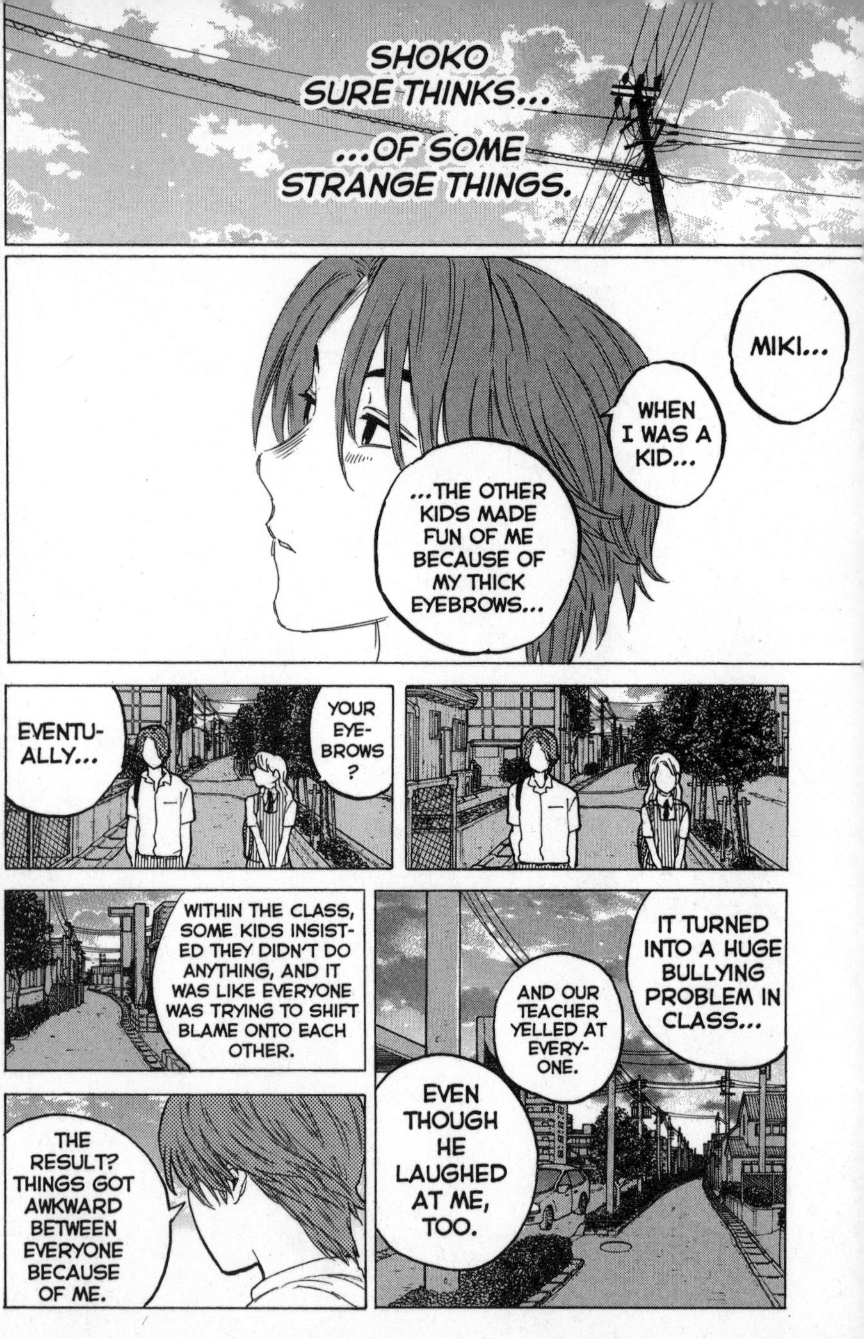
SHOKO SURE THINKS...
...OF SOME STRANGE THINGS.
MIKI...
WHEN I WAS A KID...
...THE OTHER KIDS MADE FUN OF ME BECAUSE OF MY THICK EYEBROWS...
YOUR EYE-BROWS?
EVENTU-ALLY...
IT TURNED INTO A HUGE BULLYING PROBLEM IN CLASS...
AND OUR TEACHER YELLED AT EVERY-ONE.
EVEN THOUGH HE LAUGHED AT ME, TOO.
WITHIN THE CLASS, SOME KIDS INSIST-ED THEY DIDN'T DO ANYTHING, AND IT WAS LIKE EVERYONE WAS TRYING TO SHIFT BLAME ONTO EACH OTHER.
THE RESULT? THINGS GOT AWKWARD BETWEEN EVERYONE BECAUSE OF ME.

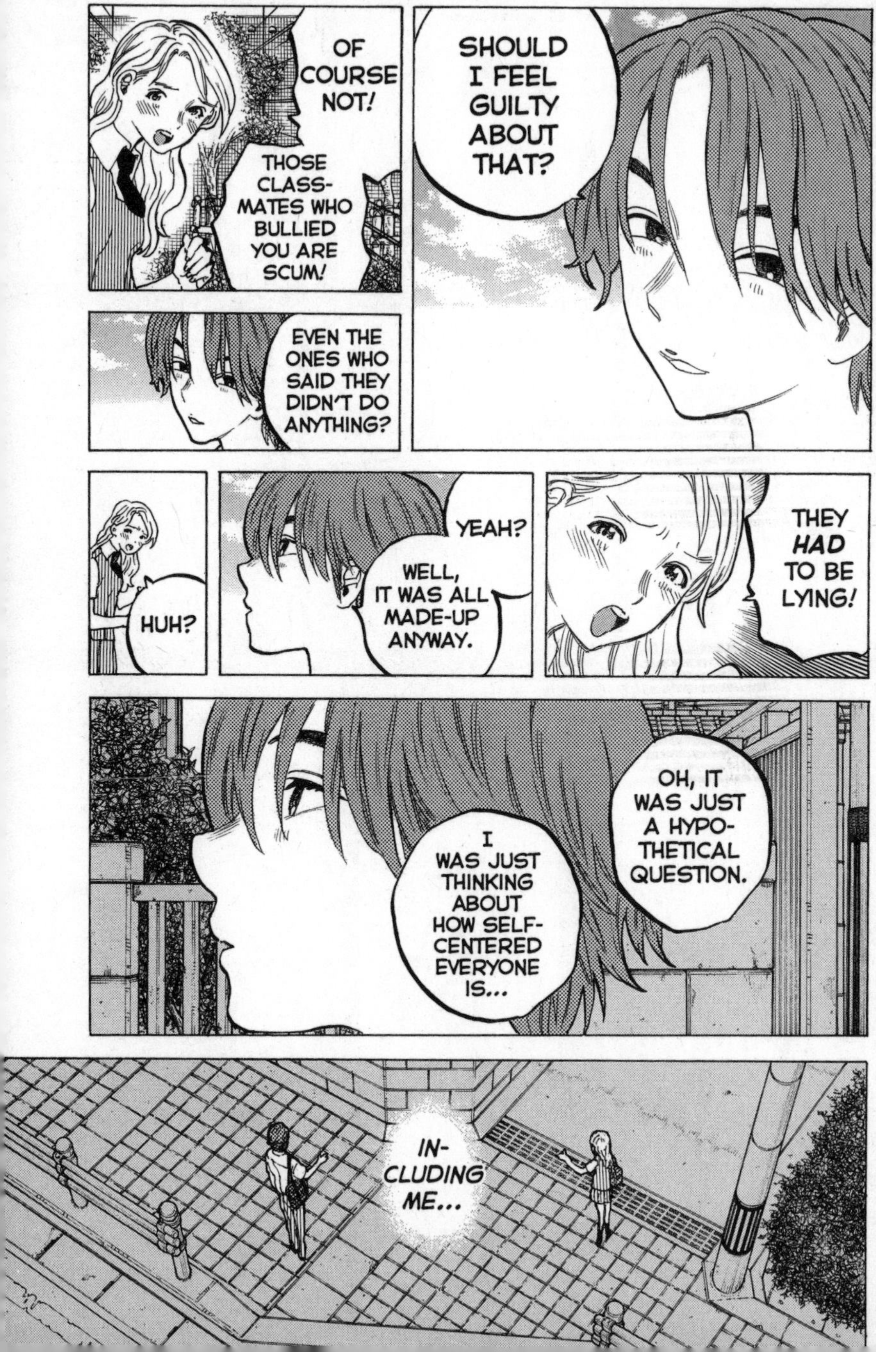
SHOULD I FEEL GUILTY ABOUT THAT?
OF COURSE NOT!
THOSE CLASSMATES WHO BULLIED YOU ARE SCUM!
EVEN THE ONES WHO SAID THEY DIDN'T DO ANYTHING?
THEY *HAD* TO BE LYING!
YEAH?
WELL, IT WAS ALL MADE-UP ANYWAY.
HUH?
OH, IT WAS JUST A HYPOTHETICAL QUESTION.
I WAS JUST THINKING ABOUT HOW SELF-CENTERED EVERYONE IS...
INCLUDING ME...

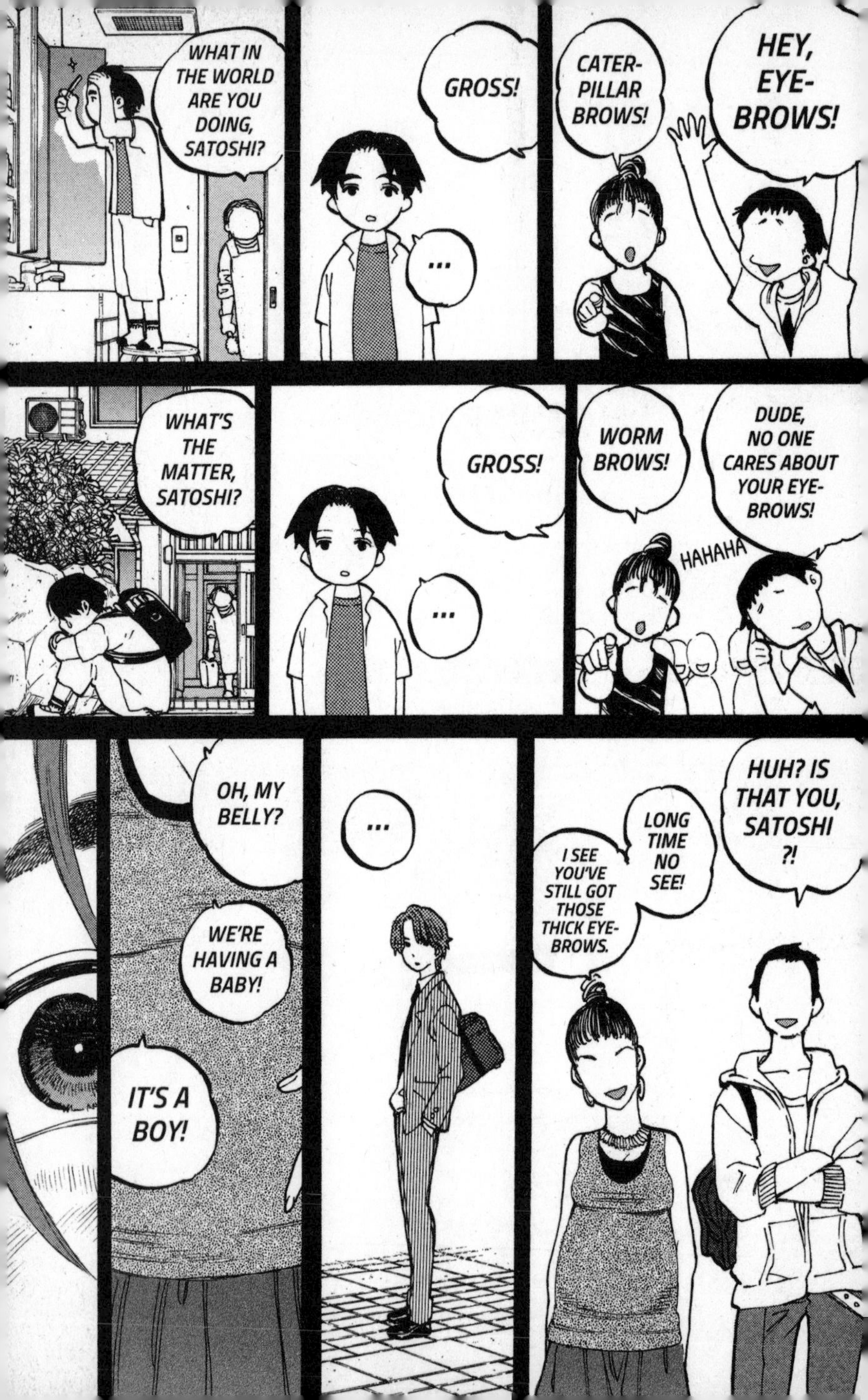
HEY, EYE-BROWS!
CATER-PILLAR BROWS!
GROSS!
...
WHAT IN THE WORLD ARE YOU DOING, SATOSHI?
DUDE, NO ONE CARES ABOUT YOUR EYE-BROWS!
WORM BROWS!
HAHAHA
GROSS!
...
WHAT'S THE MATTER, SATOSHI?
HUH? IS THAT YOU, SATOSHI ?!
LONG TIME NO SEE!
I SEE YOU'VE STILL GOT THOSE THICK EYE-BROWS.
...
OH, MY BELLY?
WE'RE HAVING A BABY!
IT'S A BOY!

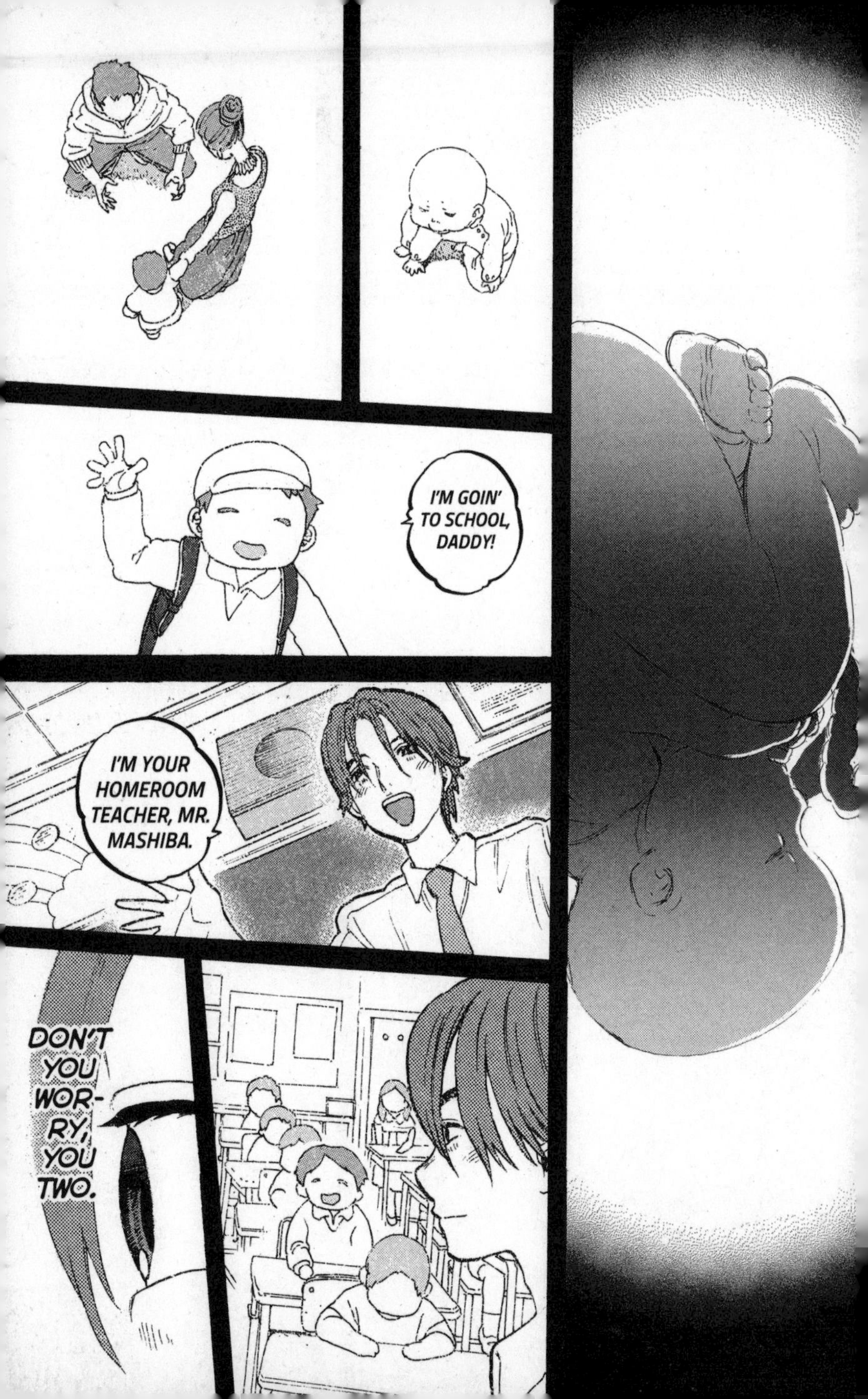
I'M GOIN' TO SCHOOL, DADDY!
I'M YOUR HOMEROOM TEACHER, MR. MASHIBA.
DON'T YOU WOR-RY, YOU TWO.

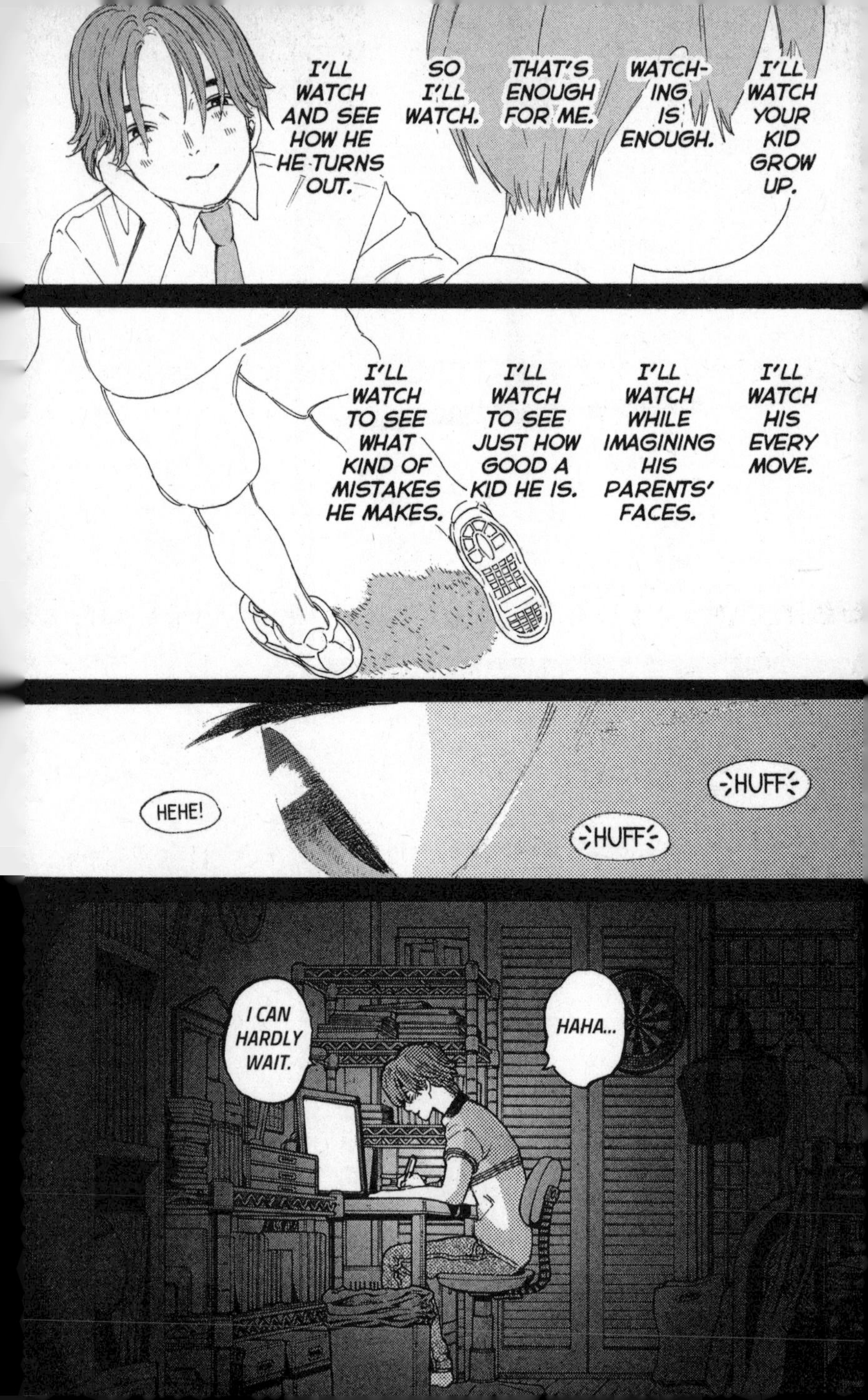
I'LL WATCH YOUR KID GROW UP.
WATCH-ING IS ENOUGH.
THAT'S ENOUGH FOR ME.
SO I'LL WATCH.
I'LL WATCH AND SEE HOW HE HE TURNS OUT.
I'LL WATCH HIS EVERY MOVE.
I'LL WATCH WHILE IMAGINING HIS PARENTS' FACES.
I'LL WATCH TO SEE JUST HOW GOOD A KID HE IS.
I'LL WATCH TO SEE WHAT KIND OF MISTAKES HE MAKES.
HUFF
HUFF
HEHE!
HAHA...
I CAN HARDLY WAIT.

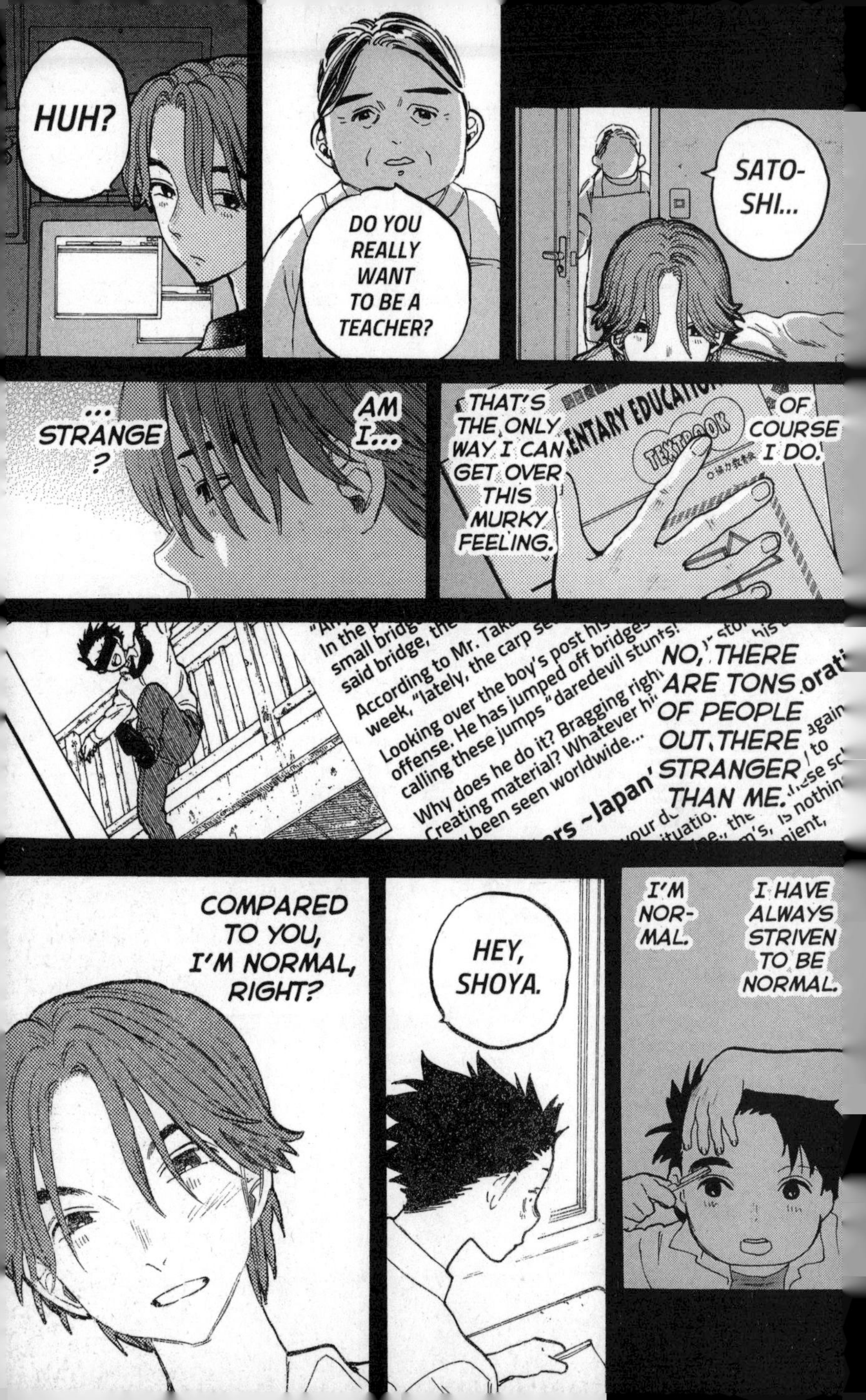
SATO-SHI...
DO YOU REALLY WANT TO BE A TEACHER?
HUH?
OF COURSE I DO.
THAT'S THE ONLY WAY I CAN GET OVER THIS MURKY FEELING.
TEXTBOOK
AM I...
... STRANGE?
NO, THERE ARE TONS OF PEOPLE OUT THERE STRANGER THAN ME.
I HAVE ALWAYS STRIVEN TO BE NORMAL.
I'M NOR-MAL.
HEY, SHOYA.
COMPARED TO YOU, I'M NORMAL, RIGHT?

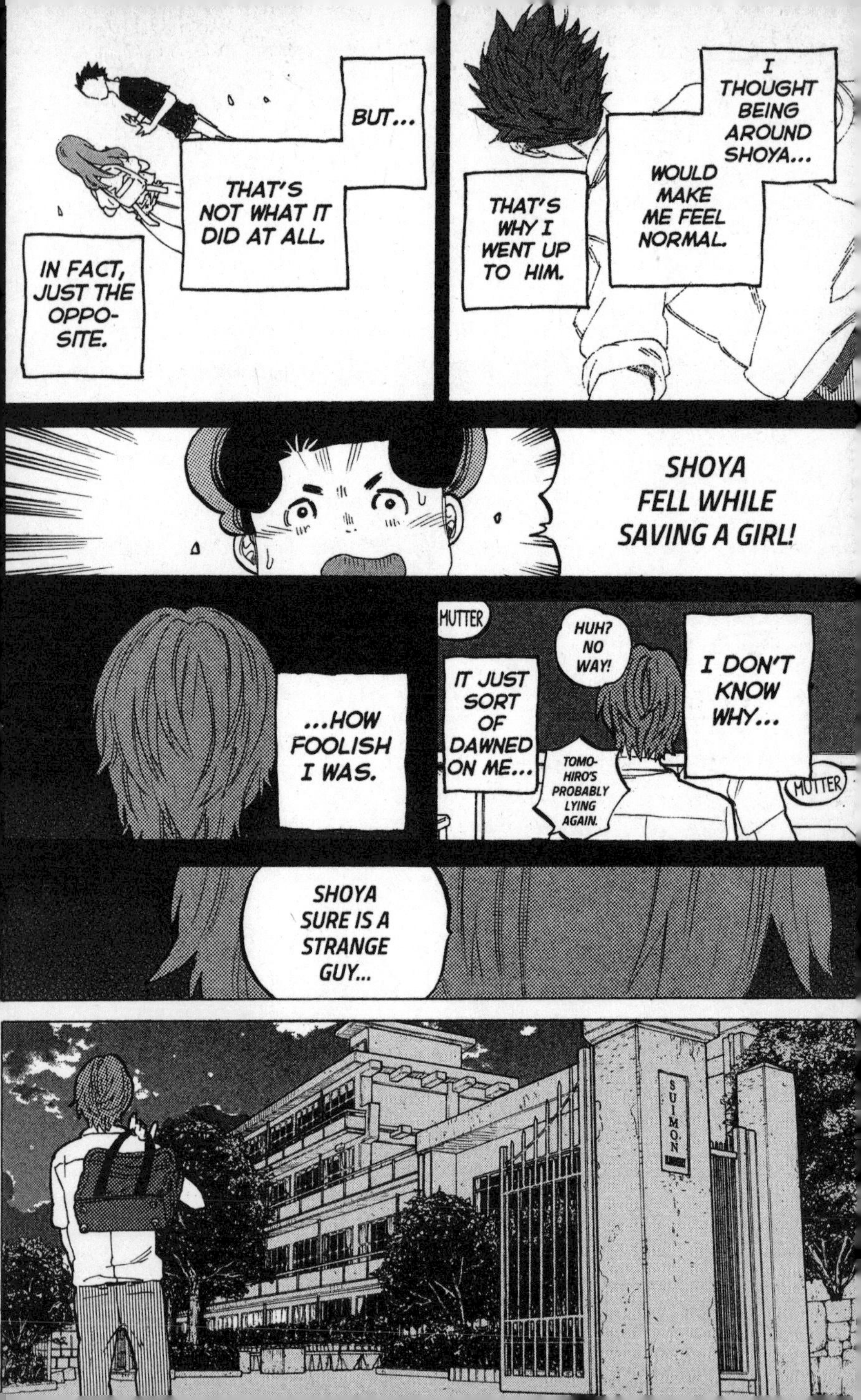
I THOUGHT BEING AROUND SHOYA...
WOULD MAKE ME FEEL NORMAL.
THAT'S WHY I WENT UP TO HIM.
BUT...
THAT'S NOT WHAT IT DID AT ALL.
IN FACT, JUST THE OPPO-SITE.
SHOYA FELL WHILE SAVING A GIRL!
I DON'T KNOW WHY...
MUTTER
HUH? NO WAY!
IT JUST SORT OF DAWNED ON ME...
TOMO-HIRO'S PROBABLY LYING AGAIN.
MUTTER
...HOW FOOLISH I WAS.
SHOYA SURE IS A STRANGE GUY...
SUIMON

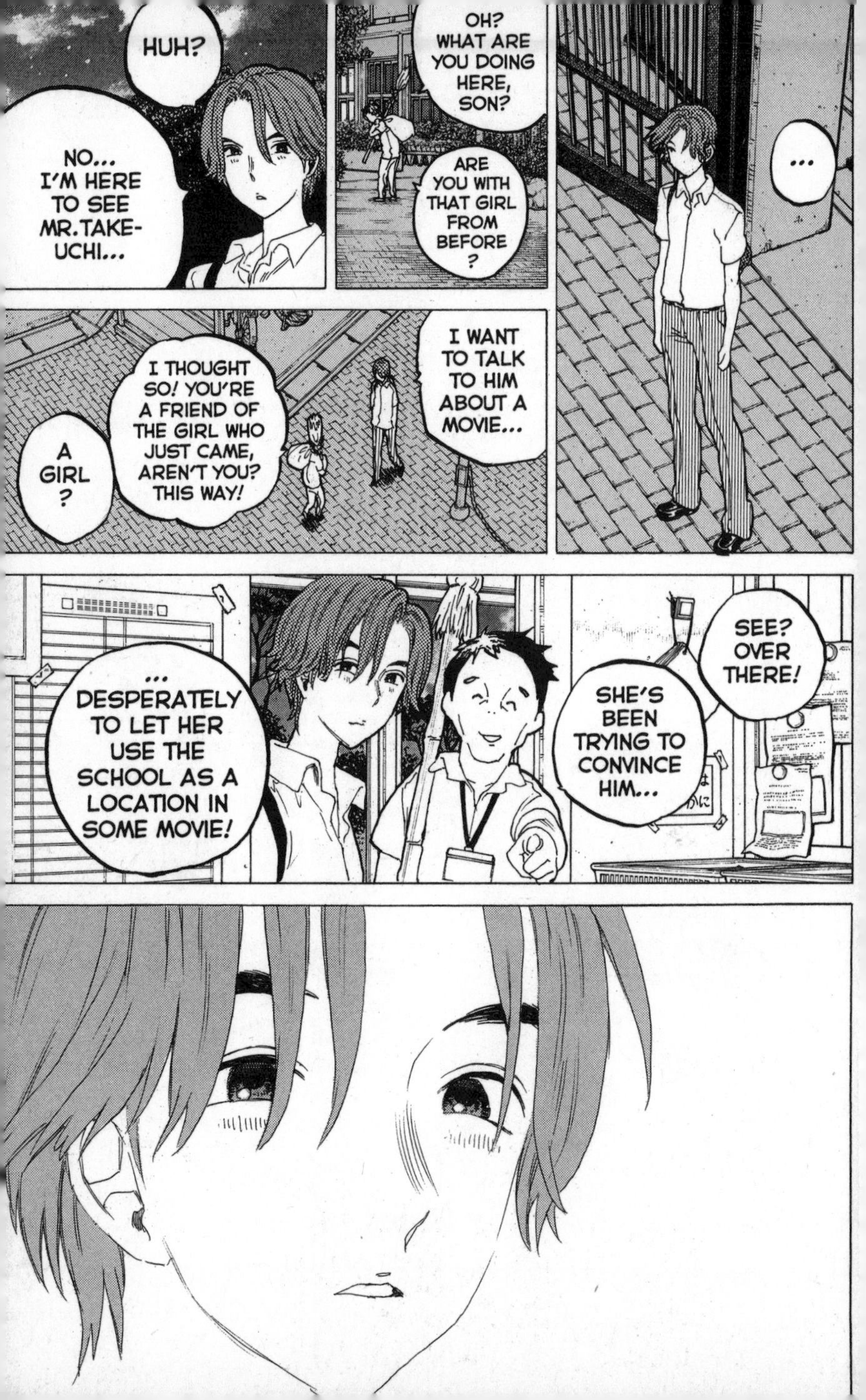
...
OH? WHAT ARE YOU DOING HERE, SON?
ARE YOU WITH THAT GIRL FROM BEFORE?
HUH?
NO... I'M HERE TO SEE MR.TAKE-UCHI...
I WANT TO TALK TO HIM ABOUT A MOVIE...
I THOUGHT SO! YOU'RE A FRIEND OF THE GIRL WHO JUST CAME, AREN'T YOU? THIS WAY!
A GIRL?
SEE? OVER THERE!
SHE'S BEEN TRYING TO CONVINCE HIM...
... DESPERATELY TO LET HER USE THE SCHOOL AS A LOCATION IN SOME MOVIE!

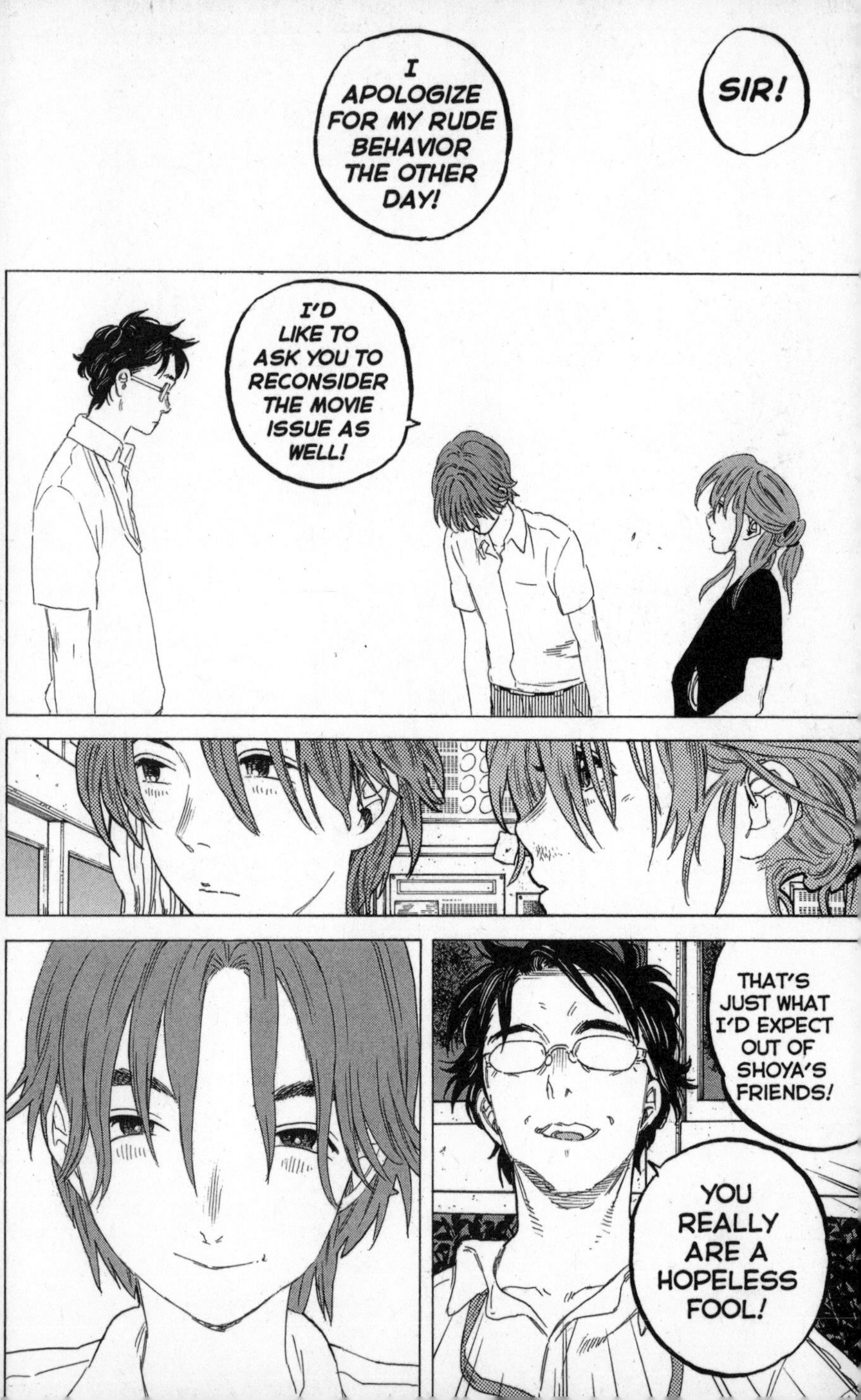
SIR!
I APOLOGIZE FOR MY RUDE BEHAVIOR THE OTHER DAY!
I'D LIKE TO ASK YOU TO RECONSIDER THE MOVIE ISSUE AS WELL!
THAT'S JUST WHAT I'D EXPECT OUT OF SHOYA'S FRIENDS!
YOU REALLY ARE A HOPELESS FOOL!

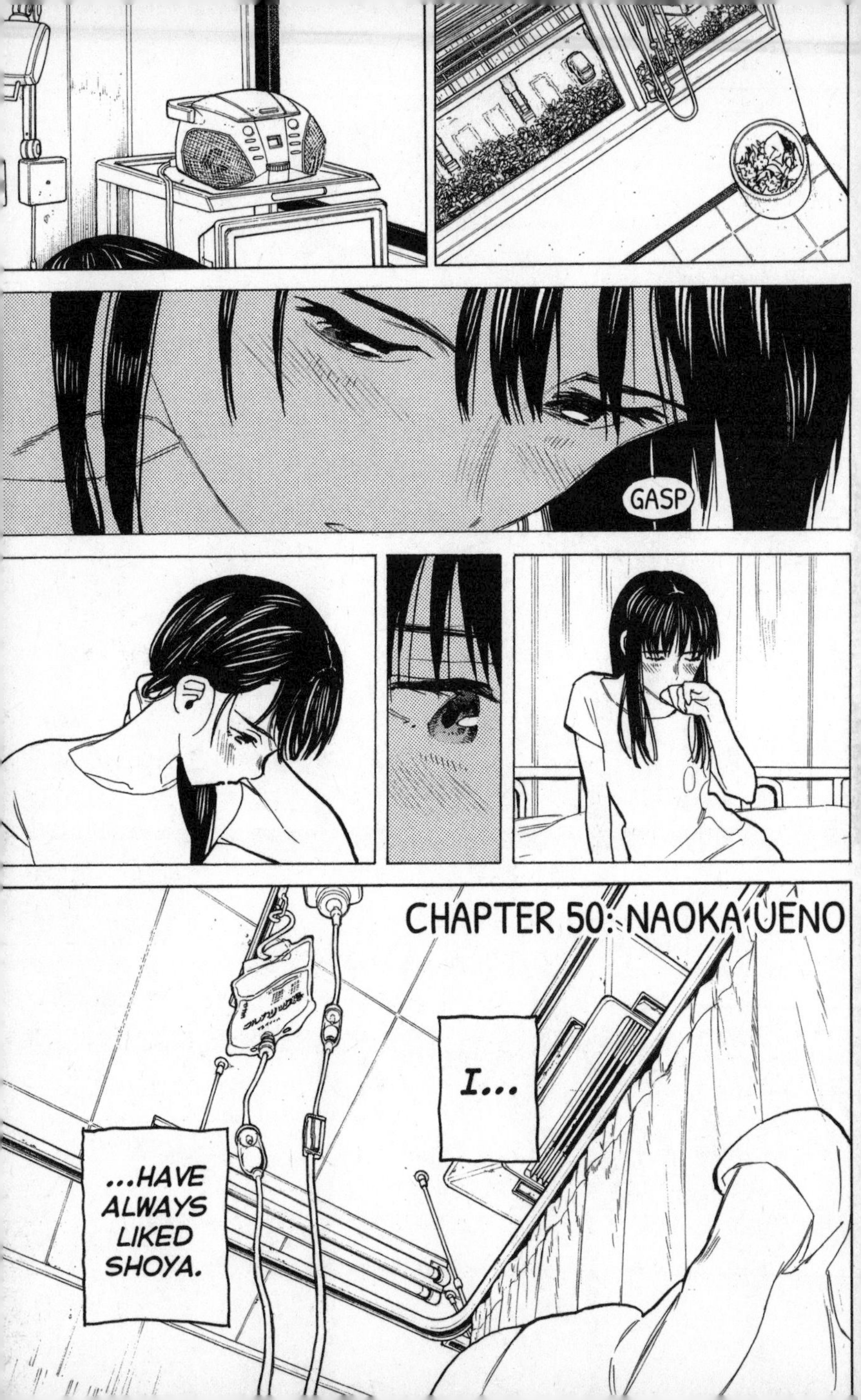
GASP
CHAPTER 50: NAOKA UENO
I...
...HAVE ALWAYS LIKED SHOYA.

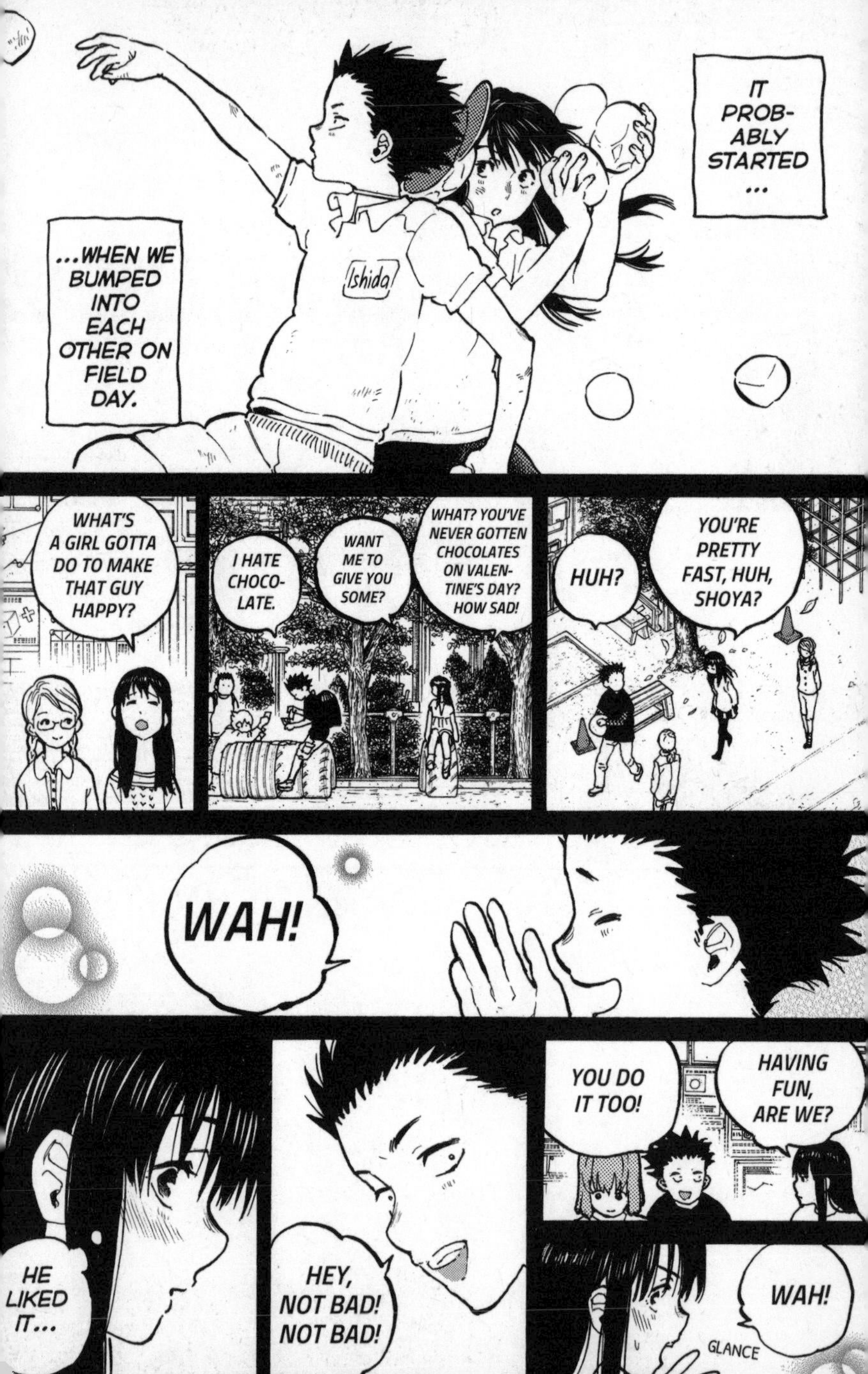
IT PROBABLY STARTED...
Ishida
...WHEN WE BUMPED INTO EACH OTHER ON FIELD DAY.
YOU'RE PRETTY FAST, HUH, SHOYA?
HUH?
WHAT? YOU'VE NEVER GOTTEN CHOCOLATES ON VALENTINE'S DAY? HOW SAD!
WANT ME TO GIVE YOU SOME?
I HATE CHOCOLATE.
WHAT'S A GIRL GOTTA DO TO MAKE THAT GUY HAPPY?
WAH!
HAVING FUN, ARE WE?
YOU DO IT TOO!
WAH!
GLANCE
HEY, NOT BAD! NOT BAD!
HE LIKED IT...

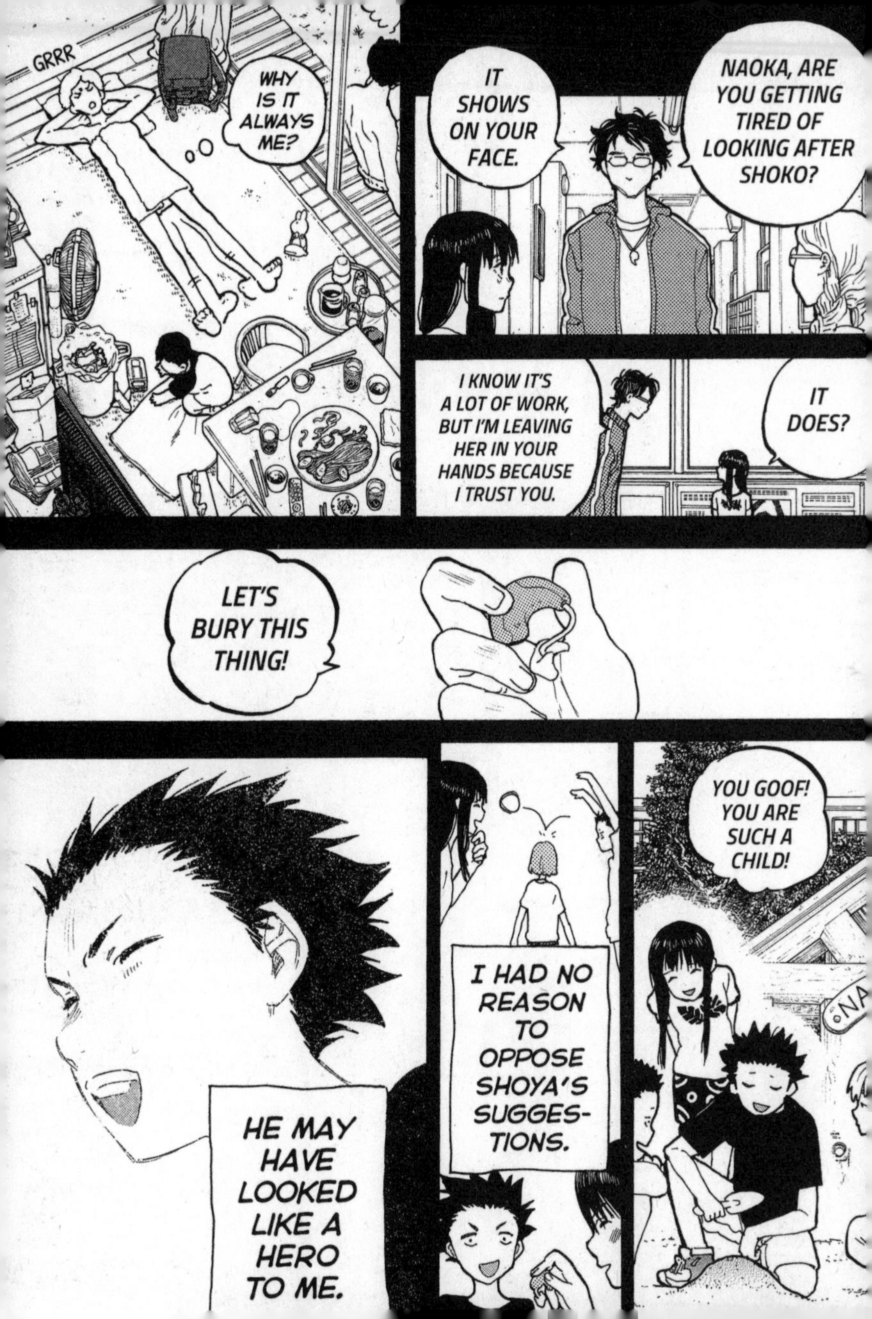
NAOKA, ARE YOU GETTING TIRED OF LOOKING AFTER SHOKO?
IT SHOWS ON YOUR FACE.
IT DOES?
I KNOW IT'S A LOT OF WORK, BUT I'M LEAVING HER IN YOUR HANDS BECAUSE I TRUST YOU.
WHY IS IT ALWAYS ME?
GRRR
LET'S BURY THIS THING!
YOU GOOF! YOU ARE SUCH A CHILD!
I HAD NO REASON TO OPPOSE SHOYA'S SUGGES- TIONS.
HE MAY HAVE LOOKED LIKE A HERO TO ME.

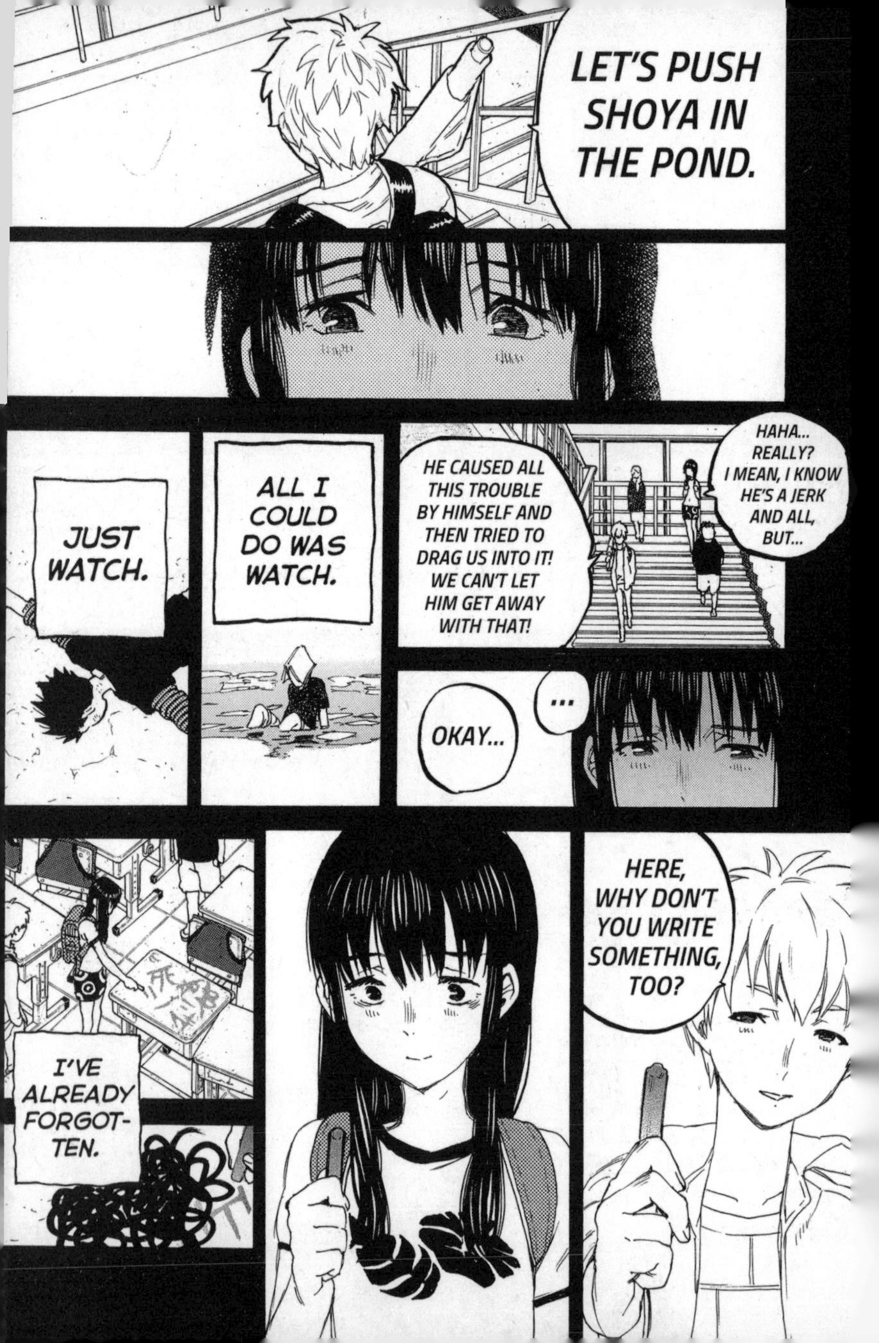
LET'S PUSH SHOYA IN THE POND.
HAHA... REALLY? I MEAN, I KNOW HE'S A JERK AND ALL, BUT...
HE CAUSED ALL THIS TROUBLE BY HIMSELF AND THEN TRIED TO DRAG US INTO IT! WE CAN'T LET HIM GET AWAY WITH THAT!
...
OKAY...
ALL I COULD DO WAS WATCH.
JUST WATCH.
HERE, WHY DON'T YOU WRITE SOMETHING, TOO?
I'VE ALREADY FORGOT-TEN.

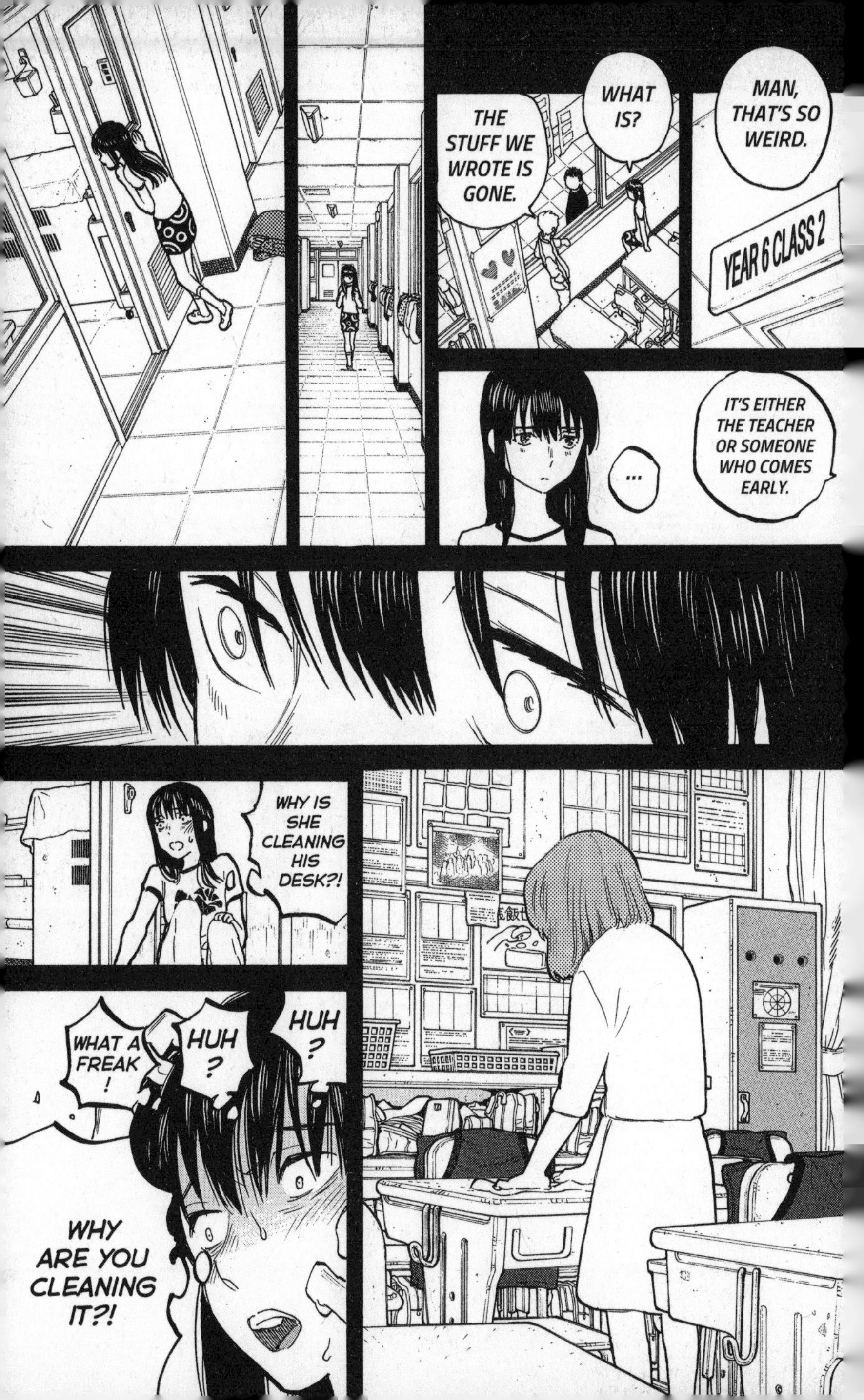
YEAR 6 CLASS 2
MAN, THAT'S SO WEIRD.
WHAT IS?
THE STUFF WE WROTE IS GONE.
IT'S EITHER THE TEACHER OR SOMEONE WHO COMES EARLY.
...
WHY IS SHE CLEANING HIS DESK?!
HUH?
HUH?
WHAT A FREAK!
WHY ARE YOU CLEANING IT?!

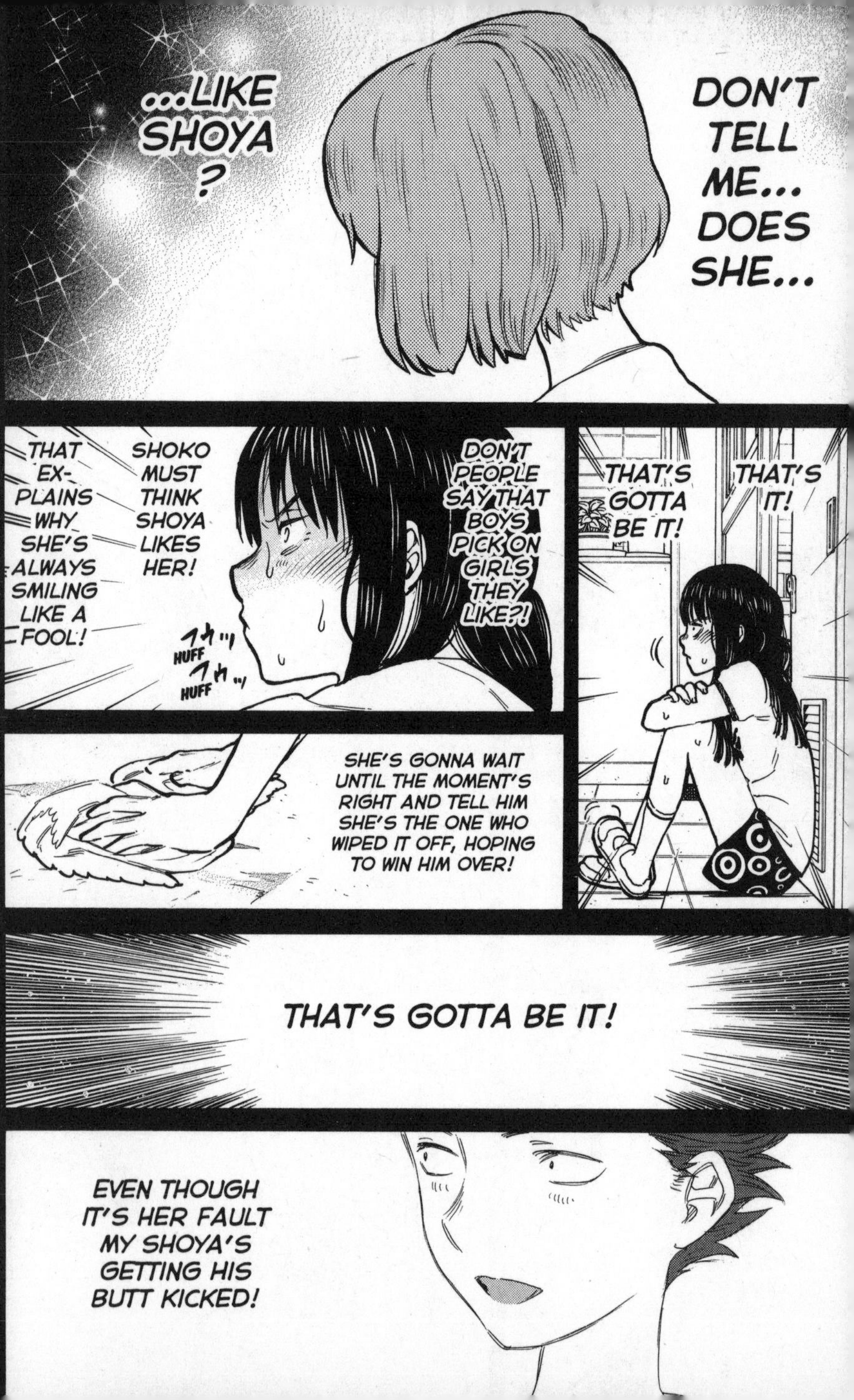
DON'T TELL ME... DOES SHE...
...LIKE SHOYA?
THAT'S IT!
THAT'S GOTTA BE IT!
DON'T PEOPLE SAY THAT BOYS PICK ON GIRLS THEY LIKE?!
SHOKO MUST THINK SHOYA LIKES HER!
THAT EX-PLAINS WHY SHE'S ALWAYS SMILING LIKE A FOOL!
HUFF
HUFF
SHE'S GONNA WAIT UNTIL THE MOMENT'S RIGHT AND TELL HIM SHE'S THE ONE WHO WIPED IT OFF, HOPING TO WIN HIM OVER!
THAT'S GOTTA BE IT!
EVEN THOUGH IT'S HER FAULT MY SHOYA'S GETTING HIS BUTT KICKED!

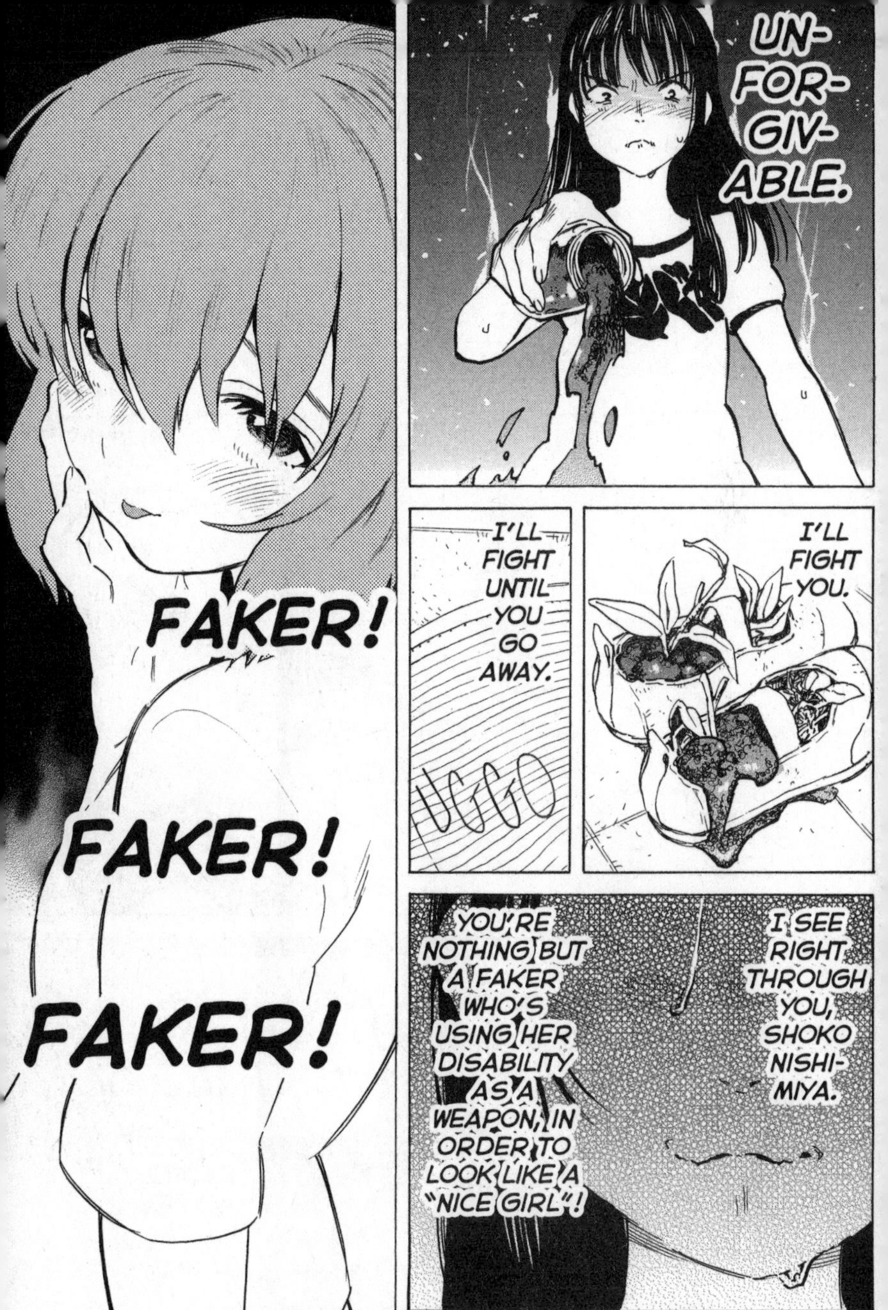
UN-FOR-GIV-ABLE.
I'LL FIGHT YOU.
I'LL FIGHT UNTIL YOU GO AWAY.
I SEE RIGHT THROUGH YOU, SHOKO NISHI-MIYA.
YOU'RE NOTHING BUT A FAKER WHO'S USING HER DISABILITY AS A WEAPON, IN ORDER TO LOOK LIKE A "NICE GIRL"!
FAKER!
FAKER!
FAKER!

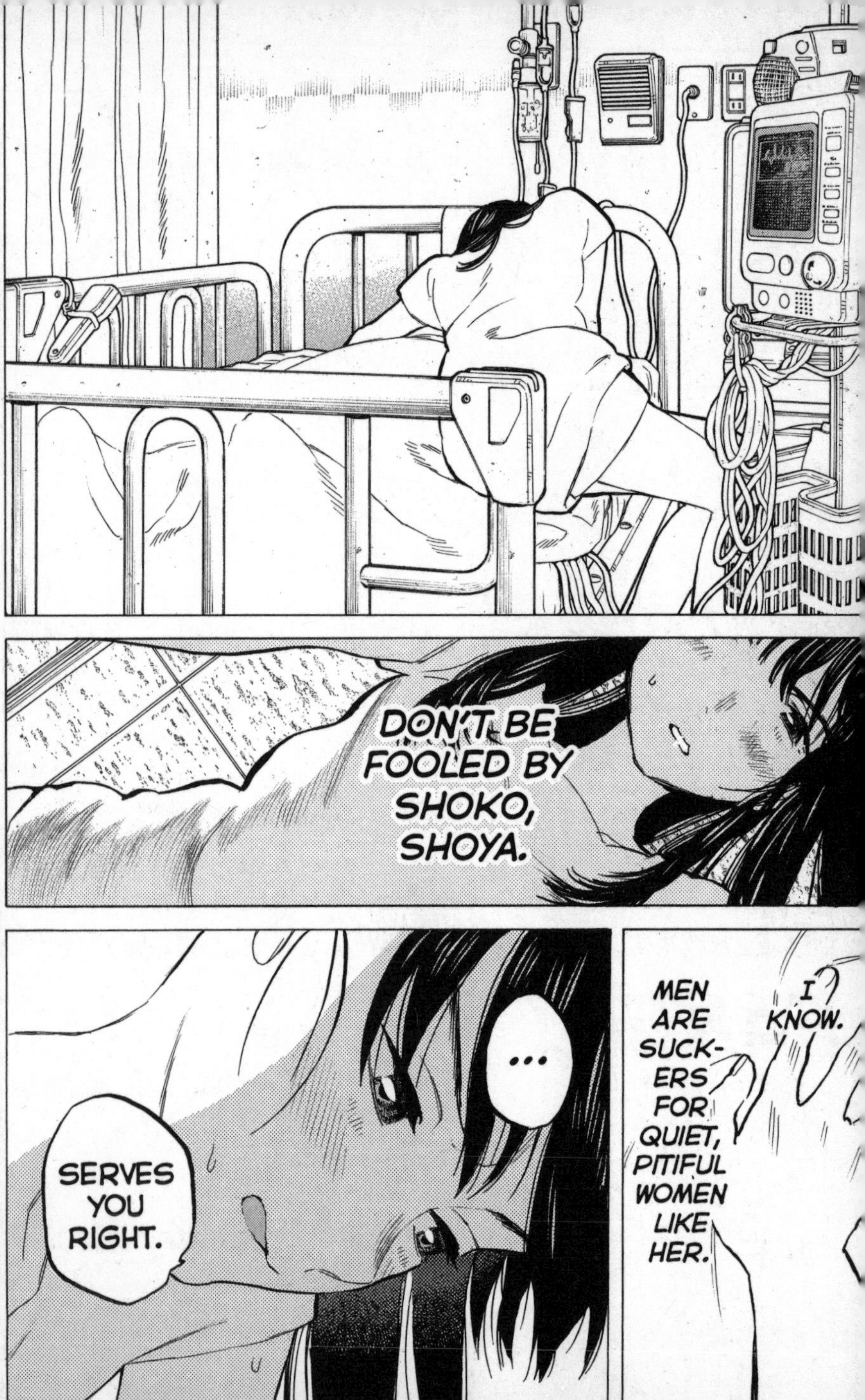
DON'T BE FOOLED BY SHOKO, SHOYA.
I KNOW.
MEN ARE SUCKERS FOR QUIET, PITIFUL WOMEN LIKE HER.
...
SERVES YOU RIGHT.

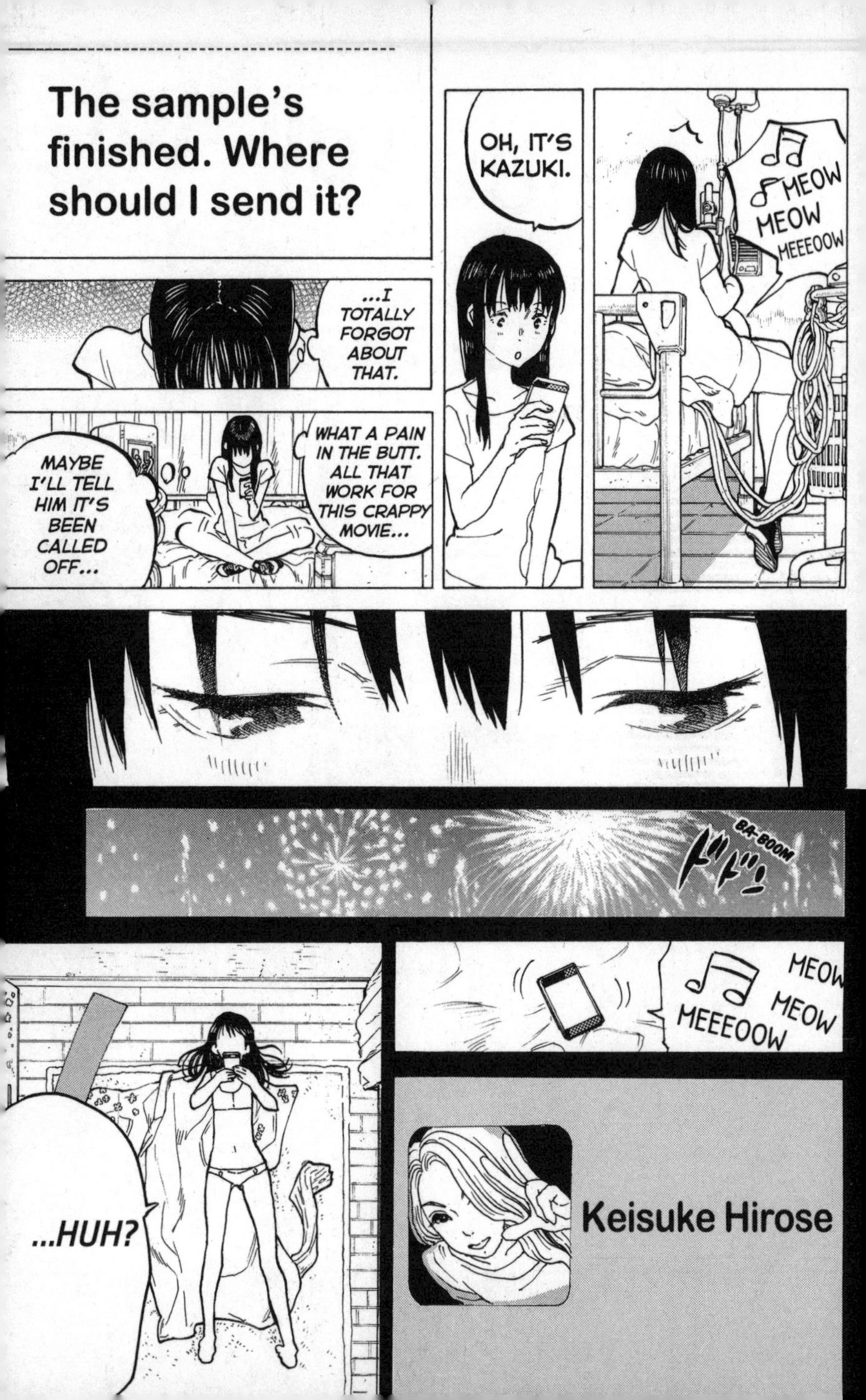

MEOW MEOW MEEEOOW
OH, IT'S KAZUKI.
The sample's finished. Where should I send it?
...I TOTALLY FORGOT ABOUT THAT.
WHAT A PAIN IN THE BUTT. ALL THAT WORK FOR THIS CRAPPY MOVIE...
MAYBE I'LL TELL HIM IT'S BEEN CALLED OFF...
BA-BOOM
MEOW MEOW MEEEOOW
Keisuke Hirose
...HUH?

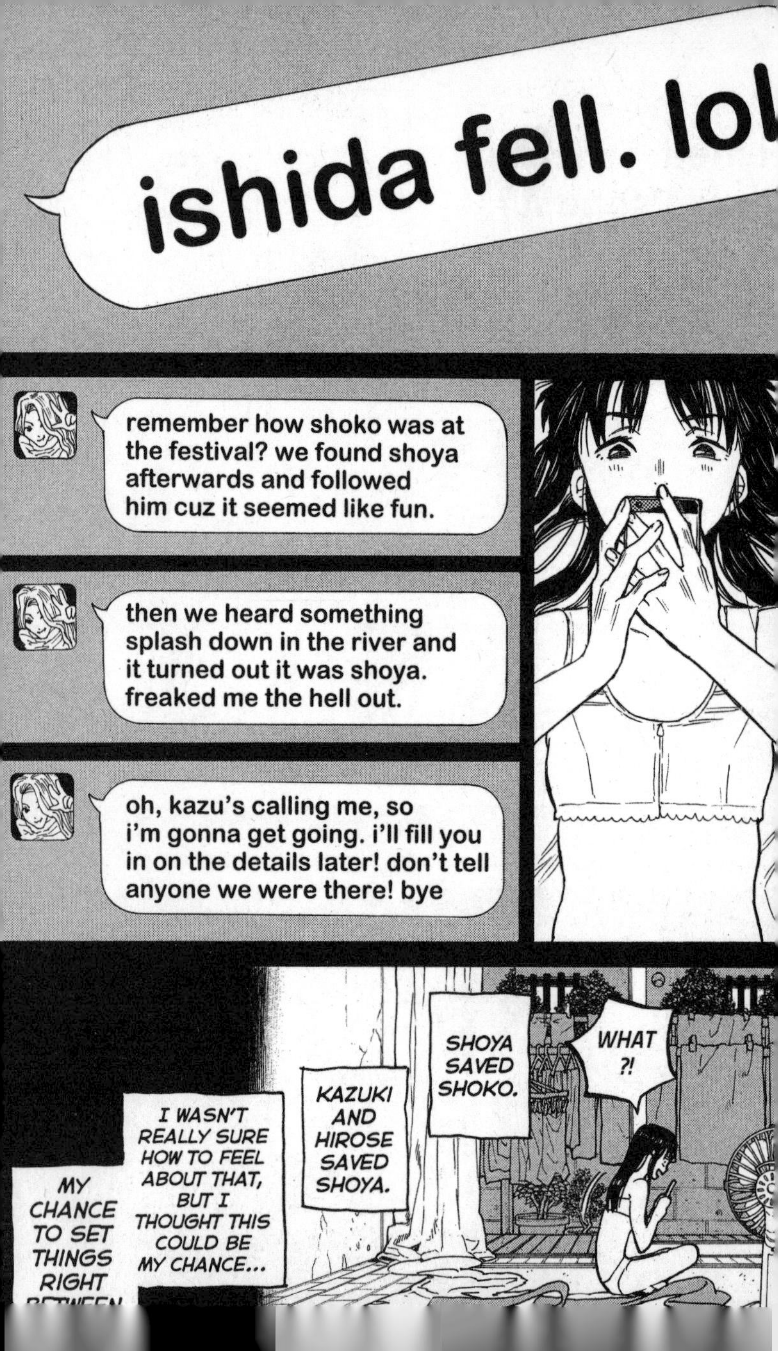
ishida fell. lol
remember how shoko was at the festival? we found shoya afterwards and followed him cuz it seemed like fun.
then we heard something splash down in the river and it turned out it was shoya. freaked me the hell out.
oh, kazu's calling me, so i'm gonna get going. i'll fill you in on the details later! don't tell anyone we were there! bye
WHAT ?!
SHOYA SAVED SHOKO.
KAZUKI AND HIROSE SAVED SHOYA.
I WASN'T REALLY SURE HOW TO FEEL ABOUT THAT, BUT I THOUGHT THIS COULD BE MY CHANCE...
MY CHANCE TO SET THINGS RIGHT

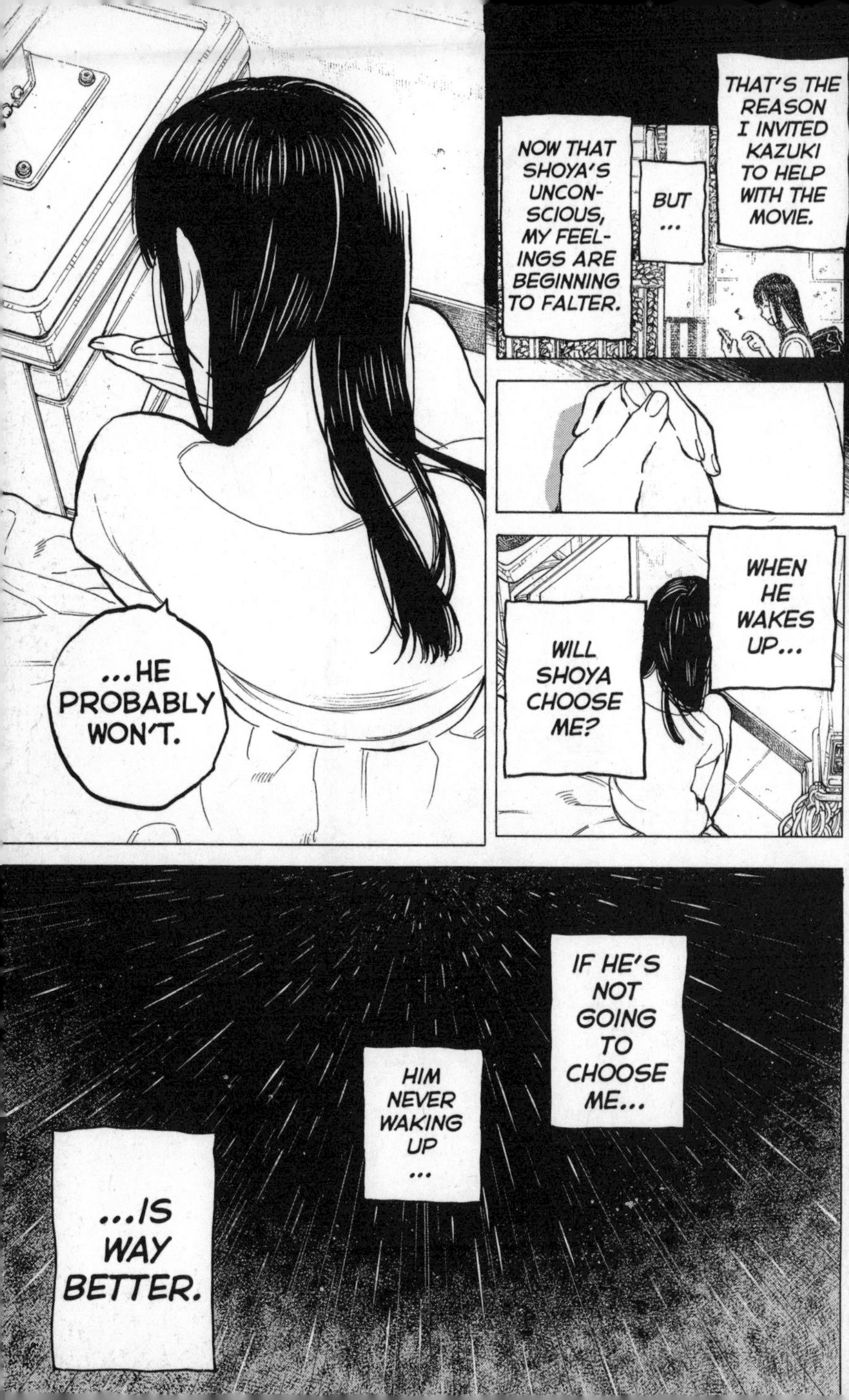
THAT'S THE REASON I INVITED KAZUKI TO HELP WITH THE MOVIE.
BUT...
NOW THAT SHOYA'S UNCONSCIOUS, MY FEELINGS ARE BEGINNING TO FALTER.
WHEN HE WAKES UP...
WILL SHOYA CHOOSE ME?
...HE PROBABLY WON'T.
IF HE'S NOT GOING TO CHOOSE ME...
HIM NEVER WAKING UP...
...IS WAY BETTER.

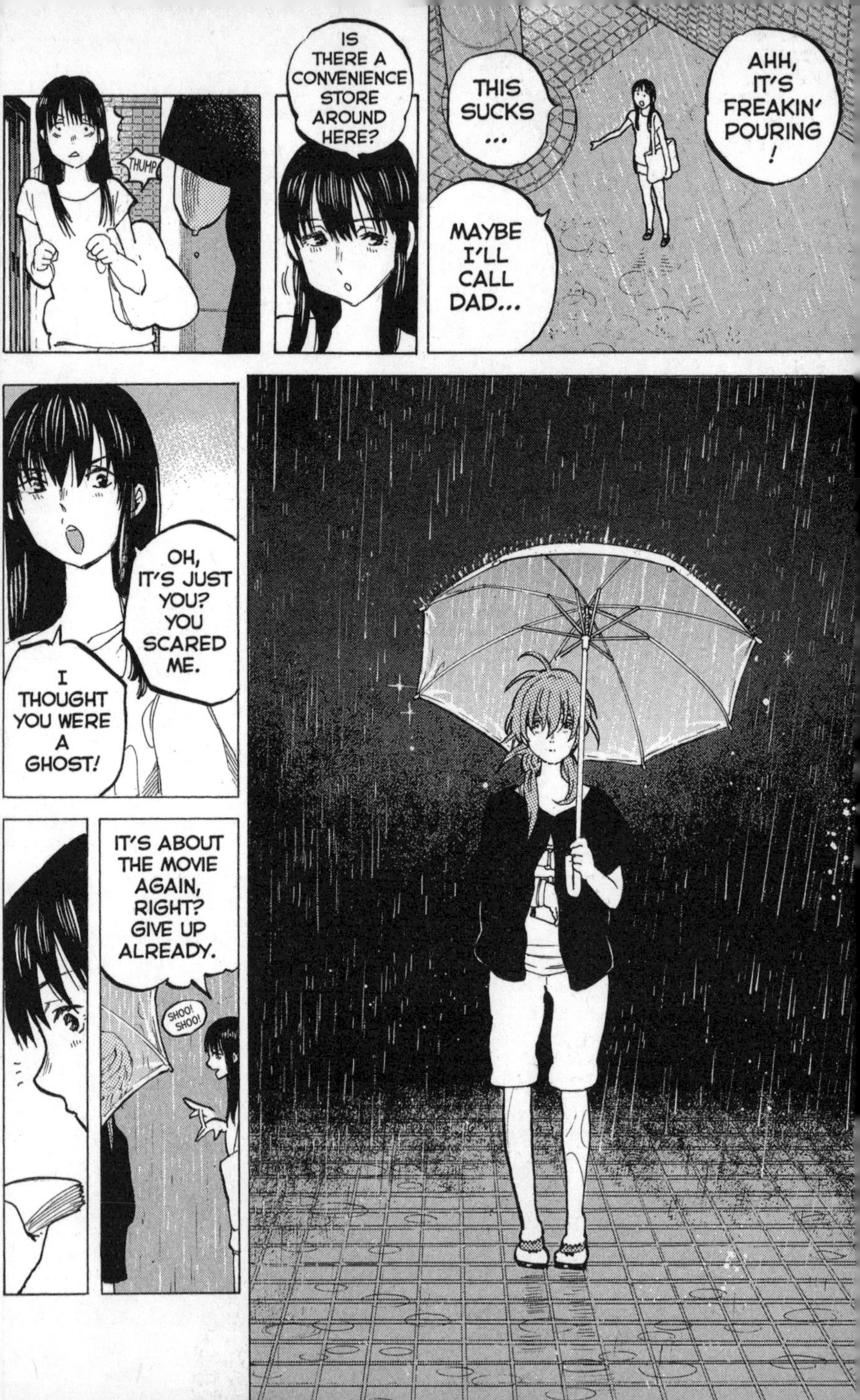
AHH, IT'S FREAKIN' POURING!
THIS SUCKS...
MAYBE I'LL CALL DAD...
IS THERE A CONVENIENCE STORE AROUND HERE?
THUMP
OH, IT'S JUST YOU? YOU SCARED ME.
I THOUGHT YOU WERE A GHOST!
IT'S ABOUT THE MOVIE AGAIN, RIGHT? GIVE UP ALREADY.
SHOO! SHOO!

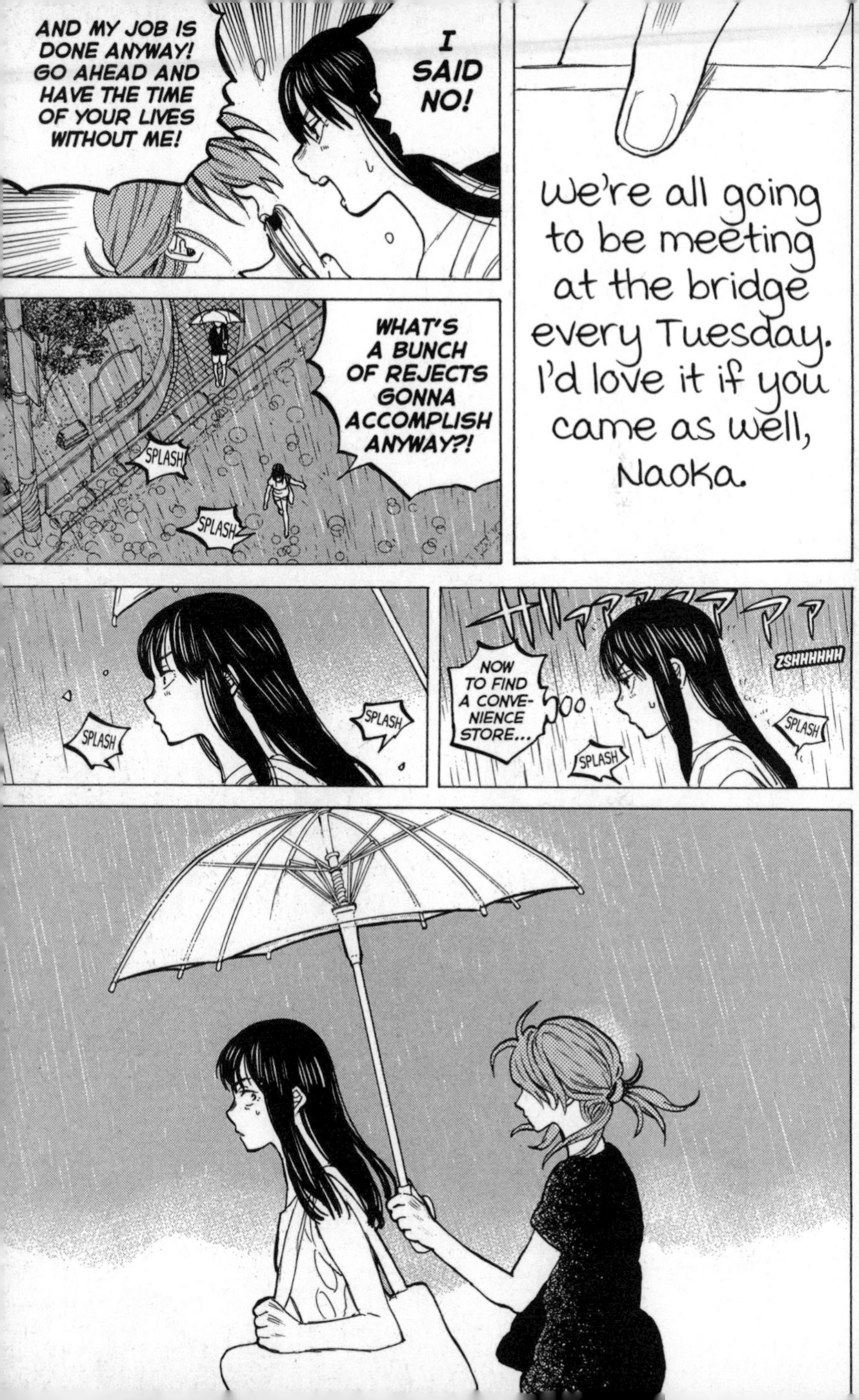
We're all going to be meeting at the bridge every Tuesday. I'd love it if you came as well, Naoka.
I SAID NO!
AND MY JOB IS DONE ANYWAY! GO AHEAD AND HAVE THE TIME OF YOUR LIVES WITHOUT ME!
WHAT'S A BUNCH OF REJECTS GONNA ACCOMPLISH ANYWAY?!
SPLASH
SPLASH
ZSHHHHHH
SPLASH
NOW TO FIND A CONVE-NIENCE STORE...
SPLASH
SPLASH
SPLASH

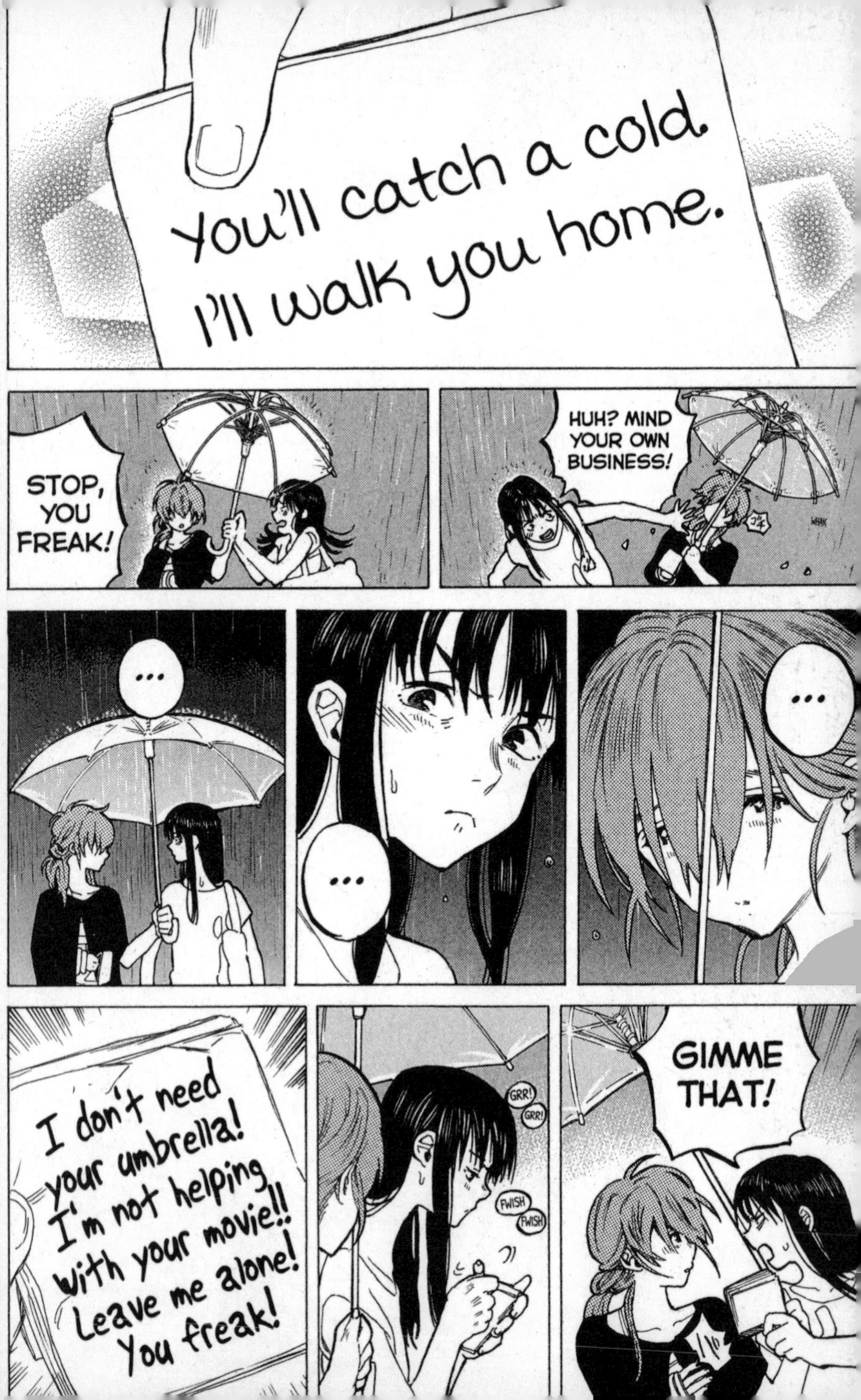

You'll catch a cold.
I'll walk you home.
HUH? MIND YOUR OWN BUSINESS!
WHAK
STOP, YOU FREAK!
...
...
...
GIMME THAT!
GRR! GRR!
FWISH FWISH
I don't need your umbrella! I'm not helping with your movie!! Leave me alone! You freak!

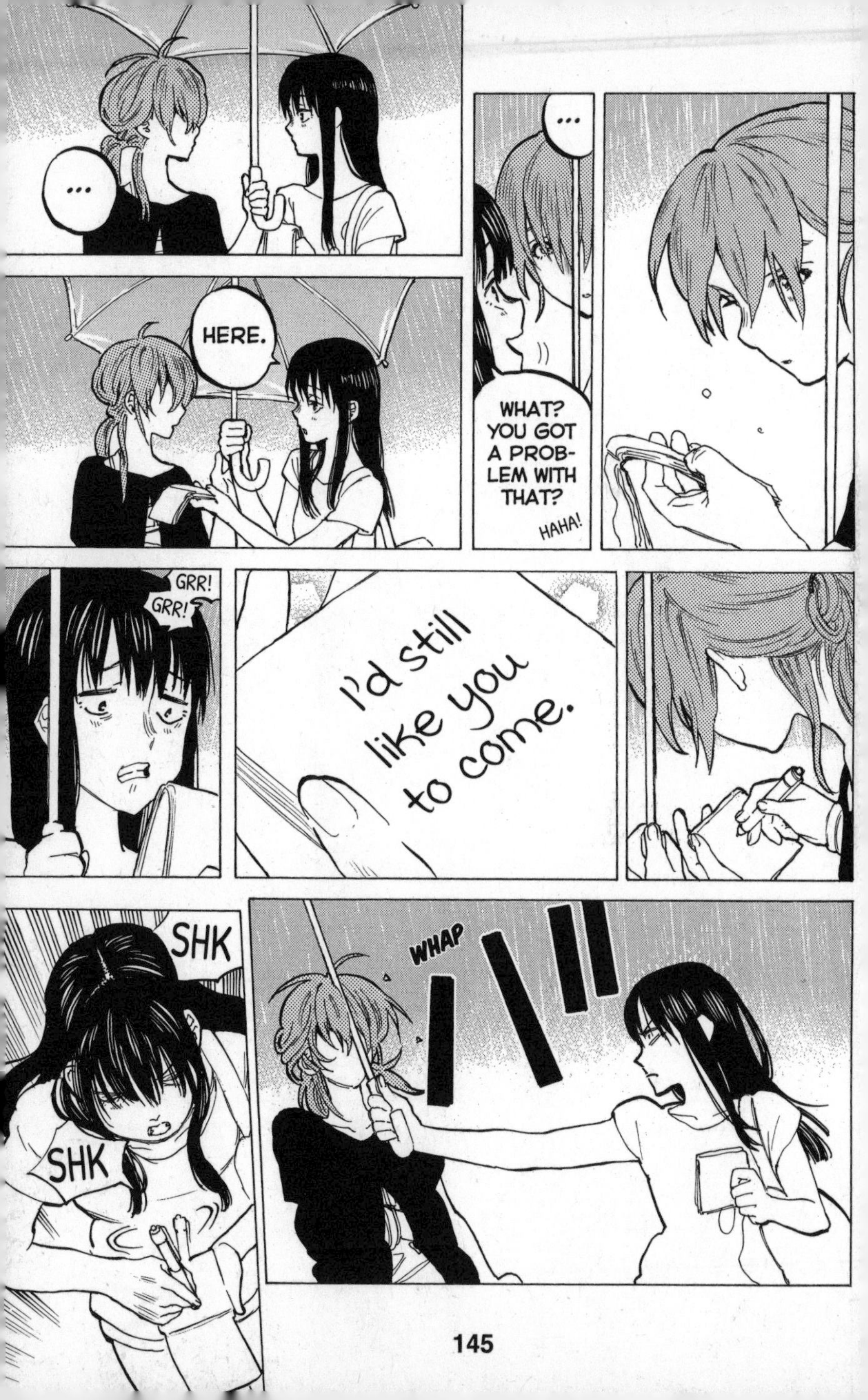
...
WHAT? YOU GOT A PROB- LEM WITH THAT?
HAHA!
...
HERE.
I'd still like you to come.
GRR!
GRR!
WHAP
SHK
SHK

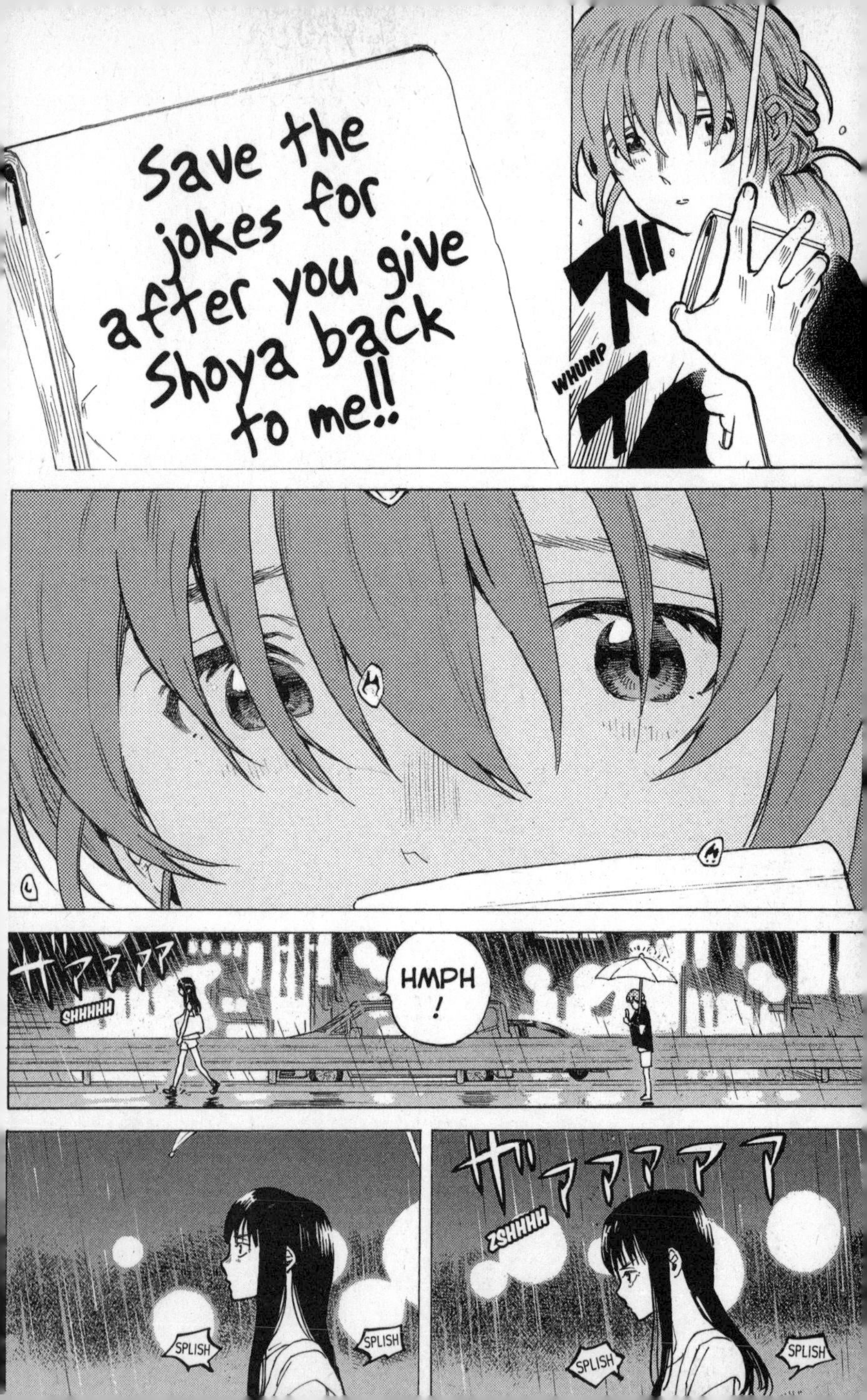

ズイ
WHUMP
Save the jokes for after you give Shoya back to me!!
ザァァァァ
SHHHHH
HMPH!
ザァァァァァァ
ZSHHHH
SPLISH
SPLISH
SPLISH
SPLISH

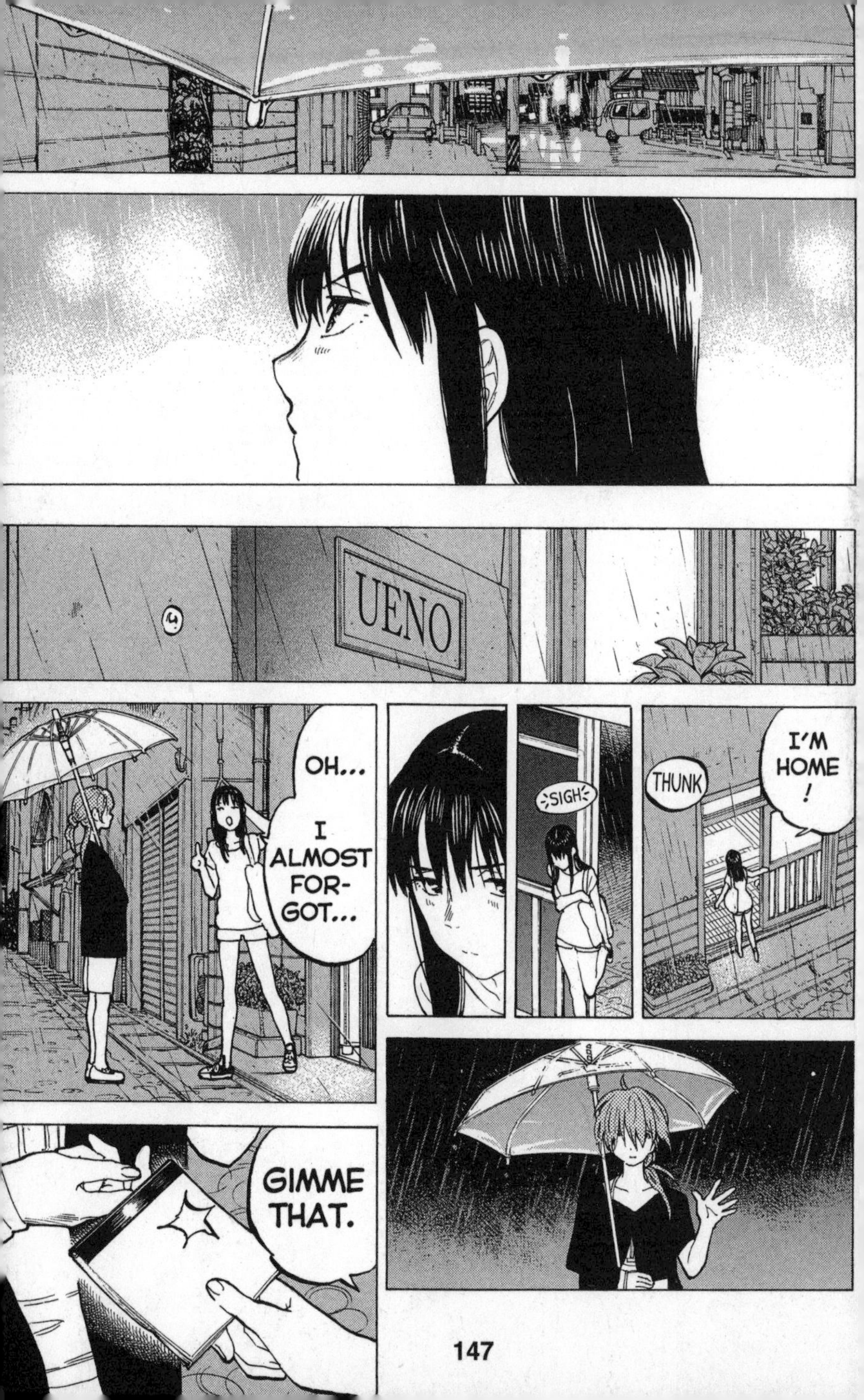

UENO
I'M HOME!
THUNK
SIGH
OH...
I ALMOST FORGOT...
GIMME THAT.

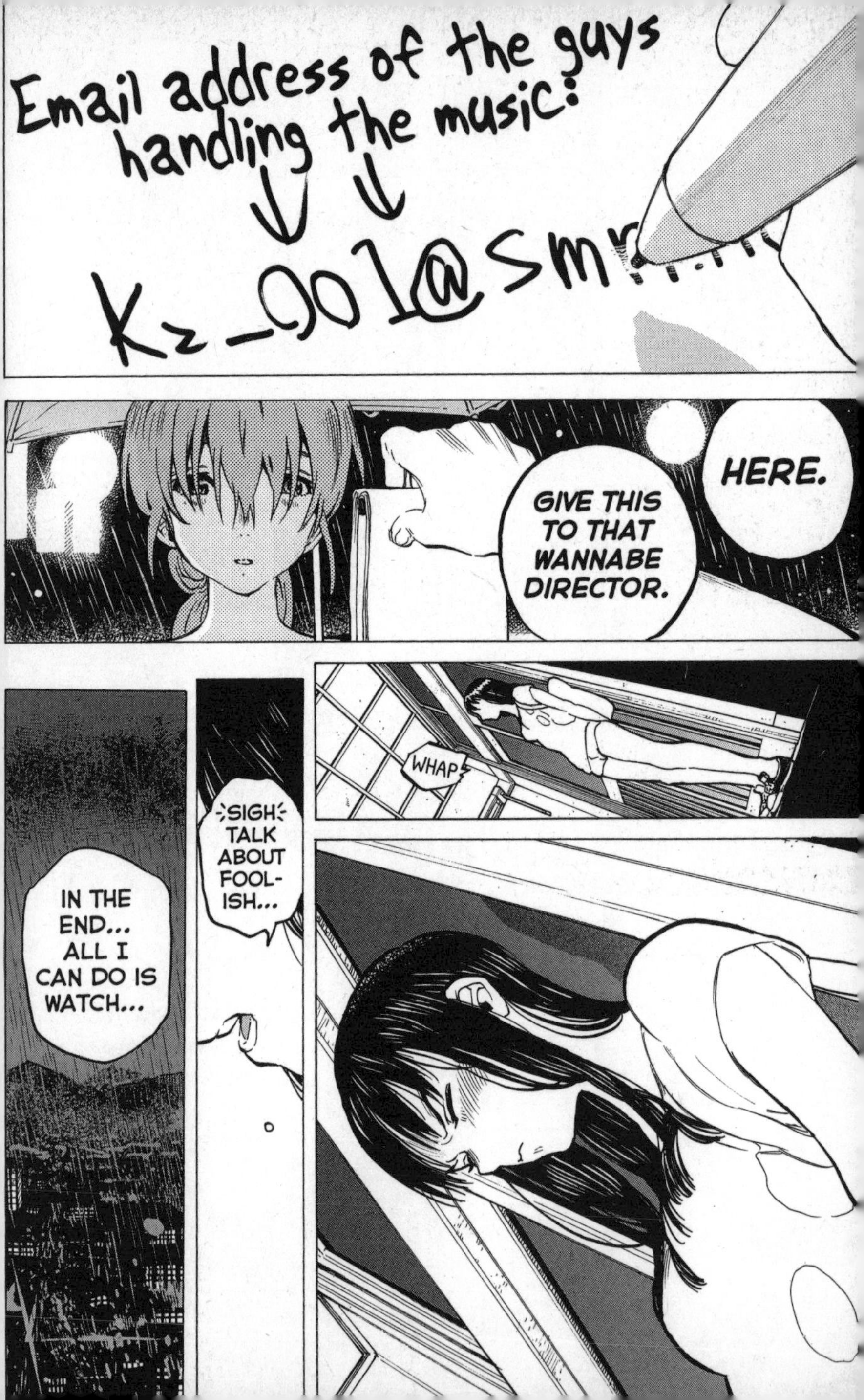
Email address of the guys handling the music:
Kz_901@smr
HERE.
GIVE THIS TO THAT WANNABE DIRECTOR.
WHAP
SIGH
TALK ABOUT FOOL-ISH...
IN THE END... ALL I CAN DO IS WATCH...

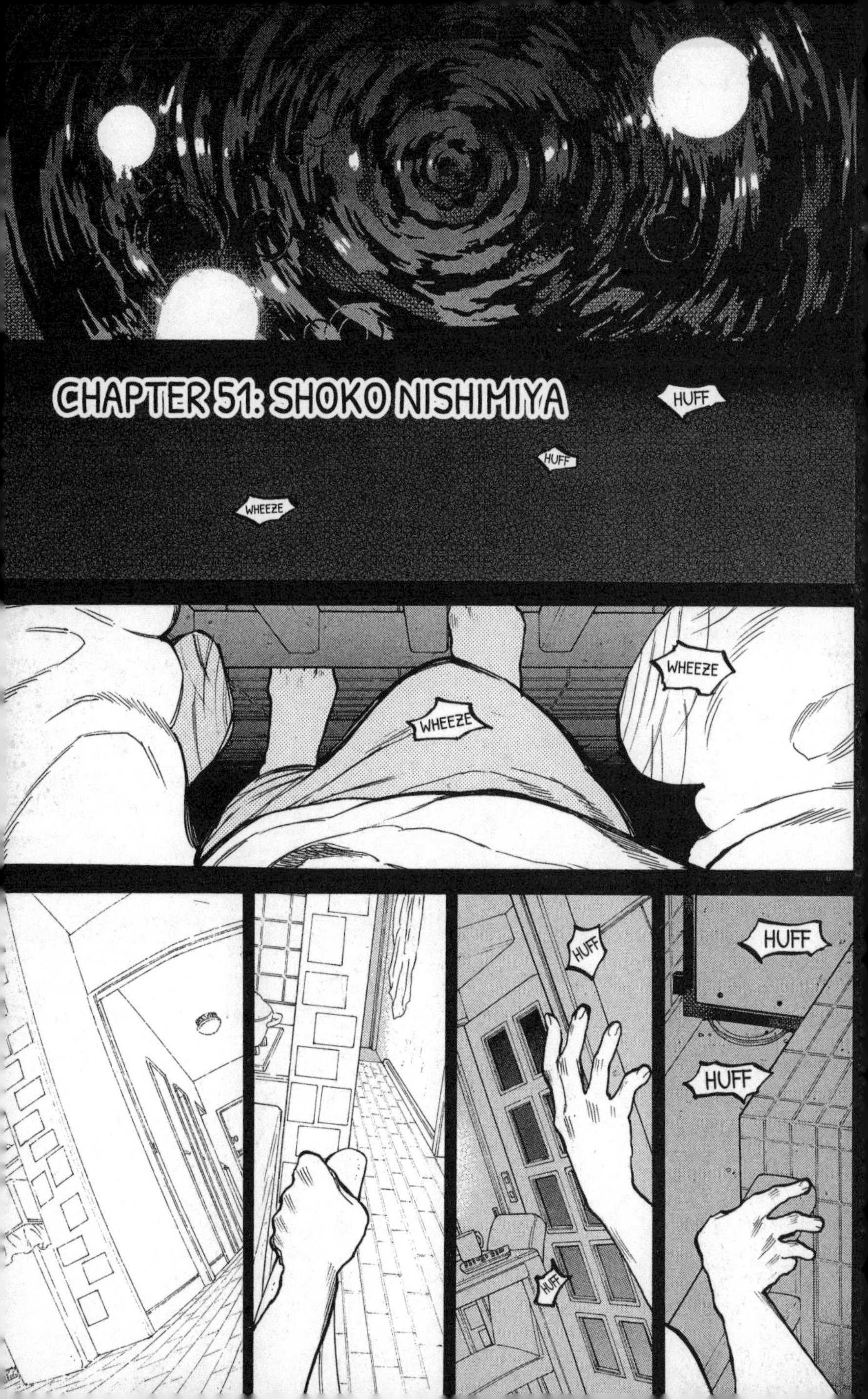
CHAPTER 51: SHOKO NISHIMIYA
HUFF
HUFF
WHEEZE
WHEEZE
WHEEZE
HUFF
HUFF
HUFF
HUFF

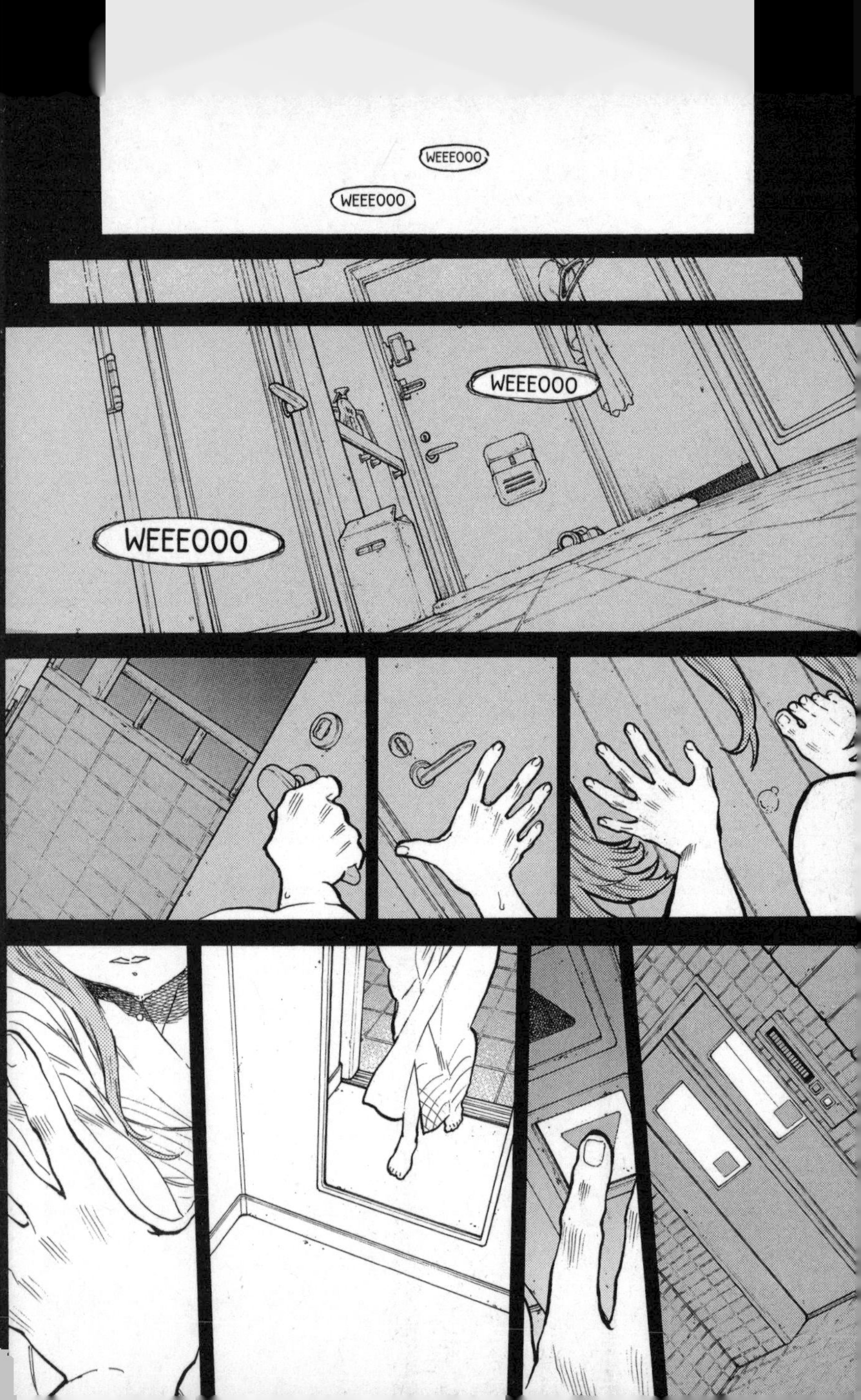
WEEEOOO
WEEEOOO
WEEEOOO
WEEEOOO

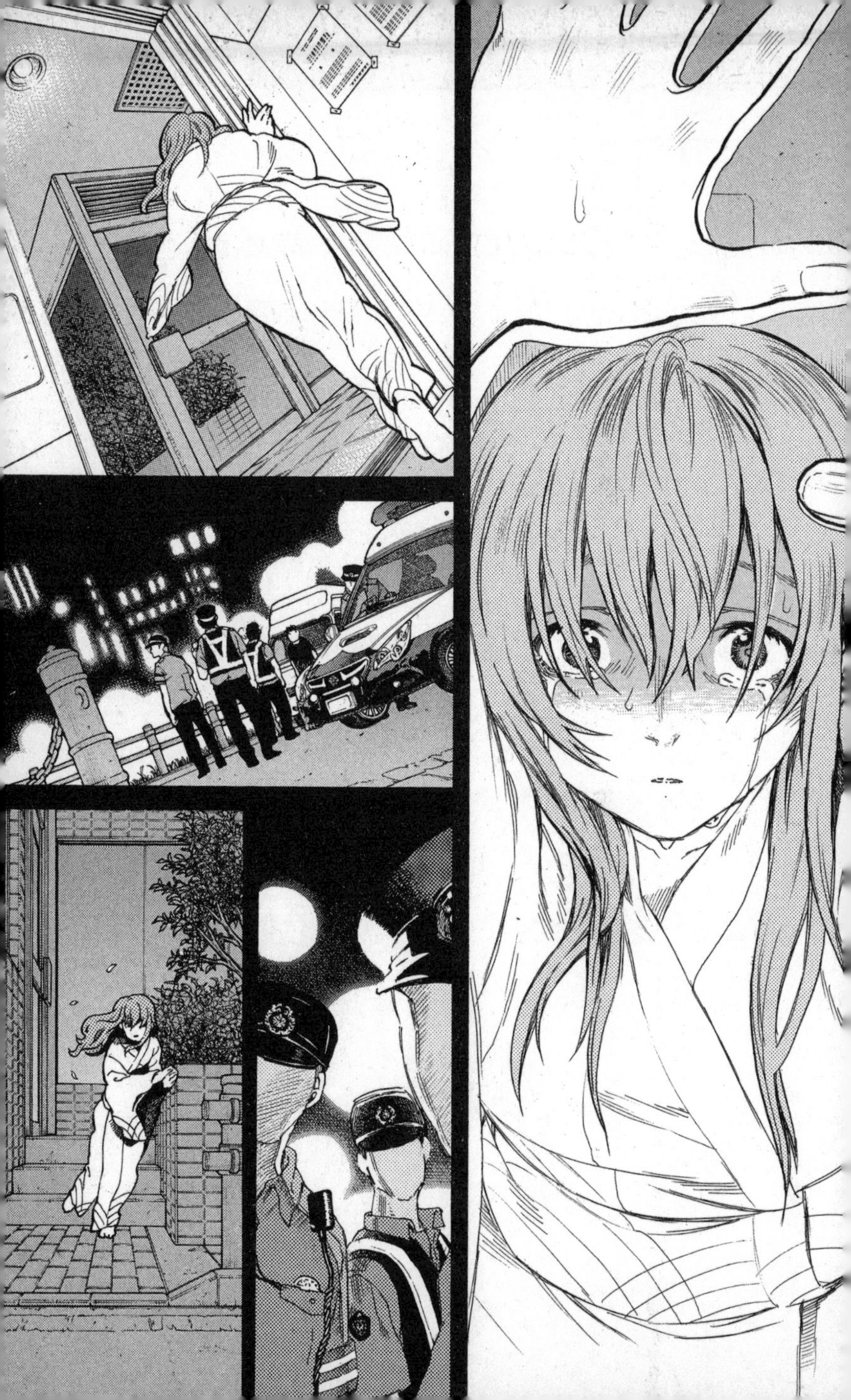

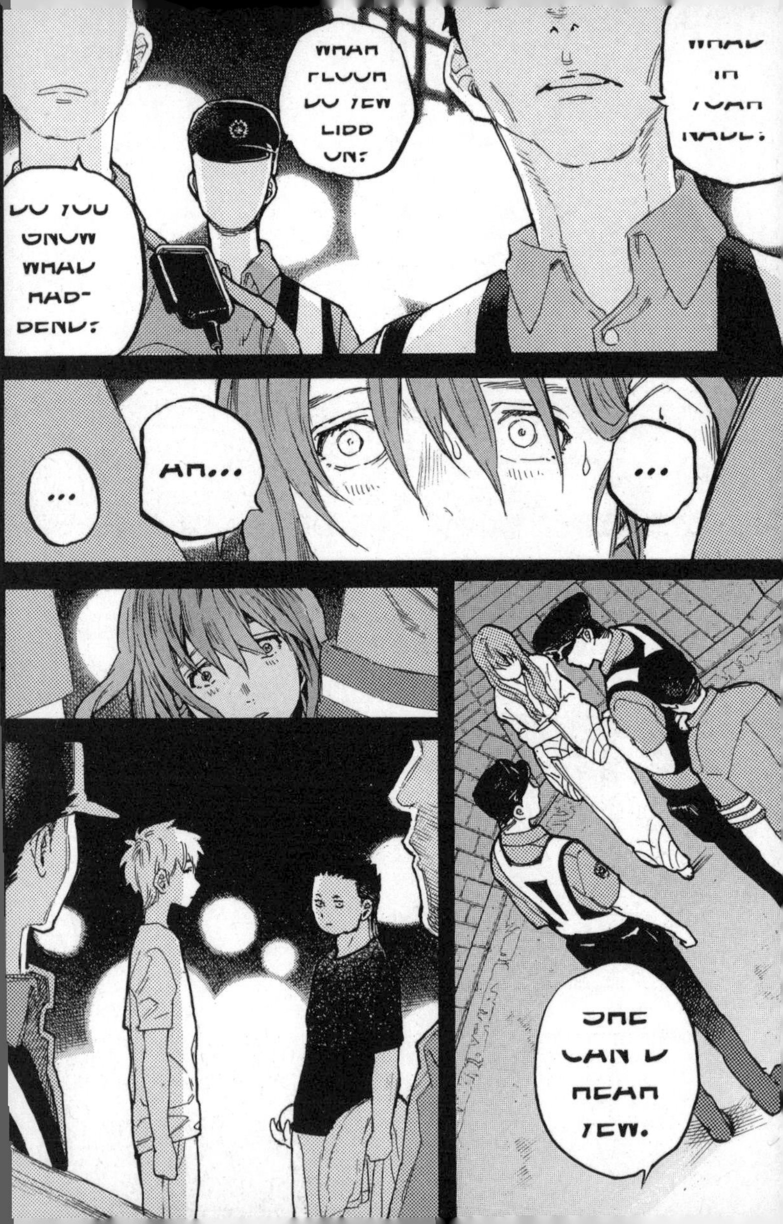
WHAD IN YOAH NADE?
WHAH FLOOH DO YEW LIBB ON?
DO YOU GNOW WHAD HAB-BEND?
...
AH...
...
SHE CAN'D HEAH YEW.

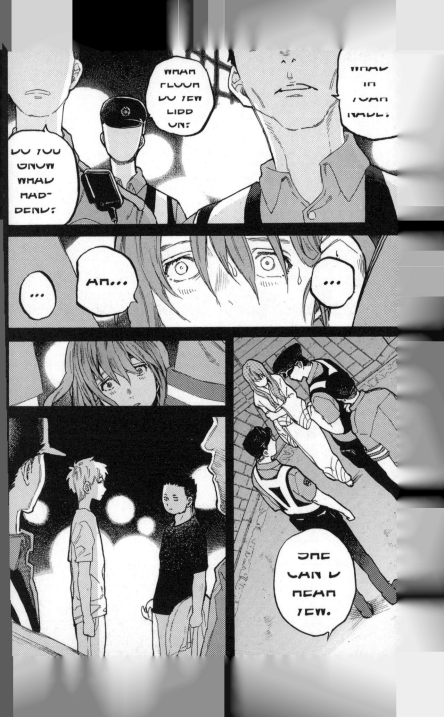

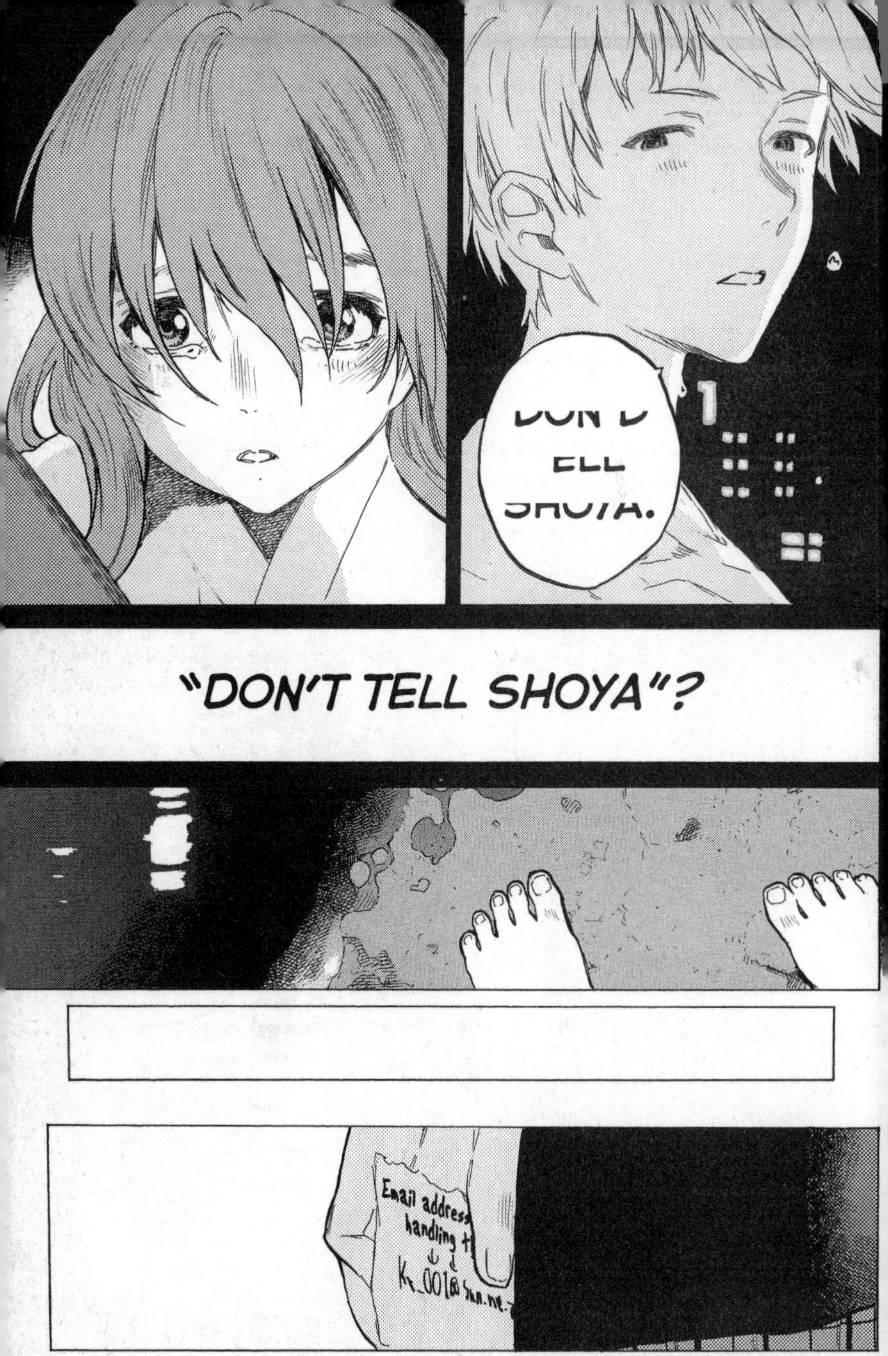
DON'T TELL SHOYA.
"DON'T TELL SHOYA"?
Email address
handling t
Kt_001@

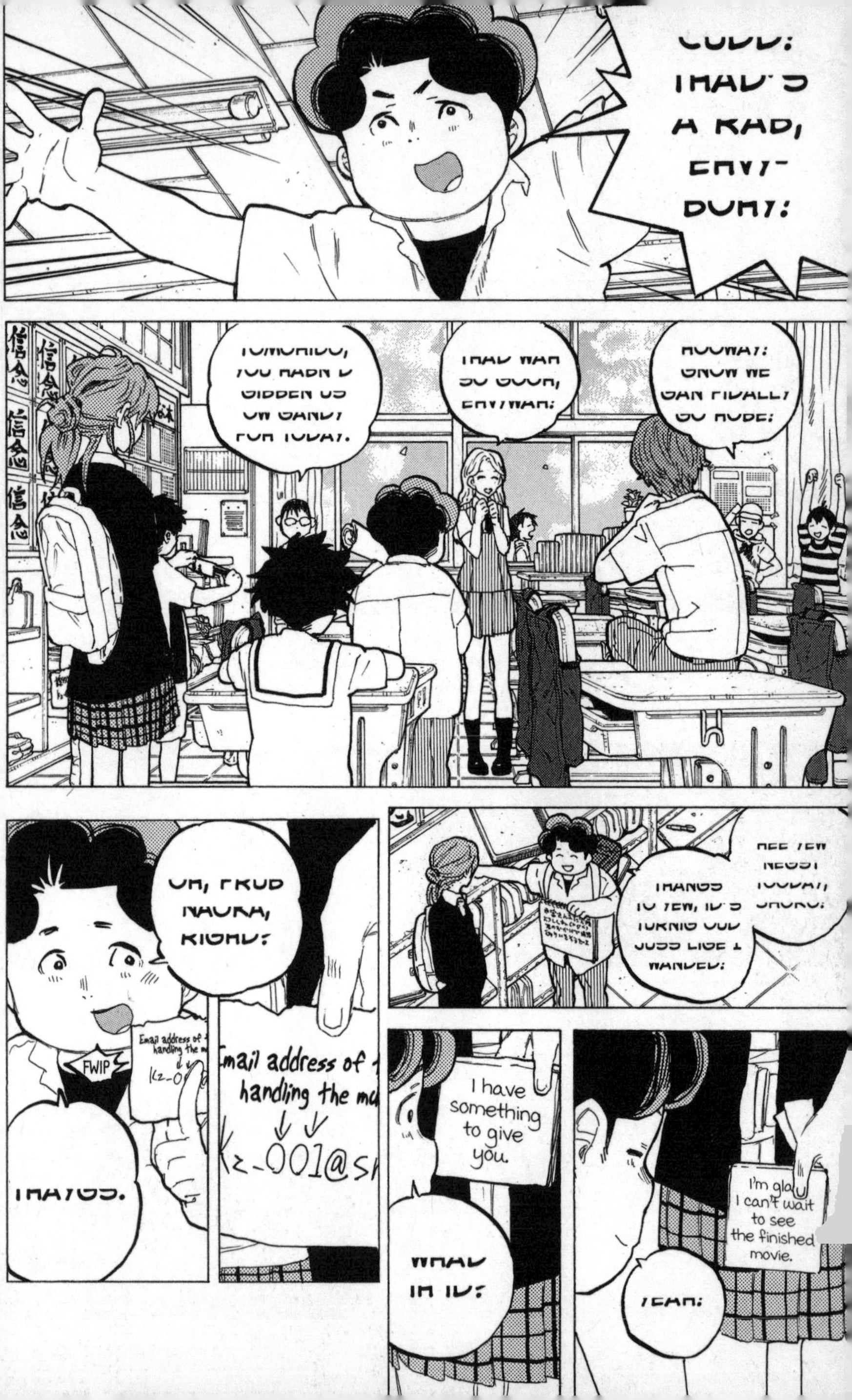
I'm gla
I can't wait to see the finished movie.
I have something to give you.
Email address of handling the mu
Kz-001@s
Email address of handling the m
Kz-0
FWIP

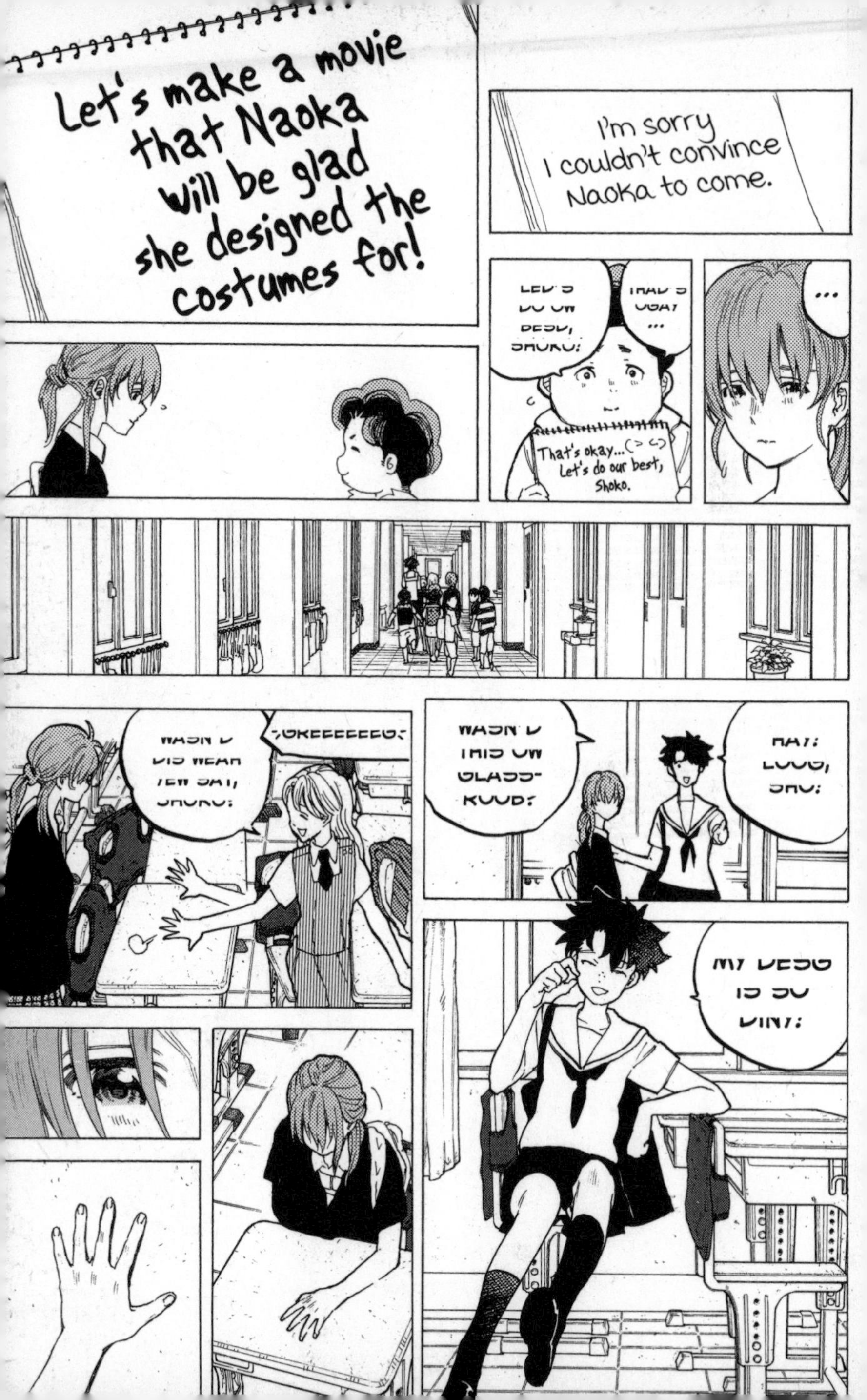
I'm sorry I couldn't convince Naoka to come.
Let's make a movie that Naoka will be glad she designed the costumes for!
...
LEVD'S DO OW BESD, SHOKU!
THAD'S OGAY ...
That's okay... (> <) Let's do our best, Shoko.
HAY! LUUG, SHU!
WASN'D THIS OW GLASS-ROOB?
WASN'D DIS WEAH YEW SAT, SHOKU!
~GREEEEEEG!
MY DESG IS SO DIRY!

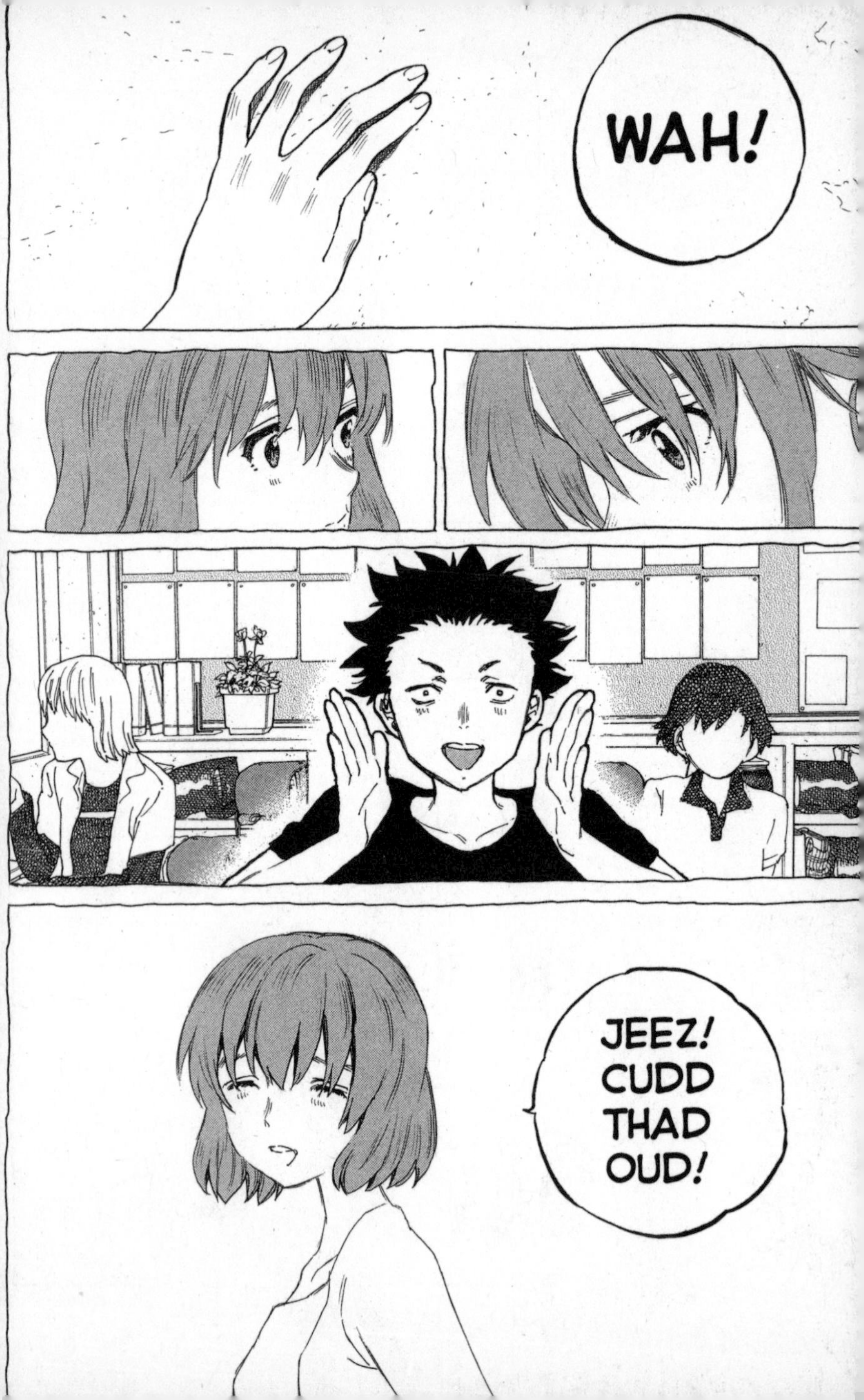
WAH!
JEEZ! CUDD THAD OUD!

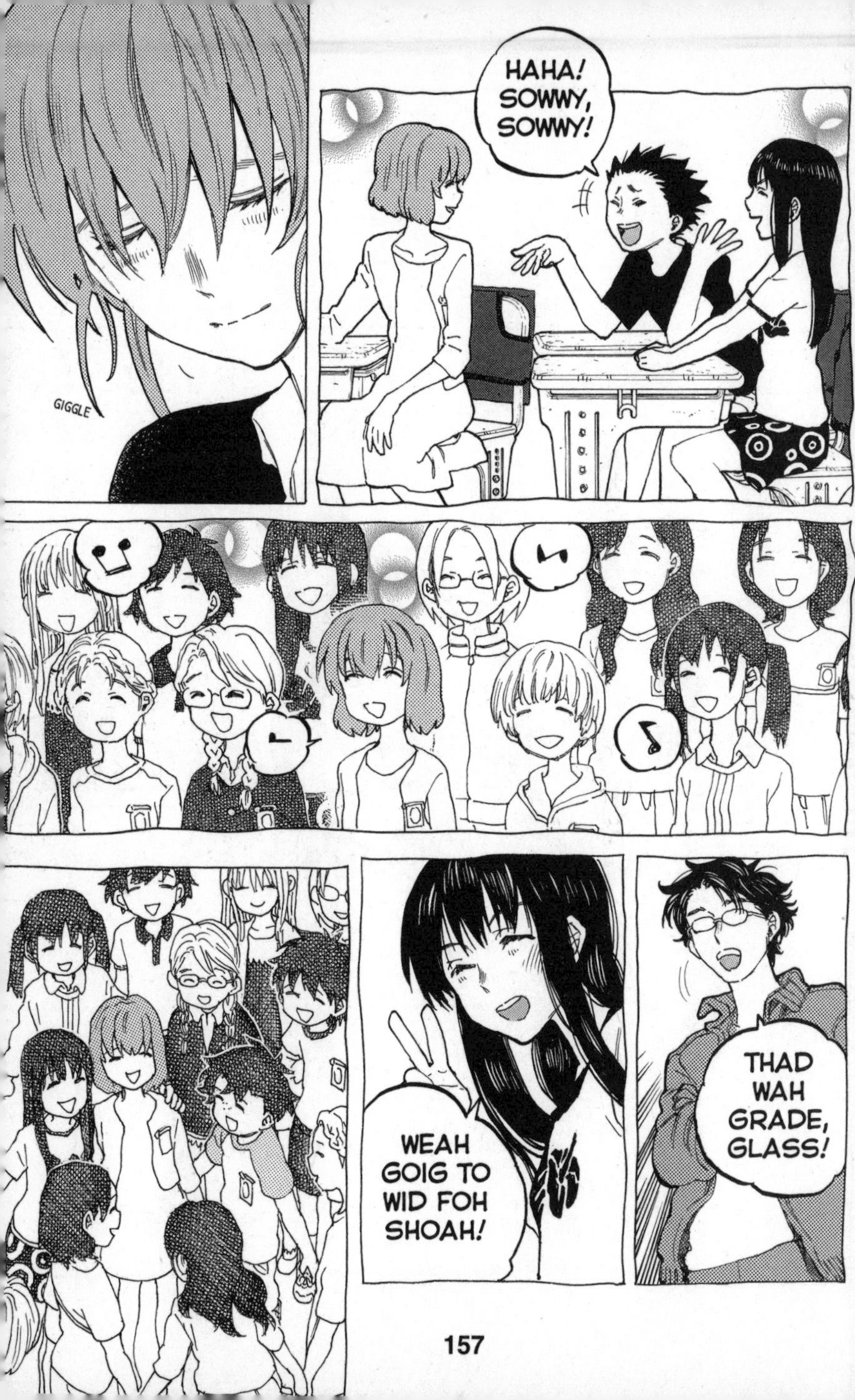
HAHA! SOWWY, SOWWY!
GIGGLE
THAD WAH GRADE, GLASS!
WEAH GOIG TO WID FOH SHOAH!

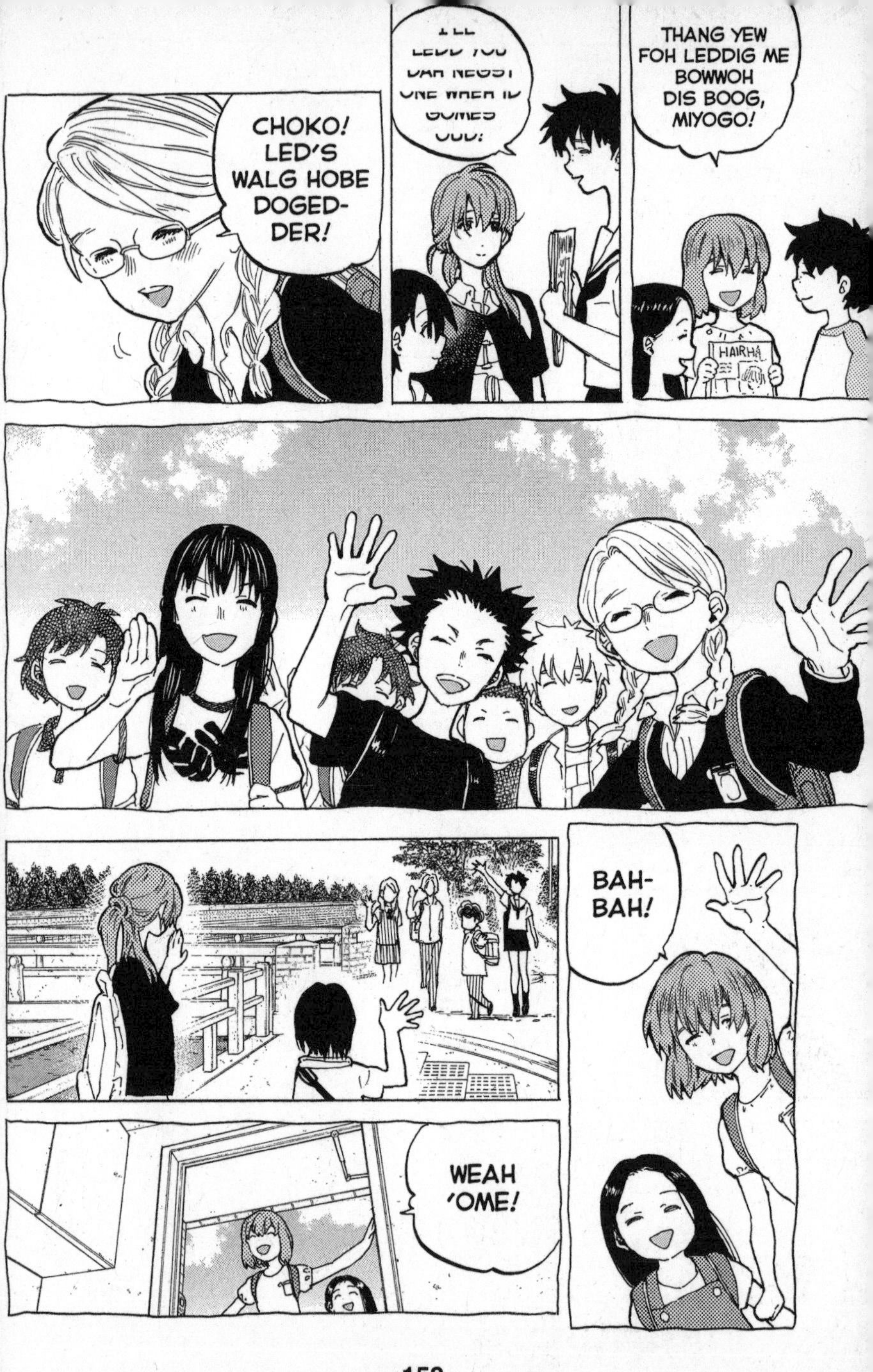
THANG YEW FOH LEDDIG ME BOWWOH DIS BOOG, MIYOGO!
HAIRHA
I'LL LEDD YOU DAH NEGST ONE WHEN ID GOMES OUD!
CHOKO! LED'S WALG HOBE DOGED-DER!
BAH-BAH!
WEAH 'OME!

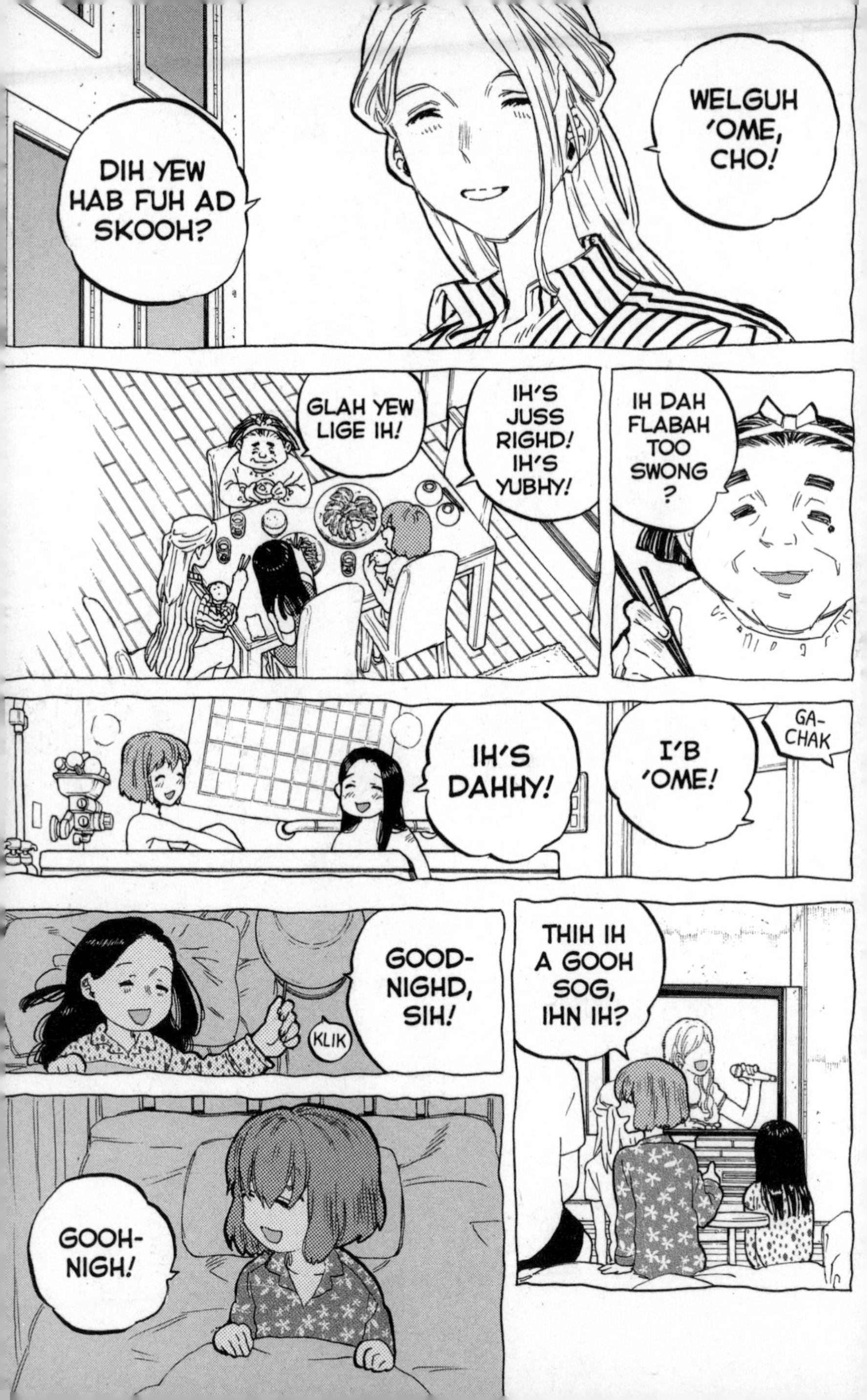
WELGUH 'OME, CHO!
DIH YEW HAB FUH AD SKOOH?
IH DAH FLABAH TOO SWONG ?
IH'S JUSS RIGHD! IH'S YUBHY!
GLAH YEW LIGE IH!
GA-CHAK
I'B 'OME!
IH'S DAHHY!
THIH IH A GOOH SOG, IHN IH?
GOOD-NIGHD, SIH!
KLIK
GOOH-NIGH!

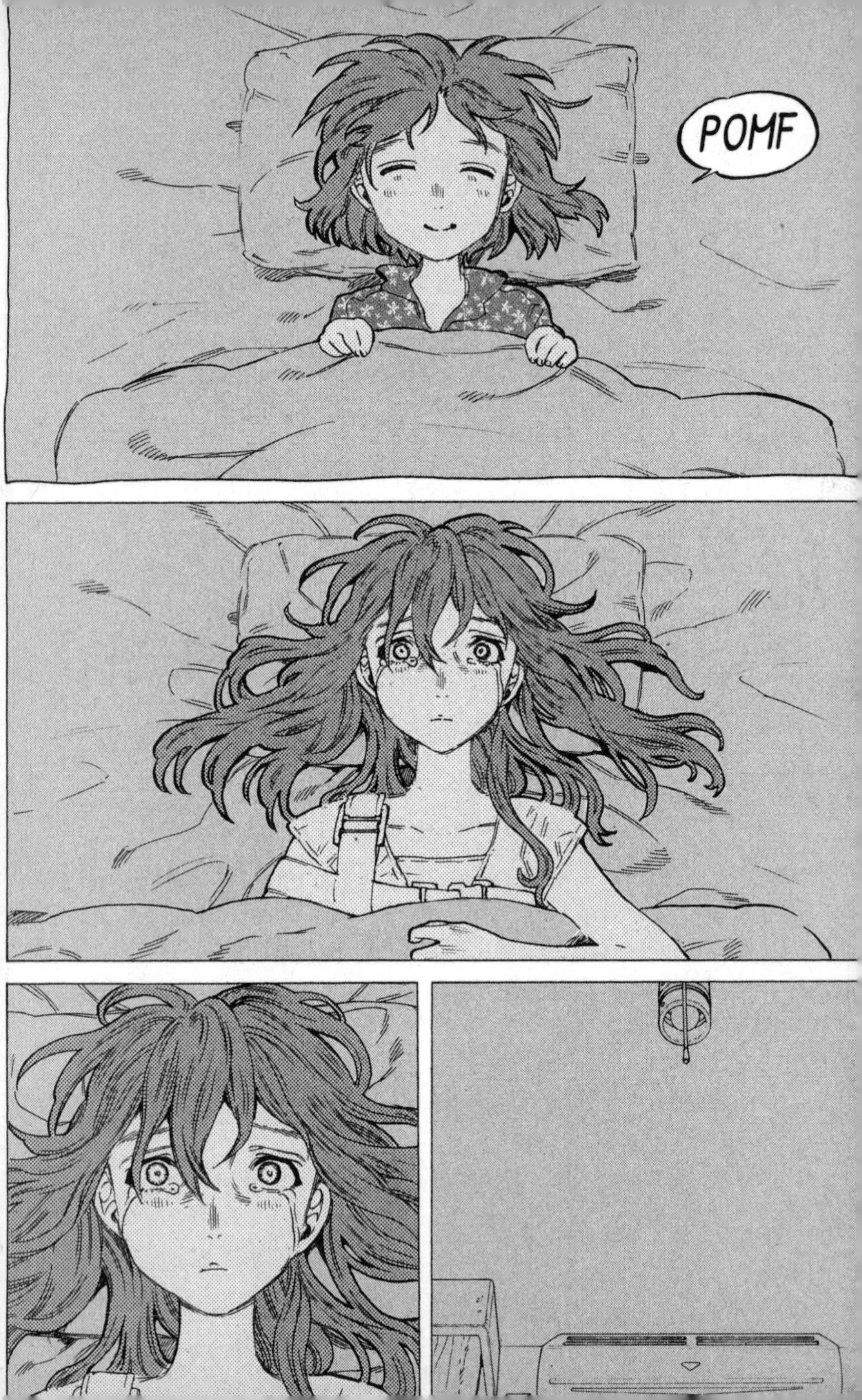
POMF

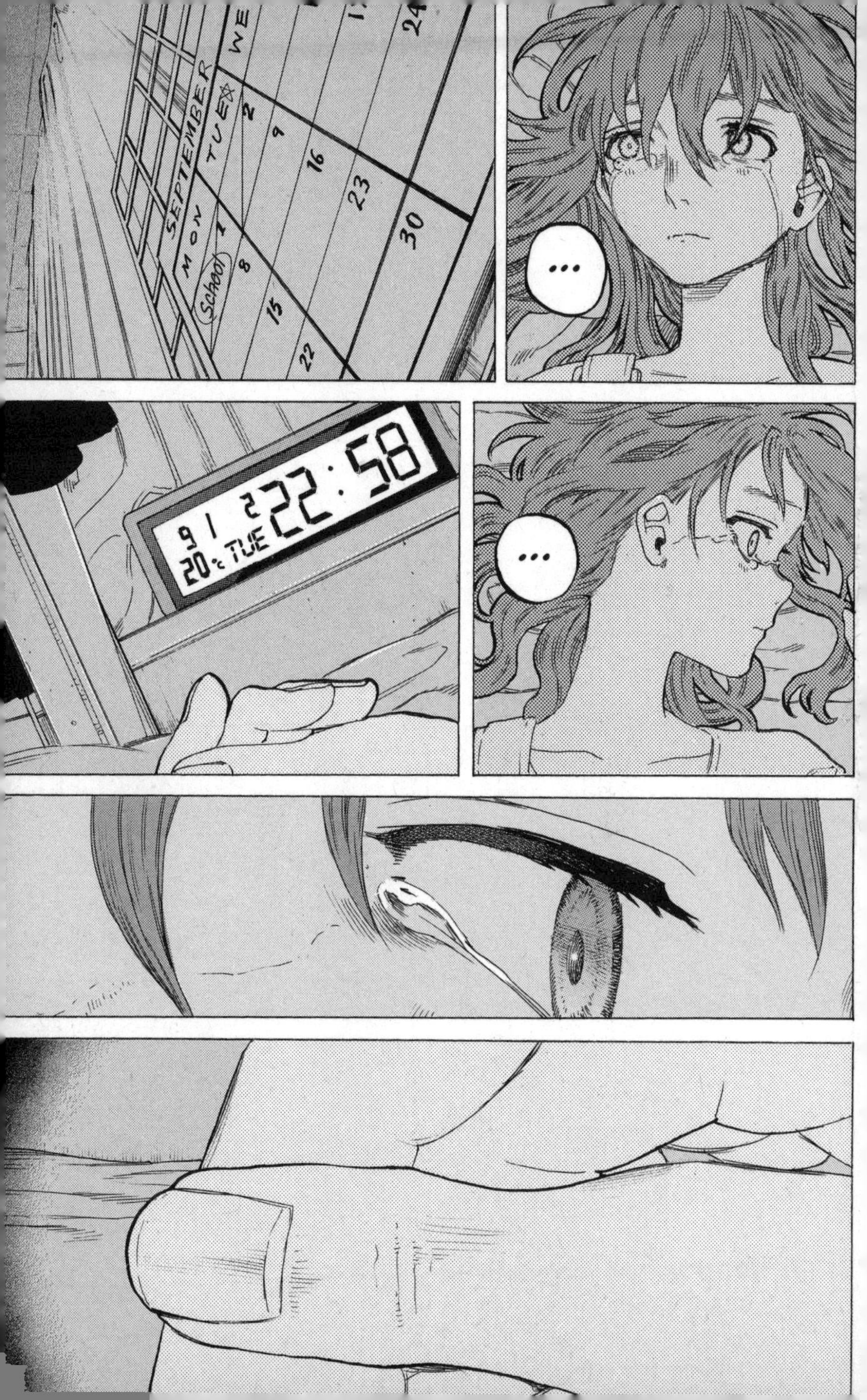
...
SEPTEMBER
MON TUE WE
School
...
9 1 2 22:58
20°c TUE

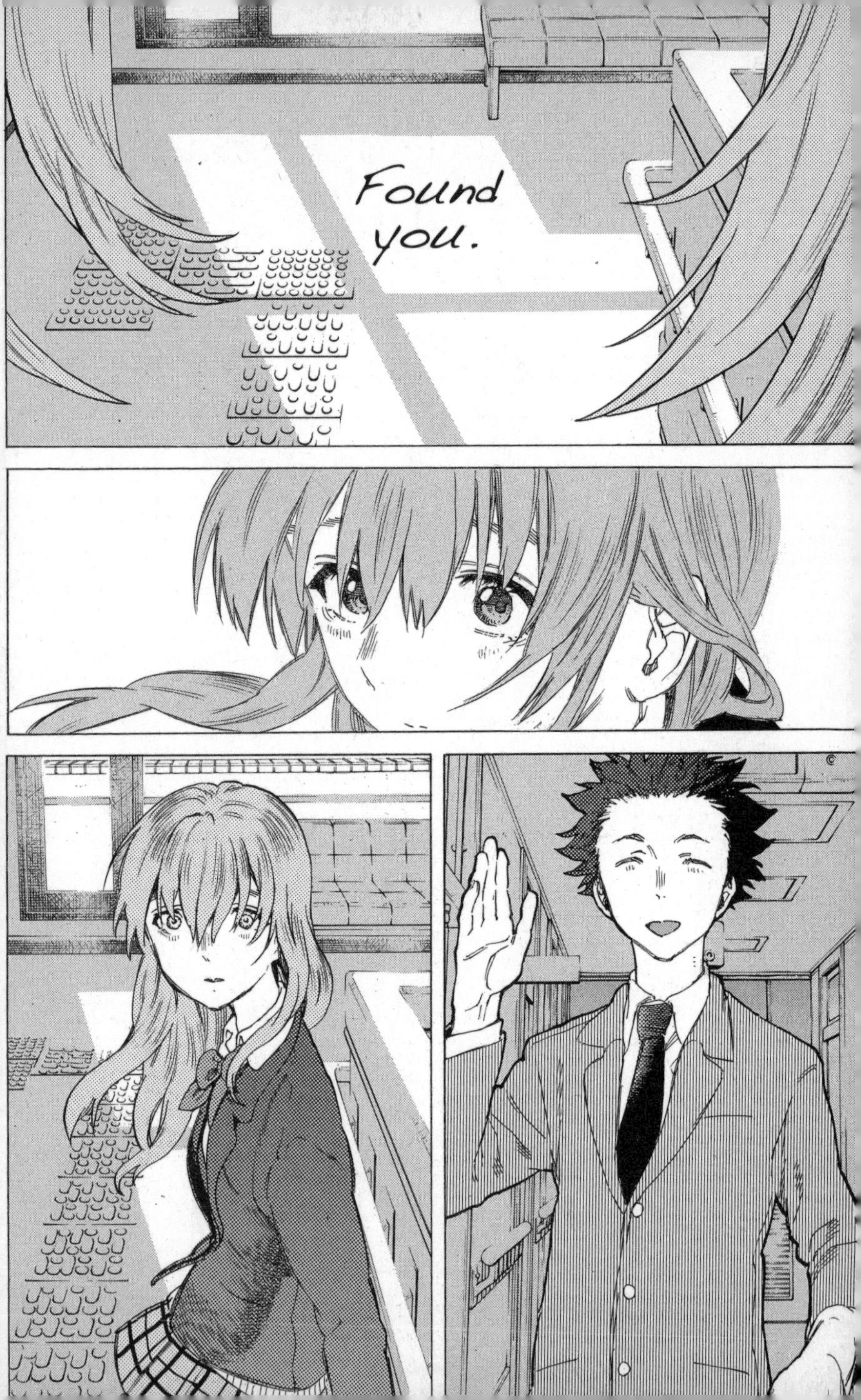
Found you.

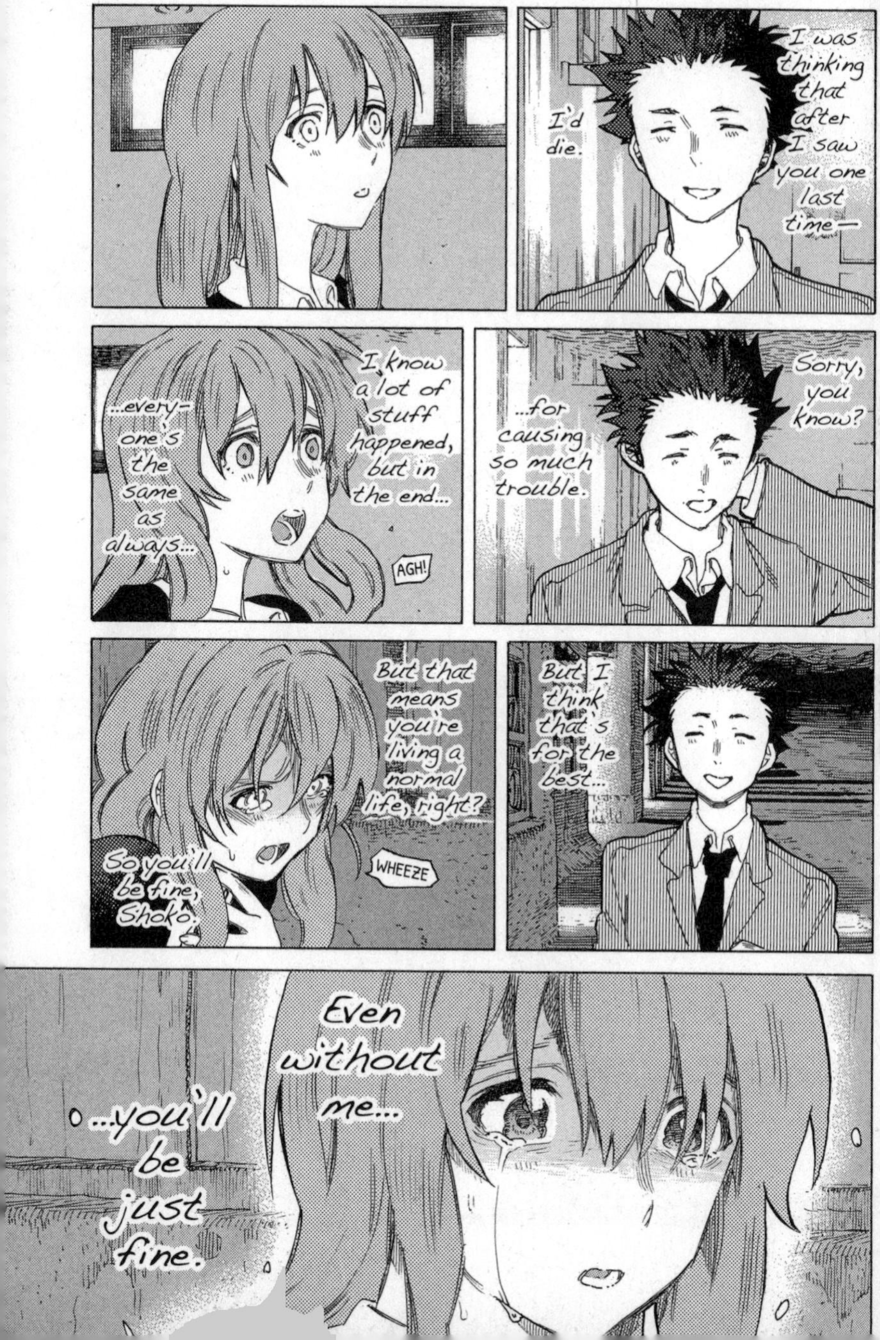
I was thinking that after I saw you one last time—
I'd die.
Sorry, you know?
...for causing so much trouble.
I know a lot of stuff happened, but in the end...
...everyone's the same as always...
AGH!
But I think that's for the best...
But that means you're living a normal life, right?
WHEEZE
So you'll be fine, Shoko.
Even without me...
...you'll be just fine.

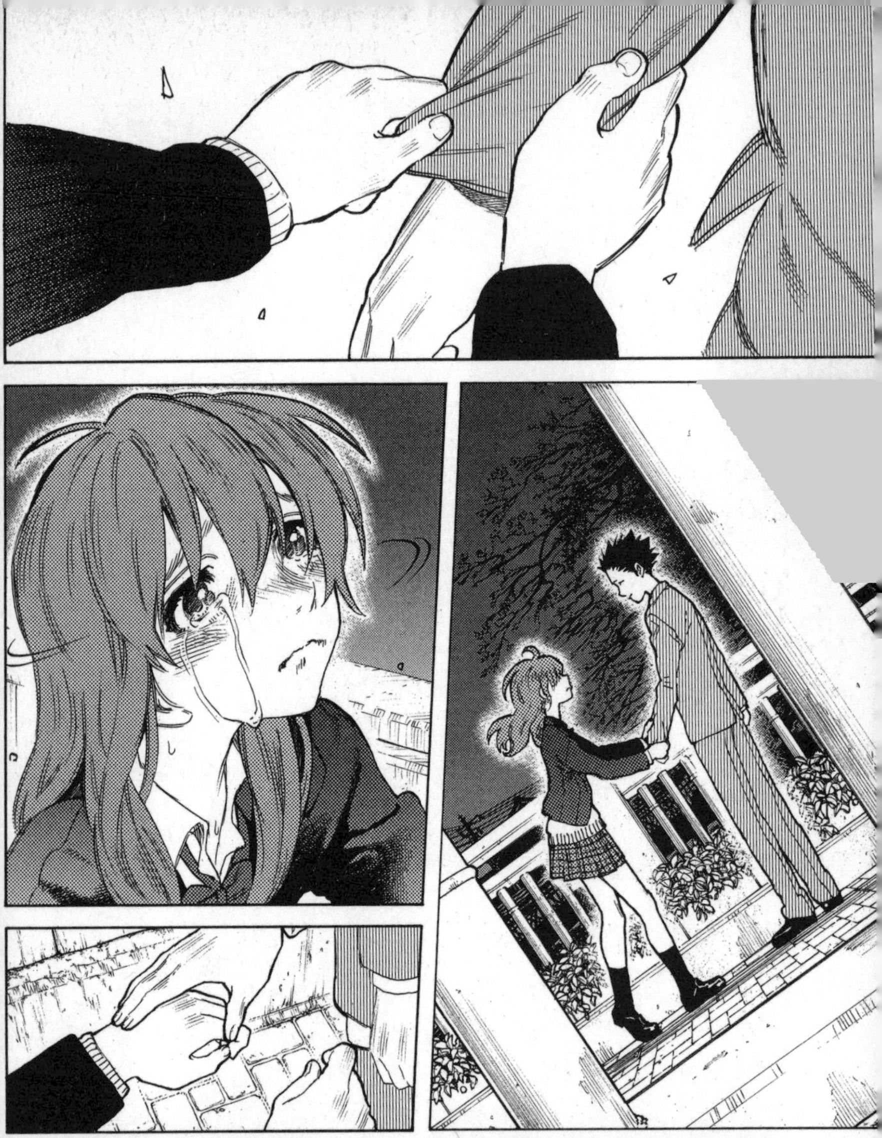
Tuesday is almost over.

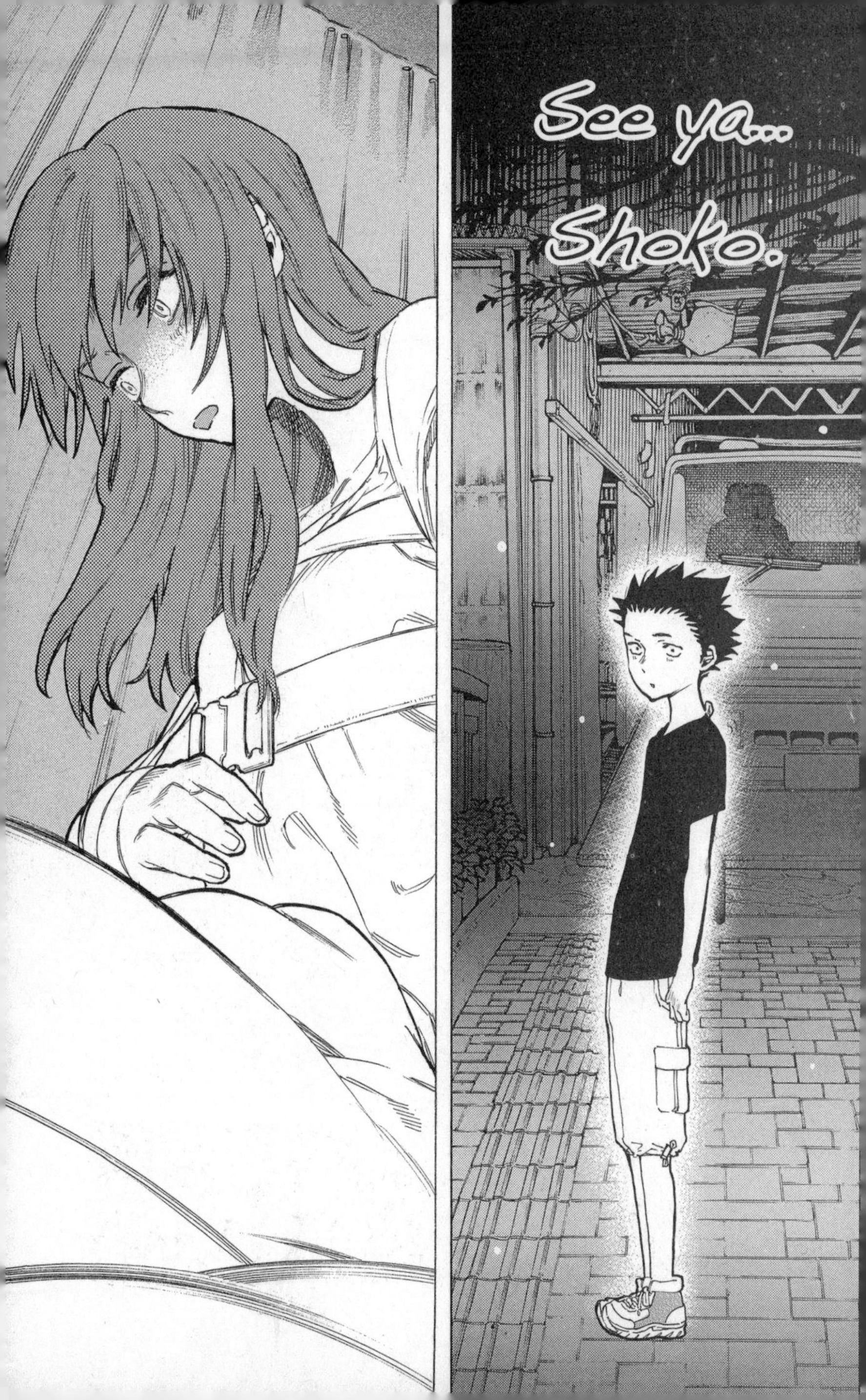
See ya...
Shoko.

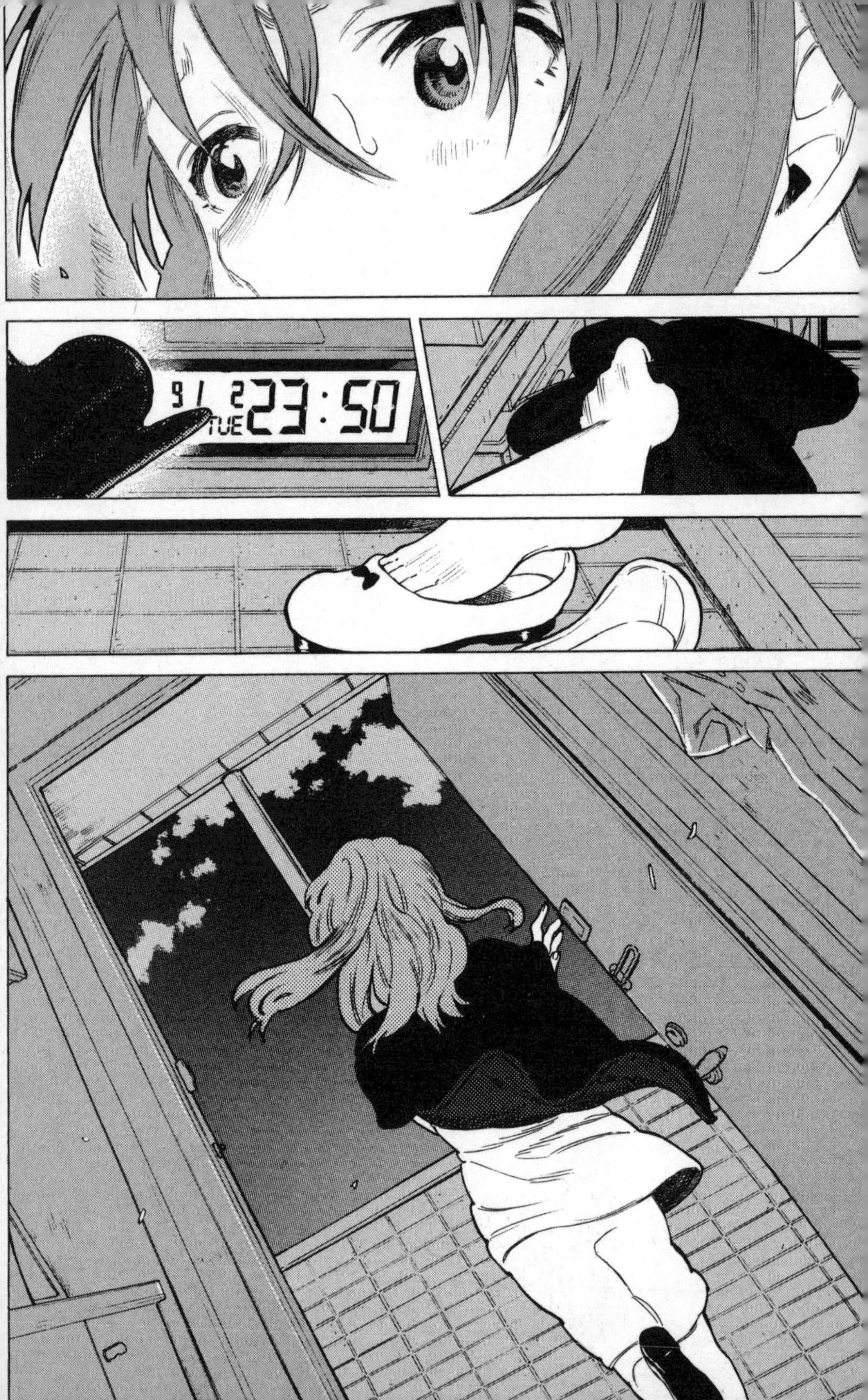
9/2
TUE 23:50

CHAPTER 52: SILENCE

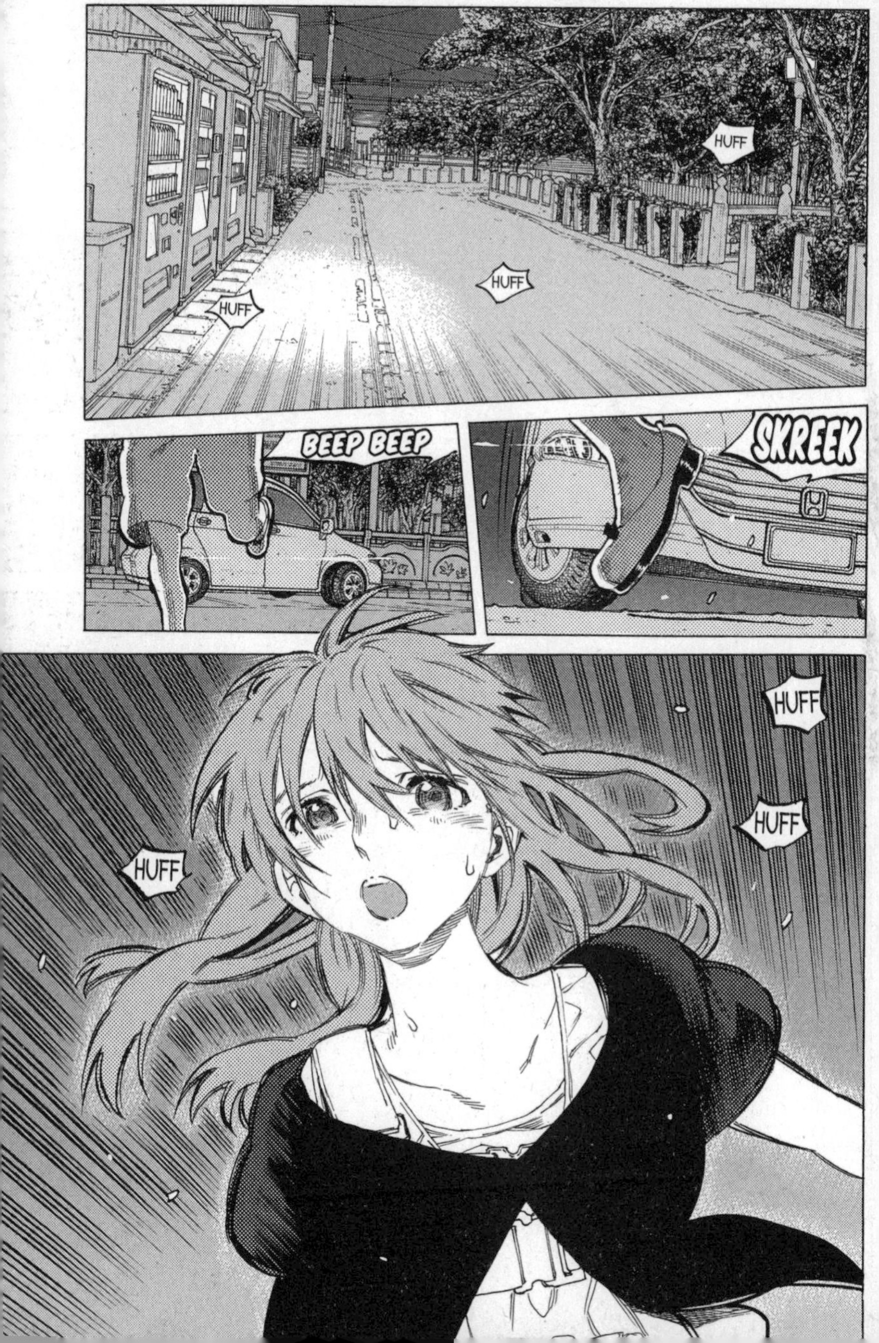
HUFF
HUFF
HUFF
SKREEK
BEEP BEEP
HUFF
HUFF
HUFF

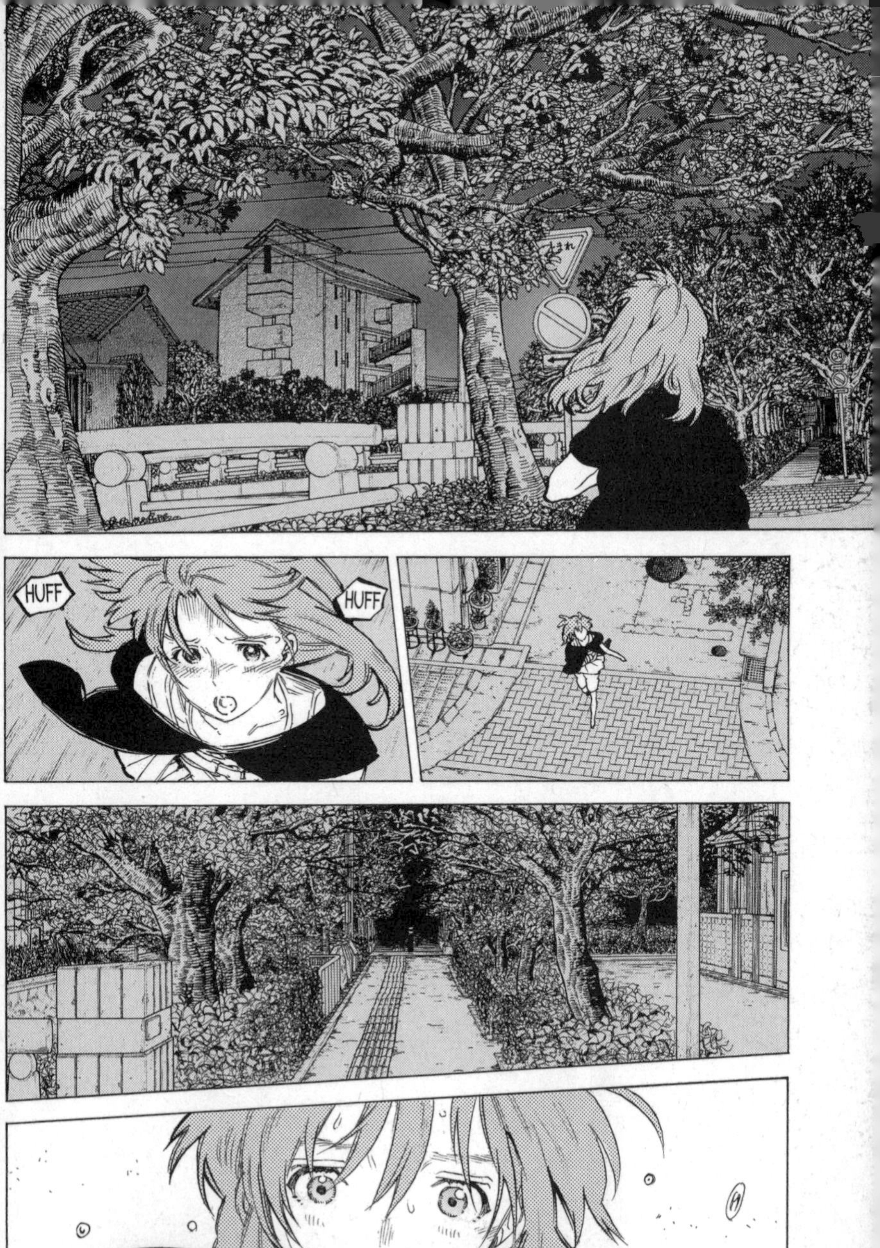
HUFF
HUFF

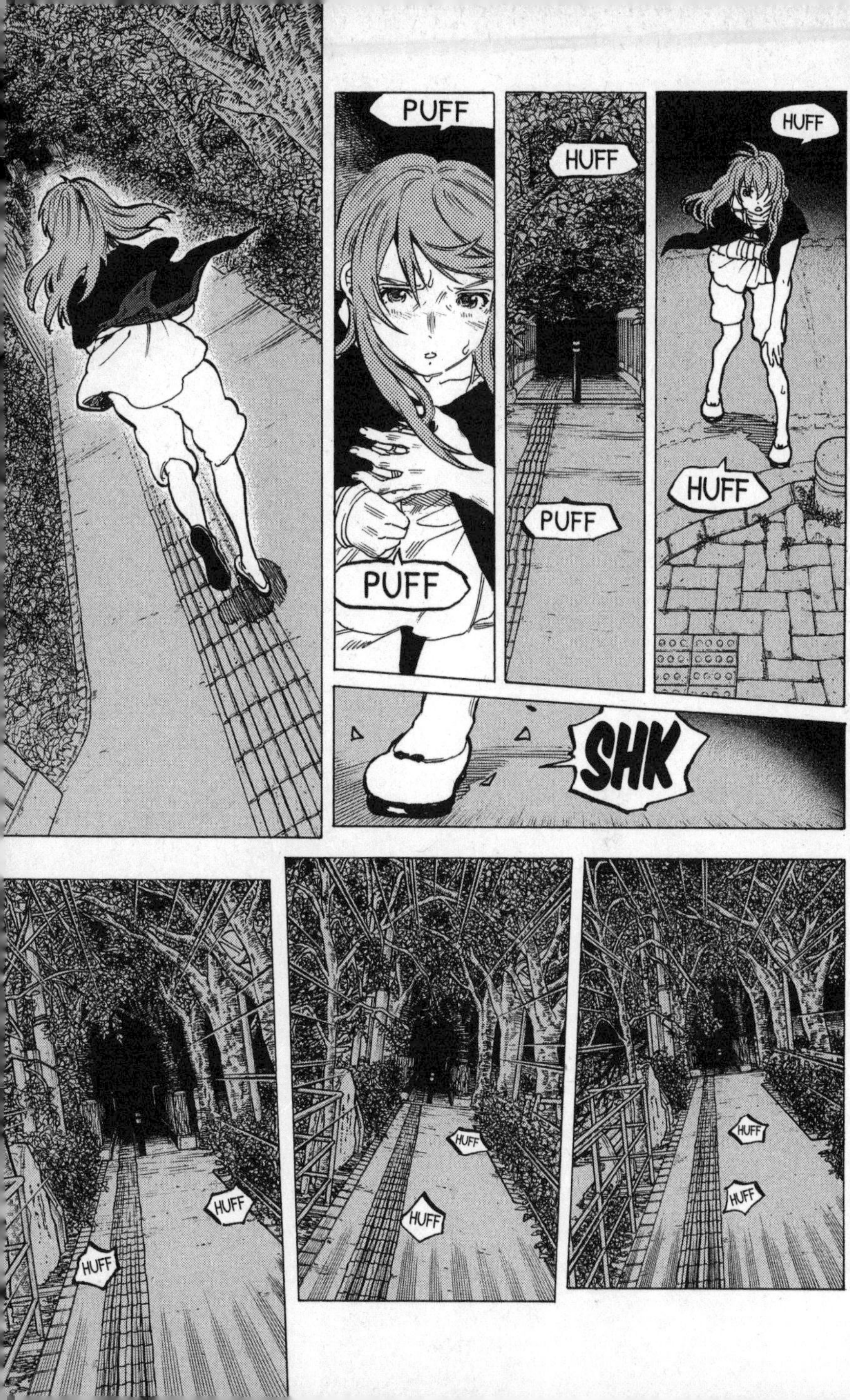
HUFF
HUFF
HUFF
PUFF
PUFF
PUFF
SHK
HUFF
HUFF
HUFF
HUFF
HUFF
HUFF

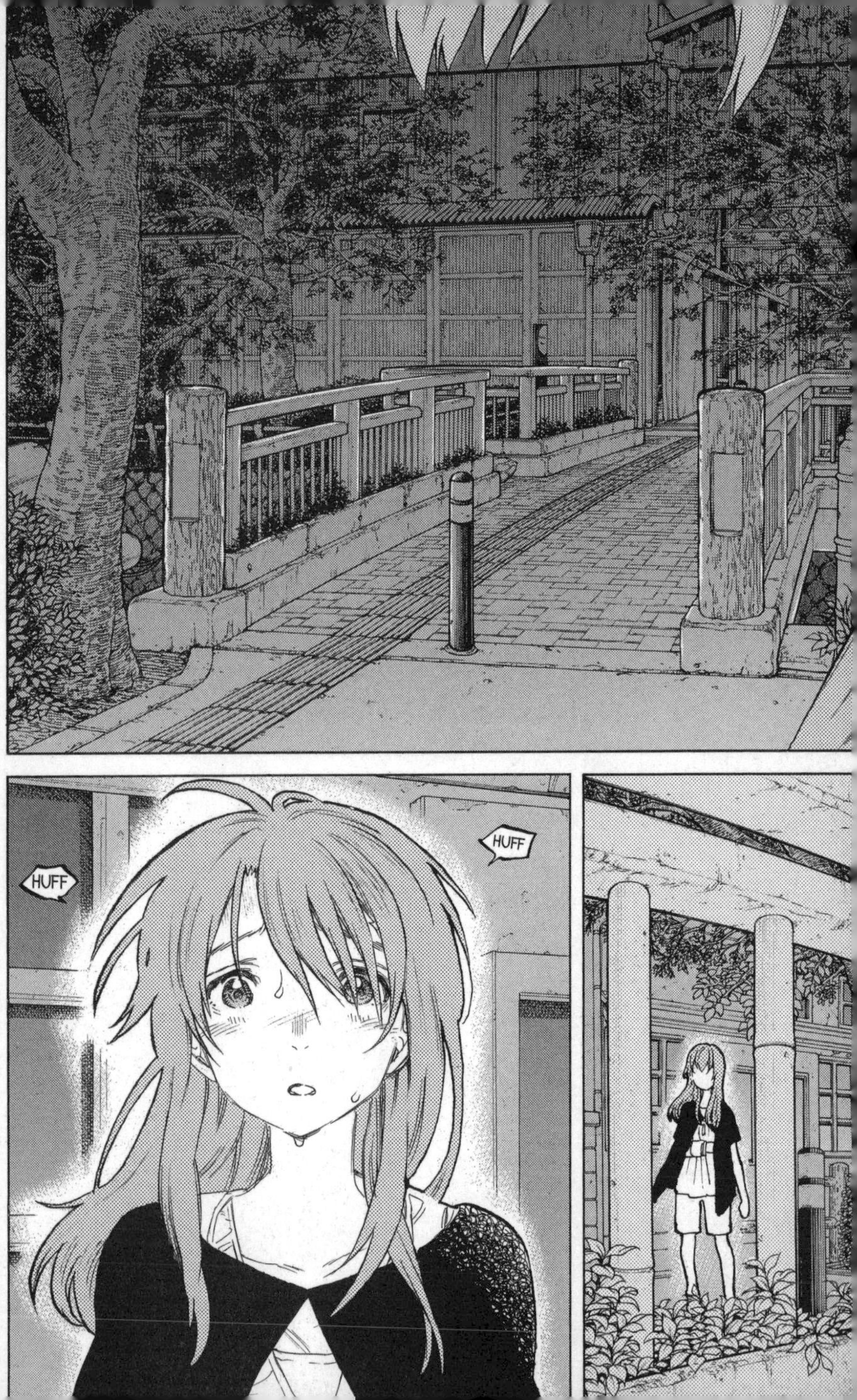
HUFF
HUFF

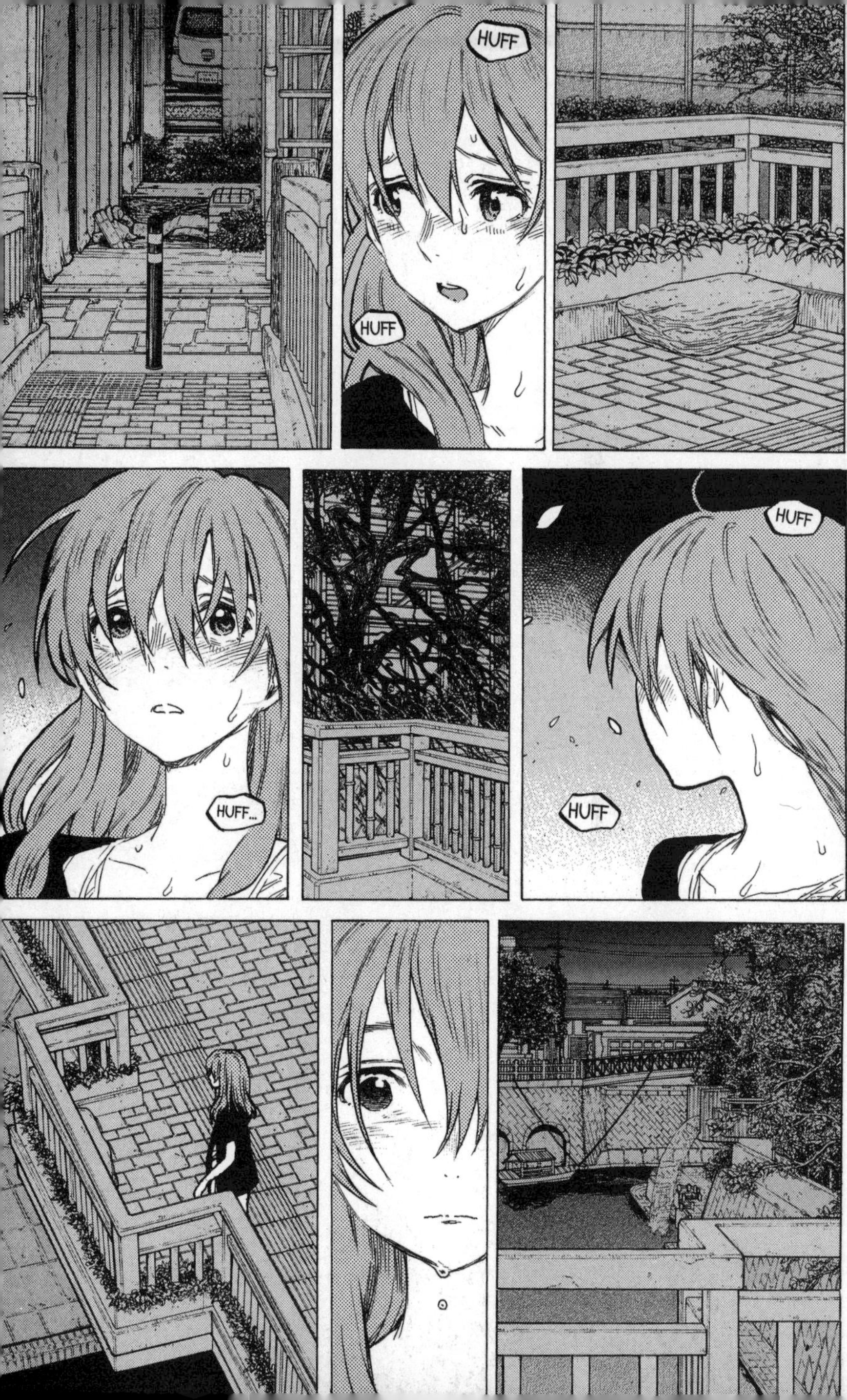
HUFF
HUFF
HUFF
HUFF
HUFF...

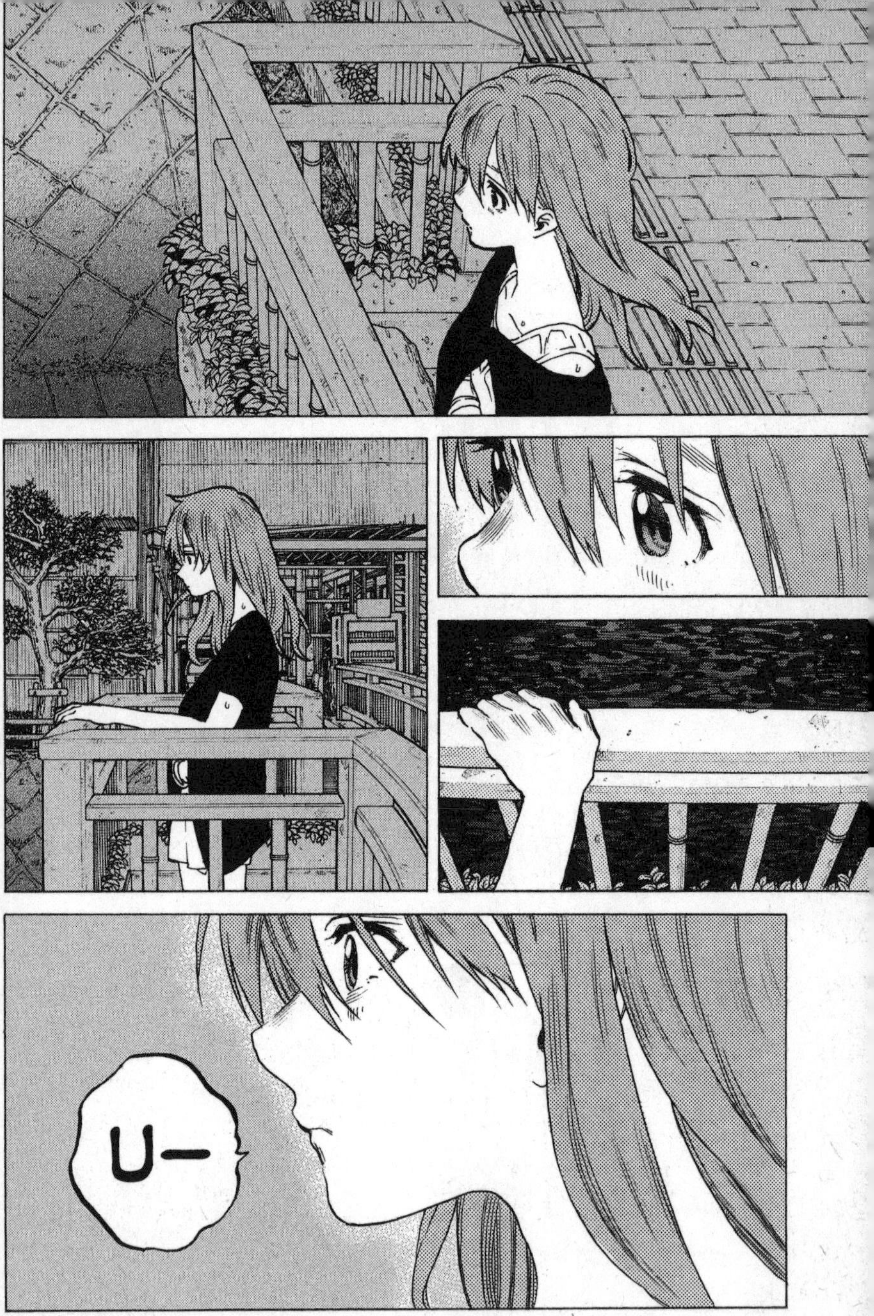
U–

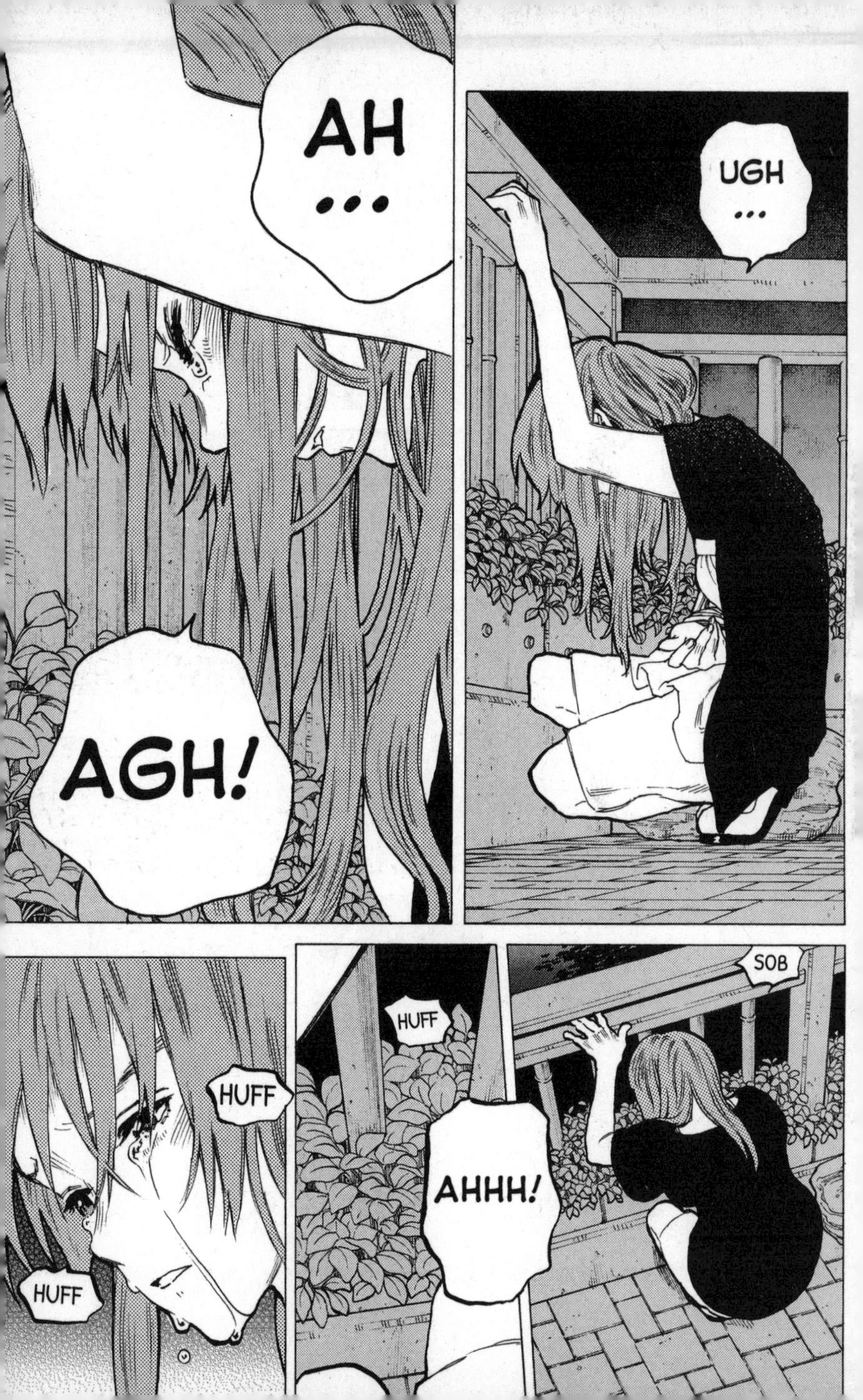
UGH ...
AH ...
AGH!
SOB
HUFF
AHHH!
HUFF
HUFF

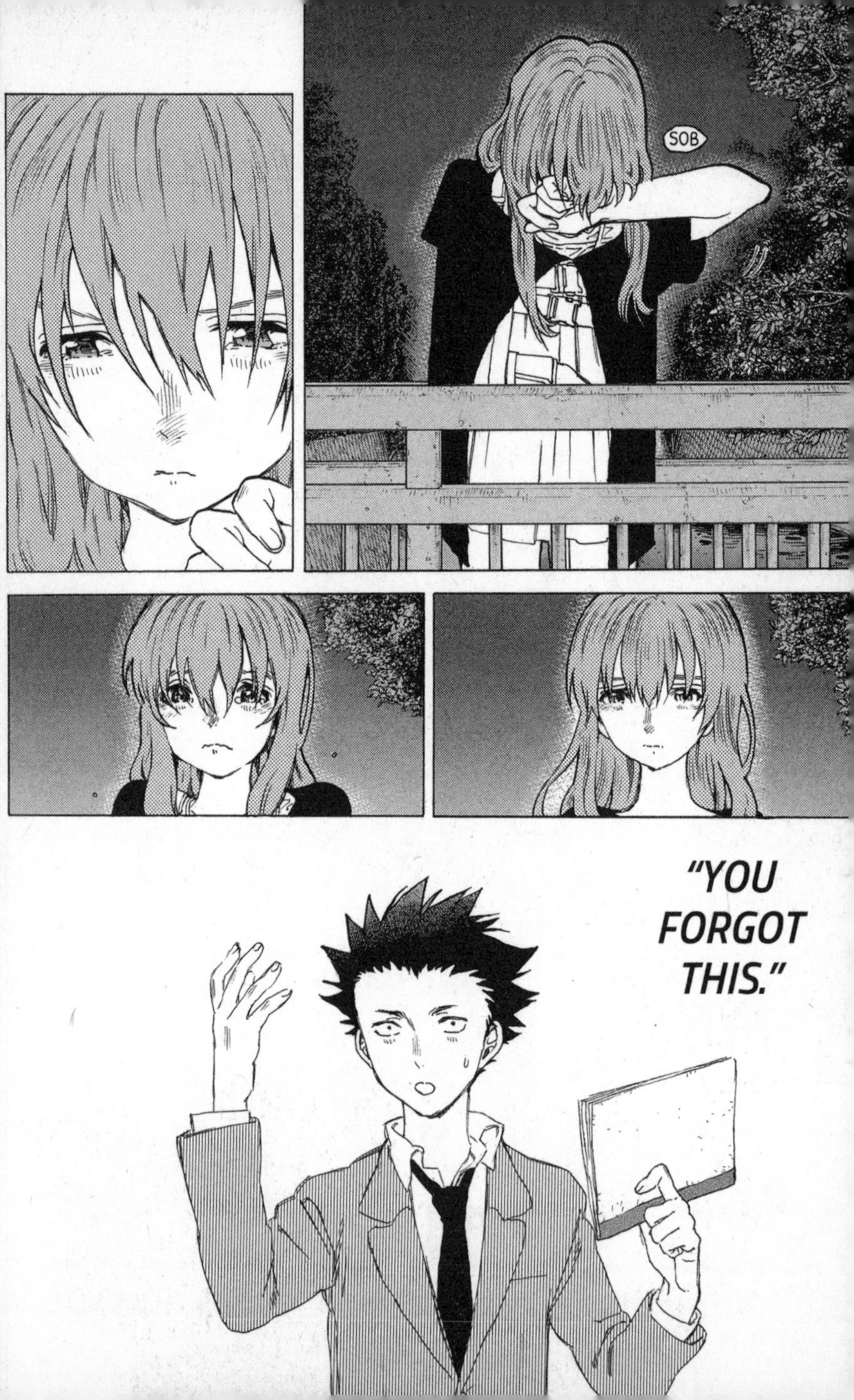
SOB
"YOU FORGOT THIS."

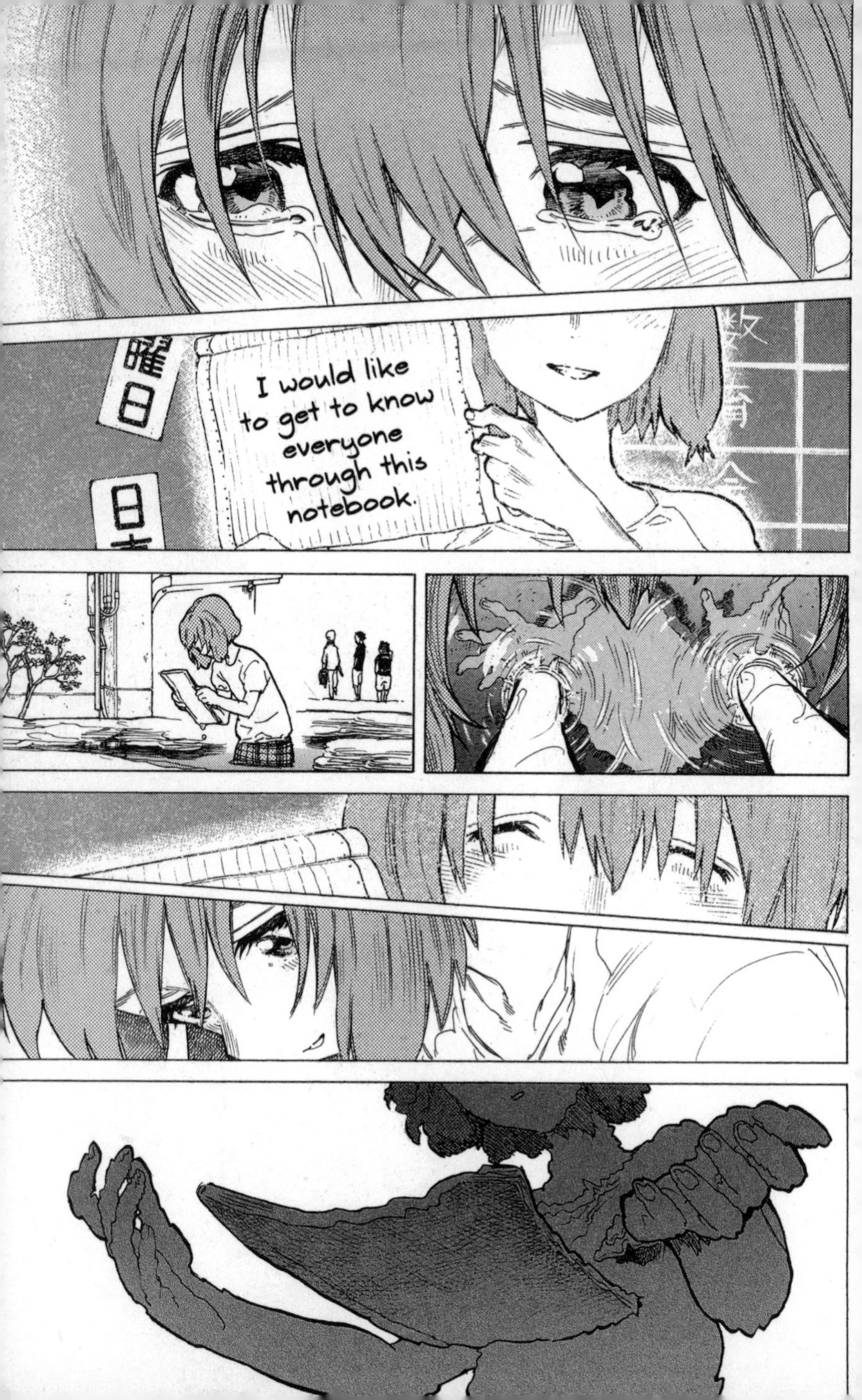
I would like to get to know everyone through this notebook.

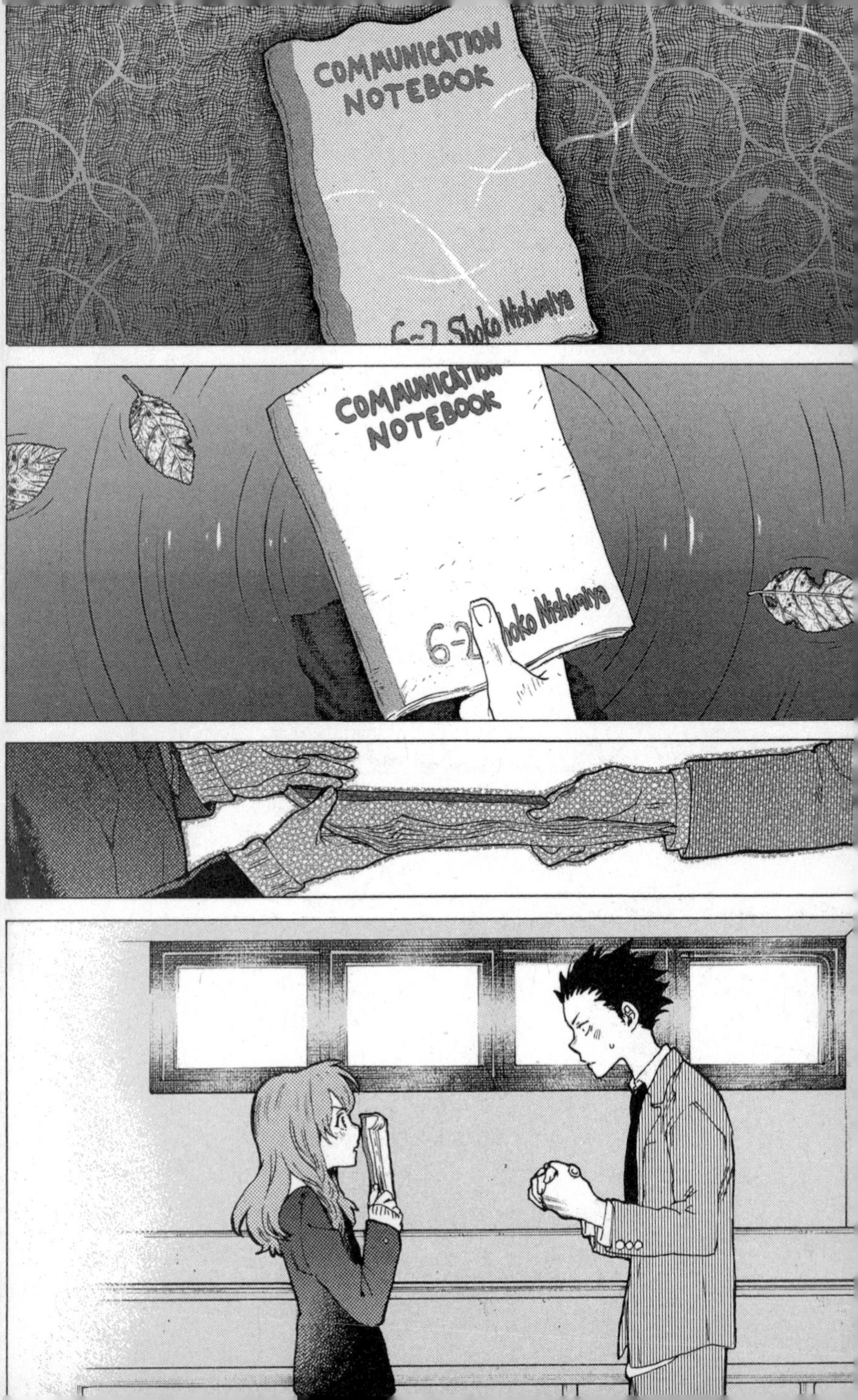
COMMUNICATION NOTEBOOK
6-2 Shoko Nishimiya
COMMUNICATION NOTEBOOK

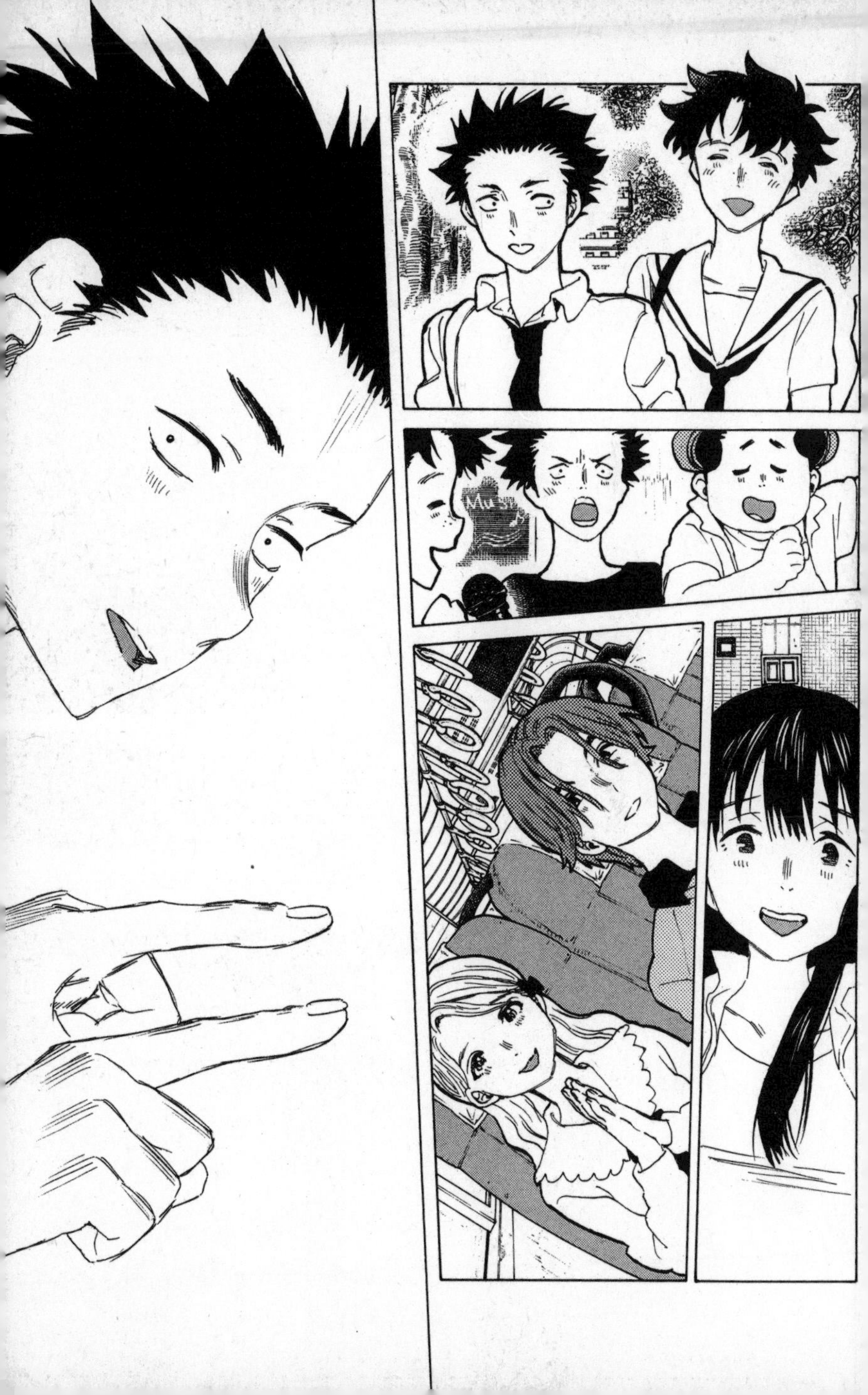

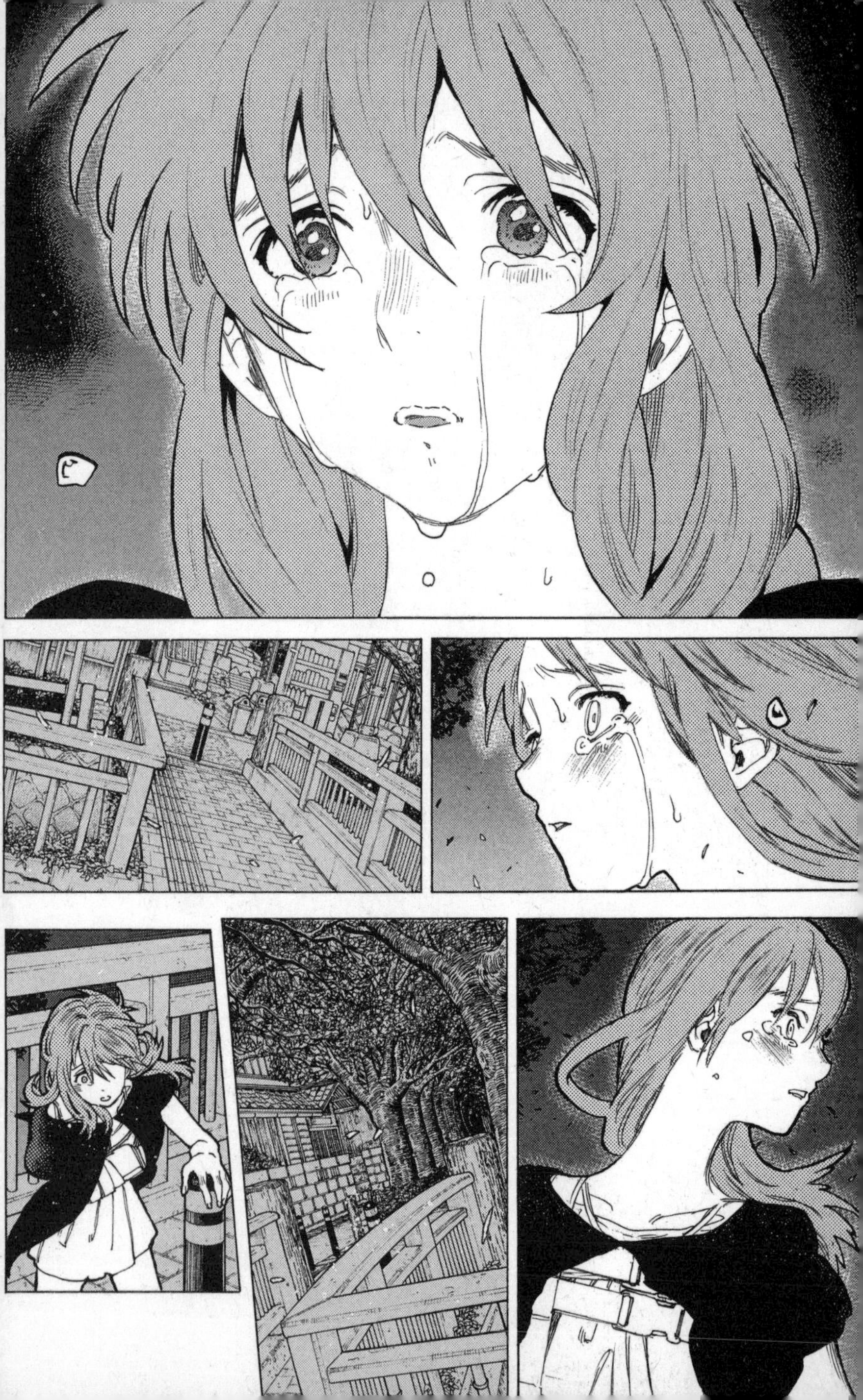

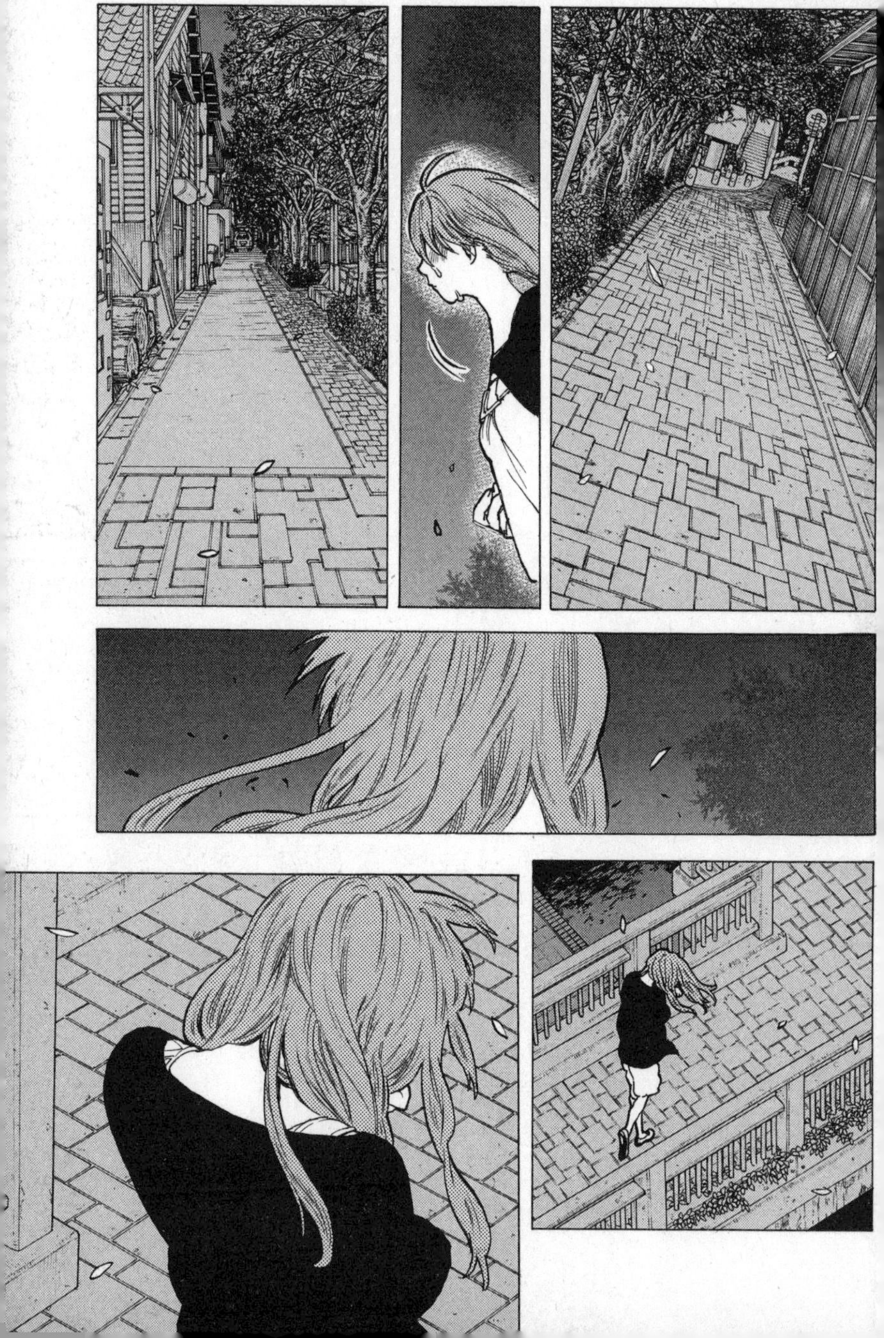

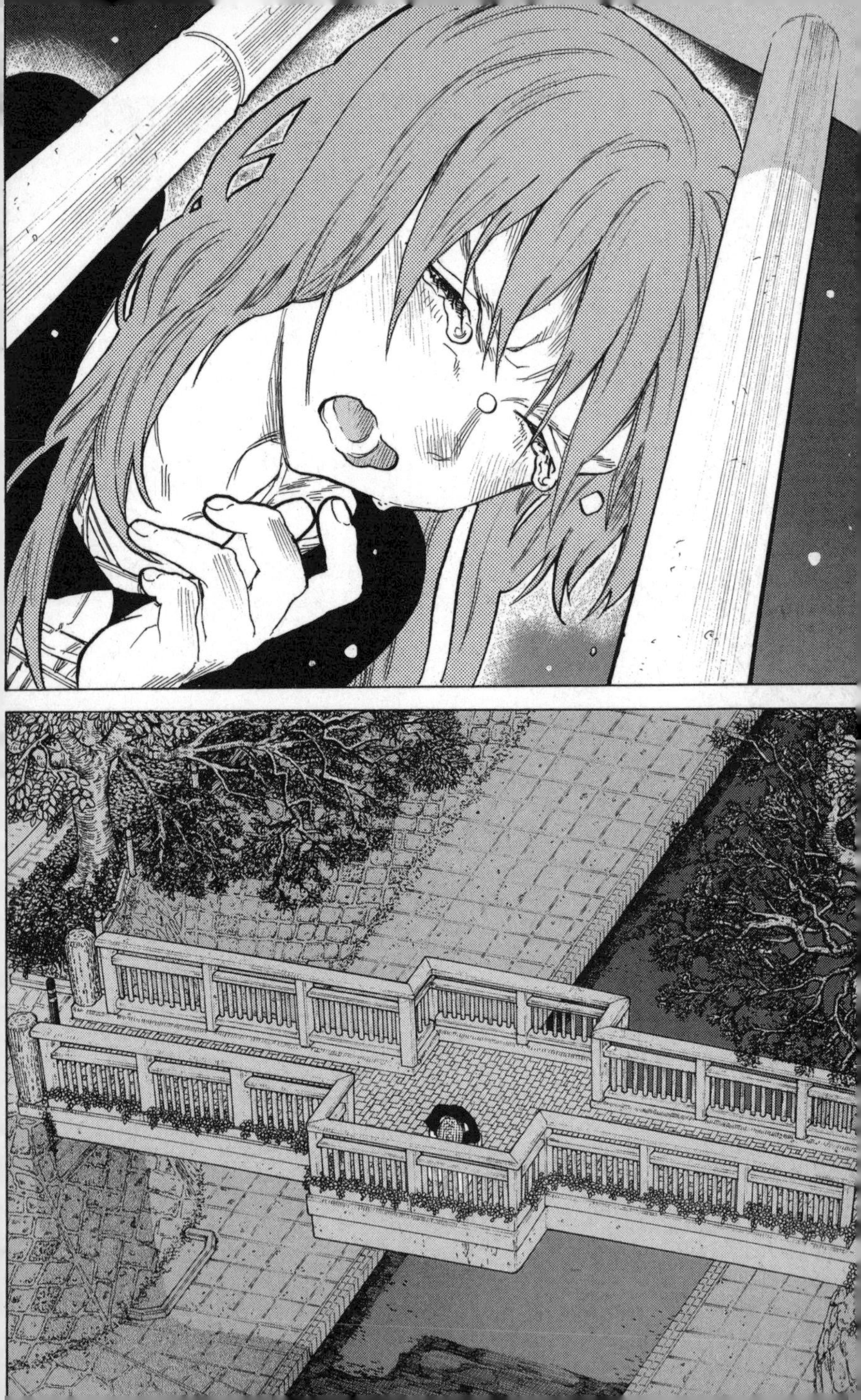

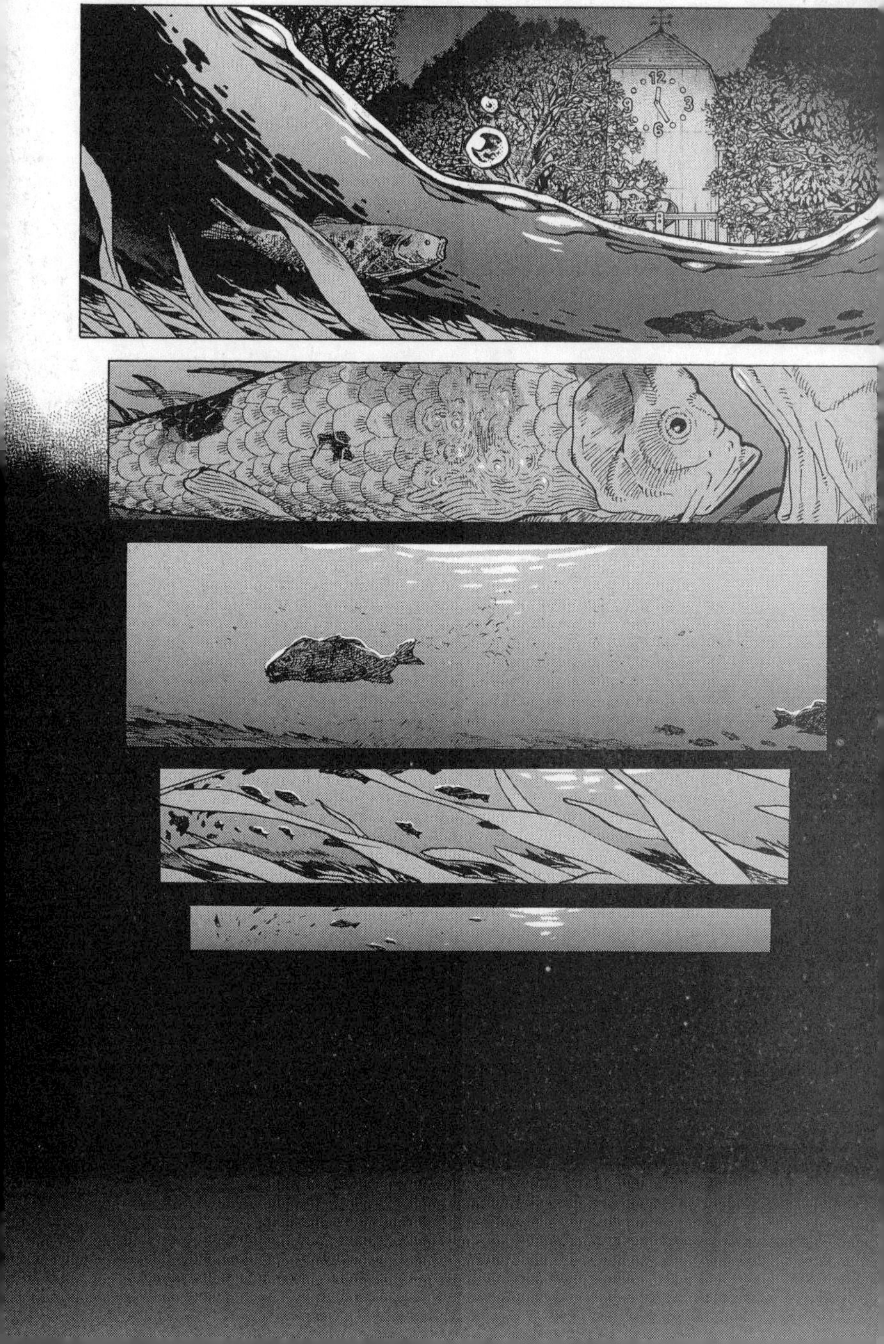

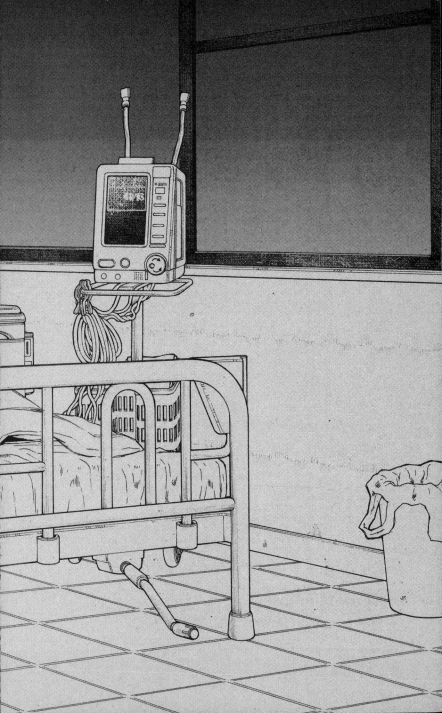

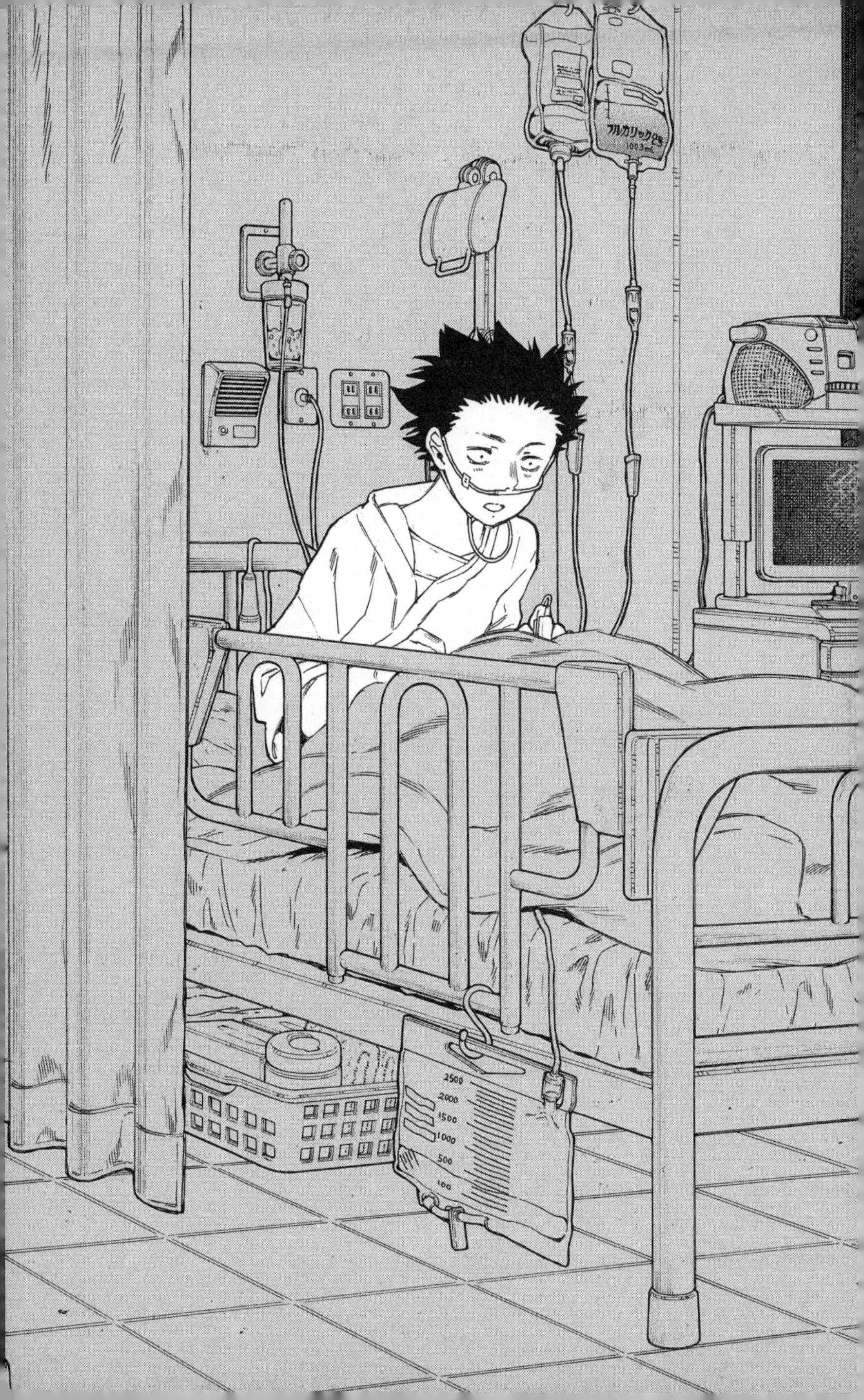
フルカリック2号
1003mL
2500
2000
1500
1000
500
100

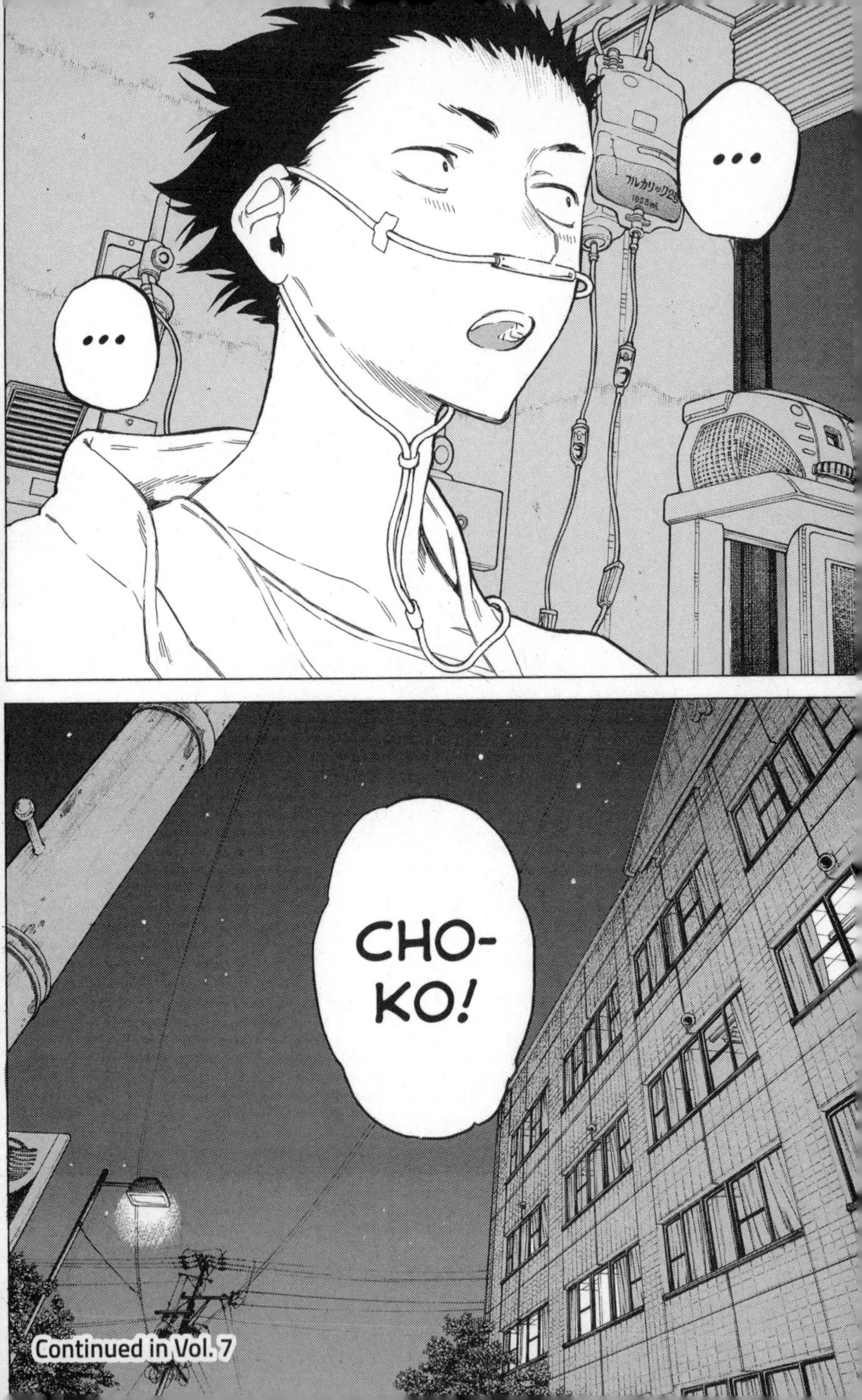
...
...
CHO-
KO!

Continued in Vol. 7

a Silent Voice

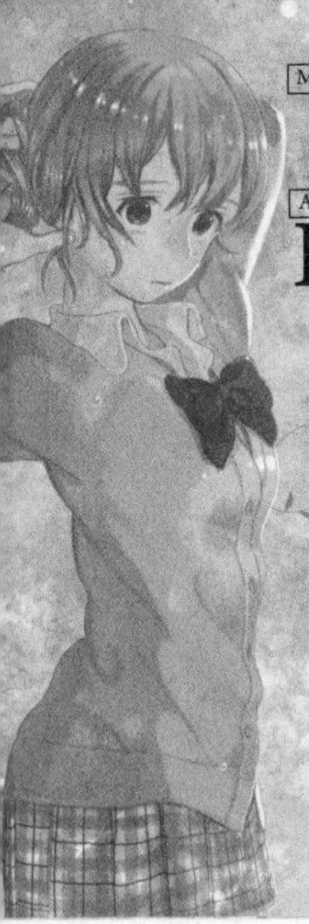

Manga Author

Yoshitoki Oima × Kasumi Arimura

Actress

A Silent Voice Interview

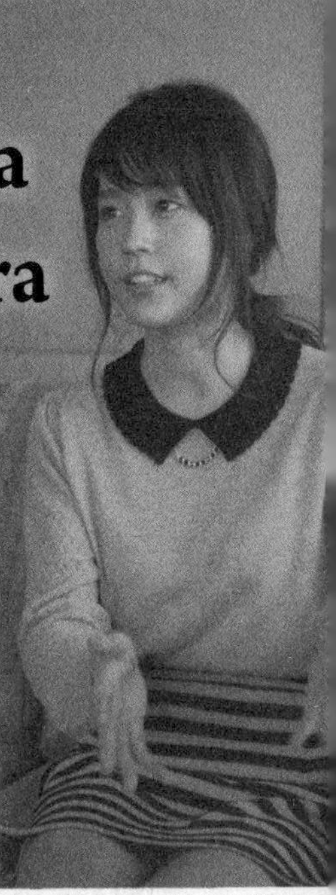

*This interview first appeared in Weekly Shonen Magazine July 2014.

Kasumi Arimura, who is well-known for her role in the TV drama, *Ama-chan*, is in popular demand for TV dramas, movies, and commercials. She also happens to be a huge fan of shonen manga, a genre often geared towards young boys. When we asked her what she thought of *A Silent Voice*, she spoke to us intimately, regarding her own experiences. We now bring you a special interview featuring both her and the author, Yoshitoki Oima.

We asked Ms. Arimura to read the second volume of *A Silent Voice* in preparation for this interview.

—To start, we would like to ask you about your thoughts on *A Silent Voice* as a whole.

Arimura: Can I speak frankly?

Oima: Of course.

Arimura: It was painful to read. The bully becomes the bullied, has insults written on his desk, and his schoolwork thrown around. I really felt the pain of seeing him trying to deal with both his classmates and his family and being unable to say who was at fault and who wasn't.

Oima: Thank you for saying that. I'm surprised at how closely you read it.

Arimura: I tried to think about how I would have behaved under the same circumstances. It may not have quite reached the level of "bullying," but that sort of thing did happen around me as well.

"Even in real life, your turn to be bullied comes around." –Arimura

Oima: It happened to you as well?

Arimura: From elementary school to around junior high school, some kids would ignore me and talk about me behind my back. They'd tell me, "don't get so full of yourself!" And would gossip about me whenever I spoke to guys. But it wasn't all the time. They would do it on rotation according to their leader's whims...

Oima: Then your turn would come up.

Arimura: Exactly. The thing I noticed when reading *A Silent Voice* was that it featured a lot of very believable scenes. There were many scenes where I wasn't sure how I would have acted in the same situation. Is the story based on actual experiences?

Oima: Yes, there is a certain truth at the root of it that I've witnessed myself. I fleshed out the story while recalling the atmosphere and feelings I had back then. However, in the story, I occasionally take things in more extreme directions, so it isn't 100% as it happened.

Arimura: Classmates pretending not to see and shifting targets depending on their own status in the class... That was so true to life it got me wondering.

> *"I wanted to depict the emotions behind bullying, and how they change."*
> **–Oima**

Oima: Which characters did you like and dislike while reading the comic?

Arimura: I liked the new friend, Tomohiro, who appeared in the second volume. He gives a great answer when asked about the definition of friendship. I feel like life is so much better when there's at least one optimistic person like that around you.

Oima: Was there a character you couldn't stand?

Arimura: The ones that bother me are Shoya's former friends who turned their backs on him. I'd hate to think they stay that way once they grow up, too.

Oima: I am thinking of eventually drawing these characters in their current, more grown-up state. I feel like I have to portray the changes in emotions for everyone surrounding this one incident of bullying.

Arimura: No matter what happens to her, Shoko doesn't get mad, does she? When someone does something mean to her, she is the one who still reaches out to the bully. Seeing her do that pains my heart...

Oima: She's a little mysterious, isn't she?

Arimura: Heheheh. She is. Very mysterious. She's very upfront and doesn't get worked up, which I think is so cool, but I wonder what she's really thinking. I know this is selfish, but I hope Shoko won't get mad over little things in future volumes...

"I can sense Shoko's kindness through her expressions." –Arimura

Arimura: But I bet that since she doesn't get mad often, when she does, you can tell just how serious she is.

Oima: (Nods)

Arimura: I never had it as bad as she did, but as someone who has been in a similar situation, I can really sympathize with the way her kindness creeps into her eyes or the corners of her mouth. It made me think, "Yeah, some things do make you make that expression," you know? It made me want to portray Shoko Nishimiya someday.

Oima: Thank you so much. When you read so deeply into my work, I actually get so embarrassed. (Laughs)

—Come to think of it, you'll be appearing in the TV drama based on the manga, *Shitsuren Chocolatier (Heartbroken Chocolatier)*.

Arimura: Since it's based on a prior work, I'll be trying not to stray too far from the "taste" of the original work in my performance. Naturally, this work has its fans and a creator, so I don't want to betray their expectations.

Oima: That is one of the difficulties in works based on something else. You can't help but compare them to the original.

Arimura: Even if you try to come up with a plan for your performance beforehand based on the script and original work, you can show up on set and it's not quite what you had imagined or maybe the other actors' performances aren't what you saw in your head. When that happens, I try to prioritize what's happening on set.

Oima: I think I know what you mean. If something feels wrong when moving from the storyboarding to the inking phase, I'll rewrite or redraw things based on that.

—*A Silent Voice* **was remade from what was first published as a one-shot (a single-issue comic). Afterwards, it was redrawn again so it was fit for serialization (a story published in chapters).**

Oima: It was difficult work, but I think it allowed me to start serialization with the story in its best possible form. And it's all thanks to the readers who supported me back when it was a one-shot. I was defiant and was able to draw it just how I wanted.

Arimura: Perhaps in performing a work, creating a work, and even in human relationships (which includes bullying), the most important thing is having a sensitive heart.

Kasumi Arimura

Born 1993. Well-known for her performances in dramas such as: *SPEC~First Blood* and *Ama-chan.* Her first photo collection *Shin·Kokyu (Deep Breaths)* is on sale now.

Photography: Maki Oe
Styling: Yumiko Segawa
Hair & Makeup: Izumi Omagari
Organization: Tatsuya Matsuura + Manami Shimakage (Baba Planning)
Design: Saya Takagi (Red Rooster)

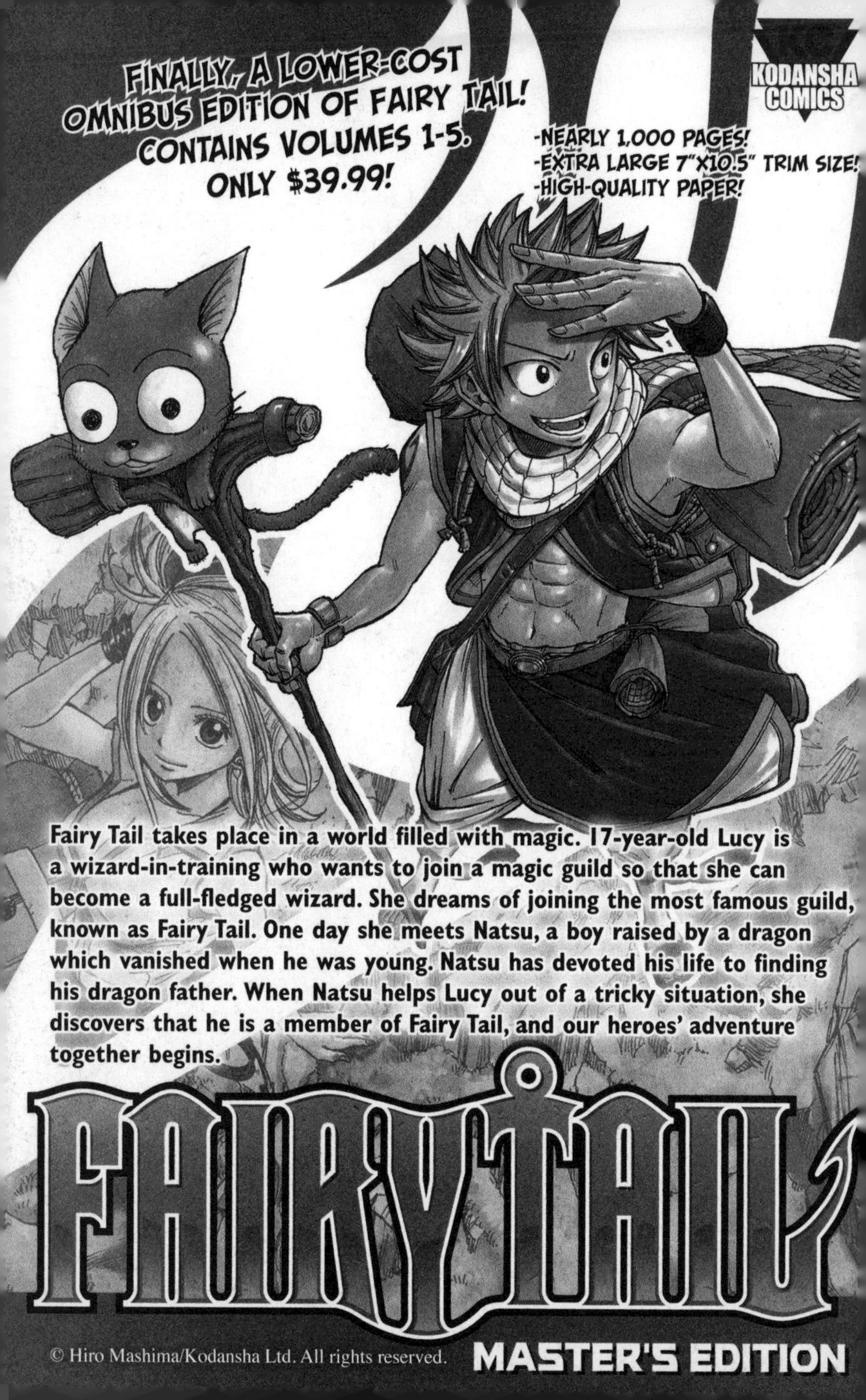
KODANSHA COMICS
FINALLY, A LOWER-COST OMNIBUS EDITION OF FAIRY TAIL! CONTAINS VOLUMES 1-5. ONLY $39.99!
-NEARLY 1,000 PAGES!
-EXTRA LARGE 7"X10.5" TRIM SIZE!
-HIGH-QUALITY PAPER!
Fairy Tail takes place in a world filled with magic. 17-year-old Lucy is a wizard-in-training who wants to join a magic guild so that she can become a full-fledged wizard. She dreams of joining the most famous guild, known as Fairy Tail. One day she meets Natsu, a boy raised by a dragon which vanished when he was young. Natsu has devoted his life to finding his dragon father. When Natsu helps Lucy out of a tricky situation, she discovers that he is a member of Fairy Tail, and our heroes' adventure together begins.
FAIRY TAIL
© Hiro Mashima/Kodansha Ltd. All rights reserved.
MASTER'S EDITION

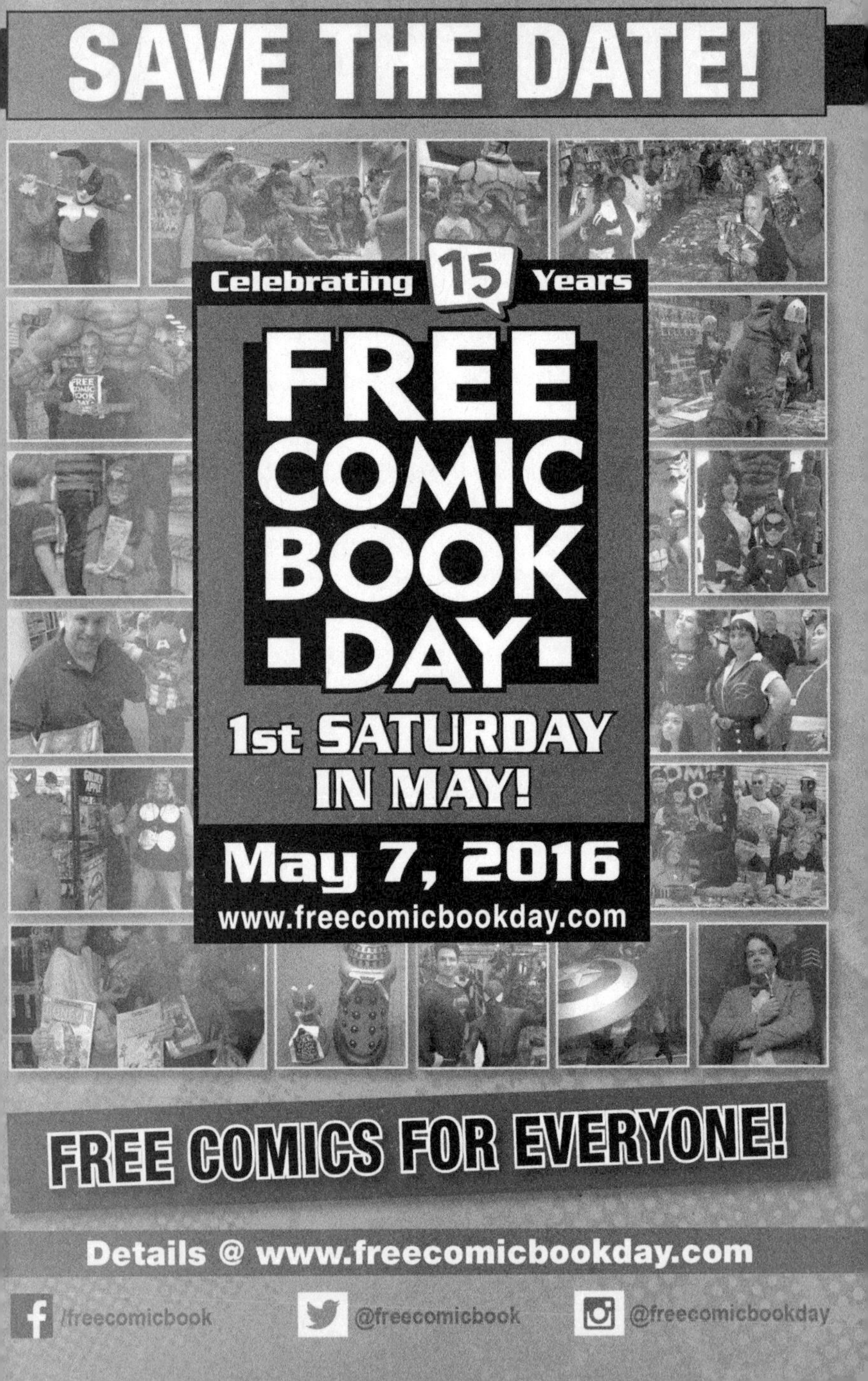
SAVE THE DATE!
Celebrating 15 Years
FREE COMIC BOOK DAY
1st SATURDAY IN MAY!
May 7, 2016
www.freecomicbookday.com
FREE COMICS FOR EVERYONE!
Details @ www.freecomicbookday.com
/freecomicbook
@freecomicbook
@freecomicbookday

A Silent Voice volume 6 is a work of fiction. Names, characters, places, and incidents are the products of the author's imagination or are used fictitiously. Any resemblance to actual events, locales, or persons, living or dead, is entirely coincidental.

A Kodansha Comics Trade Paperback Original.

Published in the United States by Kodansha Comics, an imprint of Kodansha USA Publishing, LLC, New York.

Publication rights for this English edition arranged through Kodansha Ltd., Tokyo.

First published in Japan in 2014 by Kodansha Ltd., Tokyo, as *Koe no katachi* volume 6.

ISBN 978-1-63236-061-8

Printed in the United States of America.

www.kodanshacomics.com

9 8 7 6 5 4 3 2

Translation: Steven LeCroy
Lettering: Steven LeCroy & Hiroko Mizuno
Additional Touch-up: James Dashiell
Editing: Haruko Hashimoto
Kodansha Comics edition cover design by Phil Balsman

TOMARE! STOP

You're going the wrong way!

Manga is a completely different type of reading experience.

To start at the beginning, Go to the end!

---

hat's right! Authentic manga is read the traditional Japanese way— om right to left, exactly the opposite of how American books are ead. It's easy to follow: Just go to the other end of the book and read ach page—and each panel—from right side to left side, starting at he top right. Now you're experiencing manga as it was meant to be!